QUEER AMERICA

QUEER AMERICA

A GLBT History of the 20th Century

Vicki L. Eaklor

GREENWOOD PRESS
Westport, Connecticut · London

Library of Congress Cataloging-in-Publication Data

Eaklor, Vicki Lynn.
   Queer America : a GLBT history of the 20th century / Vicki L. Eaklor.
     p. cm.
   Includes bibliographical references and index.
   ISBN 978–0–313–33749–9 (alk. paper)
1. Gay men—United States—History—20th century. 2. Lesbians—United States—History—20th century.
3. Bisexuals—United States—History—20th century. 4. Transgender people—United States—History—
20th century. 5. Homosexuality—United States—History—20th century. 6. Gay liberation movement—
United States. 7. Gay rights—United States. I. Title.
HQ76.3.U5E35 2008
306.760973'0904—dc22   2007048218

British Library Cataloguing in Publication Data is available.

Library of Congress Catalog Card Number: 2007048218
ISBN: 978–0–313–33749–9

First published in 2008

Greenwood Press, 88 Post Road West, Westport, CT 06881
An imprint of Greenwood Publishing Group, Inc.
www.greenwood.com

Printed in the United States of America

The paper used in this book complies with the
Permanent Paper Standard issued by the National
Information Standards Organization (Z39.48–1984).

10 9 8 7 6 5 4 3 2 1

To all the GLBT people who are in this book
And to all those who are not

CONTENTS

PREFACE

There are many ways to tell the story of GLBT (gay, lesbian, bisexual, and transgendered) Americans. For some, it is an account of progress—of coming out and coming into the nation's history as important if not always valued participants. Others expect, or tell, a tale of persecution and victimization, relieved only by the heroism of those who endured and the courage of those who tried to change society's views and laws. To others yet it is a list of famous people, already in the histories but not as GLBT people. These versions are neither completely valid nor completely bogus, and in fact complement each other. The history here includes these elements but seeks to be more textured; neither progressive nor regressive, it is the story of GLBT people and the conditions in which they lived during the last century. It is as much a survey of U.S. history since 1900 as those taught in every U.S. school and college, though through different eyes at times.

CONTENT AND ORGANIZATION

Themes

Limiting this volume to the 20th century conveniently allows it to bypass some of the stickier problems explained in Chapter 1. While issues of sexual identity before 1900 are fairly complex and often hotly contested, there is general agreement among scholars regarding a discernible "timeline" beginning around the turn of the 20th century. At that time the United States was witnessing the medicalization of sexuality and the more common use of the homosexual/heterosexual binary to classify people, phenomena that serve as constants in this history for the entire century. Hopefully, what is lost in treating only the 20th-century United States is gained in attempting to balance breadth, depth, clarity, and brevity in a single volume work.

The main theme of this book is that of change within the continuity provided by a heterosexual/homosexual divide. At the same time, we shall see that some of this history and its people cannot be so easily categorized. Additional themes are those of class, race, ethnicity, and gender as they not only intersect with this history but are integral and defining forces within it. The idea that some "progress" has occurred toward community formation and agitation for equal treatment among GLBT people will be inescapable in the later chapters, but again this is no simplistically progressive history. This story is not one of a simple linear development from the "darkness" of an oppressive society in which GLBT people hid to the "light" of visibility, movement formation, and civil rights activism. Indeed, what the 20th century demonstrates is the overlapping nature of these and many other elements and their refusal to follow a neat path.

The story proceeds chronologically, though, from the turn of the 20th century to the first few years following 2000. It is intended to be comprehensive rather than definitive, combining the breadth of an encyclopedia with the flow of a narrative, but a narrative that need not be read in order or cover-to-cover. Selected topics and people are treated with some detail, but more as examples of the richness of GLBT history than because they are necessarily more important than others. Topics and subtopics were chosen according to the years under consideration; not every issue appears in every chapter though a few, like politics or media, bear repeating due to the speed and number of developments in the latter part of the century. In addition, some facts are repeated here and there to lessen the need to refer to other chapters or the index. General context is provided in each chapter as well, to aid the casual reader whose knowledge of U.S. history might need refreshing, and especially to demonstrate how fully GLBT history *is* U.S. history. In sum, this is designed as a "one-stop" handbook to U.S. GLBT history of the 20th century but hopefully it will not be the only stop. If there has been progress it is in the number of works now available in this field, as demonstrated by the extensive Bibliography.

Eras and Chapter Overview

The question of periodization is an interesting one in this context. Much is revealed when any history is partitioned, since the dividing lines imply some rationale. Here, as is often the case, a concern for legitimate "eras" is combined with basic practicality, resulting in a story divided very roughly by decades. This works especially well in the post–World War II era, usually considered a period in itself in both U.S. and GLBT history because of the drastic changes brought about by the global war. Among those changes was discernible and sustained organizing that began as a "homophile" movement and blossomed into the multifaceted movements of the present. For that reason alone, although this is not solely a history of organizing and politics, the postwar era demands comparatively more attention.

As it turns out, after 1945 GLBT life, like American life generally, follows contours determined by such events as the Cold War, the activism of the 1960s and 1970s (and the flourishing of gay and lesbian culture in the 1970s especially), a backlash against liberalism and radicalism in the 1980s, and the result of regrouping and reorganizing in the 1990s. While the division is not strictly into ten-year periods, there is an attempt to make each of the five postwar chapters (4, 5, 6, 7, and 8) both manageable and cohesive around one or more themes. For the material before 1945, two chapters (2 and 3) examine important developments in GLBT life and culture while acknowledging such events as World War I, the "Roaring 20s," the Great Depression of the 1930s, and World War II. Chapter 1 explains some of the key questions involved in reading and writing this history and a concluding chapter treats selected topics of the years 2000–2005 and attempts to bring some aspects of the story full circle.

FEATURES

Introductory Stories

History is more alive when we remember that we are studying real people. Chapters 2 through 9 begin with short vignettes, each focusing on one or more people who illustrate a significant point or event in U.S. GLBT history. Additional individuals are very briefly profiled throughout the book, to remind us that at the root of ideas, forces, and other grand historical themes there are always people.

Nine important debates are included in this volume, one at the end of each chapter. These debates might be one, two, or all of three kinds: those among historians and other scholars (some of whom are G, L, B, or T); those among GLBT people (some of whom are scholars); and those reaching "the public." The aim is to explain the sides of those debates and suggest additional reading or other resources for the interested reader. Each one features an issue that pertains to the material and/or the time frame under consideration, though the topic may also be relevant in years before or after those covered by the chapter.

Images

Throughout the book are several photographs and other images to supplement the narrative. Several considerations went into their selection, beginning with what is available and in what forms. Beyond that there has been an effort to represent the variety of GLBT people and events across the century.

Timeline

In light of the general aim of this volume, to provide a balance of depth and breadth in a relatively small space, a Timeline is provided for quick reference. It is not intended to be exhaustive but it is an attempt to place a wide range of events in GLBT history in relation to each other. A few items outside the United States are included, as are several reference points or related developments (wars, elections, landmarks in civil rights and women's rights, etc.) to provide context.

Resources and Index

In addition to the sources cited in the notes for each chapter is a list of Suggested Resources that pertains to the material in that chapter (sources cited in notes are not repeated in these lists). For the readers' convenience, sources cited and mentioned throughout, as well as additional suggestions, are provided in the extensive Bibliography preceding the Index. Print sources are divided into two categories: Anthology, Primary, and Reference; and Articles, Books, and Papers. Last is a list of films by title and including the date only. Rounding out the attempt to provide a useful one-volume work is a comprehensive index.

ACKNOWLEDGMENTS

There were many times in the two-plus years it took to complete this book that I thought I must have been insane to take it on as the sole author. Fortunately, there were people along the way who provided help, advice, or just an ear. Many thanks go to the staff of Herrick Library at Alfred University for quickly providing me with materials through Interlibrary Loan, and to all of the photographers, writers, and activists who provided images, often with great kindness and generosity. I am indebted to Greenwood Press for believing in this project, and to Sarah Colwell for initiating the process and helping me through the first stages; I am especially grateful to Kaitlin Ciarmiello at Greenwood for her incredible work helping me locate and acquire images, and for her encouragement when I most needed it. My colleagues at Alfred University, in and beyond the Division of Human Studies, were brave enough to ask how the book was coming and indulged me as I moaned and groaned about it. Thanks so much to good friends Leisa Meyer, Marc Sackman, and Pat Sweeney for always listening, and to Crystal Lehman for her conversation, insights, and time spent finding pictures. I am ever indebted to my mother, Josie Eaklor, for her humor and unfailing support. Words cannot express the level of my gratitude to my partner, Pat O'Brien, for always being there and for enduring this process with me. Her love and encouragement through many years will never be forgotten, nor will her sage advice as a medical professional that put me on a healthier track (appointments and book available at www.realnaturalmedicine.com). The rest of our family are our animal companions, without whom life would be dull: our dogs Miracle and Spirit and cats Lucky (1992–2006), Beamer, Shamus, Sunshine, and especially my little Buddy (1988–2007), who I miss every day and who I hope went to a place where his sight and wanderlust were restored.

ABBREVIATIONS

ACLU	American Civil Liberties Union
ACT UP	AIDS Coalition to Unleash Power
AIDS	Acquired Immune Deficiency Syndrome
APA	American Psychiatric Association
CARE Act	Comprehensive AIDS Resources Emergency Act
CDC	Centers for Disease Control
CRH	Council on Religion and the Homosexual
DADT	"Don't Ask, Don't Tell" policy of the U.S. military
DOB	Daughters of Bilitis
DOMA	Defense of Marriage Act
DSM	*Diagnostic and Statistical Manual of Mental Disorders*
ENDA	Employment Non-Discrimination Act
FTM	female-to-male
GAA	Gay Activists Alliance
GAU	Gay Academic Union
GLAAD	Gay and Lesbian Alliance Against Defamation
GLBT	Gay, Lesbian, Bisexual, and Transgendered
GLF	Gay Liberation Front
GLSEN	Gay, Lesbian and Straight Education Network
GMHC	Gay Men's Health Crisis
GRNL	Gay Rights National Lobby
HRC(F)	Human Rights Campaign (Fund later dropped)
ILGA	International Lesbian and Gay Association
LLDEF	Lambda Legal Defense and Education Fund
MCC	Metropolitan Community Church
MTF	male-to-female
NCOD	National Coming Out Day
NCOP	National Coming Out Project
NGLTF	National Gay and Lesbian Task Force
NGRA	National Gay Rights Advocates
NGTF	National Gay Task Force
PFLAG	Parents, Families, and Friends of Lesbians and Gays
SLDN	Servicemembers Legal Defense Network

TIMELINE: 1890–2005

This timeline includes key events in the history of the GLBT United States. Additional items, such as wars, elections, landmarks in civil rights and women's rights, etc. are listed to provide context and reference points. Items are chronological by year, then alphabetical under each year.

1890   Battle at Wounded Knee between U.S. cavalry and Native Americans

Hull House, founded by Jane Addams to provide programs for workers, is underway in Chicago

National American Woman Suffrage Association formed

1892   Alice Mitchell murders Freda Ward in Memphis, TN

Earliest known use of the word "heterosexual" in the United States, in the *Chicago Medical Recorder*

Richard von Krafft-Ebing, *Psychopathia Sexualis* (1886) translated and published in the United States

Grover Cleveland elected president

1893   Magnus Hirschfeld, German homosexual rights pioneer, visits the United States

Frederick Jackson Turner delivers the "Frontier Thesis"

World's Columbian Exposition in Chicago

1895   Trials of Oscar Wilde in England; he is found guilty of "gross indecency" and serves two years in prison at hard labor

1896   *Plessy v. Ferguson*: Supreme Court declares segregation legal

William McKinley elected president

1897   Magnus Hirschfeld cofounds Scientific Humanitarian Committee in Berlin

1900   William McKinley reelected president

1901   Havelock Ellis, *Studies in the Psychology of Sex* (1897–1928) begins publication in Philadelphia

McKinley assassinated; Teddy Roosevelt becomes president

1904 Teddy Roosevelt elected president

1905 Sigmund Freud, *Three Essays on the Theory of Sexuality* published

1906 German homosexual emancipationists begin their visit in the United States

1908 Edward Prime-Stevenson, *The Intersexes* published, an early American defense of homosexuality

William H. Taft elected president

1910 Magnus Hirschfeld introduces the term "transvestite"

White Slave Traffic Act (Mann Act), passed by Congress

1912 Heterodoxy, an all-women's feminist club, begins meeting in Greenwich Village

Woodrow Wilson elected president

1913 Congressional Union (later, National Woman's Party) founded

16th Amendment adopted, establishing Congress' right to tax incomes

17th Amendment adopted, establishing the direct election of senators

1914 British Society for the Study of Sex Psychology founded

Magnus Hirschfeld, *Homosexuality in Men and Women* published

The Little Review founded in Chicago by Margaret Anderson, begins publication (to 1929)

World War I begins (United States enters 1917)

1916 Woodrow Wilson reelected president

1918 World War I ends

1919 Magnus Hirschfeld founds the Institute for Sexual Science in Berlin

18th Amendment adopted, and Volstead Act passed, establishing Prohibition beginning in 1920

1920 Warren G. Harding elected president

19th Amendment adopted, establishing women's suffrage nationwide

1923 Magnus Hirschfeld introduces the term "transsexual"

1924 Chicago Society for Human Rights chartered

Calvin Coolidge elected president

1925 Alain Locke, leader of the Harlem Renaissance, publishes *The New Negro*

1926 *The Captive,* a play with lesbian content, opens on Broadway

Richard Bruce Nugent, a Harlem Renaissance writer and artist, publishes "Smoke, Lilies, and Jade," credited as the first gay African American short fiction in print

1928 Radclyffe Hall, *The Well of Loneliness* published in United States and generates controversy

Herbert Hoover elected president

1929 Great Depression begins

1930 Hollywood Production Code, banning references to homosexuality, is adopted

1930–1931   "Pansy craze" reaches its peak in New York City

1931   Blair Niles, *Strange Brother* published, a novel depicting gay life

1932   Franklin D. Roosevelt elected president

1933   Charles Henri-Ford and Parker Tyler's novel of gay life, *The Young and the Evil,* published

New Deal begins

Prohibition ends, with the 21st Amendment, repealing the 18th

20th Amendment adopted, changing the dates executive and legislative terms begin

1934   Paul Cadmus' painting, "The Fleet's In!" stirs controversy and is removed from an exhibition

The Children's Hour, a play with lesbian content, opens on Broadway

1935   Committee for the Study of Sex Variants founded in New York City

1936   FDR reelected president

1939   World War II begins (United States enters 1941)

1940   FDR reelected president

1942   CORE (Congress of Racial Equality) founded

1944   FDR reelected president

Lillian Smith, *Strange Fruit* published

1945   Death of FDR; Truman becomes president

Veterans' Benevolent Association, for lesbian/gay veterans, founded in New York City (to 1954)

World War II ends

1947   Institute for Sex Research (Kinsey Institute) founded at Indiana University

National Security Act

Red Scare begins with investigations of communism in Hollywood and in the State Department

Jackie Robinson is the first African American to play major league baseball

Truman Doctrine expresses the intention of containing the spread of communism

Vice Versa, the first lesbian newsletter, published by "Lisa Ben"

1948   Executive Orders demand racial integration of the military and fair employment practices in the federal government

Alfred Kinsey, *Sexual Behavior in the Human Male* published

United Nations approves a *Universal Declaration of Human Rights*

Harry Truman elected president

Gore Vidal, *The City and the Pillar* published

1950   Lavender Scare underway when it is revealed that ninety-one homosexuals had been fired from the State Department as "security risks"

Korean War begins (to 1953)

Sen. Joseph McCarthy claims the State Department is full of communist employees

1951   Donald Webster Cory (Edward Sagarin), *The Homosexual in America* published

Mattachine Society, conceived by Harry Hay since 1948, founded in Los Angeles

Stoumen v. Reilly: CA Supreme Court upholds the right of bars to serve homosexuals, in a case brought by the Black Cat bar in San Francisco

22nd Amendment adopted, limiting presidential terms

1952 APA (American Psychiatric Association) lists homosexuality as a "sociopathic personality disturbance" in its first *DSM (Diagnostic and Statistical Manual)*

ONE, Inc. founded

Dwight Eisenhower elected president

Immigration and Nationality Act (McCarran-Walter Act) bans homosexual immigrants

Claire Morgan (Patricia Highsmith), *The Price of Salt* published

1953 Executive Order 10450 makes homosexuality grounds for dismissal from federal employment

Christine Jorgensen returns to the United States after male-to-female surgery in Denmark

Alfred Kinsey, *Sexual Behavior in the Human Female* published

ONE magazine begins publication (to 1968)

Rosenbergs, Julius and Ethel, are executed for passing atomic secrets to the USSR

1954 *Brown v. the Board of Education*: Supreme Court declares school segregation unconstitutional, reversing U.S. racial policy

1955 Daughters of Bilitis founded in San Francisco

Boise, ID: antihomosexual "witch-hunt" conducted

Mattachine Review begins publication

ONE Institute founded in Los Angeles to fulfill educational and other goals of ONE, Inc.

Rosa Parks arrested in Montgomery, AL

1956 James Baldwin, *Giovanni's Room* published

Dwight Eisenhower reelected president

Jeannette Foster, *Sex Variant Women in Literature* published

Allen Ginsberg, *Howl* published

Evelyn Hooker begins publishing studies of nonpatient homosexuals, paving the way for homosexuality ceasing to be classified as a mental disorder

Ladder begins publication in San Francisco (to 1972)

1957 Ann Bannon, *Odd Girl Out* published

SCLC (Southern Christian Leadership Conference) founded

1958 Daughters of Bilitis chapter formed in New York City

1959 Cuban Revolution brings Fidel Castro to power

1960 Daughters of Bilitis sponsor the first national lesbian conference, held in San Francisco

Clackum v. the U.S.: U.S. Court of Claims declares Fannie Mae Clackum's 1952 dismissal from the Air Force for lesbianism invalid

John F. Kennedy elected president

SNCC (Student Nonviolent Coordinating Committee) founded

1961 "Freedom rides" on Southern buses test the reversal of segregation laws

Illinois is first state to repeal its sodomy law

Mattachine Society of Washington, DC founded

Motion Picture code revised, allowing depictions of homosexuality

José Sarria is the first openly gay person to run for public office, in San Francisco

23rd Amendment adopted, allowing electors for the District of Columbia

1962 Crisis over Soviet missile sites in Cuba brings Cold War tension to a peak

Janus Society founded in Philadelphia (to 1969); publishes *Drum* magazine (1964–1969)

Students for a Democratic Society members write "The Port Huron Statement"

Tavern Guild founded in San Francisco

1963 Betty Friedan, *The Feminine Mystique* published

East Coast Homophile Organizations founded

John F. Kennedy assassinated, November 22; Lyndon Johnson becomes president

March on Washington for Jobs and Freedom

John Rechy, *City of Night* published

1964 Civil Rights Act creates the broadest protection yet against racial and sexual discrimination

Council on Religion and the Homosexual formed in San Francisco

Life magazine story, "Homosexuality in America," June 26

Lyndon Johnson elected president

Pickets for gay rights, the first ever, at U.S. Army induction center (9/19) and at Cooper Union (12/2), both in New York City

Jane Rule, *Desert of the Heart* published

Society for Individual Rights founded in San Francisco

24th Amendment adopted, abolishing the poll tax

Randy Wicker is the first openly gay guest on a TV talk show, *The Les Crane Show*

1965 Council on Religion and the Homosexual (San Francisco) holds press conference to report harassment by police at its New Year's Ball

Dewey's restaurant in Philadelphia is the site of the first gay sit-in

Griswold v. Connecticut: Supreme Court upholds right to privacy within marriage

Homosexual Law Reform Society founded in Philadelphia

Malcolm X assassinated

Picket for gay rights Independence Hall, July 4 (Annual Reminders, held through 1969)

Pickets for gay rights also at the White House (4/17, 5/29, 10/23), the United Nations (4/18), the Civil Service Commission (6/26), the Pentagon (7/31), the State Department (8/28), and Grace Cathedral in San Francisco (9/26)

San Francisco's first drag ball held; attendees are forced to cross a police picket line

Vietnam War is "Americanized" by sending 180,000 combat troops by the year's end

1966 Harry Benjamin, *The Transsexual Phenomenon* published

Black Panthers founded in Oakland, CA

Compton's Cafeteria riot in San Francisco, in which trans people fought police harassment

NOW (National Organization for Women) founded

North American Conference of Homophile Organizations meets in Kansas City

1967   *The Advocate* begins publication in Los Angeles

Black Cat bar in Los Angeles raided; several patrons injured and organized protests followed

Boutilier v. Immigration Service: Supreme Court upholds a gay Canadian's deportation

Homophile Action League founded in Philadelphia

"The Homosexuals," a CBS Special reported with Mike Wallace, airs

Loving v. Virginia: Supreme Court declares laws against interracial marriage unconstitutional

Oscar Wilde Bookstore opens in New York City, the first gay bookstore in the United States

Student Homophile League at Columbia University becomes first such group formally recognized

25th Amendment adopted, specifying executive succession to office

1968   APA revises its classification of homosexuality to a "non-psychotic mental disorder"

Civil Rights Act expands protections and enforcement of Civil Rights Act of 1964

Mart Crowley, *The Boys in the Band* opens off Broadway

Democratic National Convention, held in Chicago, sparks violence when police clash with protestors

Robert Kennedy assassinated

Martin Luther King, Jr. assassinated

Metropolitan Community Church originates in Los Angeles

Miss America Pageant is the subject of feminist protests

MPAA (Motion Picture Association of America) film rating system replaces Hollywood Production Code

Richard Nixon elected president

Tet Offensive in Vietnam creates more opposition to the war

1969   *GAY,* a weekly paper, begins publication (to 1973)

Gay Activists Alliance founded

Gay Liberation Front founded in New York City, July

Isabel Miller (Alma Routsong), *A Place for Us* (later, *Patience and Sarah*) published

Stonewall riot, June 27–28

Woodstock Festival held in New York State

1970   Anniversary march of Stonewall

Jack Baker and Michael McConnell apply for a marriage license in Minneapolis; *Look* magazine runs a story on them January 26, 1971

Daughters of Bilitis disbands as a national organization; local chapters continue

First gay studies class taught at University of Nebraska by Louis Crompton

Kent State University is the site of the "May 4 Massacre" when Ohio National Guard troops kill four students and wound nine during an antiwar protest

National Organization for Women purges lesbians from its New York chapter

Radicalesbians form and write "The Woman Identified Woman"

Task Force on Gay Liberation (now the GLBT Round Table) is formed within the American Library Association and is the first academic/professional caucus

Unidos, a lesbian/gay Chicano/a group, founded in Los Angeles

Carl Wittman, "Refugees from Amerika: A Gay Manifesto" published

1971 *The Empty Closet* begins publication in Rochester, NY

Gay Activists Alliance of Washington, DC founded

Frank Kameny runs for Congress, the second openly gay candidate for public office

NOW "acknowledges the oppression of lesbians as a legitimate concern of feminism"

26th Amendment adopted, changing the minimum voting age from 21 to 18

1972 Atlanta Lesbian Feminist Alliance founded

Democratic National Convention includes two openly gay/lesbian speakers

Equal Rights Amendment passed in Congress; sent to states for ratification (fails, 1982)

Gay Community Services Center opens in Los Angeles

First gay studies program, California State University at Sacramento

Lesbianism course taught at SUNY-Buffalo by Madeline Davis

Del Martin and Phyllis Lyon, *Lesbian/Woman* published

Ms. magazine begins publication

National Bisexual Liberation Group formed in New York City

Richard Nixon reelected president

Origins of Parents and Friends of Lesbians and Gays, incorporated in 1982

Survey of Gay and Lesbian Literature taught at San Francisco City College

First gay synagogue opens in Los Angeles

Title IX of the Education Amendments bans sexual discrimination in publicly funded
    education

United Church of Christ ordains first openly gay minister in any major Christian
    denomination

1973 APA removes homosexuality from its list of mental disorders

Rita Mae Brown, *Rubyfruit Jungle* published

Casablanca Records founded and becomes biggest disco label (to 1984)

Caucuses formed in Modern Languages and Psychology

Dignity founded, for Catholic gays and lesbians

Alix Dobkin's album *Lavender Jane Loves Women* released

Gay Academic Union founded in New York City

Lambda Legal Defense and Education Fund founded in New York City

Metropolitan Community Church in Los Angeles burned to the ground by arsonists,
    January 27

Naiad Press founded (to 2004)

National Gay Task Force founded in New York City

Olivia Records founded

Our Bodies, Ourselves published in its first commercial edition

Roe v. Wade: Supreme Court declares abortion legal in most circumstances

Vietnam War ends and American troops are withdrawn

Watergate scandal reveals covert operations and a cover-up; leads to Nixon's resignation

1974   Combahee River Collective, an African American feminist group, founded in Roxbury, MA

"Equality Act" introduced in Congress, the first attempt at national gay rights law

Integrity founded, for Episcopal gays and lesbians

Journal of Homosexuality begins publication

Lesbian Connection begins publication

Nixon resigns from the presidency; Gerald Ford becomes president

Elaine Noble elected to MA State House and Kathy Kozachenko elected to Ann Arbor City Council, both open lesbians

Salsa Soul Sisters formed in New York City

Sociologists' Lesbian and Gay Caucus formed

Allan Spear, MN state senator, comes out

Patricia Nell Warren, *The Front Runner* published

1975   Bisexual Forum founded in New York City

Caucuses in psychiatry and public health founded

Committee on Lesbian and Gay History founded

Gay American Indians founded

Dave Kopay, retired professional football player, comes out

Sgt. Leonard Matlovich, discharged for being gay, appears on the cover of *Time*, September 8

Saigon falls to communists; renamed Ho Chi Minh City

Cris Williamson's album *The Changer and the Changed* released

1976   *The Advocate* International Conference

Jimmy Carter elected president

Caucuses formed in nursing and social work

Jonathan Ned Katz, *Gay American History* published

Gay Rights National Lobby founded

Girth and Mirth founded for "Bears," gay and bisexual men with body and facial hair

First Michigan Womyn's Music Festival

National Gay Rights Advocates founded in San Francisco

1977   Dade County struggle over gay rights law: passed (January); Save Our Children campaign; law repealed (June)

Lesbian Rights Project founded (later, National Center for Lesbian Rights)

Harvey Milk elected to be San Francisco Supervisor

National Lesbian and Gay Health Foundation founded

Soap introduces gay character Jodie Dallas

Senior Action in a Gay Environment founded

White House staff holds first-ever meeting with lesbian/gay leaders

1978   California voters defeat antigay Proposition 6 (Briggs initiative)

Disneyland holds its first Gay Day

Gay and Lesbian Advocates and Defenders founded in Boston

Gay rights laws repealed in Eugene, OR, St. Paul, MN, and Wichita, KS

International Lesbian and Gay Association founded

Armistead Maupin, *Tales of the City* published in book form; five more books in the series follow

Harvey Milk and George Moscone murdered, November 27

NAMBLA (North American Man/Boy Love Association) founded

Effort to repeal Seattle's gay rights law fails

1979   A Different Light bookstore opens in Los Angeles

"Gay Liberation" statue commissioned; installed in Greenwich Village, 1992

Hetrick-Martin Institute founded

Moral Majority Coalition founded

National March on Washington for Lesbian and Gay Rights, October 14

National Third World Lesbian and Gay Conference

Radical Faeries hold their first "spiritual conference"

Sisters of Perpetual Indulgence make their debut in the Castro district, San Francisco

1980   Black and White Men Together founded

Democratic Party platform committee writes antidiscrimination statement including "sexual orientation"; gay and lesbian caucus nominates openly gay African American Mel Boozer for vice president and he delivers a speech at the convention

Gay and Lesbian Civil Rights Bill reintroduced in Congress

Harry Benjamin International Gender Dysphoria Association founded

Human Rights Campaign Fund founded

Ronald Reagan elected president

Adrienne Rich, "Compulsory Heterosexuality and Lesbian Existence" published in *Signs*

Gene Ulrich, openly gay, elected mayor of Bunceton, Missouri

1981   AIDS first reported, in *San Francisco Chronicle*: "A Pneumonia that Strikes Gay Males," June 6

AIDS reported in *New York Times*: "Rare Cancer Seen in 41 Homosexuals," July 3

Cherríe Moraga and Gloria Anzaldúa, *This Bridge Called My Back* published

Vito Russo, *The Celluloid Closet* published

1982   Glenn Burke, retired professional baseball player, comes out

Harvey Fierstein's play *Torch Song Trilogy* opens and runs for three years

Gay Games first held, in San Francisco, August

Gay Men's Health Crisis founded in New York City

HRCF dinner in New York City: former vice president Walter Mondale speaks, October

Wisconsin becomes first state to pass a law banning discrimination based on sexual orientation

1983   John D'Emilio, *Sexual Politics, Sexual Communities* published

Dykes to Watch Out For comic strip, by Alison Bechdel, begins its long run

Lesbians of Color Conference, the first on a national level, meets in Malibu, CA

Medical rights ordeal of and Sharon Kowalski and Karen Thompson begins; resolved 1991

People with AIDS Coalition founded

Gerry Studds is out as first openly gay congressman

1984   Discovery of virus causing AIDS; later named HIV

Ronald Reagan reelected president

1985   AIDS Civil Rights Project added to National Gay Rights Advocates

Congress passes an act authorizing the U.S. Surgeon General to close bathhouses

Gay and Lesbian Alliance Against Defamation founded in New York City

Harvey Milk High School opens in New York City, April 1

Larry Kramer's play *The Normal Heart* opens in New York City

Rock Hudson dies of AIDS

Unity Fellowship Church Movement originates in Los Angeles

1986   Antigay amendments introduced to bills in Senate, August

Joseph Beam, *In the Life* published

Bowers v. Hardwick: Supreme Court upholds Georgia's sodomy law

FTM International founded

Gay Activists Alliance of Washington, DC adds "Lesbian" to its name

National Gay Task Force adds "Lesbian" to its name and moves its headquarters to Washington, DC

New York City passes nondiscrimination law

Simpson-Mazzoli Act passes, removing the "sexual deviation" clause used to exclude homosexual immigrants

Walter Williams, *Spirit and the Flesh,* published

1987   ACT UP founded

Asian/Pacific-Islander Lesbian and Bisexual Network founded

Congressman Barney Frank comes out

NAMES Project AIDS Memorial Quilt begins

National March on Washington for Lesbian and Gay Rights, October 11

New York Times begins using "gay" in place of "homosexual," July 15

Randy Shilts, *And the Band Played On* published

1988   Claudia Brenner injured and her partner Rebecca Wight is killed by gunman while hiking the Appalachian Trail

George H. W. Bush elected president

National Coming Out Day begins as an annual event, October 11

National Black Lesbian and Gay Leadership Forum founded

1989   Day Without Art initiated, December 1

Martin Duberman et al., *Hidden From History* published

First Gay and Lesbian Studies Department, San Francisco City College

National Latina/o Lesbian, Gay, Bisexual, and Transgender Organization (LLEGÓ) founded

National Lesbian and Gay Law Association founded

Lesléa Newman, *Heather Has Two Mommies* published

Old Lesbians Organizing for Change founded

Bob Paris, former Mr. Universe, comes out and marries Rod Jackson

Webster v. Reproductive Health Services: Supreme Court upholds restrictions on abortion

1990 AEGIS (American Educational Gender Information Service) founded

Americans with Disabilities Act passed by Congress

Gay, Lesbian and Bisexual Veterans of America, Inc. founded (later, American Veterans for

Equal Rights)

Judith Butler, *Gender Trouble* published

Hate Crimes Statistics Act passed

Journal of the History of Sexuality begins publication

Longtime Companion (film) opens in theaters

Mautner Project founded

National Bisexual Conference held for the first time

National Lesbian and Gay Journalists Association founded

North American Bisexual Network (later, BiNet USA) formed

"Outing" controversy

Dave Pallone, major league umpire, comes out

Queer Nation founded in New York City

Ryan White CARE (Comprehensive AIDS Resources Emergency) Act passed

1991 CLAGS (Center for Lesbian and Gay Studies) of the City University of New York opens

Day of National Coordinated Action, protesting military antigay policy, April 10

Estate Project founded

Gay and Lesbian Victory Fund founded

Gay and Lesbian Civil Rights Bill reintroduced in Congress with 110 cosponsors

Lesbian AIDS Project founded

National Lesbian Conference in Atlanta

Persian Gulf War ("Operation Desert Storm")

Studies claiming genetic basis for sexuality begin to be published

Cheryl Summerville fired from Cracker Barrel Old Country Store for being lesbian

1992 Alliance of Lesbian and Gay Health Clinics founded

Colonel Margarethe Cammermeyer discharged from the Army after more than twenty-five years of service; wins reinstatement in 1994

Bill Clinton elected president

"Children of the Rainbow" curriculum controversy begins in New York City

Colorado voters approve antigay Amendment 2

k.d. lang comes out

Leslie Feinberg, *Transgender Liberation* published

In the Life, a gay and lesbian TV show, premiers

Lesbian Avengers founded in New York City

Oregon voters defeat antigay Measure 9

Roy Simmons, retired professional football player, comes out

Transgender Nation founded

27th Amendment adopted, banning midterm congressional pay increases

1993 Roberta Achtenberg, openly lesbian, becomes assistant secretary of Housing and Urban Development

Tony Kushner's play *Angels in America* opens on Broadway

"Camp Trans" is pitched outside of Michigan Womyn's Music Festival in protest of its "Womyn-Born-Womyn Only" policy

"Don't Ask, Don't Tell" (DADT) policy passed, September; in effect 1994

Melissa Etheridge comes out

Hate Crimes Sentencing Enhancement Act passed

Intersex Society of North America founded

Log Cabin Republicans founded in Washington, DC

March on Washington for Lesbian, Gay and Bi Equal Rights and Liberation, April 25

Newsweek runs cover story on "Lesbians Coming Out Strong," June 21

Oval Office meeting between President Clinton and lesbian/gay leaders

Philadelphia (film) opens in theaters

SLDN (Servicemembers Legal Defense Network) founded

Brandon Teena murdered

1994 Antigay measures in Idaho (Proposition 1) and Oregon (Proposition 13) defeated in elections

First national Lesbian Health Roundtable

Gay Games IV held in New York; Olympic diver Greg Louganis comes out during the Games

Hate Crimes Sentencing Enhancement Act passed

Sheila Kuehl, openly lesbian, wins a seat in the California Assembly

Northern Exposure episode has TV's first same-sex wedding

Stonewall 25 celebrated

1995 Antigay initiative in Maine defeated

OutThere (entertainment personnel) formed in July

Ryan White CARE Act renewed

1996 *Baehr v. Miike* (formerly *Baehr v. Lewin*): Hawai'i Supreme Court rules in favor of same-sex marriage

Bill Clinton reelected president

Defense of Marriage Act passed

Employment Non-Discrimination Act defeated in a 49-50 Senate vote

Hate Crimes Statistics Act renewed

The International Gay & Lesbian Review begins, online

Protease inhibitors, for treating HIV/AIDS, introduced

Romer v. Evans: Supreme Court declares Colorado's antigay Amendment 2 unconstitutional

1997 APA questions "conversion therapy" for lesbians and gays

Ellen DeGeneres comes out, appears on the cover of *Time,* April 14

Ellen DeGeneres' TV character Ellen Morgan comes out, April 30

ENDA reintroduced in Congress

Hate Crimes Prevention Act introduced in Congress

James Hormel, openly gay, nominated to be ambassador to Luxembourg

HRC holds its first National Dinner and Awards; President Clinton gives keynote address

Journal of Lesbian Studies begins publication

1998   Tammy Baldwin is the first open lesbian elected to Congress

Executive Order bans antigay discrimination in federal government

"Ex-gay" ads run, sponsored by right-wing Christian groups

Hawai'i constitutional amendment passes banning same-sex marriage

Maine's gay rights law repealed by voters

Matthew Shepard, an openly gay student, dies from injuries of an antigay beating, October

Will & Grace, a TV sitcom with a gay lead character, premiers

1999   Billy Bean, retired professional baseball player, comes out

Boys Don't Cry (film) opens in theaters

Gay and Lesbian Pride Month (June) declared by President Clinton

James Hormel sworn in as ambassador to Luxembourg, June 29

Impeachment trial of President Clinton; not convicted

2000   *Boy Scouts of America v. Dale*: Supreme Court rules that Boy Scouts can exclude gay people

George W. Bush becomes president in a contested election

Gay and Lesbian Pride Month (June) again declared by President Clinton

Millennium March on Washington for Equality, April 30

Queer as Folk premiers on Showtime

Vermont legislature approves civil unions for same-sex couples

2001   *Journal of Bisexuality* begins publication

Terrorists attack the United States at the World Trade Center and the Pentagon, killing nearly 3,000 people, September 11

2002   Death of gay rights pioneer Harry Hay

Esera Tuaolo, retired professional football player, comes out

here! TV, aimed at GLBT viewers, established

2003   *The Ellen DeGeneres Show* and *Queer Eye for the Straight Guy* premier

Goodridge v. Massachusetts Department of Public Health: Massachusetts Supreme Court declares same-sex marriage constitutional

Lawrence v. Texas: Supreme Court overturns *Bowers v. Hardwick* (1986)

V. Gene Robinson, openly gay, elected bishop by Episcopal Diocese of New Hampshire

War in Iraq ("Operation Iraqi Freedom") begins

2004   Antigay marriage amendments pass in eleven states in November elections

George W. Bush elected president for a second term

The L Word premiers on Showtime

Same-sex marriage available in Massachusetts, May

2005   *Brokeback Mountain,* a movie about gay cowboys, opens

Connecticut legalizes civil unions for same-sex couples

Death of lesbian/gay rights activist Jean O'Leary

Sheryl Swoopes, WNBA player, comes out

1 WHAT IS GLBT HISTORY?

Early in 2005 a *New York Times* book reviewer asked the provocative question, "Was Lincoln Gay?"[1] It was a response to yet another Abraham Lincoln biography, but this time a study of the Great Emancipator's close personal relationships, including those with men. That such a book not only could be written and published, but also gain the attention of the venerable *New York Times* are results of developments of the 20th century. The term used—gay—and the fact that there is no easy answer to the question, are no less products of the same century. What this suggests is that remarkable changes occurred in one hundred years of U.S. history as seen through a lens focused on GLBT (gay, lesbian, bisexual, and transgendered) people and issues. This volume is an attempt to present those changes in order to gain a richer understanding of both our past and our present.

In these opening years of the 21st century in the United States, perhaps no topic is more divisive than homosexuality, particularly when it is coupled with the deeply rooted concept of civil rights. Controversy over ex-presidents' sexuality, although hotly debated at times, pales next to recent debates surrounding same-sex marriage, for example. In 2004, a president was elected who publicly supports a constitutional amendment that would prohibit such marriages, and eleven states added amendments to their constitutions banning same-sex marriage. The marriage debate, in turn, is but part of a larger discussion over issues crucial to American life, such as the role of law in the lives of individuals, relationships among law, economics, and morality, and the values thought to distinguish and define us. Just a year previously, thirteen states, Puerto Rico, and the U.S. military still had laws prohibiting sodomy until the U.S. Supreme Court ruled such laws unconstitutional in the 2003 decision *Lawrence v. Texas* (reversing the 1986 Supreme Court decision in *Bowers v. Hardwick*). On the other hand, only two years after the *Lawrence* decision, Maine joined fifteen other states offering some sort of legal protection to GLBT people.[2] This is a mixed, and confusing, bag. While questions of progress—whether things are getting better, worse, or staying the same—are interesting, they are quite subjective and less important to historical inquiry than explaining how we got to this point. This volume is in part a modest attempt to do just that.

A NOTE ON TERMS

One source of current confusion is terms, each of which reflects the mentality and concerns of the times in which it gained currency. A variety of words has been used over the last one hundred years to describe desire, affiliation, behavior, and identity that is not exclusively opposite-sex and/or that violates standard gender assumptions. This has been no simple linear development, however, with one term replacing another in a dominant language. Instead, many words are and have been used simultaneously but by different populations, exposing the ethnic, class and other fault lines of American culture, into which any facile narrative might be swallowed. "GLBT," representing "Gay, Lesbian, Bisexual, and Transgendered," has largely replaced "homosexual" among activists and scholars, but it is not a simple substitution since GLBT includes more possibilities than only those who previously might have been termed homosexual. For most of the 20th century, the "homosexual" was the primary focus of both medicine and law, and the word now represents to many the stigma usually implied when doctors, lawyers, and other public officials used the term. "Gay" had been known for decades, but only entered more public use (among nongay people, that is) in the 1960s and 1970s; this change was signaled in 1987 by the *New York Times* when it officially replaced "homosexual" with "gay."[3] As feminism and lesbian feminism became greater forces in the 1970s and after, "lesbian" was added as a result of women's demand for visibility, and similar claims followed for those identifying as bisexual and transgendered. The evolution of terminology, then, is significant in the way it reflects the way choices offered Americans regarding their sexual identity have both narrowed (into homosexual) and broadened (in GLBT, etc.) in one hundred years. GLBT was chosen for the title, rather than homosexual or queer, to be both current and historical—to represent contemporary thought and the order in which activists have come to add terms to define their cause. At the same time, because it often would be ahistorical to use GLBT, or each singly (Gay, Lesbian, Bisexual, Transgendered), for people or events preceding the words' usage, the language used at the time has been adopted throughout the narrative.

What about that loaded term "queer"? The sources of its various connotations will be examined here to show why it remains controversial. In part there is a generation gap: many men and women who came of age after World War II, out or not, continue to have painful memories of "queer" as connoting the worst imaginable pervert. As one man remembers,

...the movement to reclaim the term queer is a little, well, *queer* to me. When I was growing up in a small Midwestern city in the 1970s, being called a queer was an insult of the highest order. For a boy, it meant not only being accused of liking other boys, but was also a damning indictment of how one operated within his gender.[4]

The name-calling had consequences beyond the personal. During the Cold War, people lost jobs by the hundreds for mere suspicion of homosexuality because "queer" and "commie" were linked in the minds of policy makers at the highest levels. Younger activists and scholars, especially those involved in developing queer theory (see Debate, Chapter 9), believe the stigma can be removed through associating it with visibility and pride, and so the debate continues.

GLBT HISTORY TODAY

The field of GLBT/queer history has mushroomed to a level unimaginable when John D'Emilio first published his groundbreaking *Sexual Politics, Sexual Communities* in 1983. As apparent in the Bibliography, there are now hundreds of books available in the area to everyone from the casual browser to the serious scholar. Additionally, the Committee on Lesbian and Gay History, an affiliate of the American Historical Association celebrating its 30th anniversary in 2005, recently reported that there are more than eighty dissertations completed or in progress in the field, up from none in less than twenty-five years.[5]

The vast majority of work in GLBT history so far has been in both U.S. history and, within that, the 20th century. Detailed studies of particular eras or topics by George Chauncey, Dudley Clendinen, and Adam Nagourney, Lillian Faderman, Eric Marcus, and many, many others have added immeasurably to our knowledge in this field. For a comprehensive treatment one can turn to the *Encyclopedia of Lesbian, Gay, Bisexual, and Transgender History in America* and for an excellent overview to Leila Rupp's *A Desired Past: A Short History of Same-Sex Love in America.* Oddly, though, there is yet nothing in between—a comprehensive survey of 20th-century GLBT American history aimed at the general reader. This book attempts to fill that gap, and balance the purposes of a chronological narrative with those of a reference work and a handbook of topics, people, and issues.

WHAT *IS* GLBT HISTORY?

To ask this question is to delve into the meaning of history itself. Implied in the inquiry are multiple questions: What *is* the story? Who or what should be included and why? What is the theme and how should the story be organized? In some ways, answers to these are no different than for other groups in U.S. history. There are important differences also, however, that reinforce the very need for this particular history.

U.S. History and GLBT History

To many people, main themes of U.S. history are not only its internal politics and rise to world power status—important themes indeed—but also the changing composition of its population and the extension of political, social, and economic rights or opportunities to groups previously denied them. The quest for rights, particularly equality under the law as defined in the 14th Amendment to the U.S. Constitution, has been a driving factor in our history and helps define us as Americans. When people have chosen certain characteristics—race, class, religion, ethnicity, sex—and determined that those characteristics have been used to deny them equality, they are said to be operating in a system of identity politics. Ideally, gains are made when people relate to a certain group based on one attribute over others, and can be a bloc effective in the political process. Labor organizing is one example. Since the early 19th century, many people who work for wages have felt they could have a voice only when they were organized. This demanded that men and women think of themselves as wage earners first and anything else—men or women, white or not, etc.—as secondary to their self-image. What many women and nonwhite men found, though, was that they were less welcome in labor organizing, and so identified more fully with their sexual or racial identities.

Sexuality is a relatively recent development in all this, but the history of people thinking of themselves primarily in terms of homosexual or heterosexual (and later GLBT and/or queer) follows the general patterns of U.S. history and history writing. After World War II, all GLBT people may or may not have accepted themselves, but those who did adopted a concept of themselves as a "minority" deserving of the same rights as "straight" Americans. The way in which they did so follows important patterns of U.S. historical thought, bringing GLBT Americans into a "mainstream" of the driving forces of our history, not just as victims but as actors in their destinies. In this way GLBT history is similar to other minority histories, be they of African Americans, women, laborers, or any other self-defined group.

GLBT history is not just the struggle for rights, though, any more than women's history is confined to the suffrage movement or African American history to slavery. Like those other histories, it also relates people simply living their lives "the best they knew how" regardless of the terms they or others use for them, regardless of their own sense or oppression or freedom.[6] Like all minority histories, that of GLBT Americans intertwines significantly with "traditional" political history to become not merely an interesting side shows but part and parcel of the central narrative. Finally, none of these histories could have developed without a corresponding group identity, first formulated and then projected backward in time.

In other words, one way of thinking about doing GLBT history is as a history similar to those of other marginalized people. The subjects may be different, but there are common themes in all these of self-definition, pride, community formation, and political action that help to organize a narrative. None of this was as possible before the advent of the new social history of the 1960s and 1970s. At that time, contemporary politics and the writing of history, always allied, merged more obviously than in previous years. The ongoing African Americans movement for the civil rights, a revitalized women's movement, and many others helped stimulate the quest for a broader, more inclusive U.S. history than usually taught. As these histories developed, they in turn helped spur the movements for social change. In this respect, gay history (as it was first called) became an almost predictable result of an increasingly vital set of movements, from gay rights, to gay liberation, lesbian feminism, and on to current configurations.

While GLBT history is yet another in a growing list of minority histories, there are factors that distinguish it from these other histories and make it more problematic. One concerns the risks that have been involved in teaching and learning it while another is the historical visibility or "presence" of the proposed subjects. What these factors seem to share, at root, are both homophobia and heterosexism.

One governing theme of 20th-century homosexual history has been homophobia, loosely defined as the fear and hatred of homosexuals. Its sources seem varied, some deeply rooted and some relatively recent, but none constant throughout American history. Regardless of its origins (see Chapter 2 Debate), the stigma eventually attached to homosexuality affected all areas of thought, including history. More subtle but no less powerful has been the effect of heterosexism, or the assumption that everyone, past or present, is "straight" unless "proven" otherwise; what we have called heterosexuality, in other words, has been the default condition, supported further by the notions of its "normalcy" as opposed to any "deviant" sexuality. The burden of proof in this situation falls on those who would suggest someone is *not* heterosexual rather than on *any* claims of *any* type of sexuality. Different though related, homophobia and heterosexism are equally effective in enforcing silence and invisibility, which return the favor by maintaining homophobia and heterosexism.

This has put GLBT historians in an awkward position; a position, like the history itself, both similar to and distinct from that of other minority historians. An interesting phenomenon attached to all branches of social history has been the strong association of the history written with the historians writing it. This is understandable in light of the fact that members of marginalized groups not only have been the first to reconstruct their pasts but sometimes have sought continued control over the process. The idea is not that only a member of the group can write its history but that the same power relations that kept the history hidden in the first place should not be replicated in more powerful people co-opting (as some see it) the narrative for their own purposes. The resulting dilemma for so-called minority histories has been between relinquishing control over them in order to get them taken more seriously, or controlling them only to have them portrayed as mere accompaniments to questionable, even dangerous political movements.

At its most dismissive, however, the question implied is, "Who else but ____ (fill in the blank—women, African Americans, Native Americans, queers, etc.) would be interested in doing ____ (fill in blank with same word chosen before) history?" Not only does this reinforce the notion of a "real" history (i.e., the story of straight, white, male, middle-class people as they engage in politics and war) versus other histories tainted by some agenda, it also highlights the unique and precarious position of GLBT history and historians. *Are* historians of GLBT people themselves gay, lesbian, bisexual, or transgendered? Very often the answer is yes, just as it is for those other histories, but the ability to hide this particular identity and the possible repercussions in refusing to hide are what complicate both the history and its practice. In 1992, for example, the Committee on Women Historians of the American Historical Association conducted a survey of lesbian and gay historians. According to the Committee's report, 70 percent of their respondents faced antigay prejudice, 43 percent noted some form of discrimination, and 34.6 percent were told to avoid publishing on gay/lesbian topics. "Homophobia," asserted the report, "can push graduate students out of the profession and respected teachers out of history departments." It went on to state that although "a surprising number (63.9%)" of gay and lesbian professors reported being out to their colleagues to some degree, they then faced conflicting expectations: "demands from students to be role models, while colleagues may prefer them to keep a low profile."[7] Although things have improved somewhat in higher education, GLBT public school teachers in most communities risk their jobs by coming out. In this climate, students, regardless of their self-identification, can be hindered from inquiring into GLBT history, or even showing the slightest interest.[8]

Whether one specializes in GLBT history as a scholar or is merely an attentive student, then, there are risks many might prefer to avoid. Again, these are similar to those faced by most people studying minority histories in the last decades of the 20th century, as historians of marginalized groups have repeatedly faced derision at the least and unspoken blackballing at the worst, until their fields were shown to have merit. The pace at which this occurred paralleled the political and social gains made by those groups, and so GLBT history is no different in that respect. The difference, perhaps, is that GLBT people still face discrimination, job and personal insecurity, and violence in American society to a degree still more acceptable than that faced by many others. The result has been a kind of Catch-22: had no stigma ever been attached, there would be an easily accessible record of GLBT people (or maybe no such categories), but less, if any, need to tell it.

Who to Include and Why?

If silence and invisibility, rooted in homophobia and heterosexism, have complicated the construction of a GLBT narrative, so have more complex theoretical issues. These can be illustrated by returning to the question of "Was Lincoln Gay?" The combination of a 19th-century person with a 20th-century term encapsulates the main problems faced by students and scholars of what we currently call GLBT history. While the minor controversy such a question seems to create whenever it is raised about a respected American of any century reveals a deep-seated prejudice against all things GLBT—it often has been viewed as an "accusation" intending to discredit the person—such controversy also reflects serious debates among the most sympathetic scholars. There are at least three possible answers to "Was Lincoln Gay?": yes; no; and we are not sure. Taking each response in turn illustrates the theoretical complications facing anyone involved in doing GLBT history.

Yes, Lincoln was gay. This claim, or any reference to someone who existed before either "gay" or "homosexual" was available to them as a category, implies belief in a linear history, or one plotted along a line, any point in the line being related to others both before and after it. In Western European and American tradition, linear history has often been equated with progressive history, though the two are not automatically identical. Progressive history promotes the notion of an ascending line of human accomplishment: that in knowledge, human rights, and other areas, the closer we are to the present the greater the progress away from such things as authoritarianism in politics, economics, and religion. Progressive history became especially popular in 19th-century Europe and America, when the spread of democracy and technology, for example, seemed to promise unlimited advances, and it continues to influence historical thought.

In this case "gay" as understood in the late 20th century is projected backward to include those that exhibit the desires, behaviors, and/or self awareness, even if the language differs, of what is presumed to be an ahistorical "gayness." This has been termed a more essentialist argument and it has been a popular approach, especially among activists (see Debate). This may be due in part to the advantages of biography generally, since that genre is a tried and true window into all types of history and a perennial favorite with general readers. More important, the effort to "find the queers in history" offers role models to counter extremely negative stereotypes that arose immediately upon the definition of homosexuality. Labeled "deviants" from the start, homosexuals, as we shall see, were linked with sin, crime, and/or illness (mental and physical) throughout most of the 20th century, and have often been considered a danger to children. Including revered people in a homosexual narrative is seen to challenge those stereotypes. This was the logic at work, for example, when Supreme Court Justice William O. Douglas wrote, in his dissenting opinion in a 1967 case regarding the exclusion of homosexuals from immigration to the United States:

> To label a group so large "excludable aliens" would be tantamount to saying that Sappho, Leonardo da Vinci, Michelangelo, Andre Gide, and perhaps even Shakespeare, were they to come to life again, would be deemed unfit to visit our shores.[9]

This same logic—finding and noting gay, lesbian, or bisexual heroes might help destigmatize homosexuality—is at work in a poster celebrating National Coming Out Day. It features photos of people considered prominent or "achievers," such as Willa Cather, Cole Porter, and Eleanor Roosevelt. Underneath the photos it reads, "Assume that all

UNFORTUNATELY, HISTORY HAS SET THE RECORD A LITTLE TOO STRAIGHT.

James Baldwin/Writer
1924 - 1987

Willa Cather/Writer
1873 - 1947

Errol Flynn/Actor
1909 - 1959

Michelangelo/Artist
1475 - 1564

Edna St. Vincent Millay/Poet
1892 - 1950

Cole Porter/Composer
1891 - 1964

Eleanor Roosevelt/Social Activist
1884 - 1962

Bessie Smith/Singer
1894 - 1937

Walt Whitman/Poet
1819 - 1892

Virginia Woolf/Writer
1882 - 1941

Assume that all important contributions are made by heterosexuals, and you're not only thinking straight, but narrow.
Sexual orientation has nothing to do with the ability to make a mark, let alone make history.

NATIONAL COMING OUT DAY
OCT. 11, 1988

This poster, "A Little Too Straight," represents efforts to reclaim famous individuals as part of GLBT history. Among the messages that instill pride are that one can be queer and achieve great things. Pictured are (top, L to R) James Baldwin, Willa Cather, Errol Flynn, Michelangelo, Edna St. Vincent Millay, and (bottom, L to R) Cole Porter, Eleanor Roosevelt, Bessie Smith, Walt Whitman, Virginia Woolf. (© Laurie Casagrande)

important contributions are made by heterosexuals, and you're not only thinking straight, but narrow. Sexual orientation has nothing to do with the ability to make a mark, let alone make history."

Such efforts not only have the potential to generate pride among members of a relatively young movement, but also represent important issues in doing this or any history. Foremost among those issues are visibility and evidence. As is the case with many other neglected histories, simply filling in gaps of knowledge in the interest of a more complete story has been a primary objective. Many of the first GLBT histories, then, were conceived as projects of discovery, as revealed in such titles as *Becoming Visible, Hidden from History,* and "Who His Lesbian History?"[10] The rationale was that the GLBT people were there all along but for various reasons, including heterosexist assumptions and homophobia, they had all but disappeared from the record; either they were invisible, or they were present but assumed to be heterosexual.

Visibility past and present is linked in turn to the question of evidence. In this respect, GLBT history becomes more problematic than that of women or ethnic minorities, for example, because the latter categories are generally more stable over time (there is little debate over who was or was not a woman, whether one hundred or one

DEBATE: IS HOMOSEXUALITY HISTORICAL?

When we say something is "historical" we mean more than that it happened in the past or that it is especially important. Rather, it means it has a distinct beginning that might be traced, and was the product of specific historical conditions. Jonathan Ned Katz, for example, makes the case that sexuality in general is historical in his examination of *The Invention of Heterosexuality*.[11] To suggest that heterosexuality was invented places it in a context and denies it a privileged place as a "given": as a product of human history rather than something "natural" it becomes historical. Since the 1980s historians and theorists have debated the historicity of homosexuality—and consequently sexuality in general—with early positions defined as "essentialist" and "social constructionist."

Essentialism is rooted in the idea that there are constants in human existence, same-sex attractions and actions being among them, that are more basically similar than the differences that changes across time and place create. This is not to be confused with biological essentialism, however, which is the "nature" position as opposed to "environmental" or "nurture" arguments in an entirely different debate over the origins of sexuality (see Chapter 8). This general position is represented in such works as Judy Grahn's *Another Mother Tongue* and Rictor Norton's *The Myth of the Modern Homosexual*.[12] In the latter work, the "myth" is "that 'the homosexual' is a distinctive new species invented in the modern age."[13] As represented by these scholars, the paradox of homosexuality is that it has a history that can be traced back in time indefinitely, but it is not "historical"; that is, it is a human constant but not a human creation. Whether "true" or not, this position has played an important role in the politics of the 20th century, supporting the model of homosexuals as a distinct minority within a system of identity politics. That is, possessing a traceable linear past contributes greatly to the concept of the homosexual as a type of person who, as a constant of all human societies, is likely to remain so in the present and future.

Other scholars, originally termed social constructionists, caution against creating, in John D'Emilio's words, "the myth of the 'eternal homosexual.'" Sharing the idea that sexuality, like gender, race, and other factors, is something devised by human beings in various ways, they believe that to be a homosexual the way the term was understood in the 20th century requires certain conditions, assumptions, and ideas be present. For D'Emilio and many others, one of those conditions is capitalism, for example, with its attendant developments of class consciousness, urban life, the possibility of geographic mobility and economic independence, and so on.[14] Constructionists do not deny that same sex *behavior* has always existed in some form, but disagree with essentialists that one or more terms, if coined relatively recently, will accurately position people who lived in different circumstances. In general, the more "distant" subjects are from 20th-century Western European or American culture (ancient Greek society, Asian cultures, and Native American nations), the more problematic the label "homosexual" is to constructionists. There is further debate *among* constructionists over whether a unique identity based on same-sex desire, attraction, or behavior can be found before the modern era, and if so, what words to use. It is around these issues that arguments over "sexual preference" and "sexual orientation" also arise, with the latter designation viewed as more of a fixed identity. Probably the majority of theorists consider themselves constructionists but acknowledges that the position can be problematic politically. If notions of sexuality vary over time and place, have changed and are thus changeable, then is there really a "homosexual" that can be the object of human rights legislation?

In the early 21st century discussion is no longer polarized into simple "essentialist versus constructionist" or "behavior versus identity" camps, but has become more nuanced even while continuing to raise more questions than it answers. David Halperin aptly summarized the debate when he recently wrote, "...even after constructionists claimed to have won it, and essentialists claimed to have exposed the bad scholarship produced by it, and everybody else claimed to be sick and tired of it, the basic question of the historicity of sexuality has remained."[15] (See also Debate, Chapter 9)

thousand years ago). However, in Lincoln's or any other subject's case the immediate question following a claim of homosexuality or bisexuality is, "How do you know that?" The very question is an expression of heterosexism while the proposed answers reflect important debates over not just evidence but the nature of sexuality itself and its relationship to love, desire, activity, and so on.

The fact that heterosexuality has become the "default" assumption for people past and present has immeasurably complicated the task of the historian. It places the burden of proof on those asserting nonheterosexuality for any figure rather than asking for proof of *any* type of sexuality. In a lighthearted piece for the *Gay Community News,* Charley Shively illustrated this well when he suggested that George Washington might have been gay.[16] Although Shively's evidence was sketchy and relied on associations more than any proven declarations or activity on Washington's part, he raised a crucial question in the process: How do we know Washington (or anyone) was *heterosexual?* He demonstrates that evidence for any sexuality can be elusive once we reexamine our assumptions about what constitutes "proof."

No, Lincoln was not gay. Setting aside a knee-jerk "he was a great man he couldn't have been gay" response, there are thoughtful objections among GLBT historians to blithely attaching the term to Lincoln or, again, to anyone else living prior to recent decades. These arguments range from a more absolutist position, that the labels homosexual, gay, and lesbian are appropriate only for those who have had access to them (and, ideally, adopted them), to a kind of case-by-case approach (Lincoln might not have been gay but someone of the same era might qualify, or vice versa). Originally termed social constructionists (see Debate), their positions are more varied than those of "essentialists" and arguments occur *within* this group over when various sexual identities emerged and why. Nonetheless, they generally agree that we should be cautious about glibly extending a linear "gay history" backward too far into the past.

We are not sure we want to call Lincoln gay. Proponents of this position would likely have much in common with the constructionists, but may be more open to placing Lincoln along some kind of continuum. In other words, the position is less one of uncertainty than it is the sense that Lincoln (and many others) belongs somewhere in a GLBT or queer history but not necessarily as simply "gay." The idea here would be to try and understand his sexuality as he understood it himself, and in terms familiar to those of his time and place. This is not a simple task, but one potentially more revealing than forcing the terms or concepts of a later era onto an earlier time.

As Americans entered the 20th century, it appears that a variety of possibilities were gradually eliminated in favor of a simplistic heterosexual/homosexual dichotomy. As the century passed that duality then expanded again to include ideas and identities born of particular times and circumstances. This is that story and more.

NOTES

1. Richard Brookhiser, "Was Lincoln Gay?" reviewing C.A. Tripp, *The Intimate World of Abraham Lincoln* (New York: Free Press, 2005) in *New York Times Sunday Book Review,* January 9, 2005, http://www.nytimes.com/2005/01/09/books/review/09BROOKHE.html.

2. As of September, 2005, sixteen states and the District of Columbia had laws banning discrimination based on sexual orientation in housing, public accommodation, and/or employment: Wisconsin, Massachusetts, Hawaii (employment only), Connecticut, New Jersey, Vermont, California, Minnesota, Rhode Island, New Hampshire, Nevada (employment only), Maryland, New York, New Mexico, Illinois, and Maine.

3. New York State Newspaper Project of the New York State Library, http://www.nysl.nysed.gov/nysnp/nytlucey.htm.

4. John D. Poling, in CLGH *Newsletter* of the Committee on Lesbian and Gay History, Fall 2003, 15. [permission to use quote granted]

5. *Newsletter* of the Committee on Lesbian and Gay History, Spring 2005, 8.

6. Quote from Judy Grahn poem, "A History of Lesbianism" from *The Work of a Common Woman: The Collected Poetry of Judy Grahn, 1964–1977* (New York: St. Martin's Press, 1980), 54.

7. Anna Clark et al., *Report* on the Survey of Lesbian and Gay Historians by the Committee on Women Historians, January 31, 1993. Typescript.

8. My own experience reinforces this. I have had survey courses in American history "shut down" during lectures on the gay rights movement; normally lively interactions cease and students seem afraid to engage in discussion, perhaps for fear of appearing *too* engaged.

9. *Boutilier v. Immigration Service, 387 U.S. 118.* Douglas, in turn, relies on Freud in his note to the passage:

> Sigmund Freud wrote in 1935: "Homosexuality is assuredly no advantage, but it is nothing to be ashamed of, no vice, no degradation, it cannot be classified as an illness; we consider it to be a variation of the sexual function produced by a certain arrest of sexual development. Many highly respectable individuals of ancient and modern times have been homosexuals, several of the greatest men among them (Plato, Michelangelo, Leonardo da Vinci, etc.). It is a great injustice to persecute homosexuality as a crime, and cruelty too. If you do not believe me, read the books of Havelock Ellis." Ruitenbeek, *The Problem of Homosexuality in Modern Society* 1 (1963).

The full text of the decision can be found at http://laws.findlaw.com/us/387/118.html.

10. Kevin Jennings, ed., *Becoming Visible: A Reader in Gay & Lesbian History for High School & College Students* (Boston: Alyson, 1994); Martin Duberman, Martha Vicinus, and George Chauncey, Jr., eds. *Hidden from History: Reclaiming the Gay and Lesbian Past* (New York: New American Library, 1989); Lillian Faderman, "Who Hid Lesbian History?" in *Lesbian Studies: Present and Future,* ed. Margaret Cruikshank (Old Westbury, NY: The Feminist Press, 1982), 115–21.

11. Jonathan Ned Katz, *The Invention of Heterosexuality* (New York: Dutton, 1995).

12. Judy Grahn, *Another Mother Tongue: Gay Words, Gay Worlds* (Boston: Beacon Press, 1984); Rictor Norton, *The Myth of the Modern Homosexual: Queer History and the Search for Cultural Unity* (London: Cassell, 1997).

13. Back cover.

14. John D'Emilio, "Capitalism and Gay Identity," in *Making Trouble: Essays on Gay History, Politics, and the University* (New York: Routledge, 1992), 3–16; quote on p. 5.

15. David M. Halperin, *How to Do the History of Homosexuality* (Chicago: University of Chicago Press, 2004), 105.

16. Charley Shively, "Was the Father of Our Country a Queen?" *Gay Community News,* July 1–7, 1990.

SUGGESTED RESOURCES

Black, A. (Ed.). (2001). *Modern American queer history.* Philadelphia: Temple University Press. See especially John Howard's Introduction and articles by Estelle B. Freedman and Vicki L. Eaklor.

D'Emilio, J. (1992). Not a simple matter: Gay history and gay historians. In *Making trouble: Essays on gay history, politics, and the university* (pp. 138–147). New York: Routledge.

Eaklor, V.L. (1998). Learning from history: A queer problem. *Journal of Gay, Lesbian, and Bisexual Identity, 3*(3), 195–211.

Rupp, L. (1999). *A desired past: A short history of same-sex love in America.* Chicago: University of Chicago Press. See chap. 1 especially.

2 INTO THE 20TH CENTURY

New York City, 1906. Otto Spengler, a director of the Scientific Humanitarian Committee of Berlin, gives a lecture to the German Scientific Society on "sexual intermediates." The Committee, cofounded in 1897 by Dr. Magnus Hirschfeld, was working to change attitudes regarding homosexuality and reform the German penal code, which criminalized homosexual acts under paragraph 175. Following his talk, Spengler reported, a lawyer declared "that homosexuals belong in prison," and used that comment as an example that much more education was needed on homosexuality in the United States "where such educated people are so stupid. . . . Now, people just faint when the subject is broached."

The following year an anonymous writer from Boston sent a letter of support to the Scientific Humanitarian Committee. In part, the writer mentioned "how many homosexuals I've come to know! Boston, this good old Puritan city, has them by the hundreds." The letter further explained the situation:

> *Here, as in Germany, homosexuality extends throughout all classes, . . . Reliable homosexuals have told me names that reach into the highest circles of Boston, New York, and Washington, D.C., names which have left me speechless with astonishment. I have also noticed that bisexuality must be rather widespread.*
>
> *There is astonishing ignorance among us of the Uranians [homosexuals] I've come to know about their own true nature. This is probably a result of absolute silence and intolerance, which have never advanced real morality at any time or place. But with the growth of population and the increase of intellectuals, the time is coming when America will finally be forced to confront the riddle of homosexuality.*[1]

The two observers above reveal some significant aspects of GLBT history in the United States at the turn of the century. First is the simple fact the term "homosexual" was by then in use, at least by a few people in urban areas, and that there were people applying the term for themselves. Also, both describe an oppressive atmosphere for homosexuals, and reflect the belief that education would create more tolerance. Finally, the influence of European thinkers on the subject is apparent, particularly the influence of Magnus Hirschfeld and the German homosexual emancipation movement. Despite the information crossing the Atlantic, however, the United States would be perceived as relatively less open to sexual variety than many places in Europe at different times in the 20th century. This chapter lays the groundwork for understanding these and other developments and attitudes that characterized U.S. GLBT history as the new century opened.

The history of GLBT people in the United States is often divided into two broad eras, divided at roughly 1900. This is more than mere convenience, since by 1900 a medical model of sexuality was gaining currency in the Western world. As reflected above, that model resulted in the creation of the categories homosexual, heterosexual, and bisexual that came to dominate sexual discussions for most of the 20th century. At the same time, earlier ways of thinking, often determined by class, ethnicity, or geography, continued to survive alongside the newer concepts, resulting in a surprisingly diverse array of possibilities for self-identification. In fact the 20th century, though it is the era of remarkably successful GLBT rights movements and visibility, also witnessed as much contraction as expansion of options for sexual definition.

In order to better understand the language and developments of the 20th century, then, we must look at least briefly at the various legacies of the nation's colonial beginnings through the 19th century. As Spengler noted about his audience that included lawyers, doctors, and ministers, for example, many educated people viewed homosexuals as criminals by the early 20th century, even as the anonymous letter reveals the existence of many such newly classified people in U.S. cities. Both situations are rooted in earlier developments, as was the concept of sin attached to same-sex acts. The newer construct of illness only added a third association to homosexuality rather than replace any older ones. The result was a triad of sin, crime, and sickness when it came to defining homosexuality, designations that overlapped and continued to dominate most discussions for the next one hundred years. At the same time, not all of the older associations were necessarily negative, since same-sex attractions and activity, as recently as the 19th century, sometimes did not necessarily carry any stigma at all. It is a complicated picture, made more complex in the 20th century by the effort to subsume so many different antecedents and attitudes under the single rubric "homosexual."

COLONIAL LEGACIES

It is now well established that two old worlds met when Europeans began arriving at the shores of the Americas. As Europeans established colonies in what became the United States it was a process involving both cooperation and conflict with natives, and one that combined old ideas and new circumstances in a volatile mix. Although a close look at those encounters is far beyond the present purpose, some attention to the groups involved and their attitudes and actions toward each other sheds some light on later developments.

The cultures that collided—native, a variety of Europeans, and African, were not merely different from each other. At times it seems that the values of the Europeans were opposite to those of the cultures they encountered, a situation made tragic by the assumption of superiority on the part of Europeans—now generally termed ethnocentrism—and their ability eventually to dominate the hemisphere. It is well known that European ideas concerning monotheistic religion, imperial politics, land ownership, and legitimate labor, for example, were strange to the native inhabitants. Less obvious is that the differences between the cultures included assumptions about women's and men's proper roles and behaviors, creating a situation, in Leila Rupp's words, of "competing sexual and gender systems."[2]

Europe before Contact

"The Spain that Christopher Columbus and his crews left behind just before dawn on August 3, 1492, as they sailed forth from Palos and out into the Atlantic, was for most of its people a land of violence, squalor, treachery, and intolerance. In this respect Spain was no different from the rest of Europe." This assessment, by historian David E. Stannard, may seem harsh, but captures something of the reality of many Europeans of the late 15th century, including those who would sail abroad.[3] In a brief consideration of this era, a few points are relevant: Europeans, though very different from and frequently at war with each other, might be considered here as a group, sharing more similarities than any of them shared with natives; among those similarities were concepts of religion, politics, and economics and, especially important, the lack of separation among those arenas; and the roots of those similarities lie in the shared history and developments in Europe in the centuries prior to contact. The major players in the race for trade with "the East"—Portuguese, Spanish, French, Dutch, and English—succeeded in establishing themselves around the world, with all but the Portuguese establishing themselves in the area that became the United States. A full consideration is not possible here, but some general outlines, with emphasis on the English experience, illustrate a context for a lasting concern with sex and gender that reverberated well into the 20th century.

In the quotation above, Stannard was quick to note that his was no rehashing of a "Black Legend" against Spain (in which the Spanish were considered more cruel than other Europeans), but a consideration of a Europe in turmoil and the people it produced. Ironically, this same era of violence and intolerance was also that of a scientific revolution and a Renaissance, and all elements combined in a mix that produced the people and ideas that would pave the way for expansion into the Americas. While the Renaissance and scientific revolution produced the ideals, means, and economics (in the form of budding capitalism), equally important were struggles and concepts inherited from previous centuries.

In particular, the less savory elements of European colonization are usually associated with the religious and political warfare of the Reformation and related conflicts over sin, heresy, and witchcraft. Europeans had been at war with one another for centuries before Martin Luther, and later Jean Calvin, helped bring about the religious dissention of the 16th century called the Protestant Reformation. What is important to remember here is that there were long-standing class divisions and political struggles that also found expression through religious war. Rather than any "separation of church and state" the situation was the opposite: political and religious power were intertwined and the institutions of one were used to support those of the other. For this reason, a sin against God or the church could be viewed as treason, or an act of treachery against the state, and vice versa. While church and state each had their institutions of justice, at times they acted in concert—with the church accusing and trying the person and the state carrying out the sentence—to punish those deemed dangerous to orthodox belief: Catholics punished Protestants, Protestants punished Catholics, and everyone went after heretics and witches.

The dynamics of sex and gender in this era would have effects far beyond the 16th and 17th centuries. It is now well known that the vast majority of those executed as witches in Europe were women, for example, and those accused sometimes did not fit into their assigned gender roles; that is, they might be considered more independent or outspoken than women should be. In addition, there was often a sexual dynamic to their supposed relationships with Satan and demons. Similarly, there is some evidence to suggest that one attribute associated with heretics was their willingness to engage in sex acts prohibited by orthodox religion. Finally, it is very telling that one consistent accusation launched at outsiders, from ancient times to modern, was the danger posed to children. Both Christians and Jews were accused (by Romans and Christians, respectively) of killing babies, while witches and heretics endured these charges, as well as the more subtle view that they might lure children into their practices. In other words, in the world that produced explorers and colonists, "deviant" sexual practices were linked to people considered dangerous to both church and state, and those dangers extended to influences on the next generations. As we shall see, these deeply rooted ideas may help to explain some of the later attitudes and treatment of GLBT people.

Collision and Dominance

Although European contact with natives often included collaboration, particularly during the earliest contacts, the eventual "victory" of Europeans in establishing lasting colonies all too regularly was coupled with tragic results for non-Europeans. At best, natives faced enforced acculturation or displacement and at worst virtual slavery (though technically outlawed in New Spain and never defined as such in British colonies) and extermination. Africans, of course, met similar fates as captive immigrants. Patterns of conquest and settlement were similar in many ways, and all imperial nations—Spain, France, the Netherlands, and England—left their marks on the Americas. Since our focus is on the later United States, however, the British colonies of the Atlantic seaboard demand particular attention.

As English settlers established colonies in New England, the mid-Atlantic, and the South in the 16th and 17th centuries they naturally relied upon the familiar institutions of family, church, and government. Although these varied in structure, colonists shared basic assumptions about them and the relationships, even if they differed widely on colonial governance or which Christian denomination was the "correct" one. Perhaps the overriding institution of all was patriarchy, or a power structure in which males are dominant over women and children. From the patriarchal family came ideas about a well-ordered society, which often was thought of as a large family. Since patriarchy assumes the dominance of men over women, it works in concert with strict gender rules, rules of masculinity and femininity that prescribe appropriate behavior for each gender.

Legal codes also varied from colony to colony but again there was general agreement on the source of law: the Christian Bible and English common law, the latter developed through centuries of practice and precedent. To the New England Puritans, for example, the very purpose of law and government was to support the establishment of what they considered a godly community. Like nearly all their fellow Europeans, they had no concepts of separating church and state, or of individual rights. Rather, to the Puritans the individual was a servant of God and the community (though men and women might fulfill this purpose in different ways). Family, church, state, and eventually school all were designed to aid in keeping the covenant, a special relationship with God the Puritans believed they possessed. Certainly not all colonists were Puritans, but the reliance on biblical interpretation as a basis for law was not unusual. In particular, buggery was a capital crime among the English and thus in the colonies. Buggery included both sodomy (anal intercourse, whether male–male or male–female) and bestiality (intercourse between a human and animal). Terms and laws varied from colony to colony—in New Haven sex between women was expressly outlawed—but in general were designed to discourage nonreproductive sexual activity. Importantly, what the laws reveal is the attitude that same-sex acts were just that: acts, which were all the more threatening because anyone, not just a specific type of person, could be tempted into engaging in them. This fit the prevailing views that (1) all people were inherently sinful and in need of control in order to preserve the social and moral order, and (2) the role of law was to uphold a Judeo-Christian version of morality. Overall, though, only five people were executed for sodomy during the colonial period. Because conditions changed by the 20th century, those same sodomy laws could be interpreted as directed at specific people rather than acts, and therefore discriminatory. By that time, concepts of rights and identity had developed that would have been completely foreign to the colonists.

The people that English adventurers and later colonists encountered along the eastern coast of North America represented a variety of cultures and languages, as did the natives throughout the interior of the Americas. One constant, however, is the opposing worldview of natives when compared to Europeans, a fact Europeans used to justify their actions over the centuries. At the root of these differences was spirituality. Just as Christianity functioned for Europeans, out of native religions arose concepts of the natural world and the proper roles of all living things. Where Europeans saw a rigid hierarchy, with humans over nature, men over women and children, and God over all, however, the native view professed more interdependence. Humans were as much *part of* nature as other beings rather than dominant *over* them. Further, while both systems have creation stories and creator gods, native religions infuse all nature with spirit and are generally polytheistic. These differences fueled an already tense situation in which Europeans' desire for land and laborers led to their exploitation of both in the Americas. "Property" was among the fundamental rights of Englishmen, for example, and came to define their "freedom" in many ways; it was also the source of goods and people that would define their wealth and status. To natives, land was (and is) sacred ground possessing spiritual qualities in the life supported there.

The conflict over land and resources spawned many others between the cultures. Eventually, any variation from European conceptions might be used to justify exploiting, displacing, and exterminating natives when not causing those actions in the first place. In this light, the natives' sex and gender systems were but one more reason to consider them inferior people, ripe for conquest. In particular, there is and was a place in most native cultures for "two-spirit" individuals, who today would be called transgendered. These are people whose gender appearance and behavior does not match their biological sex, through cross-dressing, performing tasks of the other sex, and/or acting as sexual "wives" or "husbands" to persons of the same sex. Where Europeans saw "devilish" and "sinful" things, natives saw people behaving in accordance with their own inner spiritual natures. At times these *berdache,* as French explorers called males, were also shamans who commanded respect as having special spiritual powers. Historians disagree over the actual roles and effects of cross-gendered natives, and men in particular, but their very presence indicates a tolerance of sex and gender diversity not found in the colonizers. Equally significant, some historians suggest a relationship between this diversity and the relatively greater power of women in many native societies. That is, respect for feminine power, whether embodied in men or women might enhance a greater respect for diversity generally, as does a belief in many possible spiritual paths. What we do know is that Europeans found intolerable both the power of women (when they recognized it) and the sexual and gender variety they often encountered; more reason to "civilize" or conquer those who allowed them.

The collision of cultures persisted, of course, through the centuries between first contact and 1900, as Euro-Americans settled the interior and Pacific coasts. Only as native populations dwindled from disease, starvation and war, dropping to about a quarter million by 1890, did attitudes regarding both native cultures and sexuality begin to change. Apparently the 18th-century "noble savage" was much less threatening as an ideal than a living being, and so the concept became increasingly attractive as actual natives disappeared. Added to this was the development of anthropology in the 1800s. Although they never escaped the biases of their own cultures, early anthropologists contributed to the attempt to observe and record mores and practices, including those of sex and gender, with less judgement and persecution.

By 1900 some of the changing ideas about sex, gender, and natives were combined in the notoriety of We'wha, a Zuni "two-spirit" person. Born around 1849 in the southwest, We'wha was a biological male who represented a genuine mixture of masculine and feminine as understood by Zunis. Ethnologists James and Matilda Coxe Stevenson "discovered" We'wha and obtained valuable cultural information from him/her. S/he achieved national fame due to a visit to Washington, DC in 1886, where s/he engaged in cultural and political diplomacy with the U.S. government. Before his/her death in 1896, however, We'wha had been arrested by U.S. soldiers in a confrontation over governmental authority on native land.

If information about the sex and gender structures of native societies is scattered, and too heavily based on European reports, such is also the case of the cultures from which Africans were taken and transported to the Americas. Further, the question of what attitudes and practices survived under slavery—sexual or otherwise—has long been controversial. In general, African cultures from which slaves came were similar to those of natives in having a place for some same-sex and/or cross-gender behavior. Sodomy among Africans is reported, for example, and in some cultures sex with an older man might be part of an adolescent male's initiation process. Eventually, though, he would be expected to behave in a "heterosexual" way, as the 20th century would understand it, partnered with a woman and fathering children.

In the colonial era, legal records hint at practices but, as is often the case, reflect only the cultural ideas of the lawmakers. Those records show punishment of the occasional "Negro" for sodomy, for example, but nothing about the concepts of those punished. They also support the theory that a two-caste racial system was developing in North America well before the 19th century, in which only blacks could be enslaved and only whites could possess all the freedoms of citizenship. As part of this racial division, sodomy continued as a capital crime for blacks/slaves but for not whites/free people in some colonial and state legal codes.

For an understanding of later developments in the United States the mythology of African American sexuality created by the enslavers and their descendants is as important as actual practices. Stereotypes emerged early and continued through U.S. history regarding the supposedly greater sexual prowess or desire of both men and women of African descent. These notions clearly served the dominant race by shifting blame to slave women when they bore the masters' children, and by portraying black men as dangerous to white women. Also, for white racists, their ideas that (a) blacks were more sexual and (b) sex was less rational and more animalistic further supported their foregone conclusion that white dominance over blacks was natural. By the mid-nineteenth century, when slaves numbered about four million and free blacks about 500,000, sex and race were fully intertwined with images of the "exotic" and "forbidden" and all this merged with Victorian sexual reticence into a powerful jumble. This may have helped create an atmosphere in which same-sex activity also would be associated with blacks, in the same complicated web of attraction/repulsion that characterized white racial thinking of the early 20th-century Jazz Age. Such association also may have contributed to later homophobia among some African Americans as they attempted to offset centuries of using sexual "otherness" against them.

THREE REVOLUTIONS

Political

The American Revolution, as the political birth of the United States, also became the touchstone for later generations seeking to define themselves and their country's role in the world. To some degree, the unique nature of that identity—what Americans have told themselves about themselves—may have contributed in surprising ways toward a society seemingly obsessed with proper gender roles as the 19th century became the 20th century.

Undoubtedly an American identity was taking shape long before the shots fired in 1775. This is revealed not only in the Declaration of Independence the following year, but also in the ability of the empire's opponents to rouse and maintain a spirit of rebellion, and eventually to emerge as victors. The ideals stated (if not always obeyed then or later), became the center of the self-image 19th-century Americans would develop and bequeath to their 20th-century descendants. The various ideals, deriving from sources as various as 17th-century English politics, the 18th-century "Age of Reason" in Europe and, very likely, the example of the Iroquois (Haudenosaunee) League, were codified by the early 19th century and subsequently lumped under the rubric "republican ideology." In brief, this concerned the special demands placed on citizens of a republic, whose government ideally was to exist only for the protection of "natural rights" (especially life, liberty, and property). From this base came the tenets of "liberalism" as the term was understood throughout the 19th and most of the 20th centuries: representative, constitutional government, in which the rule of law is supreme; separation and balance of power within a central government; separation of church and state; and "free trade" without government control or interference. In the United States, social order and natural rights have been viewed as equally important, resulting in a tension between them. In very general terms, "conservatives" have been those concerned more with maintaining order, and liberals more with protecting individual rights. Liberty, defined differently over time and by different people, emerged foremost among those rights, and equality joined them in an uneasy balance by the mid-nineteenth century.

Lincoln, of course, expressed this well in the *Gettysburg Address* in 1863, when he described the United States as a "nation, conceived in liberty and dedicated to the proposition that all men are created equal." Just as important are his closing words, in which he expressed the determination that the United States "shall not perish from the earth" since that was exactly the fear of many Americans. Republics, Americans had been taught, did not seem to last very long by historical standards—a couple of hundred years at most—and this raised questions about what caused their demise. Naturally, opinions varied widely, and throughout the 19th century there were repeated debates over the definition of citizenship and, especially, just how much democracy and freedom a republic could withstand before it dissolved into a meaningless heap of individuals. While 19th-century liberals feared the concentration of power into the hands of the few, conservatives feared the potential of "mobocracy" that they believed could arise out of extending citizenship too quickly and broadly. The end result, they believed, was not anarchy, but instead the opposite: the rise of demagogues (one or more) whose only qualification for office was their ability to appeal to "the people." There was general agreement, however, that a republic depended upon a virtuous citizenry and this originally meant those who were willing to sacrifice something for the greater good; that living in a republic demanded attention to the whole and not just to personal liberty.

During the 19th century this 18th-century concept of virtue gradually merged with one rooted in Judeo-Christian concepts of "morality." This was not necessarily new in the 19th century, since Puritans, for example, had seen their enterprise as part of God's plan for the world, and Thomas Jefferson had further universalized the colonial rebellion by linking the rights of Englishmen with human rights. However, a new evangelical fervor was infused into Americans during the Second Great Awakening that swept the country in the first half of the 19th century, strengthening the link already forged between Christian and "American" standards of behavior. Popular histories at the time portrayed the United States as the creation of the Christian God (though it was not clear what denomination He was), and the civil life of the nation as the unfolding of His plan—for the United States and the world.

In this way America had a "civil religion" not unlike that of the ancient republics, in which the devotional and the political were often indistinguishable. Not only was God invoked at public gatherings of all kinds, but at those gatherings (like that at Gettysburg in 1863) the sacred and secular were interchangeable. In this atmosphere, and in a manner reminiscent of 16th-century Europe, "sin" could be treasonous, or at least politically suspect; now "good" citizenship virtually required profession of Christianity, and the Protestant variety at that, while the loyalty of all others (including Catholics) would be questioned for decades. As we shall see, even in the more secular 20th century, the vestiges of 19th-century civil religion would be apparent in many ways, from inherited legal codes that outlaw "unchristian" sexual behaviors such as sodomy to the equation of "immoral" with "un-American."

At the same time, the Second Great Awakening was only one of the many factors that have led historians to label the early 19th century an "age of reform." Beginning just as the last founders were dying in the 1820s, this era would become the first round of a cycle of significant reform activity that repeats roughly every other generation: 1830s; 1860s (Civil War and Reconstruction, to some, more "revolution" than reform); 1890s–1900s (Progressivism); 1930s (New Deal); 1960s. The causes of any or all of these are never clear, but in the early 19th century, it appears that rapid changes contributed to both the hope and the fear that is revealed in so many projects for the improvement of the country.

Early 19th-century America saw expansion in every sense of the term. The population grew sixfold, from five million in 1800 to over thirty million in 1860, while the Western boundary of the United States shifted to the Pacific Ocean by 1850. New means or routes of transportation and communication—roads, canals, telegraph, and of course the railroad—arose to alter the countryside, and altered the countryside while the number of newspapers, magazines, and books would explode throughout the century.

As if these were not enough, the political and economical realms experienced their own expansion. Property qualifications for voting were eliminated by 1830, enlarging the base of white male voters age twenty-one and older, and industrial capitalism was rapidly developing from its 18th-century roots in New England. By the end of the century, suffrage was extended to all males twenty-one and older, and an urban and industrial economy was well on its way to replacing the agrarian lifestyle of generations. At the least Americans were ambivalent about all this. Some viewed these changes as proof of genuine progress and God's special favor while others worried about their effect on the still new republic. Could a republic be spread over such a large area of land? What qualifications *should* one have to vote? Can a republic also be industrial and capitalist? If democracy is extended too far, what will assure an ordered society? Many Americans worried over all these questions as the nation grew, contributing to an outburst of reform activity.

Activists called for a wide range of changes to ensure the nation's survival. Abolitionists believed that slavery was the largest stain on the nation, and that God would withdraw His support if it were not eliminated, while other worked against slavery for more political or pragmatic reasons. Temperance advocates and diet reformers worried over the physical and spiritual health of Americans, prisons and hospitals came under scrutiny, and a political movement for women's rights was born. Laborers began to organize, tax-supported public schools arose to train good citizens, and dozens of secular and religious utopian communities came and went, each with its own vision of a better United States.

Complicating this picture further was the uneasy relationship between the states and the federal government. Since the end of the revolution, in fact, Americans had debated that relationship, considering it a vital question as they fashioned constitutions. States' rights advocates emerged before 1800, fearful of too much centralized authority. Among their descendants were New England Federalists in 1814 and southern Democrats in 1860 who so feared federal power that they advocated secession from the country; the latter group claimed to have accomplished this in forming the Confederacy, accelerating the onset of the Civil War. Although the end of that war may have resolved the issue of leaving the Union, the argument over state versus federal authority, especially in questions of civil rights, only intensified in the 20th century.

These changes and responses affect later GLBT history in several ways. First, it is important to note the apparent anxiety caused by both the promise and the realities of 19th-century American life. The self-imposed pressure on the United States to succeed (by whatever definition) was tremendous, while its self-image as God's chosen nation added an apocalyptic dimension to potential failure. (This helps explain why the Civil War, for example, was viewed by so many Americans as a universal struggle literally of biblical proportions.) As both revivalists and reformers responded to these changes, they would create and adopt techniques eventually used by all movements in U.S. history. Some were organizational: societies founded local and state chapters and some gathered in national meetings; circulars, magazines, and other print media were created; activists (abolitionists especially) endured violence and engaged in ever more drastic actions, from demonstrations (against the return of fugitive slaves) to attempting to start a slave insurrection. All these techniques were adopted in some fashion by later U.S. activists, including GLBT activists.

Equally important are the assumptions and rhetoric of reform inherited as a legacy of the 19th century. At their root most reforms and movements, no matter how secular their cause, have something of revivalism in them. Evangelicals preached their messages in hopes of converting others not just to thinking, but to *feeling* that their message was right. Their goal was to inspire others to action, internal or external. Paradoxically, despite their message of the inherent sinfulness of humans, the preachers revealed in their expectation of conversions a faith in others' potential for goodness.

Eventually, whether the topic was alcohol, slavery, votes for women, or labor organizing, leaders "preached" their messages in a similar way, with identical hopes of "converting" others to their causes; as "good" people at heart, others surely would see and feel the "rightness" of the cause. This basic faith in Americans' sense of justice and fairness (as different activists have interpreted those words) would underlie virtually every movement for rights in the United States from this era forward, including that for GLBT rights.

Finally, this era's legacy of fear and anxiety over rapid political and social changes may help to explain Americans' preoccupation with gender roles then and since, a preoccupation inseparable from later attitudes towards GLBT people. Gender roles cannot be understood, however, without a closer look at the drastic transformation of the economy in the 19th century and its effects throughout society.

Economic

The industrial revolution that began in 18th-century England and the United States blossomed fully in the 19th century, affecting all realms of life. Industrialization, capitalism, and urbanization developed hand-in-hand, each supporting and encouraged by the other two. Rural life did not disappear by 1900, of course, but the outlines of an agrarian *economy* were by then altered forever. It was not that all of America became industrial, in other words, but rather that the nation's markets and producers became interdependent as never before, and increasingly more of those markets were urban and international. By 1900, even farming itself was well on its way to becoming another big business with farmers at the mercy of economic as well as natural forces.

Changes in concepts of labor and the family were as much by-products of industrialism as the type and place of labor performed. In some interpretations, the interdependent family of the self-sufficient farm was gradually replaced by both the idea and reality of the male breadwinner. Families had always been patriarchal, but now the *economic* role of women and children was transformed from producers to dependents and consumers. As a (predominantly white, urban) middle class developed, women and children, without an economic role, had little if any legal agency as well. When a woman married, in fact, she and her property, including any children she might bear, became her husband's property. Now the home, or "private sphere" was the domain of the middle-class wife, who was expected to provide a haven in which her husband could escape the nasty "public sphere" of business and politics. The sexes were consigned to different social worlds, as were the accompanying genders, or sets of roles and behaviors. That is, masculine gender attributes were to coincide with biological maleness and feminine attributes with femaleness. Sex and gender were supposed to match exactly and the characteristics of each were appropriate (even necessary) to its sphere and complementary of the other in a balanced society. Men needed to be masculine, meaning physically and intellectual strong, aggressive, competitive, and rational. Women were to serve humanity by protecting the feminine virtues of spiritual strength, passivity, cooperation, compassion, and emotion. Barbara Welter summed up these traits in her classic examination of the antebellum "Cult of True Womanhood" as piety, purity, submissiveness, and domesticity.[4] Further, when men and women were geographically outside their spheres, they were expected to carry them along, so to speak. Women, of course, left their houses and entered public space, but a "good" woman took along her femininity, just as a man did not leave his masculinity at the office. These gendered codes of behavior, and their rigidity, are key to understanding later attitudes and behaviors of both those deemed "homosexual" and their opponents.

The uncompromising nature of gender division in the United States, in fact, was observed as early as the 1830s. In his famous commentary on the United States, *Democracy in America,* Alexis de Tocqueville praised the differences between European and American notions of the "Equality of the Sexes." "There are people in Europe," he wrote, "who, confounding together the different characteristics of the sexes, would make man and woman into beings not only equal but alike." In the United States, however, such was not the case:

> The Americans have applied to the sexes the great principle of political economy which governs the manufacturers of our age, by carefully dividing the duties of man from those of woman in order that the great work of society may be the better carried on.
>
> In no country has such constant care been taken as in America to trace two clearly distinct lines of action for the two sexes and to make them keep pace one with the other, but in two pathways that are always different.[5]

It is no accident that Tocqueville saw this in the context of democracy, which was seen by many as a social leveler. Equality was feared as much as celebrated, particularly by those who felt that traditional class boundaries, together with the authority of church and divine-right government, had helped stabilize society and prevent chaos. It is possible that gender (and race) "replaced" a rigid class system in a country experiencing the level of political and economic change and dissention—over expansion, slavery, the federal/state relationship, etc.—as did the United States in the early 19th century. Eve Kornfeld nicely summarized the situation in her study of Margaret Fuller:

> Paradoxically, their construction of more rigid gender boundaries reconciled many middle-class Americans to the tremendous social changes and fluidity of the early nineteenth century. Developed by and for northern middle-class men and women to anchor their own identities in a world of flux, the doctrine of separate gender spheres also formed their standard for understanding and judging the lives of others. Gender norms allowed an elite threatened by political democratization and economic mobility to distinguish itself from the rest of society. Clearly articulated gender spheres became a mark of worth and civilization in a confusing world.
>
> Thus Indians were perceived as "savage" because of their refusal to abandon communal economies (in which women participated and sometimes dominated) in favor of private property held by individual males.... Similarly, the poor were condemned as indolent, immodest, and immoral for their failure to separate family life from public life and to keep their women and children out of the workplace, off the streets, and in the home. They, too, seemed unwilling or unable to assume the polarized gender roles that many middle-class Americans considered most natural, most civilized, and most their own.[6]

As Kornfeld suggested, gender cannot be fully separated from the categories of race and class. This situation would not only be inherited by 20th-century Americans, but used by them to continue to marginalize those outside the idealized white, rigidly gendered middle class. Even after the crisis of the Civil War was resolved in favor of the Union, the republic faced the upheaval of Reconstruction and even more rapid industrialization. Masculine qualities were essential, it seemed, to fulfilling the duties of citizen and capitalist, while those feminine were their opposite. For those who believed this, effeminate men and masculine women were both threats in their own ways, undermining in one case and usurping in the other the "normal" arrangements.

This may help explain the eventual hostility against both groups, which only intensified in the 20th century once sexuality was defined by gender conformity.

Finally, there is another, more positive, side to urban, industrial capitalism and its role in GLBT history. The rapid growth of cities represented significant economic opportunities as well as changes, and increasingly larger populations. People moved from the American countryside and from overseas, finding ways to form or join communities on the one hand or remain anonymous on the other. Both situations contributed to GLBT activity and identity, as described further in Chapter 3.

Social

In addition to the drastic changes created by the creation of the United States and the industrial revolution, in 1865 the end of slavery signaled yet another revolution in American life. Since slavery was an institution that organized legal, economic, and social relations among people, its absence meant a reevaluation and restructuring of all those relations. To further complicate the picture, American slavery had been so intertwined with Anglo-American racism against Africans that the legal end of slavery was only the beginning of potentially new racial relations in the country. The eras known as Reconstruction (1865–1877) and Redemption (1877–1945) represent the efforts toward greater equality and the backlash against those efforts, respectively.

For our purposes, Reconstruction produced both legal and social activism that influenced all subsequent thought and activity around the issue of civil rights. At that time the debate over equality between the races produced questions, arguments, court cases, and three constitutional amendments concerning the rights of U.S. citizens. The 14th Amendment in particular would be used in the 20th century as the basis for new interpretations of individual rights. Less formally but just as influential were the organized movements and variety of methods and arguments African Americans and their allies created to demand enforcement of the new laws and liberties. Although civil rights as a movement is usually associated with the years following World War II, its structure was built on the groundwork laid during Reconstruction. When GLBT people adopted a "minority model" and came to demand equal rights in the 20th century they relied on that foundation, knowingly or not.

ORGANIZING PERSONAL LIVES IN THE 19TH CENTURY

The gender division in the middle class limited the behavior of both men and women in many ways, and there was a general concern with conformity to the norms of the class. Those norms, however, have not been static over time. The strict nature of gender roles, in fact, likely contributed to the "homosocial" worlds of Victorian men and women, making it easier in some ways to develop and maintain varieties of same-sex relationships that only later would be considered abnormal. A consideration of relevant 19th-century ideas and practices highlights some of the changes that distinguish the 20th century from the previous years.

Although it is customary to divide human interaction into public and private spheres (and the Victorians added gender to these, as we have seen) actual life is rarely that tidy. Also, it should be noted that "private" life is usually circumscribed in some ways by institutions of the public arena. Laws, for example, establish legal behavior and/or legal relationships and once that occurs the line between public and private is blurred.

Marriage

Marriage, when applied to same-sex couples, was among the most controversial topics of the late 20th century. One reason is the combination (and sometimes confusion) of religious or spiritual marriage with legal marriage. In the first, an organized church usually sanctions the union while in the other it is the government (individual states, in the United States) that claims the exclusive right to determine who is "married" and controls the process by issuing licenses. (This control is evident in the usual marriage ceremony when an official, sacred or secular, pronounces the couple married "by the authority vested in me by the state of ____.") This combination of religious and legal definitions of marriage in the United States predates the 20th century, and the 19th, and is a result of centuries of specific developments over the course of Western European history. In other words, marriage is "historical" as it is already defined in this volume. While 19th-century marriage closely resembles its earlier and later counterparts, there are also elements particular to those years in American history. Those elements clarify both the changes and the debates of the 20th century by revealing possibilities of the 19th century.

One way to look at 19th-century marriage is to consider it as an economic and social institution as well as a spiritual and legal one. This requires thinking about the reasons for marriage, or what each person expected from it. Given the gendered world of the middle class, marriages might be divided into "his" and "hers." Men sought "good" wives and potential mothers who would provide a private haven for the family. Women, in the middle class in particular, had little recourse outside marriage to economic survival, and no real legal standing once they were married. This forced them to seek someone who could and would support them and their children. This is not to say that no one married for love in the 19th century. However, there were other, more pressing considerations in that world that could override mere mutual attraction.

Just as marriage is not absolute proof of love, neither is it proof of sexuality. As noted in Chapter 1, it is difficult to discuss sexuality in the 19th century using 20th-century terms, yet the question of whether someone was homosexual or not is often raised. In these cases, being married, and producing children, are often equated with heterosexuality (an assumption exploited by actors and others in the 20th century). The parallel is assuming that homosexuals will be found among only the "old maids" and "confirmed bachelors," past and present. However (and setting the difficulties of using these terms aside for the moment), neither is necessarily the case. Again, 19th-century marriage was not necessarily defined by love and sexual passion, and the latter was deemed unseemly in the good wife, anyway. Though these may have been present, marriage was (and still is in significant ways) a legal and economic arrangement. Marrying and having children were no more proof of heterosexuality then than in the 20th century, since it was the norm expected of everyone. Equally important, 19th-century ideas regarding love, sex, and friendship allowed some private lives to be organized in ways that accommodated what we would now call homosexual love, with or without its sexual expression.

Friendship

Friendship, like sex and sexuality, has both universal and historical aspects. We know that friendship has always existed, but its forms and limits can vary according to time and location. It has been argued, for example, that ancient cultures considered friendship a relationship of equals; since ancient Hebrews, Greeks, and Romans viewed men as superior to women, male–female friendship was unlikely occurrence. Further (in a very early anticipation of *When Harry Met Sally*) sexual tension between men and women supposedly complicated their potential friendship, a view reappearing down to the present. Ironically, then, the assumption of opposite-sex attraction contributed to the respect given same-sex friendships in both ancient and modern times, a respect diminishing again only in the 20th century.

In 19th-century America, as in the ancient world, same-sex friendships were often very intense but may or may not have been expressed sexually. Those without a sexual dimension are usually called platonic or homosocial in nature, and those sexual on some level are labeled homoerotic. The terms "romantic" and "passionate" are also used to describe special friendships, especially those of women, and these may be either homosocial or homoerotic. There are difficulties, however, in conveniently labeling any historical same-sex relationships as "sexual" or not. As noted in Chapter 1, there is the question of evidence; not only is there usually a lack of "proof" as usually understood (someone writing about their sexual lives in diaries, letters, etc.), but historians disagree over what constitutes proof. Finally, there is the issue of interpreting past language and action using assumptions of the present, which underlies the debate between essentialists and social constructionists (see Debate, Chapter 1). For these reasons, historians argue over whether the intense friendships between men and between women should be classified as gay or lesbian, respectively.

What we do know is that middle-class Victorian Americans lived in a homosocial world of strict gender roles. Men socialized with men and women with women. Although most men and women married, their most intimate connections may have been with same-sex companions. We also know that this was acceptable as long as husband and wives fulfilled their duties to the family. Some women and men never married, of course, and some women paired up in lifelong partnerships called "Boston marriages." Undoubtedly some men had similar arrangements but the very lack of a comparable term may indicate they were less accepted. Given the assumption of men's baser, sexual nature, perhaps male partnerships were seen as automatically sexual and hence sinful. At the same time, the culture saw women in contradictory ways, as both dangerously sexual and inherently more innocent in a dualism often called "Madonna/whore" or "Mary/Eve." When women were idealized as Marys, their "marriages" were more likely seen as "pure," a view aided by the idea among some that sex without a penis was impossible anyway.

There are numerous examples of women's romantic friendships, beginning with "smashes" among schoolgirls and continuing through life partnerships, despite marriages to men of one or both women. The true extent of these friendships can never be known, but diaries and letters of lesser-known women, combined with the known circumstances of prominent educators, reformers, suffragists, and social workers suggest how common and accepted they were until late in the century. Among the more famous women in these relationships were Elizabeth Cady Stanton and Susan B. Anthony (with each other), Anna Howard Shaw, Carrie Chapman Catt, Jane Addams, and "America the Beautiful" author Katharine Lee Bates. Bates, in fact, was a faculty member at Wellesley College, where these friendships were so common they were also known as "Wellesley marriages." It was only later, though, that the women in these "marriages" would be labeled homosexual or bisexual, an indication of gendered views of "marriage"—if they were between women, sex was not assumed—and changes in thinking by the 20th century.

Despite the culture's general tolerance, not every female passionate friendship ended in a happy Boston marriage. The most notorious example of tragic consequences is the 1892 murder of Freda Ward by Alice Mitchell in Memphis, Tennessee. Both girls were teenagers, met in school, and developed a relationship initially considered typical despite its intensity. They were separated, however, when it was discovered they planned to run away and marry, with Mitchell posing a male to support Ward. Once apart from Mitchell, Ward wrote to boys and socialized with them. Fearing Ward would marry someone else, Mitchell, age 19, slit 17-year-old Ward's throat, and was ultimately committed to the state mental institution. In 1898, at age 25, Mitchell committed suicide. From her thorough study of the case, Lisa Duggan has noted that the inquiry into Mitchell's sanity was significant in revealing the state of both public and medical thinking at the very time that new sexual categories were emerging (see Constructing the Medical Model).

For men in the 19th century the situation was both similar to and different from that of women. From his study of fiction of the mid-nineteenth century, Robert K. Martin concluded that "a range of possibilities existed that could run from boyhood 'chums' to an idealized comradeship of 'knights-errant' to an anguished and guilt-ridden projection of the self onto figures of Gothic evil." Further, he noted the changes occurring in the years he studied that contributed to the mixture of images: "By the 1880s...homosexuality seems to have emerged sufficiently so that it has a public profile (certain authors, certain poems, certain subjects), while in the 1840s it was indistinguishable from other forms of male friendship."[7] For men as well as women these years provided opportunities for a variety of relationships with members of the same sex. These opportunities are apparent in real life as well as novels, and found not only in written sources but also in photos in which men are clearly comfortable with physical expressions of friendship (such as sitting in each others' laps). Soldiers, sailors, cowboys, miners, and others who found themselves in predominantly male environments have left records of intimate bonding. These occurrences are later called "situational homosexuality," but the implication that men—or women—resort to members of the same sex for love, sex, and/or companionship only when there are not enough of the opposite sex available is heterosexist. Rather, it is also possible that some people with homoerotic attractions seek out same-sex environments. (Also see Chapter 3 for community formation.) Finally, for men as well as women, passionate friendships can be found among the famous as well as the anonymous. A number of political and literary figures experienced intense male bonding, including Abraham Lincoln (see Chapter 1), Daniel Webster, James H. Hammond, Ralph Waldo Emerson, and, infamously, Walt Whitman. Some friendships, like selected ones of Hammond and Whitman, were erotic by any standards.

The years examined by Martin were also those bisected by the Civil War. Again, various attitudes are evident at that time and accentuated by the intensity of the experience for the soldiers, black and white. As depicted in the film *Glory,* for example, the "manhood" denied African American men in a racist society could be proven in battle, rendering their participation that much more important to them. Out of the war, too, came the focus on the "strenuous life" for men that, like battle, should render them fit for the rough world of industrial America. At the same time, the circumstances of war provoked expressions of intense emotions, whether directed at males, females, or loss generally. People of this era were more comfortable with men crying, sharing beds, and hugging and kissing each other, an indication of how quickly gender norms can change; once these behaviors were labeled effeminate, however, the label remained in place for the next hundred years.

While both men and women in the middle class could experience romantic friendship, the strict gender code caused some distinctions in perceptions and expectations. First, it has been easier to assume that homoeroticism underlay men's passionate friendships more than women's. Sexual desire was deemed "natural" to men (and often something to be overcome, regardless of the sex of the desired) but denied to any but "loose" or "fallen" women. In a culture and class suspicious of sex generally, male bonding, if assumed to contain sex, would be subjected to greater scrutiny than women's natural affinity for the pure in each other. Second, the cultural tolerance of male romantic same-sex attachments decreased as boys became adults. Men might continue boyhood friendships, but it would have to be alongside marriage, family, and their economic and civil responsibilities. Tellingly, there is no male equivalent to the term "Boston marriage," indicating not the absence of lifelong male partnerships but only the lack of the kind of cultural "space" for them as there was for those of women.

Women Passing as Men

It is interesting that for 19th-century women passionate friendships were not outside the norm, but passing as men (or attempting to) was. Although later Americans might see cross-gender behavior and same-sex attractions as equally "abnormal," for Victorians the threat lay not in what women did privately, in their assigned sphere, but publicly. The public life of women, especially in the middle class, was limited to activities appropriate to their gender. Advocates like Catharine Beecher, for example, were able to convince their countrymen that women could be allowed to teach young children since it was a natural extension of their maternal and moral roles. The argument was so successful that women made up the vast majority of all elementary teachers by 1900. For similar reasons reform activities were appropriate (as long as they did not get too radical or include public speaking), and women had always had a place in the arts, though in selected kinds of activities beyond the home circle. After the Civil War women could enter medicine, too, as long as they aspired to nursing and were thus answerable to a male physician. Even when women worked for pay outside the home, wages or salaries were less those paid to men—female teachers generally earned one-third to one-half the compensation of male teachers.

The economic limits placed on women, then, were one motivation for women to pass as men. This meant cutting their hair, wearing male clothing, and adopting mannerisms and anything else that would make them more masculine by their era's standards. Besides employment, the social and geographic mobility allowed men, and just plain adventure, were added attractions. Like many men, some women wanted to sail and see other lands, to fight for their country on the battlefield, or to roam freely without supervision. Finally, there were women clearly attracted to other women, who desired to live as "husbands" to them; perhaps more "male-identified" than their counterparts in Boston marriages, for them passing as men made their lives easier and possibly more fulfilling than trying to conform to feminine behaviors.

One of most fascinating examples of a cross-dressing female comes from the colonial era of Spanish America. Had she lived in the 20th century the Basque adventurer Catalina de Erauso would be called not only a transvestite (cross-dresser) but also transgendered (identifying more completely with the opposite gender) and possibly transsexual (desiring to *be* the opposite sex and gender). By passing as a male at age fifteen she escaped the convent in which she had been placed as a child and eventually made her way to New Spain. She was a soldier and clerk in South America until her sex was discovered. Remarkably, however, the pope granted her permission to dress as a man, which she apparently did after returning to the colonies, where she lived until her death around 1650. She continues to defy 20th-century categories of sexuality and gender, suggesting once again the degree to which norms can vary across time, place, class, and other factors.

The wars that marked the birth and division of the United States also had their women in uniform. During the revolutionary era, Deborah Sampson (1760–1827) achieved fame similar to Catalina's in Europe, serving in the Continental Army as Robert Shirtliff. During her eighteen months as a soldier she was wounded in battle, and contracted a fever, after which she was discovered to be female and then honorably discharged. Sampson later married, had three children, and toured the Northeast speaking about her experiences as a soldier. She received pensions from both Massachusetts and the U.S. government, and Congress voted her heirs a pension upon her death. Hundreds of females donned disguises in the Civil War on both sides, for reasons ranging from the desire to be with male loved ones to the impulse to live and act as men, and in ways then barred to women. Sarah Emma Edmonds and Loreta Velazquez left famous memoirs of their exploits posing as male spies, Edmonds for the Union, Velazquez for the Confederacy. Rosetta Wakeman fought with a New York regiment until she died of disease in 1864, at age 21. Her last letter to her family, written from Louisiana two months before her death, reads in part:

> Our army made as advance up the river to pleasant hill about 40 miles. There we had a fight.... I was not in the first day's fight but the next day I had to face the enemy bullets with my regiment. I was under fire about four hours and laid on the field of battle all night. There was three wounded in my Co. and one killed....
>
> I feel thankful to God that he spared my life and I pray to him that he will lead me safe through the filed of battle and that I may return safe home.[8]

Perhaps the most famous cross-dresser of the era was Dr. Mary Walker, a Union surgeon later awarded the Congressional Medal of Honor. Dr. Walker adopted male attire during and after the war, but differed from the passing women. Her intention was not to disguise herself as a man, but to wear male clothing as a woman. After the war and until her death in 1919 she continued cross-dressing, and wrote and lectured on various causes, including women's suffrage.

Women wore not only uniforms but whatever clothing their circumstances deemed "male" as well. There are scattered references to slave women passing as men in order to escape, and many accounts of working-class women, who led colorful lives dressing and/or passing as men in both urban areas and as miners and adventurers on the frontier. As long as there have been gender rules there have been people willing to defy them. For some women of early and Victorian America, living as men, for a few years to a lifetime, allowed them freedom and opportunities normally denied them. The situation would change somewhat in the 20th century, but not so much so quickly that passing women disappear. The presence of women dressed as men in the history of the American West should not be explained away solely as trading femininity for opportunity, though. Historian Peter Boag has noted the tendency of Western narratives to "normalize" those women in just this way and presents two challenges to us: to reconsider them as part of a history of transgenderism and to ask why the possibility "they did not consider themselves women" has been consciously avoided in the record.[9]

Dr. Mary Walker is pictured here, probably in Chicago, Illinois, with Miss Dorothy Hunt. Walker is one of many American women who have dressed in male attire, often as statements of female liberation. This photonegative was published in the *Chicago Daily News* December 2, 1912, and exemplifies the gender differences often enforced by clothing alone. (Chicago History Museum)

Limits and Laws

Despite the possibilities for same-sex romantic friendships, it would be a mistake to assume that the 19th century was a time of "anything goes" in personal relations. While there was more social space for expressing of same-sex eroticism and emotion openly, that space was defined somewhat by such factors as class, race, and age. Power, in other words, has always been a factor in who could do what with whom, and the 19th century was no different.

A case in point is that of Horatio Alger, Jr., whose name became synonymous with the self-help philosophy of the 19th century. In Alger's novels, poor urban youth succeed through a combination of hard work and often the luck of finding an older male sponsor. As historian Leila Rupp noted, "...Alger glorified the affection and support of older, powerful men for 'gentle' boys from the 'dangerous classes.'"[10] In Alger's own life, this support apparently had crossed over into sexual relations, resulting in his 1866 expulsion from his Unitarian ministry in Brewster, Massachusetts. Upon being confronted with charges that he committed with two teenaged boys "deeds that are too revolting to relate" he received them "with apparent calmness of an old offender—and hastily left town on the very next train..."[11] Alger settled in New York City where he worked for several of the newly emerging humanitarian organizations devoted to addressing urban poverty and especially its effects on children. Also at this time he began publishing the novels that would total over one hundred before his 1899 death; his books increased in popularity in the early 1900s and influenced future adolescent series such as those featuring Nancy Drew and the Hardy Boys. His story reveals something of prevailing attitudes, at least of his community, and the willingness of the community to censure the sexual offender. Importantly, had Alger's partners been older and classified as "men" (a category with no single fixed age in the 19th century) his dalliances may have been tolerated.

The legal situation surrounding same-sex acts had changed only slightly, though enforcement would wane and wax through the century. As colonies became states, sodomy and/or buggery (also called "crimes against nature") continued to be a crime in most of them, but less and less a capital one (the Carolinas were the last to drop the death penalty for sodomy, after the Civil War). Even Thomas Jefferson, during the Revolution, turned his attention briefly to Virginia's statue and proposed eliminating the death penalty in favor of lesser punishments (a bill not passed at the time):

> Whosoever shall be guilty of Rape, Polygamy, or Sodomy with man or woman shall be punished, if a man, by castration, if a woman, by cutting thro' the cartilage of her nose a hole of one half inch diameter at the least.[12]

Regardless of penalties, enforcement of sodomy laws was spotty and seemingly targeted more at nonwhite and foreign-born people until the late 19th century. At that time moral/social crusades of various types gained popularity; older laws were used to prosecute offenders and newer ones included oral sex as sodomy and outlawed "disorderly conduct," "public indecency," "lewdness," and so on. In this way, sin and crime, far from being disconnected, were bound as tightly together as they had been when natives first sighted European ships, and sexual "degeneracies" topped the list of illegal acts. It only remained for scientists to help define those acts, associate them with types of people, and add "illness" to the list of synonyms for the newly defined condition of homosexuality.

CONSTRUCTING THE MEDICAL MODEL

By the late 19th-century new professions, and the very idea of the professional, or expert, was taking hold in the western world. In the United States these new experts, who began to make their appearance during the Civil War, reflected the sense that bodies of knowledge were growing too rapidly to be mastered by any one person. Technology was equated with progress even more than before, and science was in ascendancy. Certainly not everyone became a Darwinist, but capitalists and social theorists alike found something in his ideas to forward their own goals, while more literally minded Christians entered into a long-standing debate with Darwinists over human origins.

Charles Darwin's ideas were imported, of course, as were those of Sigmund Freud and other pioneers of psychology, continuing a long tradition of exchange across the Atlantic. In the meantime, homegrown experts were also tackling illnesses of mind and body. All this combined to begin the long and complicated relationship between medical professionals and GLBT people in the United States.

The United States and Europe in the 1890s

Europe and the United States had already been in their own long and complicated relationship, lasting throughout the entire 19th century. Americans saw Europe as possessing models to be both avoided and emulated. Undemocratic forms of church and state served as constant reminders of the past Americans hoped to escape, while European literature and fine arts seemed to defy the notion that the United States was superior in all things. This ambivalence would continue into the 20th century, even as ideas and people, including those associated with new modes of sexuality, continued to flow in both directions.

Even without crucial developments in GLBT history, the 1890s signaled more than one turning point in the United States. Politically and socially it was the decade of Populism, Progressivism, and *Plessy v. Ferguson.* By 1894 the Populist Party rose from midwestern discontent to fashion a remarkably successful coalition. Urban Progressives emerged slightly later to address social issues with legal solutions, culminating in four new amendments to the U.S. Constitution (16, 17, 18, and 19) by 1920. In 1896, the U.S. Supreme Court, in the *Plessy* decision, legalized segregation between blacks and whites, further spurring organized action by African Americans and their allies. In the next two decades the Niagara movement and the National Association for the Advancement of Colored People provided a critique of Booker T. Washington's more conciliatory tone in his famous "Atlanta Address" of 1895. These kinds of differences over strategy—especially whether to "accommodate" those in power and assimilate into the majority rather than embrace and celebrate differences—have divided every movement for equality, including those of GLBT people.

Other events and causes distinguished the 1890s. The relationship between the federal government and Native Americans had further deteriorated after the Civil War due to a combined policy of forced acculturation through the Dawes Severalty Act and armed conflict in the deserts and plains. The year of the Battle at Wounded Knee, 1890, also saw the two major women's suffrage organizations merge into the National American Women's Suffrage Association, though success in the form of a constitutional amendment was still thirty years in the future. Economically, Americans experienced their worst crisis yet in the 1890s. By the end of the decade, though, many were celebrating a new American Empire following victory over Spain and the acquisition of territory in the Caribbean and Pacific. The stage was set for Frederick Jackson Turner to speculate on the meaning of America's frontier history; its supposed "closing" offered imperialists good reason to continue seeking frontiers elsewhere. Turner's speech in 1893 coincided with the World's Columbian Exposition in Chicago, a remarkable event that embodied progress in a city that, ironically, was then and later known for some of urban America's worst features.

The Chicago World's Fair, in fact, embodied many of the contradictory aspects of American culture. One of these was the historical relationship between the United States and Europe, in which Americans felt both superior and inferior to Europeans—superior in politics, business, and technology but inferior in literature and the arts. The Fair's premier engineering "exhibit," the gigantic Ferris wheel, was designed to outdo the Eiffel Tower, for example, even while much of the Fair's architecture relied heavily on European precedents. This reflected the ongoing dilemma of U.S. architects, writers, and artists who were trying to create "American" works based on highly regarded European models.

In the sciences and social sciences, there was less overt nationalism, perhaps due to the very notion of objectivity built into its disciplines, but their origins and receptions remained products of their time and place. The relatively new sciences of anthropology, sociology, and eugenics, for example, all reflected the 19th-century belief in progress through mastery of knowledge and conquest (or manipulation) of nature; eugenics especially reflected class, race, and imperial biases while touting "improvement" of the human race through genetic control. Of all the 19th-century sciences, psychiatry, psychology, and the even newer sexology had the greatest and most lasting impact on GLBT people. Information in all areas continued to flow in both directions across the Atlantic, with developments in Germany and England of particular significance for GLBT history then and since. It is interesting that some movements, such as Freudian psychology, gained tremendous acceptance in the United States while others, like homosexual emancipation, did not.

The selective nature by which ideas and movements crossed the Atlantic highlights the importance of specific histories, even as nations shared larger trends. France, Italy, and Holland, for example, were among the Western European countries that did not outlaw homosexual acts, and Paris especially featured a thriving subculture of "bohemians" (see Chapter 3). Since social and legal situations are often related, it may be that those areas less affected by Victorianism generally, and especially its specific notions of gendered spheres of influence, were less likely also to involve the state in policing some realms of sexual behavior. These differences reflect too the heightened nationalism which played out on the global stage as competition for colonies in the "New Imperial" age of the era, an age the United States was just entering. By 1914, the tensions produced by the virulent nationalism and revived imperialism of the 19th century resulted in a world war that for many is the dividing line between the Victorian and Modern eras. Many elements define that division and among them are ideas about sex and sexuality. In the decades just preceding World War I Europeans and Americans were developing and exchanging many of those ideas.

The Sexologists

In the same year as the World's Fair in Chicago, German sexologist Magnus Hirschfeld visited the United States and later included his observations in his *Homosexuality in Men and Women* (1914). The terms homosexual and heterosexual had been introduced to U.S. readers—at least those of medical journals—only the year before, and "homosexual" is usually dated from the late 1860s, when Hungarian Karl Maria Kertbeny coined it in defense of male love. Hirschfeld, Kertbeny, and other sexologists of the era were working in the specific context of legal repression. This introduces two important themes of 20th-century GLBT life: the stimulus to organize around an identity caused by discrimination, persecution, or worse; and a kind of love/hate relationship between GLBT people and professionals in law and medicine (since doctors and lawyers had power to both cause and relieve homophobia).

Hirschfeld, an openly homosexual physician, was probably the most important theorist in an impressive list of German, English, and American doctors. In Germany, a turning point came in 1871 when the newly created Second Empire adopted the Prussian legal code and its paragraph 175, which included homosexual acts between males as "unnatural fornication," and made them criminal offenses. This law, coupled with the era's faith in science, helped stimulate inquiries into same-sex love, sex, and attraction. Karl Heinrich Ulrichs, Karl Westphal, and Richard von Krafft-Ebing developed differing but related theories of sexuality, often relying on the gender norms of their day. Westphal's writings of "contrary sexual feeling" that was congenital (or inborn) were influenced by Ulrichs, who further described such feeling as basically natural and healthy. In Ulrichs' view, occasionally there was a mismatch of "soul" to body; males, whom he called "Urnings," might have female souls, and vice versa, but to persecute people born thus was "cruel, unjust and senseless."[13] Ulrichs' work also influenced that of Krafft-Ebing, a neurologist whose exhaustive study of perversions, *Psychopathia Sexualis* (1886; translated and published in the United States, 1892), represented his conviction that the appropriate response was medical correction rather than punishment.

Hirschfeld in turn rejected theories of mental illness and degeneracy. Like Ulrichs, he promoted a positive view of homosexuality as natural, and further contributed the idea of the "Uranian," a person of an "intermediate" condition or "third sex." In 1897 came his Scientific Humanitarian Committee and in 1919 he founded the Institute for Sexual Science. He continued to oppose paragraph 175, and although it was repealed in 1929 under the Weimar Republic (1919–1933), the repeal never took effect and the law remained in some form until 1994. Hirschfeld lived until 1935, having witnessed the Nazis come to power and destroy his work—literally, by burning his library. The German homosexual emancipation movement he helped create, however, had already made its way to the United States, though in fits and starts.

In England too a changing legal climate advanced sexology by stimulating literary and scientific reactions. Sodomy had been a capital offense from the 16th century to 1861, and since then punishable by life imprisonment. In 1886, amid a more general "purity crusade" also underway in the United States, the Labouchére amendment went into effect. It more broadly defined "acts of gross indecency" between two men as criminal, regardless of age or consent. It was this amendment, in turn, that precipitated the era's most sensational English trials, those of Oscar Wilde in 1895. Perhaps the nation's most eminent writer and wit, Wilde was made an example when he was found guilty and sentenced to the maximum penalty of two years hard labor, which he served in full. The trials also popularized the phrase "the love that dare not speak its name," from a poem by Wilde's companion, Lord Alfred Douglas. Wilde famously defended that love in an eloquent speech, and in doing so insisted that the "spiritual affection," between an older and younger man, was historic, noble, and without sexual meaning.

As mentioned above, in late 19th-century England and the United States, the two nations where Victorian ideals predominated, reformers had organized "purity" movements and sought to entrench their morals through law. Concerns ranged from prostitution to the birth rates of various groups (were the "wrong" people breeding too quickly while Anglo-Saxons were engaged in forms of nonreproductive sex?). In England as in Germany, sexologists emerged to challenge negative views of same-sex desire and activity.

Edward Carpenter, John Addington Symonds, and Havelock Ellis were among those in England seeking to understand sexual variation. Carpenter and Symonds both were familiar with Walt Whitman's poetry and affected by it. Both also promoted very positive views of homosexuality—Carpenter contributed to the concept of an "intermediate" sex—in response to the prevailing view even in medicine that it was abnormal and demanded a cure. Symonds, a physician, was especially concerned with revising the law to abolish penalties for homosexual acts. Of the English writers, Ellis was probably more known in the United States, and then only among budding specialists. The second volume in his *Studies in the Psychology of Sex* (1897–1928) was titled "Sexual Inversion," a label for the dominant concept of homosexuality through the next hundred years. He contributed also to the debate over the causes of "inversion" and its manifestations. That is, "inverts" were primarily people whose gender behavior did not match their biological sex, but there was debate over two issues: whether the condition was inborn or acquired, and whether same-sex attraction and gender inversion were invariably coupled. Could a "masculine" man desire other men, and if so, did that desire alone make him an invert? Regardless of the individual theory, two results of the discussions, in England, Germany, and the United States, are important. First, what was previously considered a sinful and/or criminal type of *behavior* was becoming a *type of person* who required treatment (or not) rather than incarceration. Second, it logically followed, to the new medical professionals, that they were better equipped to address the issue than lawyers, judges, and ministers.

The most influential work on sex and psychology came not from Germany or England, though, but from Vienna. The writings of Sigmund Freud, often distilled and simplified, became immensely popular in 20th-century America. One of the most controversial thinkers of his time, Freud helped end the century-long public silence surrounding sex and suggested that sexual impulses were a normal part of being human. Famous for his ideas of repression and sublimation of sexual feelings, he also proposed the ideas that humans may be born bisexual, but that "normal" development would be in *stages*—oral, anal, genital—towards sexual maturity. By these theories inverts (whom he defined more by attraction to a same-sex object choice than gender attributes) still fell into the abnormal category, as victims of arrested development. He had doubts about curing homosexuality, however, and possibly doubts about the need to do so. According to a now-famous story told by Freud's student Helene Deutsch to her grandson, Dr. Deutsch had been treating a lesbian patient. "My grandmother was disturbed," recalled Nicholas Deutsch,

> because, although the analysis finally concluded successfully—the woman could deal with various problems in her life—she was still a Lesbian. My grandmother was rather worried about what Freud would say about this turn of events. When she next saw Freud the first thing he said was, "Congratulations on your great success with Miss X." My grandmother, startled, said, "But she's still a Lesbian." To which Freud replied, "What does it matter as long as she's happy?"[14]

As Otto Spengler found in 1906, the idea that one could be well adjusted and be homosexual was not a popular view in the United States, even among professional men. Still, there had been some discussion of sexuality by then, stimulated by the same kind of scientific curiosity and possible legal reform as among the Europeans. Foremost among Americans studying sex were neurologists James G. Kiernan and G. Frank Lydston. Kiernan is credited with the first known use of the term "heterosexual" in the

United States in a medical article in 1892. Interestingly, at that time it was meant to suggest what is now called bisexuality, and was a "perversion" due to a focus on pleasure over reproduction. As Jonathan Ned Katz has illustrated in *The Invention of Heterosexuality,* both homosexuality and heterosexuality were conceived (not "discovered") relatively recently and out of the specific conditions of the late 19th century. Also, he demonstrates changes in even those concepts, until they more or less solidified into the opposition of heterosexuality-as-normal versus homosexuality-as-abnormal in the early 20th century. Kiernan, Lydston, and other American doctors considered sexual "perversions" to be biological, and, typical in an era concerned with social reform and the progress of (American) civilization, they were as concerned with their effect on American society as well as on the specific individual.

Supposed causes generated possible solutions. People committing homosexual acts continued to be arrested and jailed, but alongside that response came treatments and proposed "cures." Again, this was the product of a parallel shift in thinking from acts to types of people (perverts, inverts) and the incursion of medicine into the legal realm. The variety of treatments proposed would set the stage for the entire 20th century, and ranged from abstinence and cold baths to castration, from psychoanalysis to surgery (also see Chapter 4 for treatments). What they shared was the general view that some kind of treatment was *needed.* "Natural," as in biological, was not necessarily "normal" any more than other inherited diseases of the body or mind. A few sexologists and many self-identified homosexuals continued to argue the normality of same-sex attraction, but were overwhelmed by the immense value eventually placed on heterosexuality as a foundation of a good society.

At the turn of the 20th century, then, there were many views in the Western world about human sexuality and its variations. Sexologists described those who sexually desired people of the same sex and/or whose gender was that of the opposite sex variously as "Uranians," "deviants," "variants," and "inverts," all the while proposing these as neutral, scientific terms. Most important, their work led to a simple duality in which heterosexual was normal and homosexual abnormal; a third category, bisexual, has had meaning only in the context of these poles, and has since occupied an uneasy place between them.

SEXUAL POLITICS AT THE TURN OF THE CENTURY

The 19th century is often associated with "isms"—industrialism, liberalism, romanticism, realism, Darwinism, and so on. By the late 19th century, nationalism, imperialism, and feminism combined to create an explosive situation in the West; certainly the first two are seen as major contributors to World War I, while feminism added another dimension to a volatile situation. "Sexual politics" basically refers to the intersection of public and private worlds—ways one sphere is affected by the other—with the private dominated by concepts of sex and gender that dictated the separation of men and women, male and female.

By the turn of the century, ideas about men and women were a mix of the Victorian and the modern. There was still concern with appropriate behavior for males and females. A "cult of masculinity," for example, has been linked to imperialism abroad and feminism at home in the Western nations experiencing both. Nations as well as male individuals needed "manly" qualities to assert their authority in the world; feminists were seen as threatening to the social order needed at home by trying to undermine barriers between men and women. As Theodore Roszak put it in his classic

1969 analysis of responses to feminism,..."the last hundred years stand as the historical crisis of masculine dominance....The period leading up to 1914," he wrote,

> reads in the history books like one long drunken stag party where boys from every walk of life and every ideological persuasion goad one another on to ever more bizarre professions of toughness, daring, and counterphobic mania—until at last the boasting turns suicidal and these would-be supermen plunge the whole of Western society into the blood bath of world war. Compulsive masculinity is written all over the political style of the period.[15]

In this context feminism and lesbianism were equally dangerous and at times interchangeable. To many, lesbians were women "acting like men" regardless of their personal lives. Their public demands for the vote, property rights, access to professions and the education necessary for them made them as "manly" as anything they might do with other women in their bedrooms. At the same time, Boston marriages did come under more scrutiny, too. A newer ideal of "companionate marriage" was replacing the older homosocial world of the middle class. While this was a boon to men and women who believed marriage and sexual desire were two sides of a coin, and who wanted to socialize together, it now called romantic friendships into question as immature at best, abnormal and dangerous at worst.

The sexual politics of the era included the rise of professions and specialties within those professions; by definition, the professional was in the public sphere, and therefore male. Education and medicine provide examples of the gendered consolidation of power through the 19th century: nurturing females assisted male professionals (principals, doctors) in appropriately subservient roles. In some areas, such as childbirth, male experts gradually replaced females altogether. Power was involved in the development of the sciences of the mind and of sexual behavior also. In order to wield any power, however, the new doctors had to convince legal and penal officials that sex and gender deviants were ill, not criminal.

The creation of the medical model produced mixed results. For some, the label "homosexual" offered relief in knowing they were not alone and possible association with others like them. While some would accept the supposed need for a cure (later termed "internalized homophobia"), others chose rather to accept their difference and assert its value. The latter was the case especially in Germany, whose emancipationists influenced the first U.S. efforts at homosexual organizing (see Chapter 3).

The relationships among identity, community formation, and movements are contested, as is the idea that defining homosexuality was necessarily a positive development. Those who argue the disadvantages of the new identity focus on two aspects: the stigma attached to it, and the contraction of options for identity and lifestyle compared to those available to those with same-sex affinities in the 19th century. Whatever the intentions of the sexologists, their views entered a context in which gender was still crucial to social order, and deviance therefore threatening. Also due to this context, the medical model did not simply replace constructions of sinful and criminal behavior but was instead added to the mix, and became further justification for arrest and punishment through most of the 20th century.

Finally, it is well to remember that the origins of the medical model are contested and the impact of that model was uneven. Sexologists may have invented new terms but did so with knowledge of people (sometimes themselves) already behaving or identifying in a variety of ways. The people they described might accept those terms or not, when they even knew about them; race, ethnicity, class, and location all might

DEBATE: WHAT ARE THE ROOTS OF HOMOPHOBIA?

Scholars now believe that homophobia, or the fear and hatred of homosexuals, has a history. That is, they generally reject the idea that there is necessarily one sexuality "natural" to human beings, causing an equally "natural" aversion to all other sexualities. If this were true, then homophobia would be considered part of human nature and not have a history in terms of being created under specific circumstances at a particular time. However, not only does homophobia appear to be just as much a result of historical forces as is the heterosexual/homosexual binary, it may even be a by-product of the same forces that shaped that binary.

Within this general agreement, there are differences over the causes of homophobia, how recent it is, and to whether American homophobia is unique, in style or fervor. Certainly there are sources for antigay attitudes that predate the late 19th century and its changes in the construction of sexuality. Many believe that Judeo-Christian teachings have always prohibited homosexual acts, and it is clear that those beliefs found their way into European and American law that made those acts criminal (and punishable by death in the colonial era). According to some scholars, though, religious ideas alone may not account for the depth of antigay sentiment both inherited and developed in the last 100 years, and so historians and theorists have also considered three contexts for understanding homophobia.

First is the system of sex and gender outlined in this chapter. Suzanne Pharr, in *Homophobia: A Weapon of Sexism* notes links among sexism, heterosexism, and homophobia, arguing that each supports the others and that all are used to maintain patriarchy. Further, all three rely upon gender codes. "Who suffers from gender roles?" she asks, and answers, "Women most completely and men in part."[16] Added to this more universal explanation is a consideration of time and place. Not only was the 19th-century U.S. patriarchal, but, like other emerging industrial capitalist nations, it witnessed a growing middle class as well. Middle-class families on both sides of the Atlantic developed strict rules that demanded an exact correspondence between biological sex (male, female) and social gender traits (masculine, feminine). In this way, order was brought to societies that seemed too much in flux, particularly, perhaps, in the United States, where property, wealth, and race were being challenged as sources of social order. In such a climate it was difficult to tolerate males and females who did not keep to their respective spheres and behave in ways deemed appropriate to their sex.

Second is the duality of heterosexual/homosexual devised by the new profession of sexology in the late 19th century. Importantly, we have noted that the new duality was conceived as much in terms of gender as of sexual behavior, so that a "gender invert," male or female, would be deemed "homosexual." When these concepts were united, homosexuals came to embody the dangers already implied in breaching the gender code. It also meant that the violations were different for men and women, since the gender ideals were opposite and complementary. While men's sexual behavior (especially playing a "women's" role in sex) might be a greater factor in labeling them homosexual, women might be thought homosexual for publicly demanding their rights (a serious departure from their sphere in several ways). Either way, the determination to punish (or cure) the inverts seems to reflect the fear of chaos of a class in flux and a society amid drastic political and economic change.

Finally, there is the very specific context of American nationalism, in the form U.S. historians have called exceptionalism. The United States and its history, according to this mentality, were both unique and universal. Nineteenth-century Americans combined the older idea of the country's special relationship with a Judeo-Christian God with newer concerns of the survival of this republic as a haven for liberty in the world. The result was viewing America history not as a continuation of the European past, but as a significant (and better) departure from it, while the future held hope for all humankind. To historian Jay Hatheway, this exceptionalism, when added to the new medical model and the many uncertainties of late 19th-century America, helped create a specific and virulent strain of antihomosexual thought and action. As he succinctly stated in 2003, "The problem with homosexuality during the Gilded Age [1877–1900] was that it was fundamentally un-American, and while this sentiment may be less strongly held at the beginning of the twenty-first century, such was not the case in the latter part of the nineteenth."[17]

Whatever the roots of homophobia are thought to be, it is significant that historians are investigating them. Until recently, scholars studied homosexuality from a variety of perspectives, but rarely questioned bias against it; what caused sexual "deviance" was more a concern than what caused hostility toward it. We have come to realize, however, that the results of that hostility—persecution, discrimination, and violence—are as much a part of 20th-century GLBT history as those same results of racism and sexism are to the histories of minorities and women, and so they demand another look. (See also Debate, Chapter 8.)

determine the relationship, if any, with the newer and more limiting categories. Not everyone with same-sex desire identified, then or since, as homosexual. Neither would all homosexuals, then or since, accept the stigma, and certainly not all homosexuals ever joined a movement. As we turn to the 20th century, the variety of experiences possible among what become GLBT Americans remains an important theme.

NOTES

1. All quotations from Jonathan Ned Katz, *Gay American History: Lesbians and Gay Men in the U.S.A.,* rev. ed. (New York: Penguin Meridian, 1992), 381–83.

2. Leila Rupp, *A Desired Past: A Short History of Same-Sex Love in America* (Chicago: University of Chicago Press, 1999), 14.

3. David E. Stannard, *American Holocaust: Columbus and the Conquest of the New World* (New York: Oxford University Press, 1992), 57.

4. Barbara Welter, "The Cult of True Womanhood: 1820–1860," *American Quarterly* 18 (1966): 151–74.

5. All quotations from Alexis de Tocqueville, *Democracy in America,* vol. 2 (New York: J. & H.G. Langley, 1840; New York: Alfred A. Knopf, 1980), 211–12, from the chapter entitled, "How the Americans Understand the Equality of the Sexes."

6. Eve Kornfeld, *Margaret Fuller: A Brief Biography with Documents* (Boston: Bedford Books, 1997), 8–9.

7. Robert K. Martin, "Knights-Errant and Gothic Seducers: The Representation of Male Friendship in Mid-Nineteenth-Century America," in *Hidden from History: Reclaiming the Gay and Lesbian Past,* ed. Martin Duberman, Martha Vicinus, and George Chauncey, Jr. (New York: New American Library, 1989), 182, 180–81.

8. Lauren Cook Burgess, ed., *An Uncommon Soldier: The Civil War Letters of Sarah Rosetta Wakeman, alias Private Lyons Wakeman, 153rd Regiment, New York State Volunteers, 1862–1864* (New York: Oxford University Press, 1994), 71.

9. Peter Boag, "Go West Young Man, Go East Young Woman: Searching for the *Trans* in Western Gender History," *Western Historical Quarterly* 36 (Winter 2005): 477–97; quote p. 486.

10. Rupp, *Desired Past,* 67.

11. Quoted in Katz, *Gay American History,* 33.

12. "A Bill for Proportioning Crimes and Punishments in Cases Heretofore Capital," *The Papers of Thomas Jefferson,* vol. 2, ed. Julian P. Boyd (Princeton, NJ: Princeton University Press, 1950), 497.

13. Quoted in Jay Hatheway, *The Gilded Age Construction of Modern American Homophobia* (New York: Palgrave Macmillan, 2003), 102.

14. Quoted in Katz, *Gay American History,* 161.

15. Theodore Roszak, "The Hard and the Soft: The Force of Feminism in Modern Times," in *Masculine/Feminine: Readings in Sexual Mythology and the Liberation of Women,* ed. Betty Roszak and Theodore Roszak (New York: Harper & Row, 1969), 90, 92.

16. Suzanne Pharr, *Homophobia: A Weapon of Sexism* (Berkeley, CA: Chardon Press, 1997), 8.

17. Hatheway, *Gilded Age Construction of Modern American Homophobia,* 11.

SUGGESTED RESOURCES

Colonial America/Native America

Allen, P.G. (1989). Lesbians in American Indian cultures. In M. Duberman, M. Vicinus, & G. Chauncey, Jr. (Eds.), *Hidden from history: Reclaiming the gay and lesbian past* (pp. 106–117). New York: New American Library.

Benemann, W. (2006). *Male-Male intimacy in early America: Beyond romantic friendships.* Binghamton, NY: Harrington Park Press.

Jacobs, S.-E., Thomas, W., & Lang, S. (Eds.). (1997). *Two-spirit people: Native American gender identity, sexuality, and spirituality.* Urbana: University of Illinois Press.

Native Americans/Gay Americans: 1528–1976. (1992). Pt. IV of J.N. Katz, *Gay American history: Lesbians and gay men in the U.S.A.* (Rev. ed., pp. 281–334). New York: Penguin Meridian.

Roscoe, W. (Ed.). (1988). *Living the spirit: A gay American Indian anthology.* New York: St. Martin's Press.

Williams, W.L. (1986). *The spirit and the flesh: Sexual diversity in American Indian culture.* Boston: Beacon Press.

19th Century: Same-Sex Relations/Passing Women

Duberman, M. (1989). 'Writing Bedfellows' in South Carolina: Historical interpretation and the politics of evidence. In M. Duberman, M. Vicinus, & G. Chauncey, Jr. (Eds.), *Hidden from history: Reclaiming the gay and lesbian past* (pp. 153–168). New York: New American Library.

Edmonds, S.E. (1999). *Memoirs of a soldier, nurse, and spy: A woman's adventures in the union army (1865).* DeKalb: Northern Illinois University Press.

Faderman, L. (1981). *Surpassing the love of men: Romantic friendship and love between women from the renaissance to the present.* New York: William Morrow.

Faderman, L. (1999). *To believe in women: What lesbians have done for America—a history.* Boston: Houghton Mifflin.

Hansen, K.V. (1995, August). 'No Kisses Is Like Youres': An erotic friendship between two African-American women during the mid-nineteenth century. *Gender and History, 7,* 153–182.

Johnson, S.L. (2001). *Roaring camp: The social world of the California gold rush.* New York: W.W. Norton.

Katz, J.N. (2001). *Love stories: Sex between men before homosexuality.* Chicago: University of Chicago Press.

Passing women: 1782–1920. Pt. III of Katz, *Gay American history* (pp. 209–279).

San Francisco Lesbian and Gay History Project. (1989). 'She Even Chewed Tobacco': A pictorial narrative of passing women in America. In M. Duberman, M. Vicinus, & G. Chauncey, Jr. (Eds.), *Hidden from history: Reclaiming the gay and lesbian past* (pp. 183–194). New York: New American Library.

Smith-Rosenberg, C. (1975). The female world of love and ritual: Relations between women in nineteenth-century America. *Signs, 1,* 1–29.

Stepto, M., & Stepto, G. (Trans.). (1996). *Lieutenant nun: Memoir of a Basque Transvestite in the New World.* Boston: Beacon Press.

Velazquez, L.J. (1972). *The woman in battle: A narrative of the exploits, adventures, and travels of Madame Loreta Janeta Velazquez (1876)* (C.J. Worthington, Ed.). New York: Arno Press.

Vicinus, M. (2004). *Intimate friends: Women who loved women, 1778–1928.* Chicago: University of Chicago Press.

Young, A.F. (2004). *Masquerade: The life and times of Deborah Sampson, continental soldier.* New York: Alfred A. Knopf.

Sexuality: History and Construction

Duggan, L. (2000). *Sapphic slashers: Sex, violence, and American modernity.* Durham: Duke University Press.

Katz, J.N. (1995). *The invention of heterosexuality.* New York: Dutton.

3 SEXUALITIES AND COMMUNITIES THROUGH TWO WORLD WARS

Washington, DC, 1941. At the Howard Theatre the International Sweethearts of Rhythm sets a new box-office record. Formed in 1937 as a school band, the Sweethearts received similar receptions throughout their tours in the United States and, at the end of World War II, in Europe while entertaining African American troops. "America's Greatest All Girl Band" was one of over forty all-women jazz/swing bands; what made the Sweethearts unique was that which also put them in danger, especially in the South: they were truly "International" or interracial. Segregation was the law of the land, so the group's audiences were predominantly black, and the few white women could be arrested (and were) for their very presence.

Another unique aspect of the band was simply their musicianship: they were good. Among the band's finest players was trumpeter/singer Ernestine "Tiny" Davis, who had joined them in Chicago. Then separated from her husband and children, she had played with other all-female bands before answering an ad for the Sweethearts. Described as "the heart of the band," Davis was its star as well, and known widely in jazz circles as "the female Louis Armstrong." Ironically, Armstrong was among the band's and Tiny's fans (Count Basie and Ella Fitzgerald were others) and reportedly offered Davis up to ten times her $150/week salary to join his band. Asked later why she didn't go, she responded, grinning, "Well, I loved them gals too much." Whether or not that decision hurt her career, simply being a woman was an obstacle for most women musicians. Tiny was certainly aware of the prejudice: "I don't like to hear that 'plays like a girl' or 'plays like a sissy' stuff. I had more chops than most men . . . . So no, we never got the credit we deserved. But women have a hard time in anything. There's nothing you can do. Just keep on keeping on."

Taking her own advice, Tiny left the Sweethearts (who split up by 1949) soon after the war's end to form her own band, Tiny Davis and Her Hell Divers. Also at this time she met musician Ruby Lucas [aka Renei Phelan] and they soon became a couple. In Chicago they opened Tiny and Ruby's Gay Spot, which they ran through the 1950s. Upon Davis's death in 1994, the women had been partners for well over forty years. In the late eighties Davis was somewhat vague but hardly shocked when asked about their relationship: "Ruby came over one day [in Kansas City] and never left. Hell, she stayed for 42 years. Are we gay? Maybe we are. We have ourselves a time, I can say that."[1]

Born in 1907, Tiny Davis (d. 1994) lived through the years under consideration in this chapter, and far beyond. She witnessed the key events of the century as a member of the group recently termed the "Greatest Generation" in a best-selling book by newsman Tom Brokaw.[2] Although historians debate the notion of generations in history, there is a kind of consensus that the millions of Americans who experienced both the

Ernestine "Tiny" Davis was among the finest musicians of the swing era. She was known as "the female Louis Armstrong" and played with the all-woman band, the International Sweethearts of Rhythm. Later she formed her own band, the Hell Divers, and in the 1950s she and life partner Ruby Lucas ran Tiny and Ruby's Gay Spot in Chicago. (Courtesy of Jezebel Productions. Used by permission.)

country's worst depression and the war that followed it emerged with many shared values, hopes, and attitudes. True, there were significant differences among those old enough to recall vividly the Japanese attack on the U.S. naval base at Pearl Harbor on December 7, 1941: economic or social status, race, sex, location, and many other factors might dictate a person's specific experiences in that time, as in any other era. Depression and war did not erase those differences (and even highlighted some) but they did set in motion profound changes that affected all Americans to some degree. Just as important, that generation shaped those years—and the decades that followed—as much as those years shaped them.

The thirties and forties are as significant for GLBT history as they are for the more famous national story. Davis is a part of this history too, and represents the intersection of individual identities—in her case African American, female, and lesbian—and collective themes. The fact that her career continued after 1945, for example, highlights the more common postwar retreat of many women, including musicians, from the public sphere. That she lived openly as a lesbian after the war emphasizes not only her courage in doing so during a repressive time for homosexuals (see Chapter 4) but may equally reflect the relatively more tolerant era and cultural milieu in which she came of age. In the end, though, perhaps the most crucial point is that she and millions of other GLBT people were very much among those who, as a generation, "went on to build modern America."[3]

Even before the thirties, however, the United States was experiencing a time of rapid transformation resulting in cultural conflict. The Victorian values of a white middle class met modern urban life and "modernism" in the arts and science and resulted in clashes with social and political consequences. Despite their survival, old assumptions became more difficult to defend in light of an unstoppable world war and the country's—and world's—most severe economic depression. Many Americans emerged from the First World War disenchanted and ready to party. When the party was over, some recent cultural arrivals sustained their momentum through the century while others were all but gone, slowly departing until squeezed out by the newcomers. Among the former, the music and literature of the Harlem Renaissance are notable examples, the setting of which figures importantly in GLBT history. Another lingering guest was the binary concept of sexuality, a relatively narrow idea gathering adherents and strength well after dawn and eventually leaving little room for varieties of desire and expression of the 19th century.

LIFE IN THE CITIES TO THE TWENTIES

Urbanization and industrialization had been facts of life for many Americans long before 1900, as had their conflicting results. During and after the Civil War, however, the pace of both developments increased, in tandem and at breakneck speed, into the 20th century and beyond. Americans also had long been torn between the virtues of country life and the opportunities of the city, an ambivalence deepened by 1920 as the urban world offered some of the best and worst living conditions imaginable.

Population is one of two key factors related to understanding those conditions. Uniting the two areas is a remarkable increase in people: between 1860 and 1900 the U.S. population doubled, from thirty-one to sixty-two million (and this despite more than 600,000 lives lost in the Civil War), and by 1930 had nearly doubled again, to over 122 million. Sources of the growth included both natural increase and immigration. Until after the Civil War the majority of immigrants were from Great Britain and

Western Europe, while Eastern and Southern Europeans arrived in increasing numbers later in the century.

Also related to population issues was historian Frederick Jackson Turner's new concept of American development, the "frontier thesis." Turner had read the 1890 census report, which declared that a frontier no longer existed in the United States due to settlement west of the Mississippi River. In 1893 Turner delivered a now-famous address on "The Significance of the Frontier in American History" in which he argued that the experience of settling undeveloped land had created in pioneers the characteristics defined as uniquely American. In addition, he claimed that the very presence of "free" land (Native American rights to it were not acknowledged) offered opportunities for betterment and provided a "safety valve" that had prevented class war in the United States. Much of the message was a celebration of westward expansion, but it also raised an alarm: if the frontier era was now over, how would America sustain the values thought central to being "American"? To many observers it was no coincidence that after 1893 U.S. expansion into the Pacific and the Caribbean, though begun earlier, was promoted as essential to national development.

Finally, people were not only moving west in greater numbers, but also from the countryside to the city. Once Reconstruction was ended in the South in 1877 and those states returned to a "home rule" dedicated to white supremacy, African Americans began moving north to urban areas in search of jobs and better treatment (neither of which they necessarily received). After World War I the numbers reached about a half-million and the "Great Migration" of blacks had begun that would have a significant impact on American cultural life as well as on the economic opportunities and visibility of African Americans. This shift continued in a second wave of migration after World War II, with northeastern and midwestern states showing the most increases, particularly in their cities. Significantly, as World War I ended the percentage of Americans living in areas defined as "urban" outnumbered those in rural situations for the first time in American history (51 percent in 1920).

The other key element affecting the extremes possible in urban life was a radically altered economy. Although 49 percent of Americans still lived in rural environments in 1920, they were much less "agrarian" than their grandparents in terms of their ability to be self-sufficient landowners. Even as that dream persisted, farmers, ranchers, and others dependent on crops and animals (and land and water) had been drawn into an industrial capitalist arrangement as much as their "urban" counterparts. After the Civil War banks and railroads, while providing the links in the newly expanding and interdependent economy, also gained increased control through the mortgage terms and shipping rates offered to rural Americans. The stresses of these changes underlay the Grange movement and Farmers' Alliances of the era, culminating in the attempt of the Populist Party to draw urban workers, western miners, and farmers/ranchers into a new coalition based on their relationship to industrial power. As the 19th century became the 20th, the urban-based reform projects of Progressivism created changes at all levels, and a "Progressive mentality" influenced American imperial activities and goals.

Americans we would now term gay, lesbian, bisexual and transgendered found the times, and urban life, as full of mixed blessings as did their non-GLBT counterparts. In several cities thriving subcultures arose, and several concepts of sex and gender identity coexisted. Perhaps surprisingly, these subcultures had a very visible presence that coincided with the years before and after World War I, only to gradually go "underground" by the time the world was again at war. All the while, urban life was neither universally welcomed nor a boon for everyone. Homosexuals (as then defined by scientists) were not only targets of reformers but vital participants in some of the central movements of the day.

Capitalism, Gender, and Sexuality

Capitalism, or the pursuit of profit through investment, was not new in the late 19th century. Rather, it was the rise of machinery, mass production, and the concentration of workers in factories and the cities that combined into the industrial capitalism that distinguished a "developed" from an "undeveloped" nation. Individuals could accumulate fortunes larger than ever before imagined, though whether those that did so were "Robber Barons" or "Captains of Industry" was a subject of debate. In a now-famous 1889 essay, often called "The Gospel of Wealth," Andrew Carnegie declared wealth the "problem of our age" and predicted European-style class war unless "the ties of brotherhood [that] bind together the rich and poor in harmonious relationship" were restored.[4] Carnegie's remarks concerned the administration of great wealth by those who accumulated it, while others saw the problem in different terms, from the need for greater efficiency to the effects of industrialization on the work and lives of laborers. Efforts to organize workers began in earnest after the Civil War and achieved some success before the Great Depression. Unions promoted differing methods to better the conditions of labor; wages and working conditions always topped any list, and workers felt forced into boycotts, strikes, and even violence to protect their positions. In the meantime, middle-class reformers responded in a variety of ways to workers (often immigrants) and their conditions, from legal actions controlling their behavior to the settlement houses, exposés, and labor laws of the Progressive Era.

The "revolution" of the industrial revolution, then, actually was many sided. Machines transformed the economy and the lives of everyone, even those on farms; fewer craftsmen were needed and the many that now did the job of a few were referred to literally as "hands," reflecting the dehumanizing effects of efficiency. As examined more thoroughly in Chapter 2, no less central to the revolutionary nature of this transition were changes in the family as an economic unit, resulting in the exaggeration of separate public and private realms in the middle class. These "spheres" were clearly gendered and rigidly divided into public/male/masculine and private/female/feminine. This contributed to sexologists' concepts of "deviant" sexuality, since they tended to focus on those who violated the dictates of their sphere and the gender assigned that sphere. "Feminine" men and "masculine" women were a threat to the social/economic order, it seems, regardless of their sexual proclivities (see also Debate, Chapter 2).

Industrial capitalism has had more paradoxical effects in GLBT history than the above suggests, though. While its development likely solidified a two-sex, two-gender system that would allow less and less tolerance of variety within it, other of its changes enhanced the ability of some men and women to claim a nonheterosexual identity and to construct lives around that identity. For some, those lives included settling near and/or socializing with other "inverts" (or other terms of the era), both of which were facilitated by urban growth and nonagrarian labor. As historian John D'Emilio wrote in a 1983 essay,

> In divesting the household of its economic independence and fostering the separation of sexuality from procreation, capitalism has created conditions that allow some men and women to organize a personal life around their erotic/emotional attraction to their own sex. It has made possible the formation of urban communities of lesbians and gay men and, more recently, of a politics based on sexual identity.[5]

That politics would have to wait until two wars created additional changes in the United States and the world. In the national culture, though, before World War I there arose a politics of reform by which middle-class men and women sought to address the conditions of urban life.

Reform and Reformers

The late 19th century was the second time in U.S. history that a wave of reforms seemed to sweep through much of the United States. The first wave struck in the 1830s, propelled by evangelical fervor and secular concern for the survival of the new republic. That subsided—or was overcome, really—by the hurricane of the Civil War, and after that bloodbath the perils of finding too much wrong with America were too freshly imprinted. Still, in the decades just before and after 1900 a number of reforming efforts emerged that revived the idea of changing Americans for the better. Although the newer movements shared some characteristics with the previous ones, they differed in placing more responsibility on society rather than individuals and in seeking change through institutions more than the "moral suasion" of the antebellum years. GLBT people figure prominently in these movements, not only as Americans affected, positively or negatively, by proposed remedies but also as leaders and workers in the major reforms of the era.

Before 1900 middle- and upper-class urban men and women offered up a mixed bag of proposals. So-called Mugwumps focused their efforts on governmental corruption of the Gilded Age (1877–1900) and pushed for civil service reform (enacted nationally in 1883). Poverty was "discovered" at this time, not because it was new to American life but because its causes were now perceived as rooted more in social ills than in personal moral failures. People calling for "social justice" ranged from the few in the Socialist Party to capitalists trying to envision how Jesus would respond to the conditions of the poor. These impulses contributed to the actions and concerns of the Progressives of the next generation.

Two patterns to emerge that are relevant here are a moralistic concern with bodies and sex on the one hand and regulation by law on the other. Abortion and contraception became matters of law (as opposed to morality or religion only) for the first time in these years, for example, and states began to prohibit both (population lost during the Civil War also was likely a factor). In 1873 the Comstock Act typified the new approaches when it empowered the U.S. Post Office to serve as national censor. It outlawed a wide range of activities, including selling and lending "obscene" material and using the mail to distribute it. The definition of obscene was linked to immorality and clearly rooted in sex, but also included information on or devices for contraception and abortion. Among those prosecuted under the law was feminist Victoria Woodhull, running for president in 1872 (with VP candidate Frederick Douglass) for the Equal Rights Party. Woodhull had published a tract exposing the extramarital affair of prominent minister Henry Ward Beecher and essentially arguing for the era's concept of "free love" (freedom to divorce and marry according to sexual passion, in this case). In the mentality of the time, passion was a dangerous ideal in distracting from capitalist achievement and in potentially separating sex from procreation. The latter especially would affect the way homosexuals came to be seen as self-absorbed pleasure seekers and associated with the dangerous, irrational forces of free love.

The "purity crusade" as it has been called, encompassed other areas besides defining obscenity and regulating pornography. The public behavior of working-class men and women came under scrutiny and with it old laws were enforced and new ones passed. In a vicious cycle of reasoning, the moral and political suspicion of Catholics, Jews, and/or people not of western or northern European descent limited the economic opportunities of those groups. Their poverty, in turn, was used to further justify their outsider status. While some of these women and men turned to prostitution for income, others simply cultivated social and sexual lives in public places, there being few other arenas. Policing morality then merged with control of the "dangerous classes" to create (or more rigidly enforce) laws against cross-dressing, vagrancy, loitering, disorderly conduct, indecent exposure, and "lewd behavior." Homosexuals, bisexuals, and trans people were not necessarily singled out but those whose actions fit those categories would be arrested under such laws until throughout the 20th century.

Reform efforts of the later 19th century bled into those of the Progressive Era (ca. 1895–1920), making any clear delineation for the latter difficult. Also complicating Progressivism is that it encompassed a variety of people, views, and projects (though the people and reforms were distinctively middle-class in status and values). Loosely uniting it all as a movement was a set of attitudes as much as specific programs or accomplishments: belief in the basic institutions of family, capitalism, and democracy and a desire to make them all function more efficiently. Above all, perhaps, was a faith that the right laws passed and enforced could solve the problems of poverty at the bottom and corruption at the top of the societal ladder.

Two examples of older issues that Progressives inherited but addressed with typically legalistic solutions are prostitution and alcohol. Both had long been viewed as problems, though what kind of problem and whom to "blame" changed over time. In the 19th century prostitution was usually viewed by male and female reformers alike as caused by prostitutes—that is, by "fallen" or "loose" women who endangered upstanding American men and their families. They needed moral instruction from their betters in order to change their ways. Though this attitude remained, some reformers blamed poverty more than the women, and early feminists suggested that prostitution was simply one more form of male (and class) power. Each cause required different solutions, of course, and eventually Progressives used federal power over interstate trade to address the issue. In 1910 Congress passed the White Slave Traffic Act (Mann Act), which "forbade, under heavy penalties, the transportation of women from one state to another for immoral purposes." By the end of World War I, the older purity crusade further merged with legalism to create laws against noncommercial sex, including crossing state lines for it, and state laws against fornication.

The general attack upon sexual activity (especially that of the lower classes) figures into GLBT history in several ways. Most obvious is the contempt for sex of any kind and desire to control. This impulse coincided with the rise of sexology and the new categories of heterosexual and homosexual, with the latter defined primarily as inappropriate gender behavior and viewed as deviant (see Chapter 2). Another intersection is that of male prostitutes—also serving male clients—and GLBT history. On one level is simply sex between men, or "homosexual" sex. A more complicated story is suggested by considering gender also: in a male–male encounter only the "passive" partner (likely the prostitute, as a man playing a "woman") would be deviant in some way. This is also suggested in language of that era and before, since "gay" and "in the life" (both later related to homosexual activity) were used for prostitution generally.

Equally characteristic of Progressivism, and equally important in GLBT history, was the era's campaign against alcohol. Concern over Americans' consumption of alcohol was as old as the United States itself and accelerated with the industrial era. By 1860 a number of approaches were already "on the table" and ranged from moral suasion (the evangelically toned temperance movement) to local or state legislative action ("Maine laws"). By the early 1900s to all this was added the movement for a federal law, finally successful in 1919 with the adoption of the 18th Amendment. Ratified at the close of World War I, the amendment prohibited not drinking alcohol (still in the realm of personal freedom, even to a Progressive) but instead the "manufacture, sale, or transportation" of it. With the addition of the Volstead Act (1919), establishing enforcement of the amendment, Prohibition officially began in 1920. The era (1920–1933), called the "Roaring 20s" and the "Jazz Age," is associated with images now famous: young white people drinking and "slumming" in Harlem, people of all colors gaining access to illegal "speakeasies," and gangsters carrying machine guns protecting their "investments." Less common to the imagery now, but not then, were the homosexuals, bisexuals, and cross-dressers who played significant roles in every aspect of the era (see below, "The Jazz Age").

New Women

The term "new women" actually encompasses two generations: the suffragists and other Progressive reformers and their "daughters" of the flapper era (see below for the latter). In the years just before and after 1900 some privileged women continued in the pattern of *their* foremothers of empowering themselves by embracing their "domesticating" role. If femininity included a "civilizing" influence on the home, why not bring that role to society at large? Just as teaching small children and nursing the ill could be cast as extensions of woman's gender role—something she could carry with her into the public realm—so could Progressive causes. Women's involvement in crusades against alcohol and for relieving the conditions of the poor is well established and makes sense in light of the era's gender rules.

Less historically visible are the many LBT women who not only participated in all aspects of public life from that time to this but who in fact were at the forefront of important social change. Lillian Faderman has documented this aspect of U.S. history in her fascinating account, *To Believe in Women,* provocatively subtitled *What Lesbians Have Done for America.* She makes a solid case for her title by presenting dozens of women who were, if not self-defined lesbians, were in same-sex relationships that might be described as "lesbian" for the intimacy and sustenance the relationships provided. From Jane Addams and Mary Rozet Smith to M. Carey Thomas and Mamie Gwinn, to Dr. Emily Blackwell and Dr. Elizabeth Cushier, Faderman shows the "lesbian" influence on pioneering social work, women's higher education and women entering law, medicine, and theology. One or both members of a female couple might be engaged in activism and one, both, or neither might be exclusively involved with other women. More important were the contributions made possible by the fact of female partnerships, which allowed these women a public role *and* a private life to sustain it in ways not imaginable within heterosexual marriage. M. Carey Thomas (president of Bryn Mawr College, 1894–1922), for example, "was susceptible to both men and women." But, writes Faderman, "she recognized early that unlike her susceptibility to men, her susceptibility to women, far from threatening the 'dearest work' that lay next to her heart, would encourage it. Its corollary would be that she must make something of herself so that she would not have to rely on a man to support her."[6]

It is not just the presence of so many real or possible lesbians that creates parallels between reform history and lesbian history. As explained at the end of Chapter 2 sexology also made its appearance at this time, and fed the era's hunger for verification of all things through science. Sexologists often acted out of either genuine curiosity or a desire to liberalize views on sex and gender, but their theories were just as often adapted to the interests of purity crusaders. In the case of female inverts (as they were called) it was the presence of "male" attributes, including merely seeking a public role, that defined them. If an invert was a lesbian and inverted behavior meant seeking professional education, employment, or the vote, then any woman agitating a public cause (regardless of her sexual proclivities) could be labeled lesbian. This introduced the equation of feminism = lesbianism and the stigma attached to both that resurfaced in the 1960s. Finally, after 1900 a new middle-class emphasis on heterosexual romance, public courtship, and "companionate marriage" further disgraced both "spinsters" and female (and male) couples, moving them to the edge (or outside) of the shrinking circle designated "normal."[7]

The women's suffrage movement brings together all the strains of politics and culture described thus far. Like other causes its roots were in antebellum America and like others it experienced changes and divisions until its last phase in the legalistic Progressive Era. Feminists argued over philosophy, strategy (state versus national legislation) and even, in 1848, whether suffrage was too radical a goal. Typical American fault lines emerged along race and class, with less privileged women alienated from the larger organizations. As the suffrage movement went into its fifth decade, it first united then divided again: the two main groups merged in 1890 to form the National American Woman Suffrage Association but in 1913 Alice Paul and Lucy Burns created a more "radical" arm with the Congressional Union (later, the National Woman's Party). Important here, early and later suffragists also follow Faderman's pattern of women in couples and communities: Frances Willard and Anna Gordon, Alice Blackwell and Kitty Barry, Anna Howard Shaw and Lucy Anthony, Carrie Chapman Catt and Mollie Hay. In the end the 19th Amendment, adopted in 1920, was the result of political bargaining made possible by the World War as well as a variety of tactics before and during that time. On the heels of getting the vote came the League of Women Voters, the continued activities of women's clubs and another radical proposal, again by Alice Paul: an Equal Rights Amendment, written by Paul and introduced in Congress in 1923. During the 1920s the movement seems to recede from public view, but it is notable that lesbians were as crucial to that visible first wave as feminism and suffrage are to lesbian history.

Congregating Together

Middle-class women were not the only creators of same-sex culture in this period of transition from Victorian to modern. Other people we would now call GLBT created vibrant urban subcultures in which multiple concepts of sexuality coexisted. Just as people with the same ethnic, racial, or cultural backgrounds often created spaces in large cities in which to live and/or socialize, so did those with same-sex attractions. The presence of male "homosexual" subcultures that predate sexologists' definitions is now well documented and suggests that GLBT history is complicated by factors of geography, class, and race. Although the categories hetero/homo/bi are valuable, we know now that the GLBT past did not begin with them and then follow a simple line of progression from invisible to visible people.

In the late 19th century, several observers, often scientists, testified to the presence of homosexual subcultures in Europe and the United States. In 1889 Dr. G. Frank Lydston, a Chicago physician and criminal anthropologist, reported:

> There is in every community of any size a colony of sexual perverts; they are usually known to each other, are likely to congregate together. At times they operate in accordance with some definite and concerted plan in quest of [a] subject wherewith to gratify their abnormal sexual impulses.... The physician rarely has his attention called to these things, and when evidence of their existence is before him, he is apt to receive it with skepticism.[8]

Pioneering German sexologist Magnus Hirschfeld, who visited the United States in 1893, corresponded with Americans, as did Havelock Ellis (see Chapter 2). Hirschfeld found that "Homosexual life in the United States is somewhat more hidden than in the United Kingdom," but also published correspondence from America regarding an active underground in Boston, Chicago, Denver, New York, and Philadelphia. Similarly, Ellis quoted "a well-informed American correspondent" as writing, "The world of sexual inverts is, indeed, a large one in any American city, and it is a community distinctly organized—words, customs, traditions of its own; and every city has numerous meeting places..." The places listed were churches, cafes, streets, and clubs, the latter further defined as "dance halls, attached to *saloons,* and presided over by the proprietor of the saloon, himself almost invariably an invert [homosexual], as are all the waiters and musicians."[9]

Knowledge of these activities was buried for much of the 20th century, but due to the recent rise of GLBT studies we now know more about these early subcultures. Due to gender expectations men were better able than women to create public spaces and therefore were more visible to friends and foes alike. Occasionally claims of comparable lesbian activity is unearthed, such as that associated with prostitution in the Storyville district of New Orleans, but this was only "public" in the sense of sensationalism in the press.[10] Within cities across the United States, however, liaisons between men of the same or different social classes and races could occur in many places—Lafayette Square in Washington, DC, Levee district nightclubs in Chicago, the Barbary Coast in San Francisco, or riverfront "dives" in St. Louis. In the latter city an account of 1907 relates that African American transvestites were arrested for "carousing and dancing with white men."[11] As this suggests, cross-dressing was another feature of the subcultures, and one that contributed to organized events. African American men were holding a yearly "drag dance" in Washington, DC in the 1890s, for example. Urban drag balls grew in popularity through the twenties, as did individual performers—male and female, black, and white, straight and not—who impersonated the opposite sex. Activities in less open environments could end in tragedy, though. In Cambridge, Massachusetts, the suicide of a Harvard student led to an investigation and the exposure of a group of homosexual students holding parties attended by a variety of men from on and off campus. The students were expelled in 1920, ruining the careers of some and driving another student to suicide. Fear of exposure also plagued government worker "Jeb Alexander" whose diary records his emotional and sexual lives with men and his long-term relationship with "Dash," another DC employee.[12]

Many cities have a documented gay presence but perhaps most is known about New York, thanks to the exhaustive research of George Chauncey. In his 1994 book *Gay New York* Chauncey investigates the various meeting places for men and shows the complex interplay of classes and sexual categories in the early 20th century. Social spaces could be relatively public or private, and ranged from parks, streets, and cafeterias to rooming houses and other accommodations. Among the latter, the hotels of the YMCA (Young Men's Christian Association) "had developed a reputation among gay men as centers of sex and social life" before 1920. The term "gay" as used here is significant because Chauncey also examines the variety of sexual identities possible and the shifts that occur by the time World War II erupted. He reveals that in the working class, for men to be "normal" had more to do with gender than sex. Normal men were those with masculine traits who also took the active role in sex. They were distinguished from the "fairies" who were the passive partners and who were known by their feminine behavior and appearance. Fairies—also called "faggots" and "queens"—might adopt female names, wear makeup, and don some articles of women's clothes. Working class "normal" men tolerated them while middle-class "queers," who desired other men sexually but identified with masculinity, disapproved of the fairies' "effeminacy and flagrancy." By 1940 the term "gay" was in more general use, a linguistic change that reflected "the transition from a world divided into 'fairies' and 'men' on the basis of gender persona to one divided into 'homosexuals' and 'heterosexuals' on the basis of sexual object choice."[13] (See below for more on New York, 1920–1940.)

Regardless of specific geographies or terms what the GLBT presence across urban America demonstrates are the lesser-known facts that homosexuals existed, knew how to find each other, and formed networks. Much of our knowledge of them comes from those who saw them as a moral, criminal, or medical problem, and whose records thus also document the very intolerance that for decades obliterated them from the national story.

World War and Its Aftermath

The World War that began in 1914 was a conflict of unprecedented destruction that left its survivors reeling. By the time the 1918 armistice stopped the fighting more than nine million people were dead and the nations involved, even the victors, were less sure that they sat at the pinnacle of civilization. On one side had been the Central Powers—Germany and Austria-Hungary—and on the other the Allies—Great Britain, France, and Russia. That an assassination set the killing in motion was evidence of how precarious was the "balance of power" achieved by complex alliances. What should have remained a local conflict between Serbs and Austria-Hungary spun out of control as the alliances kicked in, bringing rivals Germany and Britain to the fields. After more than two years of neutrality the United States entered as an Ally. American soldiers went "over there" and helped defeat the Central Powers; Americans at home soon learned that questioning the effort (or much else) was a criminal act. The irony of sacrificing civil liberties in order to protect them was only one of several at war's end. Another was that the United States never joined President Wilson's pet peacetime project, the League of Nations, while the League's inability to prevent another war adds a darker tone. Most tragic, though, was that the Allies' insistence on destroying the Second German Empire, or Reich, laid the groundwork of bitterness on which the National Socialists would build the Third.

On the most basic level this war and all wars belong in GLBT history because GLBT people are no less affected than straight people by national and international upheaval. Equally basic, plenty of nonstraight soldiers have fought in those wars on all sides. Digging deeper we find that GLBT history and "traditional" national and political histories share a common denominator of gender as an underlying principle. Militarism and masculinity are mutually supportive, for example, and historians have noted a cult of masculinity (or "compulsive masculinity"—see Chapter 2) in western nations in the decades preceding World War I. Conversely, femininity (in women or men) was the antithesis of what was needed for imperial conquest, national defense, or capitalist expansion. Budding feminist movements were feared and resisted as threats to masculine power. Organizations like the Boy Scouts of America appeared at precisely this time (1910) to assure the manliness of the next generation of leaders, while President Teddy Roosevelt (1901–1909), famously preached the "doctrine of the strenuous life" to American men.[14] Significantly, gender was married to patriotism; only traitors would defy its rules. Once it ended, the simple fact of the Great War called everything, including accepted truths about gender and sexuality, into question.

Finally, the World War I years are significant for developments overseas that reverberated in U.S. queer history. In 1914 in England the British Society for the Study of Sex Psychology was founded, while in Germany Magnus Hirschfeld, father of that nation's homosexual emancipation movement, published *Homosexuality in Men and Women*. Hirschfeld went on to found the Institute for Sexual Science (1919) and it grew to an internationally recognized body through the years of the Weimar Republic (1919–1933). More than a year before the war ended, revolution in Russia eventually brought Vladimir Lenin to power in the new Soviet Union. It also brought fear of communism (or Bolshevism) to capitalist nations, which in the United States took the form of the First Red Scare (1917–1920). Congress passed Espionage and Sedition Acts that set aside First Amendment rights in a climate in which any criticism of U.S. policies was considered communist-inspired and/or treasonous. The Supreme Court upheld prosecutions under these acts, declaring, in the famous *Schenck v. U.S.* decision, that free speech did not extend to "falsely shouting fire in a theatre" and could be limited when it posed a "clear and present danger" to the country. The U.S. attorney general instituted "Red Raids" in which thousands of suspected communists were arrested and hundreds were deported. The fate of homosexuals at this time is less directly linked to anticommunism than in the Second Red Scare (see Chapter 4), but in this first go-round we see the same tendency to view any difference as threatening. Despite the freewheeling reputation of the 1920s undercurrents of tension surrounding sex, race, morality, and politics occasionally rose to the surface.

THE JAZZ AGE

Many of the cultural trends of the twenties are well known to most Americans. The entire decade was dominated by Prohibition, making anyone who produced, sold, or transported alcohol a criminal. It was not repealed until 1933 and was probably the country's most disastrous experiment in changing "immoral" behavior, since it merely added another enriching enterprise to crime syndicates. In the meantime young, privileged, white men and women were "steppin' out" to restaurants, nightclubs, and speakeasies, often in heterosexual pairs.[15] As they did so they represented a challenge to the old order in forms common to the image of the "Roaring Twenties": the clothing they wore, the music they heard, and the bootleg liquor they consumed. The voices of urban African Americans were central to the era, not merely as heard by white patrons in jazz clubs but especially when expressing their own concerns in literature, music, and fine arts. Often racial and sexual lines were crossed, blurred, or just ignored in urban areas famous for cultural experiments and youthful rebellion that were also sites for homosexual, bisexual, and cross-dressing activities. Neither these activities nor the urban subcultures supporting them were brand new, but both underwent significant change by the early thirties: definitions shifted among some, and once-visible people began to fade from public view and thus from history.

The Society for Human Rights

One of the most significant "moments" in GLBT history occurred in the midst of this era when a U.S. soldier returned from Germany and tried to establish a gay rights organization in Middle America. Chicago resident Henry Gerber had been born in Germany, emigrated as an adult in 1913 and served in the U.S. Army. After World War I he was stationed in Germany, where he remained until 1923. Berlin was then the site of flourishing gay and lesbian cultures, and the center for both the scientific investigation of sex and gender and the world's first movement for homosexual rights. Gerber was fully aware of that movement and when he arrived back in Chicago he decided to create an organization for homosexuals. Despite friends advising him "against my doing anything so rash and futile," he later wrote, "...if I succeeded I might become known to history as deliverer of the downtrodden, even as Lincoln." He managed to persuade a few friends to join him in his cause and they founded the Society for Human Rights in December of 1924, Gerber serving as secretary. Their plan included soliciting membership, holding a lecture series, and producing a publication, *Friendship and Freedom* (two issues of which were printed). They also sought the support of "prominent persons," presumably for funding and legitimacy, but without results. Gerber remembered, "The big, fatal, fearful obstacle seemed always to be the almost willful misunderstanding and ignorance on the part of the general public concerning the nature of homosexuality."

The Society lasted only until mid-1925, brought to an end in the midst of scandal fueled by the press in the wake of the arrest of board members. SHR vice president Al Meininger, married and bisexual, had been arrested for engaging in homosexual sex, and a newspaper story ran claiming to expose a "strange sex cult." Gerber and the group's president were also arrested, "guilty just by being homosexual," according to Gerber. Though nothing ever came of his arrest, it led to the loss of Gerber's job as well as money spent on legal fees. Gerber moved to New York City, served again in the army until 1942. From the demise of the SHR to his death in 1972, well into gay/lesbian liberation, Gerber wrote articles and books advocating legal reform and promoting the concept of homosexual rights. The Gerber/Hart Library in Chicago, founded in 1981, bears his name.[16]

Blues and Jazz

The growing popularity of blues and jazz artists signaled the "arrival" of forms derived from slave life even as the descendants of that life faced ongoing discrimination and persecution. No longer literally owned by others, African Americans continued in galling servile roles whether as share-copping farmers or urban entertainers. Terrorism and violence, often associated only with Reconstruction, remained a constant—the number of lynchings of black people peaked in the 1890s (at an average of 110 per year) and decreased only gradually through the first quarter of the 20th century.[17] The Supreme Court upheld segregation as national policy in 1896 and voting rights were nonexistent in many places. In the midst of this situation musical and poetic forms from slavery or before met urban environments as a result of black migration to cities,

German immigrant Henry Gerber settled in Chicago, served for the United States in World War I, and returned to Chicago influenced by the German homosexual emancipation movement. He founded the short-lived Society for Human Rights, the first organized attempt in the United States to improve the medical and legal status of homosexuals. (Chicago History Museum)

preferably in the North. Like so much in this book, this is a familiar story, as are the musical forms now considered quintessentially American. The queer presence in all this, though, so central to fully appreciating it, is often omitted.

Female blues singers of the early 20th century provide an example of the queer dimension to a more familiar story and of the erasure of that queerness until recently. Songs like "Prove It On Me Blues" and "B.D. [Bulldyker] Women's Blues" contained overtly lesbian lyrics, while "Foolish Man Blues" and "Sissy Blues" refer to (effeminate) gay men. Typically, it was gender that signaled queer, so that a cross-dressing performer like Gladys Bentley (a woman who wore tuxedos for her act) was and is recognized as lesbian. Many others were lesbian or bisexual in their personal if not public lives, including the great figures of the era: Alberta Hunter, Ma Rainey, Bessie Smith, and Ethel Waters. As Mabel Hampton recalled of her own years in the blues scene at the time, "'all of them women was gay. All those women was gay.'"[18] The point is not to sensationalize their lives but to reclaim them for this history. More important, it is to suggest that this knowledge is important to understanding the lives of African American women and, in this case, their music and their cultural environment.

Bessie Smith is an excellent example. She and Jack Gee were married in Philadelphia in 1923. Several weeks earlier Smith had signed a contract with Columbia Records after her first recording, "Down Hearted Blues," sold a million copies. That classic blues song had lyrics that could be adapted to describe either sex, and Bessie was known to use both versions; it began (emphasis added to alternate words):

Gee, but it's hard to love some-one when that some-one don't love you.

I'm so disgusted, heartbroken, too.

I've got those down hearted blues.

Once I was crazy 'bout a *man/gal.*

He/She mistreated me all the time.

The next man/gal I get he's/she's got to promise to be mine, all mine.[19]

The words described her own life. Bessie's relationships, including her marriage, were stormy ones; she and Jack both had other women and both were jealous people (Bessie reputedly beat up a chorus girl rumored to have been with Jack while she was away on tour, and then went after Jack with a gun). Upon beginning an affair with chorus girl Lillian Simpson, she warned Ruby Walker, "Whatever you do, you better not tell on me and Lillian [to Jack]."[20] By the time she and Gee split in 1929, Bessie Smith's career had peaked, classic blues were less popular, and the nation was six months away from its biggest financial crash. Before and since her tragic death as the result of a 1937 car accident Smith was acknowledged as the "Empress of the Blues."

The development of jazz also occurred amid a culture that defied many social norms. Like blues, it was distinctively African American, but performed and consumed by both blacks and whites. It took decades for jazz to be regarded as "serious" music due to its racial origins, the sexual associations with the music ("jazzing," in fact, was slang for having sex and the music was played in brothels), *and* the white sexualization of black people. Like many aspects of the twenties, it was the very "forbidden" nature of jazz that made it attractive to rebelling white youth. More specifically, there were certainly queer musicians contributing to jazz and swing: trumpeter Tiny Davis (in the opening story); transgendered pianist/saxophonist Billy Tipton, revealed to be female only at his death in 1989; and the more famous gay songwriter Cole Porter.

New York, New York

Jazz and the culture of the jazz age was distinctively urban, and probably the most famous and most studied metropolis in this respect has been New York City. Certainly Chicago, New Orleans, and many other cities deserve a place in any picture of the 1920s, but it was New York that gave the United States the Harlem Renaissance, and to New York's Greenwich Village that many freethinkers were drawn. In between, Times Square became the mecca of Americas seeking entertainment of all kinds. GLBT Americans were a significant and visible presence in all of these areas; without them the creative lights of New York would have burned less brightly.

The Harlem Renaissance of the twenties and thirties is known for the remarkable works produced by African American writers, artists, intellectuals, scholars, and musicians. They championed the "New Negro" who looked to her/his own past and experience rather than white culture as the source of inspiration and content. Blues and jazz (above) were very much a part of this, as was their component of queer people and expression. Just as so many of the blues singers were "in the life" and sang about it to some degree, many of the major figures of the Renaissance were gay, lesbian or bisexual. Among them were acknowledged leader Alain Locke, poets Countee Cullen, Alice Dunbar-Nelson, Angelina Weld Grimké, Langston Hughes, and Georgia Douglas Johnson, and novelists Claude McKay, Wallace Thurman, and Blair Niles (whose *Strange Brother* depicts gay life), and sculptor (James) Richmond Barthé. Rarely did these individuals and others work in only one medium. James Weldon Johnson was a

Writer and artist (Richard) Bruce Nugent was among the many prominent queer figures of the Harlem Renaissance. This drawing (undated) is among several Nugent did for a proposed production of the Gilgamesh epic that would have emphasized a homoerotic element in the relationship between Gilgamesh and male companion Enkidu. (Design for "Gilgamesh" by Richard Bruce Nugent © 2002 Thomas H. Wirth.)

composer, novelist, and poet, and Richard Bruce Nugent was a writer and artist. Nugent's story, "Smoke, Lilies, and Jade" is now known as the first gay African American story to be published (1926) and he also produced paintings and illustrations, many with homoerotic themes and content.

The environment of these years in Harlem also supported queer life and expression. Drag balls like that at the Hamilton Lodge (also called the Faggots' Ball) were extremely popular with patrons of all kinds, and described by Langston Hughes as "spectacles in color." Scholar Eric Garber adapted Hughes' term to his examination of the people, social spaces, and activities in, "A Spectacle in Color: The Lesbian and Gay Subculture of Jazz Age Harlem." Garber's work brought back to light the queer element of that time and place and reopened an important line of inquiry. He noted not only the presence of GLBT people in public and private spaces—from drag balls to rent parties—but also the opportunities to form networks such as those among musicians and other entertainers.

Greenwich Village and Times Square also fostered GLBT expression and subcultures. The Village famously developed a "bohemian" style noted for radical politics and for opposition to middle-class mores. A group of feminists formed the all-female club Heterodoxy as early as 1912, for example, and their interests ranged widely. For some Village thinkers, radical sexual ideas went hand-in-hand with their politics. Some espoused "free love" for this reason (opposing legal marriage as a tool of government) while others probably just enjoyed it in practice. Same-sex desire and activity were thus more accepted here, though in the climate of experimentation the concept of fixed identities was also questioned; to bohemians one need not be labeled heterosexual, homosexual, or even bisexual. North of the Village in Times Square a highly visible "pansy craze" developed in the twenties. "Pansy" was a term commonly used to describe an effeminate man and he became another kind of entertainment "spectacle" during Prohibition. The craze peaked in 1930–1931, wrote George Chauncey, when "clubs with pansy acts became the hottest in town."[21] As the economic crisis that began in 1929 deepened (see below) a backlash developed against many "excesses" of the Roaring 20s. Also, when Prohibition ended in 1933 it brought conflicting results: "freedom" to once again open legal bars but now with strict regulation by the state through licensing. In New York, the State Liquor Authority threatened to revoke the licenses of bars that served homosexuals, driving the once-public subculture underground and into separate bars controlled by organized crime. Importantly, what this reveals is the myth of a once hidden people slowly and gradually emerging into public view from the 19th to the late 20th century. Instead, the history is more complicated, and includes periods of GLBT visibility so well submerged by the backlashes that only recently, in another era of visibility, do we know of them. In this case as Chauncey summarized, "Prohibition culture had allowed gay visibility to move into the center of New York's most prestigious entertainment district, but in the early thirties, the authorities were determined to return it to the city's periphery. In addition to ending the Times Square pansy acts and drag balls, the police tried to eradicate pansies from the streets of the square." The repeal of Prohibition, usually seen as liberating, was also "the most significant step in the campaign to exclude the gay world from the public sphere."[22]

Americans and Europeans

When George Gershwin wrote *An American in Paris* in 1928 he described musically the experience of many U.S. citizens who went abroad in the twenties and after. Some, like Gershwin, stayed only a short time while others decided to remain indefinitely. They traveled throughout Europe, but it was to Paris that artists, writers, and musicians flocked in order to experience (and create) new forms and lively conversation. In Paris, too, homosexual and bisexual people could live more openly and many were at the heart of the thriving culture.

What drew young—and often GLB—Americans were the circles of like-minded people and potential mentors for their work. Margaret Anderson and Jane Heap, for example, moved to Paris in 1923 where they continued publishing *The Little Review* until 1929. Anderson had founded the *Review* in Chicago in 1914 and it was soon "famous as a journal of literary modernism, radical politics, and avant-garde art." Writers whose work appeared in the publication included Sherwood Anderson, Djuna Barnes, T.S. Eliot, Emma Goldman, Ernest Hemingway, Ezra Pound, and Gertrude Stein. Most famously, Anderson and Heap had decided to publish James Joyce's *Ulysses* in serial form beginning in 1918 and for that were convicted for obscenity. After moving the journal to New York they went on to Paris and as lesbians "became progressively radical and public."[23]

Most famous were the salons of lesbians Natalie Barney and Gertrude Stein. Barney, an American-born poet, moved to Paris' Left Bank and in 1909 turned her home into a cultural center that became as renowned as her openly lesbian love affairs. For decades she brought together creative Americans and Europeans in lively exchanges that helped shape literature and the arts. Gertrude Stein was a Pennsylvania native who arrived in Paris in 1903 following education at Radcliffe and Johns Hopkins and brief stints in London and New York. One of several American expatriates who made their homes abroad, she was in the forefront of developing modernist literature. Modernism was distinguished by its tone of disillusion and sense of breaking from standard forms and content—free verse poetry or prose written in a "stream of consciousness" or from several perspectives, for example. Stein met San Francisco native Alice B. Toklas when Toklas visited Paris in 1907 and by 1909 the two were a couple; they remained together until Stein's death in 1946. In the twenties their circle included Sherwood Anderson, F. Scott Fitzgerald, and Ernest Hemingway and many other visited on their European travels through the 1930s. Stein's most popular work is *The Autobiography of Alice B. Toklas* (1933), depicting both their lives. The couple is portrayed also in the award-winning film *Waiting for the Moon,* released in 1987.

In 1927 Gertrude Stein also wrote an opera, *Four Saints in Three Acts,* with music by American composer Virgil Thomson, a student of Nadia Boulanger. Boulanger's studio was the destination of numerous American composers for most of the 20th century; studying with the French woman, in fact, insured a composer's recognition, especially back in the States. Those who made the pilgrimage were in the forefront of new music in America for decades and many, like Thomson, Marc Blitzstein, Aaron Copland, and Gian-Carlo Menotti, were also gay (also see Chapter 4).

Influence flowed in both directions when works as well as people crossed the Atlantic. An infamous case was that of the novel *The Well of Loneliness,* by British author Radclyffe Hall, who today would be termed lesbian and/or transgendered. First published in Paris in 1928, the *Well* traces the life and experiences of "invert" Stephen Gordon, born female but, like Hall, more naturally masculine and attracted to women. Stephen falls in love with Mary Llewellyn during World War I but in the end plots to drive Mary away so that Mary, portrayed as heterosexual, could follow her nature and be happy just as Stephen needed to follow his/hers. Although Stephen is not given a happy, riding-into-the-sunset ending, overall the novel pleads for understanding of inversion as an inborn condition and so some considered it too positive at the time. The book had been deemed obscene in England and nearly met a similar fate in the United States. Upon its American publication in late 1928 it sold well but soon was at the center of a controversy. It was seized by police in New York as obscene literature, a judgement upheld at trial. That decision was reversed by both a New York appellate court and the U.S. Customs Court in 1929, however, and the *Well* became probably the most famous lesbian novel ever written. As theories about sexuality have changed over time, so have opinions about *The Well of Loneliness,* but its ability to generate discussion in and out of the United States has not waned.

DEPRESSION, NEW DEALS, OLD IDEALS

Just six months after the *Well* was declared fit for American readers the stock market crashed and a worldwide depression began. For Americans especially, the Great Depression was a denial of fundamental truths central to the national story and arising in the agrarian past. Those who "worked hard and lived right," according to that story, had built the country and their rewards were material security and a better life for their children. The poor and homeless were equally responsible for their fates, since there appeared to be no excuse for poverty in a land filled with opportunity and, well, land—lots of it. As the United States became more urban and industrial, reformers attempted to shift the focus away from personal vice and laziness to larger causes of poverty. They were partially successful, as seen in health and housing legislation of the Progressive Era, but the older views were never completely supplanted.

With the stock market crash of 1929 came the worst economic crisis in U.S. history. Overall, unemployment reached 25 percent by 1933 and previously secure Americans found themselves homeless and hungry. Although the Hoover administration did take some steps to stop the suffering and restart the economy they were not enough. Not everyone felt the effects of the crash equally—more evidence of the imbalances in society and in industry—but no one escaped it entirely. New president Franklin Roosevelt, who had promised "bold, persistent experimentation" to end the calamity, took office in 1933 and instituted a New Deal to fulfill that promise. Meanwhile the depression had struck the rest of the world and contributed to political crises as well. GLBT people, like all people, saw their world changing; the impact on them was as both struggling citizens and as people whose sexualities would continue to be an issue, though in varying ways.

The United States and the World

Domestically, the New Deal created dozens of government programs aimed at "relief, recovery, and reform" and many were very effective in these areas. In the short term, new agencies provided temporary employment and aid to farmers and businesses while long-term planning resulted in such offices as the Social Security Administration. Opinions varied widely on the New Deal and usually fell along partisan lines. Democrats (which now included significant numbers of African American voters for the first time) largely supported the FDR administrations while Republicans were leery of assigning a larger role, and with it a larger bureaucracy, to the federal government. In a world already afraid of socialism and communism, some wondered whether the United States was falling to those ideologies. Beyond the parties, criticisms came from both the political right and left. Radicals on the right felt the New Deal went too far in the direction of economic reform and leftists were convinced (and disappointed) that no true revolution was in the works. The Old Left (as opposed to the New Left of the 1960s) gained more members in the thirties and included writers, artists, and intellectuals who often were also queer or questioned sexual and gender rules. Some would link their politics to their sexual identity and later try to organize other queer people.

Although communism and socialism remained frightening to many capitalist nations it was the rise of fascism that posed the most immediate threat in the thirties. The word comes from Mussolini's regime in Italy but is applied also to totalitarian systems elsewhere: Spain, Portugal and, most famously, Germany. The rise to power of Adolf Hitler and the National Socialists (Nazis) in 1933 ended the republican experiment of Weimar Germany and what freedom, visibility, and tolerance GLBT Germans (and visitors) had enjoyed in that brief time. One of their first projects was to destroy Hirschfeld's Institute for Sexual Science, which by then housed some 12,000 books and 35,000 pictures.[24] Also, not only did the Nazis revive and enforce paragraph 175, recriminalizing homosexual acts, by 1938 they had revised the law to include a wider range of behaviors, including kissing, touching, and even looking at another man with apparent sexual intent. By 1940 people arrested for their homosexuality were no longer sentenced to jail but sent to concentration camps as well. It is unclear how many of the 50,000 men convicted of homosexuality died in the camps, but estimates range from 5,000 to 15,000. While alive they wore triangular pink badges and were among those, like Jews and gypsies, who received the most brutal treatment. Lesbians were not prosecuted as homosexuals but may have been among those "anti-socials" who wore the black triangle.

Gender, Work, and Play

Back in the United States the ongoing depression combined with the end of Prohibition to create some mixed, often contradictory results affecting GLBT people. At the outset of the crisis in 1929 there was a sense of punishment delayed and now deserved. Those who had disapproved of the partying and open sexuality (of all kinds) saw the crisis as a rebalancing of sorts. President Hoover's treasury secretary Andrew Mellon famously expressed this view when he advised Hoover against government action; instead, said Mellon, "People will work harder, live a more moral life. Values will be adjusted, and enterprising people will pick up the wrecks from less competent people."[25] The "values" to which Mellon referred included those of traditional sex and gender arrangements, and a revival of Victorian roles occurred. Masculinity had been measured in part by the ability to make a living and now was threatened as never before. Even though (or because) more women now had to work for pay out of necessity, the blurring line between masculine and feminine behavior was redrawn. One result was a campaign to remove sexual and gender "outlaws" from public space: the "pansy craze" was over before Hoover left office. Female impersonation was banned from the stage, as were even the terms fairy and pansy from some vaudeville theatres. (Interestingly, Margaret Mitchell's original name for her *Gone With the Wind* heroine was not Scarlett but Pansy O'Hara. The publisher worried, however, that the name's association with "effeminate men" made it "offensive in the North.")[26] As mentioned above, the end of Prohibition in 1933 compounded the effects of the depression, at least in New York if not elsewhere. The public presence of fairies or pansies would no longer be tolerated as bar owners had to police their clients in order to keep their licenses. Notably this led to an even stronger identification of homosexuality with gender inversion, since the only "recognizable" gay men would be those who were overtly effeminate. Beginning in this era, periodic police raids became common, especially when officials embarked on (often politically motivated) "cleanup campaigns"; these raids continued in many cities well past World War II, as the infamous 1969 raid on the Stonewall Inn demonstrates (see Chapter 5). Where laws were different, though, the effects of newly legal alcohol also varied. In San Francisco, for example, there was no decline in the number or visibility of queer bars and new ones even appeared (such as Mona's, opened in 1936).

As important as the bars in building communities through the 20th centuries were the bathhouses. Historian Allan Bérubé has documented the evolution of the bath as a gay institution and noted four stages of development since the 1890s. They begin with the "ordinary bathhouse" in which gay sex was unusual and continue through the "favorite spot" phase to the twenties and thirties and the appearance of bathhouses that allowed sex in private spaces within them. Police raided these baths just as they did the gay bars, and continued to do so through the fourth stage of the modern gay bathhouse (designed to be exclusively gay) in the 1950s and 1960s. To Bérubé the importance of these spaces in the years preceding World War II cannot be overstated. He wrote:

> Before there were any openly gay or lesbian leaders, political clubs, books, films, newspapers, businesses, neighborhoods, churches, or legally recognized gay rights, several generations of pioneers spontaneously created gay bathhouses and lesbian and gay bars. These men and women risked arrest, jail sentences, loss of families, loss of jobs, beatings, murders, and the humiliation that could lead to suicide in order to transform public bars and bathhouses into safety zones where it was safe to be gay. In a nation which has for generations mobilized its institutions toward making gay people invisible, illegal, isolated, ignorant, and silent, gay baths and bars became the first stages of a civil rights movement for gay people in the United States.[27]

Stage and Screen

The return to Victorian values during the depression affected more than just the bars and baths in some urban areas. Queer people and references to queerness in American theatre and movies were already under attack before 1930 and only became more problematic. This too contributed to the myth that no visible GLBT culture had ever existed until the sixties and made it easier to discount that culture when it resurfaced. As noted above, drag was an aspect of urban GLBT life from the Gilded Age onward and a popular form of entertainment through the twenties. Female impersonator Julian Eltinge, for example, was among the highest-paid performers of the vaudeville era and successfully made the transition into early film. Drag never really disappeared, of course, and has resurfaced repeatedly as entertainment, but the "tone" of presenting it—from ridicule to celebration—has varied depending on the era, venue, or audience.

In the "legitimate" theatre occasionally scandal would emerge in the form of (homo)sexual content. In 1923 the English translation of Sholom Asch's Yiddish play *The God of Vengeance* opened on Broadway. Its plot includes a lesbian relationship and for that the producer, cast, and theatre owner were arrested, charged with obscenity (though later cleared on appeal). Similar controversy surrounded *The Captive,* a translation of a French play by Edouard Bourdet, and two plays by Mae West, *Sex* and *The Drag. The Captive* featured a lesbian theme and opened in late 1926. It ran for about three months but was then raided by police, who arrested the cast. No one was prosecuted, but the play closed days later. Mae West first starred in her own play, *Sex,* which was raided the same night as *The Captive* and earned her a ten-day jail sentence. Even more scandalous was *The Drag,* also in production at this time and featuring a gay male love story. It was banned from Broadway and so remained in New Jersey.

By the 1930s, then, theatre joined other venues in prohibiting public queerness. Further complicating the picture were the New Deal-sponsored Federal Arts Projects. Federal One, as they were known, included programs in art, writing, music, and theatre, and raised at least two important questions for the first time in U.S. history: What should the relationship between the government and the arts in a democracy? If the government sponsors the arts, does it then have the right to censor them? The programs introduced the revolutionary idea that even in an economic crisis the country needs the arts and is willing to support people who write, paint, and act. Some of those on the Federal One payroll—especially painters in the Art Project—remembered fondly the ability to create freely, in cooperation rather than competition with others, and make a living. All of the programs came under some scrutiny at the time (and works created in the thirties would later come under attack) but it was the Federal Theatre Project (1935–1939) that was probably most visible, and thus most closely watched. Eventually, in fact, the FTP was the subject of the first investigation of communist influence in U.S. entertainment, conducted by the Dies Committee of the U.S. House of Representatives in 1938. This was the precursor to the more pervasive Second Red Scare of the postwar era, during which suspicion of communists merged with the homophobia reared in the climate of the depression.

In the meantime at least one play appeared on Broadway with a lesbian love story, *The Children's Hour* by Lillian Hellman. It concerned two teachers at a girls' school, one of whom (Martha) is attracted to the other (Karen). A student spreads a rumor about the women's relationship, resulting in the closing of the school and in Martha's suicide. It opened in 1934 to good critical response (perhaps due to the "appropriate" suicide of the "real" lesbian) but was banned elsewhere in the country. It was adapted to the screen in 1936 as *These Three* (1936) but by then Hollywood had joined in the policing of openly queer expression, and the lesbian plotline became a heterosexual love triangle.

The reason for the change was the infamous Hollywood Code (also called the Hays Code). The history of American film is divided in different ways, according to such criteria as actors and roles, directors, economics (studios, theatres, and distribution), and technology (sound and color). A combination of these seems to explain the designation of the 1930s and 1940s as a "Golden Age": the specific personalities and stars, the studio system of production, the artistry and scope of the films, and so on. Those same years also saw the beginning of another film era, that of the Code. With respect to content—especially queer content—it generated periods of filmmaking that are useful in this context: "before the Code," "during the Code," and "after the Code."

The Code arose not from the government but out of the MPPDA (Motion Picture Producers and Distributors of America), formed in the 1920s with Will Hays at its head. In 1930 the Code was introduced as an effort at self-regulation within the industry but was not rigidly enforced. In 1934, however, enforcement began in earnest when an office was created for that purpose. For the next thirty years content in a dozen categories, such as crimes, profanity, religion, "repellent subjects" and even titles and locations, was carefully monitored. A significant portion of the Code was devoted to sex, the introduction reading, "The sanctity of the institution of marriage and the home shall be upheld. Pictures shall not infer that low forms of sex relationship are the accepted or common thing." Nine headings follow, in which "sex perversion," understood to include homosexuality, joins white slavery, miscegenation, childbirth, and children's genitalia as subjects or images barred from the screen (adultery, passion, and rape were allowed but only under strict guidelines). Motivating the studios were the conviction, on the one hand, that movies have the power to exert influence and, on the other, fear of government control or other retribution in a climate already charged with moral policing. In addition, film historians note that Jewish studio heads, aware of anti-Semitism abroad and its potential at home, were especially cautious and hoped to avoid any criticisms of their work.

From the mid-thirties on, then, the existence of GLBT culture and communities continued but much more hidden from "the public." Straight and queer Americans alike—particularly those outside the cities—could then become increasingly unaware of that history and more subject to inferences and stereotypes, usually negative in tone; small wonder that so many GLBT people of the era 1935–1965 or so would report both self-hatred and feeling like "the only one."

"Sex perverts" did not entirely disappear from films even "during the Code," though. Vito Russo in his landmark study, *The Celluloid Closet: Homosexuality in the Movies,* showed the way gay themes and characters still appeared but through their own "codes" that many GLBT viewers (and others) would recognize.[28] Even during the Code era effeminate males (pansies or "sissies"), as in roles played by Clifton Webb, Peter Lorre, or George Sanders remained in films but sometimes with more subtle mannerisms, or those that could be read as simply effete. Similarly, Marlene Dietrich famously cross-dressed on screen, Greta Garbo, Joan Crawford, Barbara Stanwyck, and Katharine Hepburn played strong, unconventional, or "hard" ("butch") women and Hepburn passed as a boy in *Sylvia Scarlet* (1935). A Code-era public use of "gay" (as queer) appears in *Bringing Up Baby* (1938) when Cary Grant, asked why he's wearing a negligee, says, "Because I just went gay all of a sudden!" (The word "gay" was used in reference to homosexuality as early as 1933 in *The Young and the Evil,* a novel by Charles Henri-Ford and Parker Tyler.)

For Hollywood insiders Cary Grant's line could be heard also as a reference, perhaps ironic, to rumors about his personal life. For a dozen years Grant shared a house with actor Randolph Scott but denied then and since that he was gay or bisexual. Similarly, Gary Cooper and openly gay Anderson Lawler shared a house, and it has been suggested that Cooper consciously changed his image from "sophisticated pretty boy to the rugged leather-faced cowboy" to avoid the fate of actors like William "Billy" Haines. Haines was a top box-office draw, and openly gay, in the late twenties but in the thirties he had to choose between his relationship with Jimmy Shields and his acting career; he chose Shields and they were life partners until Haines died in 1973. Only very recently have queer actors been able to come out, and then only a relatively few have done so. Correspondingly, professional and public interest has grown about this more hidden history of Hollywood, with several books reclaiming the possibly fluid rather than fixed sexualities of some of Hollywood's Golden Age female as well as male stars: Claudette Colbert, Marlene Dietrich, Greta Garbo, Janet Gaynor, Katharine Hepburn, and many others.[29] That homosexuality and bisexuality were part of Hollywood life may be surprising, but only in light of the enforced silence, on screen and off, for decades, and the length of that silence only increased the shock value of revealing stars' sexuality later. The Code, in other words, assisted the erasure of public knowledge of talented GLB people; the press contributed also by agreeing not to print anything but the heterosexual marriages and affairs of the stars (a practice that largely continues despite the significant changes in GLBT themes *on* screen).

Queer directors also continued to work in the Golden Age and after. George Cukor, with many excellent films to his credit, was known "inside" the business to be gay, as was James Whale, director of *Frankenstein* (1931), and *Bride of Frankenstein*

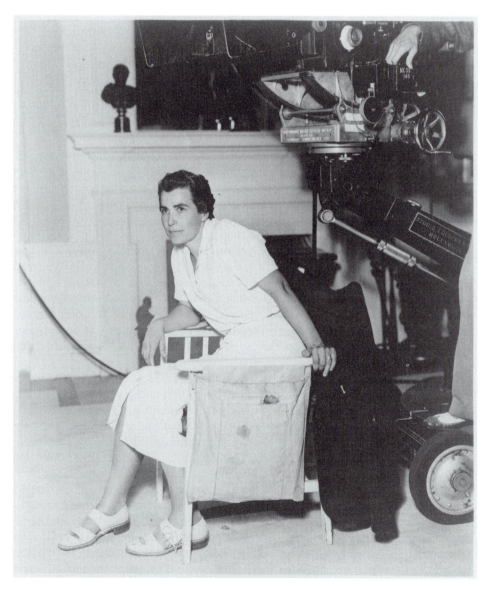

Dorothy Arzner, pictured in a film studio in 1936, remains among the few female directors in Hollywood history. Her homosexuality, like that of many Hollywood figures of the era, was something of an "open secret" but increasingly became an issue for both advocates and opponents of GLBT visibility and rights. (Courtesy Library of Congress)

(1935) (he is the subject of the 1998 film *Gods and Monsters*). While Cukor and Whale, like some actors, were "out" within the confines of Hollywood their sexuality remained unknown to middle America until scholarship of the 1970s and after (the post-Stonewall era of GLBT history) restored their full biographies also. The same is true of lesbian Dorothy Arzner, already a rarity as a female director. Arzner's credits include *Christopher Strong* (1933), *Craig's Wife* (1936), *Dance, Girl, Dance* (1940), and *Merrily We Go to Hell* (1932), and her work continues to inspire analysis. Author Boze Hadleigh could write as late as 1994 that Arzner "was and still is the cinema's leading female director" and who early in her career was considered one of the industry's "Top Ten" directors. Hadleigh interviewed Arzner in 1978, a year before her death, and asked about her reputed objection to "being called a feminist or lesbian director." She replied: "I am not a director. I'm retired. And whatever I may have been in my private life, it didn't pertain to my work, at the time, in motion pictures. You wouldn't call a woman a Democrat director? I would not."[30] Later generations would disagree about the relevance of personal to professional lives, as indicated in her very presence here.

WORLD WAR II

While many Americans were seeking news, entertainment, or escape at movie theatres, much of the world was engaged in military as well as economic struggle. The Spanish Civil War between Loyalists to the new republican government and Fascist challengers led by Francisco Franco erupted in 1936 and ended in 1939 with the Franco victorious; Japan and China went to war in 1937 (to 1945) and the Nazi government annexed Austria and demanded the Sudetenland in the next year. The 1938 Munich Agreement, in which Hitler was allowed by Britain and France to keep the invaded territory, became probably the most regretted diplomatic act of the 20th century. "Appeasing" Hitler rather than opposing his aggression was soon viewed as a mistake; the Nazis took Czechoslovakia and moved into Poland on September 1, 1939. The second world war in only a quarter-century was thus begun, and fear of appeasing dictators would haunt democratic heads of state until the present.

Similar to the situation preceding the First World War, alliances were in place or were soon made, resulting in two groups: the Axis, of Germany, Italy, and Japan; ad the Allies, comprising Great Britain, France, and eventually the Soviet Union once the Nazis broke an earlier pact with Stalin by invading the USSR in 1941. The other Ally, of course, was the United States, entering the conflict after the December 7 surprise attack on the naval base at Pearl Harbor by Japanese bombers in 1941. Engaging much of the world, the war was fought in Europe, North Africa, and on Pacific islands until 1945, when first Germany surrendered and, famously, the Japanese Empire surrendered to the Allies after the controversial decision to drop atomic bombs on Hiroshima and Nagasaki. The unleashing of atomic power only added to an already startling level of wartime destruction. Estimates of total casualties run as high as seventy million worldwide (35 percent were military casualties), and among those were over 400,000 Americans. FDR had died in April 1945, in the first few months of his fourth term as president; Harry Truman then presided over the end of the fighting and the onset of the Cold War.

Historians generally acknowledge the importance of the Second World War as a turning point in politics and diplomacy, society and culture, for much of the globe (and see Chapter 4 for more on the impact of World War II). For queer Americans, too, the war years were a watershed. Mobilizing for war meant bringing together thousands of people both within the military and in industrial and port cities, disrupting lives while providing new opportunities. For self-defined GLB people this offered the chance to socialize in their circumstances, and for those struggling with their identity it could mean their first experience of community. In historian John D'Emilio's words, writing in *Sexual Politics, Sexual Communities,* "For many gay Americans, World War II created something of a nationwide coming out experience."[31] That national moment also exaggerated a pattern of seeming opposites in GLBT history that has remained to the present: pride, visibility, and organizing on one side and backlash, erasure, and oppression on the other. While it is clear that each fed the other, "which came first" is more difficult to determine except in very specific instances, just as the chronology of identity formation, community-building, and organizing a movement also continues to be disputed among historians.

Fighting the War, Fighting the Military

In 1990, shortly before the military compromise known as "Don't Ask, Don't Tell" became a public controversy (see Chapter 8), historian Allan Bérubé published his important oral history, *Coming Out Under Fire.* In it, he combines interviews with lesbian and gay veterans of World War II with the story of the way military policy evolved toward homosexuals at that time. In particular, he notes how that policy, as it solidified, created new battles for homosexual men and women, who "discovered that they were fighting two wars: one for America, democracy, and freedom; the other for their own survival as homosexuals within the military organization."[32] The first part of the quote is important: the gay men and lesbians who entered the armed services did so out of the same patriotism that motivated their straight peers. They had been raised with the same ideals as all Americans—liberty, democracy, equal opportunity—and believed that the role of the United States was to protect those ideals in the world. They had little reason to expect that their sexuality would become an issue in this particular war (an irony when one considers the unquestioned status of this war as one fought for "freedom"). However, it did become an issue at this time, and a conflict emerged not just for homosexuals but for the U.S. armed forces as well.

By the end of World War II more than sixteen million U.S. men had enlisted or were drafted into the military. Bérubé estimated that between 650,000 to 1.6 million of these were gay men.[33] Despite their numbers and some acceptance in the ranks, both gay men and lesbians increasingly struggled to stay in the armed services through the war. At the same time, the military faced a conflict of its own making as it accepted the advice of mental health professionals and developed exclusionary policies at the very moment it needed more and more personnel. Before the first peacetime draft, passed in 1940, sexual orientation was not yet an issue to the U.S. government. However, soon the concept of a *type* rather than a *behavior* emerged in policy, thanks to psychiatry (sodomy was already punishable as a crime in the army and navy). In 1941, people designated "undesirable" for service through psychiatric screening began receiving the infamous Section eight or "blue" discharges (from the color of the paper used for them, they were discharges without paid benefits). By 1943 the category "confirmed pervert" was established and in the next year the mental health term "homosexual" replaced the legal "sodomist." Significantly, the policy that developed eventually included "latent homosexuals," an addition that further solidified the idea of a sexual *identity* (to be treated) over a criminal sexual *act* (requiring imprison-ment).[34] Equally notable is the continuing use of gender (or gender violation) to "diag-nose" the pervert: as in society at large before and after this war, masculine women and effeminate men were more likely to be targeted than "normal" acting soldiers. Though it had been around for decades through some applications of sexology, the equating of queer with crazy was now firmly entrenched in U.S. policy. Thus began the fight against the military's exclusion *and* the thirty-year struggle with the psychiatric profes-sion, the latter ending only in 1973 (see Chapter 6).

(See also this chapter's Debate: Should Homosexuals Serve in the Military?)

The Home Front

For gay men and lesbians World War II was a mixed blessing within the United States as well as for those who served overseas. Those who migrated to cities to partici-pate in the effort found not only jobs but also (as in the service) perhaps their first opportunities to meet other homosexuals. This was crucial in creating, continuing, or reviving communities and, in many areas, laying the groundwork for a rights move-ment organized around a homosexual identity. At the same time, the very visibility fostered by these conditions, as before and since, was a two-edged sword. If the war, as D'Emilio wrote, was a "nationwide coming out" it contributed also to the centrality of the medical model that classified homosexuals as mentally ill, beginning with the military but extending into mainstream culture soon after the war.

D'Emilio and others have noted also the varying effects of mobilization on men and women. The U.S. home front, in fact, is usually associated with women and with good reason:

> The female paid labor force rose by more than 6 million during the war years. For the first time, white married women and mothers of young children left their homes in large numbers to take remunerative employment. Two million women filled jobs... in war-related heavy industries;...Women made up the bulk of the civilians who migrated during the war. They moved to distant cities,...and in general engaged in a range of activities that marked their independence and signaled their departure from the normative female role.[35]

The new opportunities open to women affected every area of society; the war employed not only "Rosie the Riveters" but the Tiny Davises (see the opening story) who otherwise may never have been able to use their abilities. For Rosies and Tinys who were lesbians (as was Tiny), there was a paradox: the more "masculine" (or butch) lesbians were now more free in a way but *less* visible because less noticeable. Styles formerly suspect—wearing slacks or shorter hair—made more sense for factory work and so temporarily became acceptable for all women workers. Perhaps for the first time in their lives, butch lesbians could blend in while being themselves (though it should not be assumed here that all lesbians were butch or vice versa, only that there have always been some women both lesbian and masculine who have usually borne the brunt of antilesbian sentiment).

A New Era

The impact of World War II, then and later, probably cannot be overdrawn. Historian Alan Brinkley, in his text *The Unfinished Nation,* wrote that the war "changed the world as profoundly as any event of the twentieth century, perhaps of

DEBATE: SHOULD HOMOSEXUALS SERVE IN THE MILITARY?

The question of whether homosexuals should be soldiers reveals many of the factors involved in GLBT history in the United States. First, it is an issue that could be raised only in the 20th century, at least in this form. In its very language the question is "historical" to the degree that homosexuality itself is considered historical, as explained in the Debate in Chapter 1: a product of a specific set of circumstances rather than something universal. There have been armies and navies throughout recorded history, and there have always been same-sex activity and desire within them, but the "homosexual" as a person was a medical invention, of sorts, who became "undesirable" as a soldier only during World War II. The result, noted above in the section *Fighting the War, Fighting the Military,* was the dishonorable discharge of lesbians and gay men in the armed services, a practice that continued for decades and has influenced (as well as reflected) the way Americans have perceived homosexuals.

Second, the theme of gender, so central to understanding this history, is implicit in the question. More accurately, the question might read (for men), "Should men who are presumed to be too effeminate, lacking traits needed for effective militarism, be in the armed services?" "Presumed" is the key word because of the equation of gender inversion (having the opposite traits assigned to one's sex) with homosexuality: effeminate men were assumed to be gay, while gay men were assumed to be effeminate, in "character" if not in behavior. Gender has affected female soldiers too, but in different ways. In her book *Creating G.I. Jane* Leisa D. Meyer examined the complications facing women wanting to serve their country, and summarized her points in a later article.[36] Women, she showed, have been in a double bind. While the logic of gender would suggest that female homosexuals (if too "masculine" as women) would be *more* acceptable than gay men as soldiers, "most evidence suggests that lesbians in the military have been from four to ten times more likely [than gay men] to be targeted and discharged."[37] It appears that lesbians are unacceptable in the military because lesbians, conceived as women who violate their proper gender and place in society, are simply unacceptable everywhere. Conversely, the desire to be a soldier could be construed as masculine, so that any female enlisting might be suspected of homosexual traits. Within this gender construct the military is no place for femininity (straight women and gay men) and no place to indulge inverts (lesbians) who should change into "proper" women.

The military policy adopted during World War II perpetuated not only gender stereotypes but those regarding gay sexuality as well. Gay men were portrayed as sexual predators, unable to control a compulsion to seek sexual partners. This assumption, added to the others, led to the Defense Department conclusion that "Homosexuality is incompatible with military service.... The presence of such persons adversely affects the ability of the Armed Forces to maintain discipline, good order, and morale..."Also included were the Armed Forces' inability, with gay men in the ranks,

> to facilitate assignment and worldwide deployment of servicemembers who frequently must live and work under close conditions affording minimal privacy; to recruit and retain members of the armed forces;...and to prevent breaches of security.

The language was familiar; the same rationale was used to exclude or segregate African Americans in the U.S. military to mid-century. A 1941 Navy Department memo stated:

> The close and intimate conditions of life aboard ship, the necessity for the highest possible degree of unity and esprit-de-corps; the requirement of morale—all these demand that nothing be done which may adversely affect the situation. Past experience has shown irrefutably that the enlistment of Negroes (other than for mess attendants) leads to disruptive and undermining conditions. It should be pointed out in this connection that one of the principal objectives of subversive agents in this country in attempting to break down effective organization is by demanding participation for "minorities" in all aspects of defense, especially when such participation tends to disrupt present smooth working organizations.[38]

Due to racial prejudice, it took a 1948 Executive Order to desegregate the military. It was decades before it was fully enforced, and only after officials concluded that it was racism, not the men of color, that was the "disruptive" presence and that perhaps the wrong soldiers had been targeted. No such conclusion has yet been reached with regard to gay men and lesbians in service, and the controversy continues to the present despite a modified policy (see Chapter 8). For many, though, the question of *whether* homosexuals should serve is moot. Randy Shilts summarized the situation at the end of the 1991 in words that ring true after 2001: "In World War II, gay soldiers died on the decks of the USS *Arizona* in Pearl Harbor and spilled their blood on the sands of innumerable South Pacific islands. They died at Inchon and in the rice paddies of Vietnam. In more recent years, they parachuted into Grenada, suffocated in the rubble of Marine barracks in Beirut, and dug foxholes in the shifting sands of Saudi Arabia, Iraq, and Kuwait."[39]

any century."[40] As stated at the beginning of this chapter, the people who came of age during the Depression and experience World War II have been deemed "The Greatest Generation." Whether or not they are, it was the values of their middle-class members especially, shaped by the dual crises, that determined foreign and domestic policies and the limits of personal and public lives in the decades that followed. Central to the postwar era has been an even greater commitment to human rights as a part of U.S. rhetoric. Once hundreds of thousands of Americans (nonwhites and GLBT people included) had died fighting the notoriously bigoted fascists it became more difficult to justify discrimination and denial of rights at home. The leadership of the United States in this regard was enhanced further when former first lady Eleanor Roosevelt was appointed to chair the Human Rights Commission, the body that drafted the United Nations *Universal Declaration of Human Rights,* adopted in 1948. At home racial segregation and arbitrary voting rights, always indefensible to many, now seemed more obviously hypocritical in light of the message of liberty the United States promoted abroad as Cold War strategy. The history of limiting rights by such factors as race and sex led an "identity politics" to become deeply embedded in the U.S. system. That politics has been rooted in the promise of civil rights and organized around the "minority" identities (women, men of color, Catholics, etc.) used to deny many of those rights to individuals. The goal has been to claim the group's equal place in society by opposing discrimination and expanding its members' opportunities.

A major development of postwar GLBT history will be the application of identity politics to the situation of homosexuals. In the first half of the 20th century there were certainly queer Americans, and though driven from public spaces they had once been a noticeable presence in urban culture, at least entertaining if not completely accepted. After the First World War Henry Gerber tried to do what was possible only after the Second: organize homosexuals in order to fight prejudice against them and claim their place in society. No sooner had World War II ended, in fact, than the "first major gay membership organization in the United States" was formed in New York City, the Veterans' Benevolent Association (1945–1954).[41] A half-dozen years later momentum seemed to be building: the idea of homosexuals as a persecuted group similar to ethnic minorities was the guiding principle of both *The Homosexual in America* by "Donald Webster Cory" (Edward Sagarin) and a fledgling organization for homosexuals, the Mattachine Society. The potential of such an argument was enormous and eventually bore fruit. In the meantime the idea, born earlier, experienced a difficult development against the backdrop of the Cold War and the Red and Lavender Scares, leading many GLBT people, then and since, to regard the fifties as the darkest days for gays, ever.

NOTES

1. Information and quotes from various sources: D. Antoinette Handy, *The International Sweethearts of Rhythm: The Ladies Jazz Band from Piney Woods Country Life School,* rev. ed. (Lanham, MD: The Scarecrow Press, 1998); Marcia Froelke Coburn, "Sweethearts of Swing: The Rise and Fall of an All-Girl Band," *Reader Chicago's Free Weekly,* September 12, 1986; Patricia Smith, "'Tiny & Ruby' Relives Era of Hot Jazz and Fast Living," *Chicago Sun-Times,* October 2, 1988; and the films, *International Sweethearts of Rhythm* (1986) and *Tiny and Ruby: Hell Divin' Women* (1988). The films are available from Jezebel Productions (http://www.jezebel.org).

2. Tom Brokaw, *The Greatest Generation* (New York: Random House, 1998).

3. Brokaw, *Greatest Generation,* front flap.

4. "Wealth," *North American Review,* no. 391 (June 1889), http://www.swarthmore.edu/SocSci/rbannis1/AIH19th/Carnegie.html.

5. John D'Emilio, "Capitalism and Gay Identity," in *Making Trouble: Essays on Gay History, Politics, and the University,* ed. John D'Emilio (New York: Routledge, 1992), 7.

6. Lillian Faderman, *To Believe in Women: What Lesbians Have Done for America—a History* (Boston: Houghton Mifflin, 1999), 205.

7. Good summaries of the transition from homosocial worlds to an insistence on heterosexual coupling include Christina Simmons, "Companionate Marriage and the Lesbian Threat," *Frontiers* 4, no. 3 (1979): 54–59; and Lewis A. Erenberg, *Steppin' Out: New York Nightlife and the Transformation of American Culture, 1890–1930* (Chicago: University of Chicago Press, 1981).

8. G. Frank Lydston, *Lecture on Sexual Perversion, Satyriasis and Nymphomania* (Chicago: Philadelphia Medical and Surgical Reporter), quoted in Vern L. Bullough, *Science in the Bedroom: A History of Sex Research* (New York: Basic Books, 1994) and accessed at www2.hu-berlin.de/sexology/GESUND/ARCHIV/LIBRO.HTM.

9. Jonathan Ned Katz, *Gay American History: Lesbians and Gay Men in the U.S.A.,* rev. ed. (New York: Penguin Meridian, 1992), 50–51, quoting Hirschfeld's *Homosexuality in Men and Women* (1914), and p. 52, quoting Eliis' *Sexual Inversion* (1915) (emphasis in original).

10. Katy Coyle and Nadiene Van Dyke, "Sex, Smashing, and Storyville in Turn-of-the-Century New Orleans," in *Carryin' On in the Lesbian and Gay South,* ed. John Howard (New York: New York University Press, 1997), 54–72.

11. Charles H. Hughes, "Notes on a Feature of Sexual Psychopathy," (1907), quoted in Katz, *Gay American History,* 49.

12. For a full account of the events at Harvard see William Wright, *Harvard's Secret Court: The Savage 1920 Purge of Campus Homosexuals* (New York: St. Martin's Press, 2005); for the Washington diary see Ina Russell, ed., *Jeb and Dash: A Diary of Gay Life, 1918–1945* (London: Faber & Faber, 1993).

13. George Chauncey, *Gay New York: Gender, Urban Culture, and the Making of the Gay Male World 1890–1940* (New York: Basic Books, 1994); quotes from pp. 155, 101, and 358.

14. Theodore Roosevelt, "The Strenuous Life," delivered to the Hamilton Club, Chicago, April 10, 1899.

15. The reference is to Erenberg, *Steppin' Out.*

16. Katz, *Gay American History,* 385–97; quotes from pp. 388, 389, and 391.

17. Lynching statistics by year, 1882–1968, from the Tuskegee Institute Archives, posted at http://www.law.umkc.edu/faculty/projects/ftrials/shipp/lynchingyear.html.

18. Chloë Cooney, "'Prove It On Me': Migration, Urbanization and the Making of an Autonomous Black Lesbian Culture" (unpublished paper, 2005), quoting from Joan Nestle, ed., "The Mabel Hampton Special Collection," Oral History Transcripts at the Lesbian Herstory Archives, New York, 132–33. I am indebted to Ms. Cooney for the opportunity to read this paper.

19. Words and music by Lovie Austin and Alberta Hunter (New York: MCA Music Publishing, 1922).

20. Quoted in Chris Albertson, *Bessie* (New York: Stein and Day, 1972), 120, and see 116–21.

21. Chauncey, *Gay New York,* chap. 11: "'Pansies on Parade': Prohibition and the Spectacle of the Pansy"; quote p. 314.

22. Chauncey, *Gay New York,* 333, 334.

23. Holly A. Baggett, "'Someone to Talk Our Language': Jane Heap, Margaret Anderson, and the *Little Review* in Chicago," in *Modern American Queer History,* ed. Allida Black (Philadelphia: Temple University Press, 2001), quotes 24.

24. James Steakley, *The Homosexual Emancipation Movement in Germany* (New York: Arno Press, 1975), 105.

25. Herbert Hoover, *The Memoirs of Herbert Hoover: The Great Depression 1929–1941* (New York: Macmillan, 1952), 30.

26. Chauncey, *Gay New York,* 353, for the prohibitions against impersonators and terms. For Pansy O'Hara see Anne Edwards, *Road to Tara: The Life of Margaret Mitchell,* Author of *Gone With the Wind* (New York: Dell, 1983), 169.

27. Allan Bérubé, "The History of Gay Bathhouses," in *Policing Public Sex: Queer Politics and the Future of AIDS Activism,* ed. Dangerous Bedfellows (Boston: South End Press, 1996), 187–220; summary of stages of baths pp. 190–91 and quote p. 188.

28. Vito Russo, *The Celluloid Closet: Homosexuality in the Movies* (New York: Harper & Row, 1981; 1987); some of Russo's points and examples appear in my treatment here. Also see Harry M. Benshoff and Sean Griffin, *Queer Images: A History of Gay and Lesbian Film in America* (Lanham, MD: Rowman & Littlefield, 2006); and Lillian Faderman and Stuart Timmons, *Gay L.A.: A History of Sexual Outlaws, Power Politics, and Lipstick Lesbians* (New York: Basic Books, 2006).

29. There seems more interest in women than men, if the number of books is an indication. For examples, see Boze Hadleigh, *Hollywood Lesbians* (New York: Barricade Books, 1994); Axel Madsen, *The Sewing Circle, Hollywood's Greatest Secret: Female Stars Who Loved Other Women* (New York: Birch Lane Press, 1995); Diana McLellan, *The Girls: Sappho Goes to Hollywood* (New York: LA Weekly Books, 2000); and Darwin Porter, *Katharine the Great: A Lifetime of Secrets* (New York: Blood Moon Productions, 2004). Also see William J. Mann, *Behind the Screen: How Gays and Lesbians Shaped Hollywood, 1910–1969* (New York: Penguin Books, 2002).

30. Hadleigh, *Hollywood Lesbians,* 99, 119.

31. John D'Emilio, *Sexual Politics, Sexual Communities: The Making of a Homosexual Minority in the United States, 1940–1970* (Chicago: University of Chicago Press, 1983; 1998), 24.

32. Allan Bérubé, *Coming Out Under Fire: The History of Gay Men and Women in World War Two* (New York: The Free Press, 1990), 7. In 1994 an award-winning documentary of the same name was made, directed by Arthur Dong.

33. Bérubé, *Coming Out Under Fire*, 2–3.

34. Bérubé, *Coming Out Under Fire*, 128, 139, 142–43.

35. D'Emilio, *Sexual Politics, Sexual Communities*, 29.

36. Leisa D. Meyer, *Creating G.I. Jane: Sexuality and Power in the Women's Army Corps During World War II* (New York: Columbia University Press, 1996); Leisa D. Meyer, "The Myth of Lesbian (In)visibility: World War II and the Current 'Gays in the Military' Debate," in *Modern American Queer History,* ed. A. Black (Philadelphia: Temple University Press, 2001), 271–81.

37. Meyer, "The Myth of Lesbian (In)visibility," 271.

38. This and the preceding quote from material distributed as part of the ACLU Lesbian and Gay Rights Project's conference, "About Face: Combatting ROTC's Anti-Gay Policy," 1990.

39. Randy Shilts, *Conduct Unbecoming: Gays and Lesbians in the U.S. Military* (New York: St. Martin's Press, 1993), 17.

40. Alan Brinkley, *The Unfinished Nation: A Concise History of the American People,* 5th ed., vol. II (Boston: McGraw Hill, 2008), 725.

41. Bérubé, *Coming Out Under Fire,* 249.

SUGGESTED RESOURCES

General/Before 1920

Boag, P. (2003). *Same-sex affairs: Constructing and controlling homosexuality in the Pacific Northwest.* Berkeley: University of California Press.

Faderman, L. (1992). *Odd girls and twilight lovers: A history of lesbian life in twentieth-century America.* New York: Penguin Books.

Gustav-Wrathall, J.D. (1998). *Take the young stranger by the hand: Same-sex relations and the YMCA.* Chicago: University of Chicago Press.

Russell, I. (Ed.). (1993). *Jeb and Dash: A diary of gay life, 1918–1945.* London: Faber & Faber.

Stansell, C. (2000). *American moderns: Bohemian New York and the creation of a new century.* New York: Henry Holt.

The 1920s–1940s

Baggett, H.A. (2001). 'Someone to Talk Our Language': Jane Heap, Margaret Anderson, and the *little review* in Chicago. In A. Black (Ed.), *Modern American queer history* (pp. 24–35). Philadelphia: Temple University Press.

Beemyn, B. (2001). The new Negro renaissance, a bisexual renaissance: The lives and works of Angelina Weld Grimké and Richard Bruce Nugent. In A. Black (Ed.), *Modern American queer history* (pp. 36–48). Philadelphia: Temple University Press.

Carby, H. (1987). It jus be's dat way sometime: The sexual politics of women's blues. *Radical America, 20*(4), 9–22.

Dahl, L. (1984). *Stormy weather: The music and lives of a century of jazzwomen.* New York: Pantheon Books.

Davis, A.Y. (1998). *Blues legacies and black feminism: Gertrude "Ma" Rainey, Bessie Smith, and Billie Holiday.* New York: Vintage Books.

Estes, S. (2005). Ask and tell: Gay veterans, identity, and oral history on a civil rights frontier. *Oral History Review, 32*(2), 21–47.

Faderman, L., & Timmons, S. (2006). *Gay L. A.: A history of sexual outlaws, power politics, and lipstick lesbians.* New York: Basic Books.

Garber, E. (1989). A spectacle in color: The lesbian and gay subculture of jazz age Harlem. In M. Duberman, M. Vicinus, & G. Chauncey, Jr. (Eds.), *Hidden from history: Reclaiming the gay and lesbian past* (pp. 318–331). New York: New American Library.

Holcomb, G.E. (2007). *Claude McKay, code name Sasha: Queer black marxism and the Harlem Renaissance.* Gainesville, FL: University Press of Florida.

Middlebrook, D.W. (1998). *Suits me: The double life of Billy Tipton.* Boston: Houghton Mifflin.

Schwarz, J. (1982). *Radical feminists of heterodoxy: Greenwich Village 1912–1940.* Lebanon, NH: New Victoria Publishers.

4   QUEERS IN COLD WAR AMERICA

Cambridge, Massachusetts, 1957. Martin Duberman, completing his Ph.D. in history at Harvard University, had been struggling for years with the knowledge that he was gay. Early that year he writes in his diary:

> *I wish to change...but parallel with this desire runs the stronger current of neurotic drive and compulsion, thwarting most of my efforts to change. I can neither give up me homosexual activities, nor devote myself guiltlessly to them.*

Upon graduating Duberman would go on to teach at Yale, Princeton, and the City University of New York. He has had a distinguished career as a historian and playwright, and a leader in the GLBT movement through both activism and academics. In his autobiographical Cures, *he reflected further on this earlier period in his life:*

> *In these pre-Stonewall liberation years, a few brave souls had publicly declared themselves and even banded together for limited political purposes, but the vast majority of gay people were locked away in painful isolation and fear, doing everything possible* not *to declare themselves. Many of us cursed our fate, longed to be straight. And some of us had actively been seeking 'cure.' In my case, for a long time.*

He would continue to seek a cure through therapy for several more years, an approach typical of postwar America. As a reflective scholar, though, he also sees the complexity of that era and its mixed legacy for all Americans, including homosexuals:

> *We accepted as given that as homosexuals we could never reach "full adult maturity"... We knew we'd never qualify, and despised ourselves for it. But it's too simple to reduce "growing up gay in the Fifties" to a one-dimensional horror story.... In retrospect, I'm astonished at the tenacity with which I continued to buy into imposed, arbitrary definitions of "normalcy" and self-worth—into a state of self-abdication.... By the late Sixties my entangled cocoon did finally begin to unravel, a process greatly aided by the advent of the modern homophile movement, with its liberating new perspectives and options.*[1]

Certainly any ten or more years that is designated an era by historians has aspects of both image and reality to it. No image can contain all the complexities of a time, but neither are all images merely fiction. When we arrive fully in 1950s America, we confront this situation but perhaps in sharper relief. Like nostalgia for the "Roaring Twenties," that for the fifties seems to represent an almost desperate attempt to recall a better time of pleasure, prosperity, and overall good times. Perhaps this is understandable, since both eras shared actual similarities in what preceded and followed them. Like the twenties, the fifties came after a world war and before a time of upheaval that shook the country's confidence. While they lasted, however, both decades were characterized in part by celebration, affluence, and confidence in America and Americans.

The twenties and the fifties also share a more complicated story of cultural conflict beneath the surface of selective memory. The fifties may have offered prosperity and contentment for many in the growing middle class but the assumptions of that class were challenged fundamentally in the next decade, just as they were by the Depression following the 1920s. While the postwar image focused on consensus, the reality was a country more divided along lines of age, race, class, sex, and sexuality than the necessary Cold War propaganda would allow. In the decades since, something of this reality has been restored through accounts of youthful rebellion in words and music and those of an energized civil rights movement.

Much less famous is the birth of organized action for homosexual rights, a product of currents both positive and negative. The postwar era produced what was likely the most intense homophobia of the century, resulting in a common paradox: oppression, rather than stifling the development of successful movements, can encourage them. It is then less surprising that in the dark days of the fifties homosexuals began sustained organizing around the concept of civil rights. Although all associations formed then would not survive the changes of the ensuing decades, those early local, regional, and national efforts provided the basis for dialogues and methods lasting to the present.

IMAGES VERSUS REALITIES

The Cold War began just as the hot war—World War II—was ending. The Soviet Union, under Joseph Stalin, had joined the Allies in fighting the Third Reich and the Japanese Empire but the fault lines of that alliance were soon apparent and only widened after 1945. Even before victory in Europe and the Pacific, the traditional idea of balancing power among many nations was giving way to the polarization between the two emerging "superpowers," communist U.S.S.R. and the capitalist-democratic United States. In 1946 Winston Churchill, British prime minister warned of a communist "iron curtain" being drawn across Eastern Europe (an image that became literally concrete in 1961 when Soviets built the Berlin Wall). Anticommunism would be the dominant ideal in the United States for the next forty-five years, affecting foreign policy through those decades and dominating domestic affairs in the fifties and sixties.

Striving for Consensus

Any account of early postwar America must return to World War II with an attempt to understand the meaning of that recent experience for the people who fought it, on the battlefields and at home. In his insightful study of the politics and culture of the era John Morton Blum emphasized the way the war experience shaped the U.S. self-image, and vice versa. If the war was fought for Americans' (and the world's) political and economic security then winning implied a commitment to that security. Not only should Americans be safe from fascism but also communism, and from another Great Depression. If there was a mania against communism, and for consumerism, Blum suggested, its roots are in the perception that thousands of Americans died for not only the freedoms of the Constitution but also to ensure "freedom from want" and "freedom from fear."[2] Out of this developed a "mood" of "liberal consensus," or agreement on certain basic rights (summarized, for the most part, in the Bill of Rights) and economic principles of capitalism and free trade. At times there was more insistence on it than genuine consensus, however, that in its vehemence belied the divisions it sought to ignore or diffuse. In retrospect the United States presented "two faces" after World War II: "Confident to the verge of complacency about the perfectibility of American society, anxious to the point of paranoia about the threat of communism."[3]

A significant part of the consensus was an emphasis on consumerism. The ability—and desire—to buy products was a key element in the ongoing development of capitalism and thus an increasingly important component of the American self-image. "Freedom," long associated with free trade in liberal thought, now also included the "freedom of choice" implied by different products and represented by a proliferation of brand names. Advertising was elevated to new importance and became the symbolic (and real) profession of the new era (and also soon ridiculed by *Mad* magazine). None of this was new to the United States, since advertising and brand names had emerged in the 19th century, but the political and economic contexts had changed. Those who survived the Depression and had fought fascism were not about to have their right to make money and buy things now threatened by communists. Last, and far from least, the postwar era had television, a device with seemingly unlimited image-making potential. At its heart was advertising, which many observers claim is and was its real purpose, with programming created as "filler" to entertain consumers between the crucial content, the commercials. Certainly TV became a powerful medium, creating and transmitting notions of the "normal" American family and reinforcing the message of conformity. From the first, TV had many potential applications in U.S. life, from entertainment and consumerism to information and politics; what was seen could change the way Americans thought, what they supported, and how they voted.

The liberal consensus concerned not only foreign policy and economics but on life at home, and within the home, as well. Now familiar stereotypes of family life were at the core of the ideal: two heterosexual, legally married parents, two or more children, a male breadwinner, and a stay-at-home wife and mother. Gender distinctions, never deeply submerged, resurfaced with full force and combined with both consumerism and a revived "separate spheres" ideology: males produce (and consume or decide on expensive items), females consume that needed within the home as part of their role in maintaining the perfect family. The concept of privacy, always a class-based distinction, reached a new importance to the aspiring middle class, who would begin to link it with the liberal concept of individual rights. Some families settled in comfortable homes in suburbs of large cities (those outside New York became the model) while others aspired to this postwar version of the Jeffersonian land-owning ideal. Some tension evolved between a community of neighbors and the insular family, wherein projecting the image of happiness and perfection was supreme. Above all, the image left little room within the definition of perfection for "deviants" and "subversives" as society then defined them.

Sexology Revisited

In retrospect the fifties reveal a typical American ambivalence about sex. On the one hand, the Victorian silence on the subject had been broken by both literature and science earlier in the century. On the other, exactly what could be said or written about and in what context was still contested well into the 20th century. While the Victorians, paradoxically, may have revealed their preoccupation with sex in their refusal to discuss it openly, postwar Americans had only reached a kind of (male) adolescence in their cultural treatments. The fifties, after all, was the decade that Hugh Hefner founded *Playboy*—and featured a nude Marilyn Monroe in the first issue (December 1953). Marilyn herself signaled a new age of female imagery in films, with "sexpots" crowding out the "tough," assertive, witty women of the previous decades. "Sex," in other words, often meant women specifically, and women presented at the extremes of femininity as defined by a passive sexuality. At the same time, there was a fascination with Freudian ideas (as adapted in the United States) and a new emphasis on sex in marriage. Marriage manuals reflected a new willingness to claim the pleasures of (heterosexual, married) sex as well as the goal of procreation, and the claim was legitimized by the scientific language and approach of these "how-to" guides.

Whatever they wanted to admit, there could be no doubt that American were having sex. Between 1946 and 1964 the "baby boom" was in full swing, with seventy-six million new Americans born in those years. Amid all this activity came sex researcher Alfred Kinsey, who wanted to know not what Americans *thought* about sex but what they were actually *doing,* and eventually compiled his findings in the controversial books known as the Kinsey Reports. Kinsey, a zoology professor at Indiana University, founded with others the Institute for Sex Research (later the Kinsey Institute) in 1947. The following year, the first of the two studies appeared, *Sexual Behavior in the Human Male* (1948), followed five years later by *Sexual Behavior in the Human Female* (1953). As the titles suggest, the purpose of the research, as Kinsey saw it, was dispassionate scientific observation of the actual practices of men and women in the United States, described in the books as "outlets." He and his team began the studies years earlier and eventually accumulated data on 5,300 white men and 5,940 white women through interviews consisting of hundreds of questions. Each volume created a sensation and became best sellers. The response to each was also mixed, with particular anger directed at the second volume, perhaps due to the revelations that (white) American women were sexual at all.

The Kinsey Reports covered an exhaustive array of sexual practice, much of which the dominant culture still considered morally or legally unacceptable, or at least unprintable except as pornography. Participants were questioned about masturbation, oral sex, and anal sex, for example, as well as extramarital and premarital sex. Among the findings: 92 percent of men and 62 percent of women had masturbated; about two-thirds of the men sampled and half of the women had experienced premarital sex; and, one of the bigger bombshells, half of the male sample and a quarter of the females reported having extramarital sex. Given the lingering public silence on all things sexual this information was startling to some, as were the findings on bisexual and homosexual activity. From his subjects' interviews, Kinsey found that about 46 percent of the men and up to 14 percent of the women "reacted to" both males and females in a sexual way, and 37 percent of the males and 13 percent of the females reported same-sex activity to orgasm. These results are often grouped under "Bisexuality" and "Homosexuality" (even by sex researchers) but the headings are misleading: the terms imply *identity* whereas Kinsey was concerned exclusively with *behavior.* However phrased, though, the results of the Kinsey interviews, undoubtedly causing relief in some readers, aroused fear in others and added to an already oppressive climate for sexual nonconformists. (See the Debate for more on Kinsey's results and significance.)[4]

A lesser-known scientist who like Kinsey had begun his research before World War II was Harry Benjamin. Benjamin was born in 1885 in Berlin, center of the German homosexual emancipation movement, studied medicine in Germany, and arrived in the United States after graduating in 1912. He was long in the forefront of the scientific study of sex, advocating sexual freedom and the removal of legal barriers like antihomosexual laws. In the postwar era Benjamin became a leading expert on transgenderism and transsexuality, both of which he distinguished from transvestism (cross-dressing). He was an early advocate of using hormonal therapy and "sex-change operations" (now called sex reassignment surgery) for some cross-gendered people. Although few would have recognized Benjamin's name, transsexualism received national attention in a sensationalized way when Christine Jorgensen, born George Jorgensen in New York City, returned to the United States in 1953 after male-to-female surgery in Denmark. Indeed, Dawn Pepita Hall (previously Gordon Langley Hall) recalled that when, in the sixties, a physician at the Medical College of Charleston told Dawn s/he was a transsexual "'...I had never heard the word. Of course I had heard of sex-changes. The Christine Jorgenson [sic] story was universal.'" (Dawn went on to marry an African American man in 1969 in "South Carolina's first mixed-marriage," a widely publicized event that made the couple a target of harassment and violence.)[5] By then Benjamin had published several articles and his important book *The Transsexual Phenomenon* (1966), and his work influenced the formation of such centers as the Johns Hopkins Gender Identity Clinic. He maintained offices on both coasts and retired only in the 1970s, having pioneered research through what became the Benjamin Gender Identity Research Foundation.

Benjamin rejected theories that classified queer sexualities—now GLBT—as mental illness and, like Kinsey, conceived of sex and gender variations along a continuum of behaviors and identities. They remained in the minority of medical professionals, however. Psychiatry had gained in stature during World War II through evaluating potential soldiers and determining who was "fit" for military service (see Chapter 3). In 1952 the first *Diagnostic and Statistical Manual of Mental Disorders* (*DSM-1*) of the American Psychiatric Association was published, a professional handbook that "firmly established homosexuality as a sociopathic personality disorder."[6] Treatments, sometimes involuntary, ranged from psychotherapy to shock therapy, all with the intention, reflected in Martin Duberman's experience in the opening story, of curing the "deviant."

One professional who led the way for changing the medical model of homosexuality and removing it from the *DSM* was Dr. Evelyn Hooker, whose contributions cannot be overstated. In the midst of rampant societal homophobia *and* the beginning of lasting homosexual organizing (see below) Hooker designed studies to test whether gay men were any less "adjusted" than straight men. She used standard mental health tools like Rorschach (ink blot) tests on nonpatients, straight and gay, rather than on those who were already seeking treatments. In 1956 she presented her findings at a meeting of the American Psychological Association and also began publishing the results of her studies, paving the way for homosexuality ceasing to be classified as a mental disorder two decades later. Hooker, who died in 1996, recalled those days to Eric Marcus in a 1989 interview:

> One of the most exciting days of my life was the day I presented my paper—my study. The title was "The Adjustment of the Male Overt Homosexual." In my paper I presented evidence that gay men can be as well adjusted as straight men and that some

are even better adjusted than some straight men. In other words, as far as the evidence was concerned, there was no difference between the two groups of men in the study. There was just as much pathology in one group as in the other.... I think that the net impact of my study was felt in a number of ways.... But what means the most to me, I think...[:] If I went to a gay gathering of some kind, I was sure to have at least one person come up to me and say, "I wanted to meet you because I wanted to tell you what you saved me from."[7]

Simmering Discontent

For some GLBT people the fifties, then, were anything but "Happy Days." In that respect they were not alone, but instead shared in the realities of division and dissatisfaction. As Richard R. Lingeman put it when looking back from the 1970s, "The fifties under Ike represented a sort of national prefrontal lobotomy: tail-finned, we Sunday-drove down the superhighways of life while tensions that later bubbled up in the sixties seethed beneath the placid surface."[8] Women and youth, especially of the mostly white middle class, were among those whose frustrations eventually erupted in various ways. White women's discontent, born of a newly enforced domesticity following the war experience of paid work, was more hidden or individualized. It was soon expressed in the 1960s in Betty Friedan's *The Feminine Mystique,* though, and a revived feminist movement (see Chapter 5). For young, often privileged, people then coming of age cultural outlets provided the means of questioning society or rebelling against its values until more overtly political avenues arose in the midst of an unpopular war.

In another similarity to the 1920s, young people used music, literature, and style to counter the Victorian dictates of their parents, and again in ways charged with the taboos of race and sexuality. Like jazz, rock 'n' roll derived its rhythms and style from African American sources and provided environments for interracial mixing. African American artists like Chuck Berry and Little Richard, and R & B artists Bo Diddley and James Brown—were as popular as white singers, though it was the latter that often were considered more "sellable" to a wider (white) audience: Bill Haley and the Comets recorded the first song to hit number one on the *Billboard* chart, and Elvis Presley was the sensation of his era. Also like jazz, rock 'n' roll was associated with (forbidden) sexuality. It was openly sensual and represented a music through which young Americans could voice rebellion against some of society's rules.

While rock 'n' roll was largely heterosexual (Little Richard notwithstanding), since songs often revolved around young straight couples or heterosexual desire, the same cannot be said for the Beat Generation. Taking their name from the term coined by Jack Kerouac, the Beats were young men (and a few women, who received less attention) who wrote prose and poetry of their disillusionment with the materialism and moral dictates of the fifties. They were centered somewhat in New York but especially in San Francisco and, like their contemporary Kinsey, sexual freedom was an important part of their lives and works. Bisexual and homosexual expression, on and off the page, was significant to their subculture. Probably most famous is Allen Ginsberg's *Howl* (1956), a lengthy Whitmanesque poem that was controversial for its references to drugs and gay sex. It survived an obscenity trial, which brought the poem additional publicity. Ginsberg was gay and his lovers included fellow Beats Peter Orlovsky, William S. Burroughs, and Neal Cassady. To Jack Kerouac, author of *On the Road* (1957), sex and creativity were vitally linked, and he was involved with both women and men (including Cassady and Gore Vidal). Significantly for GLBT history, the Beats tested the limits of postwar sexual conformity and were a rare public voice celebrating queer lives at a time it was dangerous to do so.

Boiling Over

While it would be several years before the discontent of youth, women, and homosexuals would coalesce into actions that received national attention, that of African Americans in the 1950s and before established important patterns for postwar civil rights. As mentioned in the previous chapter, the time was especially ripe for exposing the gap between the image of the United States as guardian of freedoms and the realities of segregation, discrimination, and violence aimed at nonwhites at home. The World War II struggle against racist Nazis and the Cold War competition for the "Third World" made the blatant inequalities in America difficult to justify and, for some, impossible to tolerate.

Although there was some progress on racial issues by 1950, the politics of the thirties and forties was not unlike that of the early republic, in which compromises were made with southern whites (then slaveholders) in order to form the United States and get a federal government underway. By the time of FDR and the New Deal (see Chapter 3) the traditional party of southern whites—the Democrats—had expanded its appeal to diverse populations who often had little in common except economic hardship and the perception of Republican businessmen as their enemies. This included farmers, factory workers and, after 1936, African American voters, who changed parties in light of relief offered to the downtrodden by the Democratic regime. If they hoped for an end to discrimination it they were disappointed. The racial policies of the New Deal were balanced against the political need for southern support, and therefore mixed: segregation and discrimination were part of some agencies, though there were African American advisors to the president (the "Black Cabinet"). Also First Lady Eleanor Roosevelt was an outspoken advocate of racial equality, one reason FBI Director J. Edgar Hoover kept a file on her as a "subversive." A few months into FDR's third term A. Philip Randolph organized the March on Washington Movement to demonstrate against segregation and job discrimination, especially in the defense industry. News that 100,000 people would participate led to government concessions, and the march never occurred, but the idea of gathering at the nation's capital for civil rights would remain an option.

Once the war was over the time was ripe for more concerted action, and it came from both grassroots protest and the federal government, in a kind of dialogue. CORE (Congress of Racial Equality) had been founded in 1942, and fifteen years later the influential SCLC (Southern Christian Leadership Conference) appeared on the scene. In between were some of the most significant "moments" in civil rights history: Truman's Fair Deal, that included Executive Orders demanding desegregation of the military and fair employment practices in the federal government; the 1954 Supreme Court decision in *Brown v. the Board of Education* that declared school segregation "inherently unequal" and therefore unconstitutional; the civil disobedience of Rosa Parks, arrested on a bus in Montgomery, Alabama in 1955 for refusing to give her seat to a white person; and that city's bus boycott that resulted in desegregating the buses while bringing Rev. Martin Luther King, Jr. into the forefront of the movement. Congress passed civil rights legislation in 1957 and 1960, but critics saw them as ineffective and continued pressing for genuine equality. In the early years of the sixties activists added SNCC (Student Nonviolent Coordinating Committee) to the groups addressing racism and were participating in sit-ins and "freedom rides" on Southern buses, often risking (and enduring) violent attacks for their stance against segregation.

In the next decade it was postwar African American activism that provided the most immediate model for a new "militancy" among homosexuals (as they were still called). That model included not only the tactics of grassroots action (none of which was brand new) but especially the conceptual framework of identity politics. In the U.S. context, the identities are based on characteristics, such as race, religion, or sex, that society has used to justify discrimination. Usually the people without full rights or opportunities are considered inferior or unfit in some way and therefore not "eligible" for equal treatment. Identity politics, then, has been a response to the identities imposed by prejudice: racism produced a race-based movement, sexism resulted in activism by and for women, and so on. Similarly, it could be said that homophobia helped produce the gay/lesbian rights movements of the sixties and after. Importantly, those movements rest not only on theory and methods "borrowed" from civil rights but also on foundations laid by queer people themselves in the fifties within their communities and new organizations (see "A Homosexual Minority"). Something of the climate in which those communities and groups developed, however, is necessary to a fuller understanding and appreciation of their very existence.

THE POLITICS OF ANTICOMMUNISM

The history of nations is often divided into domestic and foreign, the former concerning policies within a country's boundaries, and the latter their overseas affairs. Rarely can they be separated, though, and the Cold War is as good an example as any hot war of the way the two are connected. Events overseas seemed to confirm fears at home, causing the pursuit of subversives within U.S. borders. Anticommunism became the dominant ideology of the postwar United States (along with a liberal consensus) and affected all Americans in some way. In this climate GLBT Americans became particular targets of those who believed that all "deviance" was connected.

The United States in the World

The end of World War II brought about a "bipolar" world in which the Soviet Union and the United States competed for the alliance of uncommitted areas. The ideological standoff was complicated by the new presence of atomic bombs and the demonstrations in Japan that the United States would use them to end a war or stop aggression. When the U.S.S.R. also gained nuclear power the fear of all-out atomic war was matched only by the arms buildup that seemed to guarantee it. In the meantime the Cold War affected party politics as neither Democrats nor Republicans dared seem "soft on communism." Above all, no American leader could appear to be allowing the Soviets to expand in the way Hitler had been "appeased" at Munich in 1938 (see Chapter 3).

When Harry Truman took the oath of office upon Franklin Roosevelt's death in 1945 he became not only president but also the one to decide to drop atomic bombs on Japan. His administration thus began with a strong statement, and one possibly designed as much for the Soviets as for the Axis powers to hear. By the end of 1947 key pieces of Cold War policy were in place: containment, or stopping the spread of communism with "counterforce"; the Marshall Plan of economic aid to Europe; and the creation of the National Security Council and the CIA (Central Intelligence Agency) by the National Security Act (which also replaced the War and Navy Departments with the Department of Defense). Supporting these action were the "domino theory," which pictured nations as upright dominoes that would fall one after another once the first was toppled by communism, and the assumption that economic crisis had fueled the rise of fascism in the thirties. Truman was elected in his own right in 1948 in the midst of events that seemed to confirm the wisdom of containment. Portions of Eastern Europe were under communist regimes and within the next year the Soviets successfully tested an atomic bomb. Equally chilling, a revolution in China in 1949 established communism in the world's most populous country. When North Koreans moved into South Korea in 1950 the United Nations sent troops to "contain" the incursion, 90 percent of whom were American. U.S. involvement in the Korean War (1950–1953) dominated the end of Truman's term and also provided another example, like appeasement, of precedents to avoid. However, to the critics the mistake here was not inaction, as in Munich, but weak action; "no more Koreas" indicated a dwindling tolerance for anything but all-out war against communist aggression.

During the administrations of Republican Dwight D. Eisenhower (1953–1961), a popular World War II general, and Democrat John F. Kennedy (1961–1963) Cold War tensions not only continued but also escalated. Middle Eastern nations were added to the potential dominoes that could fall and so became another site of U.S. concern. The United States had recognized the new state of Israel immediately after it formed in 1948, an action that angered Palestinian Arabs with claims on the same lands, and that conflict was placed into the larger U.S.–Soviet struggle. A crisis had previously erupted in Iran as the war was ending, and in 1953 a U.S.-sponsored coup replaced the nationalist government with the Shah that many Iranians came to despise. After conflict between Israel and Egypt the Eisenhower Doctrine extended containment to include the Middle East, stating that the United States would intervene to help a government requesting aid to repel communism there. Eisenhower's secretary of state, John Foster Dulles added the language of "liberation" and "deterrence" to Cold War policy, proposing a more proactive position. It should be clear, he thought, that America would use nuclear and air power in acts of "massive retaliation" against communism (and all communism was thought to be Soviet inspired).

Paradoxically, the standoff was increasingly characterized by races—the space race and the arms race—both of which continued well into the sixties. The space race was off and running when the Soviets launched the satellite *Sputnik* in 1957. The United States created NASA (National Aeronautics and Space Administration) the next year. When John F. Kennedy became president after a close election against Richard Nixon he addressed Congress on "Urgent National Needs," and included funding for space exploration. "I believe," he said, "that this nation should commit itself to achieving the goal, before this decade is out, of landing a man on the moon and returning him safely to the earth."[9] At his inauguration a few months earlier JFK also had announced to the world that the United States "shall pay any price, bear any burden, meet any hardship, support any friend, oppose any foe to assure the survival and the success of liberty."[10] By that time Fidel Castro was in power through a communist revolution in Cuba, and in 1962 a crisis over Soviet missile sites on the island brought Cold War tensions to a peak. Kennedy also had inherited a situation as far away from the United States, in miles and in the public mind, as Cuba was close: a struggle over the future of the divided nation of Vietnam.

Red Scares

The determination to stop the advance of communism applied inside U.S. borders as well as beyond them. The virulent anticommunism of the early postwar era resulted in America's Second Red Scare, the first one occurring on the heels of the Bolshevik Revolution (see Chapter 3). The two were similar in their opposition to leftist politics, fear of foreign influence, and efforts to curb Constitutional freedoms, but the second was broader in every way: it lasted longer, it reached into more areas of society, and it affected more people. Its dynamics are now famous since they violated cherished guarantees on the American justice system. No hard evidence was required to accuse someone of communist sympathies, and once accused a person was guilty until proven innocent. One could be guilty by association with known communists, or assumed guilty if one chose not to respond to the accusation. These factors led critics to refer to the Second Red Scare as a "witch hunt," an analogy reinforced by Arthur Miller's play, *The Crucible* (1952). Miller was one of hundreds of creative people who were targeted, reflecting the two-pronged nature of this later scare, which corresponded roughly to the East and West coasts. One prong focused on those in government and the other on arts and entertainment, especially film and television. Each branch of the scare had a profound impact on GLBT people in the United States and the effects of each lasted far beyond its heyday.

The years of fear that "Reds" were infiltrating the government are so associated with Sen. Joseph McCarthy (R-WI) that they are called the era of McCarthyism. In a now infamous act McCarthy told an audience in Wheeling, West Virginia in 1950 that he held a list of names of communists working in the State Department. Investigations of government employees had begun in 1947 but McCarthy was able to seize the spotlight and capitalize on (while contributing to) growing paranoia. The Truman administration had also instituted loyalty oaths for government employees and the practice continued under Eisenhower. To criticize U.S. policies or expose its faults was considered "un-American" and civil rights workers, among others, were placed under FBI surveillance. Further restrictions were added with the Internal Security Act (McCarran Act) of 1950, designed to identify and monitor communists in the United States, based on the rationale that "The agents of communism have devised clever and ruthless espionage and sabotage tactics which are carried out in many instances in form or manner successfully evasive of existing law."[11] The peak of the scare, perhaps, came three years later when Julius and Ethel Rosenberg were executed, having been tried and convicted of passing atomic secrets to the USSR. Many Americans who opposed communism also opposed the mentality and tactics of McCarthyism, and the Senate finally censured McCarthy in 1954 following a series of televised hearings held to investigate communism in the U.S. Army. In all, thousands of people lost their jobs or were otherwise affected by the Second Red Scare.

Several hundred of those who were fired or banned from working were screenwriters, actors, directors, and others in film, TV, and theatre. The idea was not new, since the Federal Theatre Project was subject to investigation for communist influence in 1938. The hearings that began in 1947 were broader in scope, however, and their effects lasted well beyond the fifties. The investigations of HUAC (House Un-American Activities Committee) were based on the presumption that communists would infiltrate American society in subtle ways, not only through achieving government positions but through swaying public opinion. Movies and the new medium of TV were (rightly) considered powerful tools of influence and so those who worked in them at all levels were subject to scrutiny. If Hollywood was "conquered" by communists would the citizenry be far behind? The investigations generated both the notorious blacklist of hundreds of entertainers banned from the industry, and led to jail terms for the "Hollywood Ten." Unlike the friendly witnesses such as studio heads Walt Disney and Jack Warner, actors Gary Cooper, Ronald Reagan, and Robert Taylor, and director Elia Kazan, the Ten were "unfriendly" witnesses before HUAC who objected to the methods of the Red Scare and refused to name their friends as possible communists. Most were screenwriters—Lester Cole, Ring Lardner, Jr., and Dalton Trumbo among them—and like blacklisted actors and directors their careers were stalled or ruined. Some wrote under pseudonyms, or a "front," to get their scripts into production (Woody Allen's film *The Front* is a comedic treatment of the practice and features several blacklisted people as screenwriter and in starring roles). Investigations of entertainment continued through the 1950s and contributed further to the climate of fear and suspicion.

A Lavender Scare

Less famous than the Red Scare but equally devastating in its effects was the Lavender Scare (or Pink Scare), the elimination of suspected homosexuals from government service. In his award-winning book, *The Lavender Scare,* David K. Johnson wrote, "In 1950 many politicians, journalists, and citizens thought that homosexuals posed more of a threat to national security than Communists.... By November...the 'purge of the perverts' resulted in the dismissal of nearly six hundred federal civil servants. In the state Department alone, security officials boasted that on average they were firing one homosexual per day, more than double the rate of those suspected of political disloyalty."[12] Like the Red version, the Lavender Scare actually began earlier, in 1947, and within three years ninety-one State Department employees had been fired for being homosexual. When that number, fired as "security risks," was revealed during congressional hearings in 1950, a Senate investigation followed, resulting in the report, "Employment of Homosexuals and Other Perverts in Government." The purge intensified in the fifties, and went beyond the State Department. Congress passed the Immigration and Nationality Act (McCarran-Walter Act) in 1952, banning homosexual immigrants, and the next year President Eisenhower issued Executive Order 10450, making homosexuality grounds for dismissal from federal employment. In effect, that Order further institutionalized homophobia in American society, and it was used as a basis for government hiring and firing until the 1970s.

Why did this occur? The answers are similar to those that explain the Red Scare, at least in terms of the ways both communists and homosexuals tapped into Cold War fears. At least three contexts merged at the time that heightened persecution of homosexuals: the parallel anticommunist crusade; the immediate legacy of purging lesbians and gay men from military service, through which psychiatrists gained new power in the culture; and ideas about sex that fueled a "sex crime panic." The first, the anticommunist purges, shared many elements with the Lavender Scare, especially in the common theme of infiltration by people who looked "normal" on the outside (and therefore were even more dangerous than those easily spotted), and the conviction that gays and communists posed equal serious security risks to the nation; if a homosexual was not also a communist (and vice versa), he/she might as well be. The definition as security risk hinged on the medical model, classified homosexuality as a perversion and characterized queers as mentally and morally unstable. By definition, then, "perverts" were a threat to the government and the nation. This led to the circular reasoning by which homosexuals were fired because of their potential to be black-mailed by foreign agents, while the chance of being blackmailed was caused by the stigma placed on homosexuality in the first place. Finally, in the same period there arose a "sex crime panic" reaching the status of "a genuinely national hysteria" at the end of the forties.[13] At that time the sexual assault and murder of girls in two states, added to the revelations in Alfred Kinsey's book on American male sexual behavior (see above, and the Debate), contributed to the idea of crimes motivated primarily by sexual desire. Children of both sexes were considered especially vulnerable to the perverts who possessed uncontrollable impulses, and gay men were prime targets. One of the more infamous examples occurred in Boise, Idaho, in 1955, in an event now also termed a "witch-hunt." Gay men there were subjected to a lengthy investigation after three men were charged with having sex with teenage boys. In the immediate aftermath,

> Boise's newspaper, *The Idaho Statesman,* responded to the arrests with a series of editorials demanding that prosecutors, the police and the community take action. The newspaper printed lines like "Crush the monster" and "This mess must be removed." ...The newspaper helped to ignite a witch hunt, in which many in Boise sought to rid the community of all of its gay men. More arrests followed: a lawyer, a teacher, and most sensational, the vice president of the city's largest bank. The roundup snared consenting adults as well as men who dallied with teens. By the time snow fell, scores of men had been questioned. Sixteen were charged, including one who was hauled back from San Francisco, where he had fled when the scandal broke.... [One of the sixteen] beat the charges. His steadfast denials, coupled with questions about the evidence against him, persuaded the jury to let him go.[14]

The dynamics of the sex crime furor and the Lavender Scare reached far beyond Washington, then. Another notorious case was that of Smith College literature professor Newton Arvin, detailed in Barry Werth's book *The Scarlet Professor* and in the 2006 independent film, *The Great Pink Scare.*[15] Arvin and several others were arrested in 1960 and convicted of possessing pornography and "lewd behavior" (then a code for homosexuality). Arvin was a respected author and critic and the scandal that followed, in which Arvin named other names, ruined his career and his mental health. Such actions were not confined to the North. In his account of antigay campaigns in Florida from 1956 to 1965, historian James A. Schnur summarized the common dynamics of the era. "Florida's homophobic witch-hunts served as a microcosm for cold war crack-downs throughout the nation," he wrote. "Politicians across America," he continued,

> sought to bolster the family at a time when promiscuity, adult literature, changing gender roles, and birth control became more prominent in heterosexual circles. In addition to these redefinitions of heterosexuality, Floridians faced racial crises, animosity between urban and rural regions, and unparalleled demographic growth.[16]

In Hollywood, just as there was a Red Scare there was a Lavender one of sorts. In this case, however, there was not an exact parallel. While large numbers of people were not fired for homosexuality, a general climate of homophobia prevailed in which the looming threat of unemployment, especially for stars, prevented any revelations on their part. The silence off screen, enforced by studios and agents in cooperation with the press, reflected the absence of queerness on screen, except in veiled terms; the provisions of the Hollywood Code banning references to homosexuality remained in effect until 1961. Despite that change, anything but criminal, sick, or doomed gay men and lesbians would be difficult to find on film for another decade (the film rating system of the Motion Picture Association of America replaced the Hollywood Production Code in 1968).

In general the films of the Cold War are a mixed bag, and like all films mirror their eras in what is selected as subject matter and the way it is treated. The blacklist prevented many talented people from working through the fifties and served to dampen any possible "political" statements (or anything that might be perceived as such), leading to "fluffy" romantic comedies or biblical epics like *The Ten Commandments* (1956) or *Ben-Hur* (1959). Other films, like *Invasion of the Body Snatchers* (1956), concern "alien invasion" in which the "aliens" can be read on several levels. In *Body Snatchers,* for example, the invaders literally take over the bodies of their victims and, like communists and homosexuals, they are especially dangerous because no one can tell who they are just by looking.

Before 1961 there was the occasional queer film reaching smaller audiences. The cult classic *Glen or Glenda,* featuring both transsexual and transvestite themes, was released in 1953, a product of "world's worst director" Ed Wood. Perhaps surprisingly, gay avant-garde filmmaking also began at this time, notably with Kenneth Anger's *Fireworks* (1947). In 1961 mainstream audiences could hear the word "homosexual" for the first time in a feature film in the British import *Victim.* Also that year Hollywood remade *The Children's Hour* and restored the original lesbian love story to the plot (although like the play, it still ends tragically). *Advise and Consent* (1962) pitted anticommunism directed at a secretary of state nominee against homophobia used against the main senatorial opponent of the nominee. A hidden homosexual past also figures in the plot of *The Best Man* (1964), a political drama about presidential politics adapted from the play by Gore Vidal. In 1966 Americans audiences first heard the word "lesbian" on-screen in *The Group,* in reference to the character played by Candice Bergen. Off screen if an actor or entertainer was gay, lesbian, or bisexual that fact was carefully hidden from the public. A number of actors and personalities, notably Rock Hudson, Anthony Perkins, and Liberace, were known to be gay by insiders but news or rumors of their homosexuality were quickly squelched. Unlike Liberace, who adopted an over-the-top "flamboyance" (often a code word implying homosexuality), most gay actors cultivated a masculine image and therefore fooled a public equating "perversion" with gender inversion. One of those was Tab Hunter, a teen heartthrob of the fifties who described the era in some detail in his 2005 memoir, *Tab Hunter Confidential.*[17] Hunter, in fact, was tested opposite Liberace for the film *Sincerely Yours* and reflected on that time:

> What a concept—the most extravagantly effeminate man in Hollywood, teamed with the all-American boy. What's even more outrageous is that, in 1954, the majority of the public had no idea *either* of us was gay. While I stayed in the closet, Liberace escaped "exposure" by wildly overplaying his homosexuality, turning it into a nonthreatening caricature.[18]

He also noted important context in the form of both fan magazines and the advent of gossip sheets like *Confidential,* founded in 1952. As a nod to the burgeoning youth culture, fan magazines saw teenage girls as a lucrative market and encouraged the creation of hunky teen idols who dated the current teen queens. Hunter was romantically linked with Natalie Wood, for example, stating that "America was crazy for celebrity couples. Every studio had to have its 'perfect pair.'"[19] However, the flip side of this was the potential for sensation and blackmail if the unspeakable was revealed, and that potential was tapped by *Confidential* and its imitators. The more shocking the secret the bigger the sales, and it did not get much more shocking then than hints of queer lives in Hollywood. If the Lavender Scare in Washington was one side of a coin that demanded secrecy and dishonesty from queer people, the official heterosexuality of movie stars was the other. Unlike anticommunism, these legacies affected American lives well past the end of the Cold War.

Queer Arts, American Arts

While the voices of many GLBT people were muted during this oppressive era, as a group they were never silenced entirely. As the next section, "A Homosexual Minority," illustrates, the chilly climate fostered not only fear and retreat but also significant organizing and publication on the part of self-defined homosexuals. It is also well to remember the influence of GLBT people in all realms of the American arts, at all times. The fifties were no exception, and in fact the claim that much of what is now considered important in American expression arose from queer perspectives can be shown to be true at this time.

The theatre of the era contains many examples of the interaction of queerness and the times, whether in creators' personal lives, their plots, or both. Important statements on race relations, for example, came from lesbians Lillian Smith, and Lorraine Hansberry. Smith wrote *Strange Fruit* (1944), a novel controversial for its treatment of interracial love, and it was adapted into a Broadway production in 1945. Hansberry's play *A Raisin in the Sun* (1959), about the struggles of an urban African American family, was the first by an African American woman to hit Broadway. It garnered multiple awards for both its original run and its 2004 revival, and is still considered a milestone of American theatre. Robert Anderson's *Tea and Sympathy,* premiering on Broadway in 1953, explored gender and sexuality in the story of a teenager persecuted as a "sissy" by fellow students. By that time gay writer Tennessee (Thomas Lanier) Williams, had seen several of his works produced and had received the Pulitzer Prize for *A Streetcar Named Desire* (1947). Williams, now considered one of America's foremost playwrights, went on to earn a second Pulitzer Prize for *Cat on a Hot Tin Roof* (1955). Homosexuality is a theme in *Cat on a Hot Tin Roof,* affecting the lives of main character Brick and those around him, and in Williams' *Suddenly Last Summer* (1958), in which a mother will go to great lengths to protect the secret that her dead son was gay. Typically for the time, the characters' sexuality is understood more through innuendo, and the implication of something terrible enough to hide.

Perhaps surprisingly, though, the early postwar years also saw the beginnings of what might be called a gay literature, meaning works not only written by gay men but also with gay men or gay life prominent in their subject matter. Gore Vidal's *The City and the Pillar* (1948) is considered a landmark in this respect, as are novels of African American author James Baldwin. Among Baldwin's many novels, *Giovanni's Room* (1956) was his first to feature a gay main character, and *Another Country* (1962) is important for its rare investigation into categories of race and sexuality. A year following *Another Country* (1962) writer John Rechy saw his *City of Night* published, a novel now considered a turning point in the gay literary history. It became a best seller, and did so with controversial material: the underground of gay hustlers. During these years, gay author Truman Capote was creating a new form of "reportage" from interviews collected in the wake of the 1959 murders of four members of a Kansas family. The result, *In Cold Blood* (1965), is considered the first "non-fiction novel" a form that can be seen as a forerunner of other hybrids like the docudrama.

Another genre was pulp fiction, both lesbian and gay. Definitions vary but pulp novels generally are cheaply produced paperbacks that often use sexually suggestive covers and titles to lure readers to purchase them. In postwar America any hint of queer content served the purpose and hundreds of these novels were published in the fifties and sixties. Some were books already published and then released in this form, such as Gore Vidal's *The City and the Pillar* (see above), while many associate the term with original titles written expressly for the pulp market (much like the heterosexually based "romance" novels aimed at straight women). While they offered the titillation of the sexually forbidden to straight readers they also provided at least some validation for queer readers, despite the tragic ends of most homosexual characters. Gay pulp included such works as *Whisper His Sin* (1954), by "Vin Packer" (Marijane Meaker), *The Strange Ones* (1959) by Ben Travis and the anonymously written *All the Sad Young Men* (1962). Some accounts date the origins of lesbian pulp at 1950, with the publication of *Women's Barracks* by Tereska Torres. The first queer-themed novel with a happy ending is said to be the lesbian love story *The Price of Salt* (1952) by Claire Morgan (Patricia Highsmith). An important writer in the genre is Ann Bannon, whose *Odd Girl Out* of 1957 initiated a series around the character Beebo Brinker (though Beebo does not appear in *Odd Girl Out*) that reached classic status. Another classic is the love story by Jane Rule, *Desert of the Heart* (1964), made into the film *Desert Hearts* in 1985; though definitely a period piece reflecting the moods and styles of the era, the film especially remains a favorite among lesbians seeking the same old-fashioned romance widely available to their straight sisters. Finally, a work meriting mention in this context is Jeannette Foster's *Sex Variant Women in Literature* (1956). For this study, wrote Caryn E. Neumann, Foster "deserves recognition as one of the foremothers of queer studies."[20]

There was a prominent queer presence in the fine and performing arts also—not a new phenomenon but one worth noting in this era as before. Here that presence is sometimes more difficult to pinpoint than in literature, at least in terms of obvious "content," and all the more so when abstract art or modern music is considered. In the paintings of Paul Cadmus, though, there is no such ambiguity. His career spanned much of the 20th century, from the thirties to his death in 1999. His earliest painting, *The Fleet's In!* (1934), was clearly homoerotic (as were his later works) and eventually it was removed from a New Deal-sponsored exhibit in Washington, DC. His style fell out of favor in the postwar years but he was reclaimed in the era of gay liberation as an influential pioneer. In between the thirties and the late sixties was the rise of abstract art in the United States, favored by "serious" artists but rejected as "subversive" on several levels during the Cold War. The paintings of people like Jasper Johns and Robert Rauschenberg were suspicious enough in their questioning of traditional subject and style, and the general association of abstract art with "foreign" influences.[21] The reaction had it been known then that they were not only gay but a couple for several years as well is hard to imagine. In the sixties the pop art of openly gay Andy Warhol and David Hockney once again represented recognizable objects (as abstract art had not) but threw them into question in unique ways. In performing arts the musical experiments of John Cage and the choreography of Merce Cunningham (who had a long-term relationship) are still considered among the most important innovations of the 20th century. Cage was in a long line of gay or bisexual American composers, from Charles Tomlinson Griffes (1884–1920) to Aaron Copland (1900–1990) and

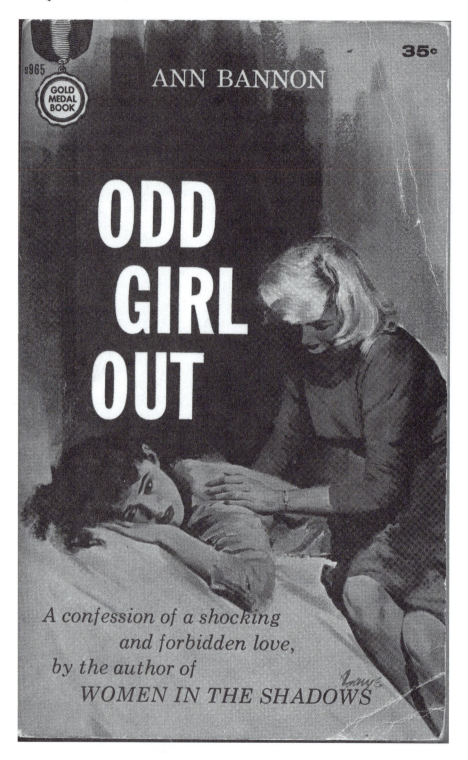

Odd Girl Out by Ann Bannon was first published in 1957 and became a classic of the lesbian pulp genre. The cover here, from the book's third printing in 1960, was the second of two paintings done by Barye Phillips after Bannon asked him for another version. (Ann Bannon)

Samuel Barber (1910–1981), to Leonard Bernstein (1918–1998) and Ned Rorem (b. 1923). The significance of these artists' sexuality, and its actual effects on their works will continue to be debated. Still, the point remains that Cold War queers made distinctive and lasting contributions to American's cultural life, and ironically were doing so in the midst of the search for their subversive influence.

A HOMOSEXUAL MINORITY

In 1983 historian John D'Emilio published a book that was instrumental in creating the field of GLBT history: *Sexual Politics, Sexual Communities: The Making of a Homosexual Minority in the United States, 1940–1970*. The term "minority" is key to understanding the change he outlined, since it designates a political relation to the rest of society. A minority group perceives itself as having less power than the majority as a result of institutionalized discrimination. That discrimination is justified by cultural biases against the group—racism, sexism, anti-Semitism, homophobia—that are based on one or more of shared characteristics—being nonwhite, female, Jewish, homosexual. Denial of equality under the law and of equal opportunities by the larger culture spark movements for civil rights, and their success appears to result from leadership, organization, and public sympathy. The relationships between individual and group identities on the one hand, and subcultures and movements on the other, continue to fascinate scholars and activists alike. Add the climate of oppression to the mix and the development of sexual identities, lesbian and gay subcultures, and organized opposition to oppression appear to form interdependently and sometimes paradoxically (oppression would seem to guarantee silence but instead breeds visibility and activism). In sorting out the relations between gay and lesbian subcultures and movement formation, D'Emilio claimed that "the subculture, or community, was the sea in which activists swam."[22] At the same time, a thriving subculture does not guarantee civil rights organizing; some would say it even undermines it, since the more secure individuals feel as a part of the community the less they may see any need for change (or, for privileged queers, the more they have at stake in the *status quo*). Despite apparently great odds against them, though, small groups of lesbian and gay men gathered to form organizations they called "homophile" and the foundation was laid for lesbian/gay rights, lesbian/gay liberation, and everything that came after them.

Communities and Identities

The formation and reformation of gay and lesbian subcultures after World War II reinforces the notion that more was going on in the fifties than met the public eye. Much like Kinsey's study in his time, recent works demonstrating a clear homosexual presence in cities, towns, and villages all over the country reveal realities of fifties America that are possibly shocking to those blinded by its shiny veneer. Within this topic, one issue scholars will continue to debate is that of identity formation, especially in relation to involvement in grassroots communities (political or not) and to external factors. In other words, do individuals seek out homosexual communities because they have already defined themselves as homosexual? If so, by what means do they arrive at that definition, or from what sources (medical professionals, novels, feeling "different" and finding others like them)? Does gender inversion (being a masculine woman or a feminine man) signify "homosexual"? Romantic feelings or sexual desire (separately or together) toward members of one's own sex? Who gets to decide and what are the implications of embracing the identity? This is not an exhaustive list, nor were the questions new in the 1950s. From this point on, though, GLBT people address them in various and increasingly visible ways that gradually sketch the contours of queer life for the rest of the 20th century.

As described in Chapter 6, older GLBT communities were revitalized and new one cropped up in the aftermath of World War II. The war had displaced thousands of Americans through mobilizing troops and war industries. In the process queer people met each other (many of them finding other like them for the first time) and decided to settle in the cities that provided employment, social opportunities, and anonymity if needed. Historians of the GLBT United States have turned increasing attention to local, urban, and regional studies, and they continue to demonstrate the breadth, vitality, and inner workings of queer communities, whether in distinct neighborhoods or through newsletters and magazines. The role of the latter in community formation is one of the areas detailed in Martin Meeker's significant contribution to the field, *Contacts Desired: Gay and Lesbian Communications and Community, 1940s–1970s* (2006).

Not surprisingly, interest has focused on San Francisco due to the political clout of its GLBT people, resulting in works such as those of Elizabeth Armstrong, Nan Alamilla Boyd, John D'Emilio, and Susan Stryker and Jim Van Buskirk (see Suggested Resources). Moving up and down the West Coast, newer studies include Gary L. Atkins' *Gay Seattle* (2003), Lillian Faderman and Stuart Timmons' *Gay L. A* (2006), and *Same-Sex Affairs: Constructing and Controlling Homosexuality in the Pacific Northwest* (2003) by Peter Boag. The Northeast has also generated important urban analyses, among them books by Charles Kaiser (New York), Elizabeth Kennedy and Madeline Davis (Buffalo), and Marc Stein (Philadelphia). Esther Newton's *Cherry Grove, Fire Island: Sixty Years in America's First Gay and Lesbian Town* (1993) shows how sex, gender, and class figure into what became a noted haven for queer people. Closer investigations of other cities—Boston, Charleston, Chicago, Denver, Minneapolis, Portland, Seattle, Washington, DC—are ongoing, as are regional works concerning the South, Midwest, and Mountain West. Rural studies reveal both similarities and differences when compared to urban situations. John Howard's work on the Deep South, for example, suggests that evangelical Protestant Christianity must be considered when evaluating GLBT communities and their politics, and responses to them.

The subfield of "urban geography" has contributed also to an appreciation of the formation and workings of queer identity and community. This includes both moderately visible neighborhoods within cities and the variety of public and private spaces created over time and in relation to circumstances. Perennial public areas for gay men in particular were restrooms (or tearooms) and parks, where they could engage in sexual activity. In Howard's account of Atlanta, he examines the politics of its parks and in the process highlights the singularity of southern religious culture and its role in queer history. "White Protestant Christianity of an evangelical variety dominated social and political life," he wrote, "and thereby began to dominate the ways in which public institutions addressed sexuality."[23] As heterosexual couples moved into public spaces like parks, city fathers added better lighting, with mixed results:

> In seeking first and foremost to shed light, and thus a measure of safety, on heterosexual couples parking on the grounds, city fathers uncovered the homosexual activity that had long been a trademark of this and other public spaces. As heterosexual courtship assumed a new visibility and legitimacy in the public sphere, homosexual men shared in that visibility, but became all the more illegitimate.[24]

Geography also intersects with considerations of sex, gender, and class. Gender constraints had always included a double standard of sexual activity for women generally, and especially "respectable" women, and that standard did not include public sex or sexually suggestive displays. The same was true of men in theory but in practice male (hetero) sexuality in general has been key to definitions of masculinity and thus an implicit part of a male public role. As class divisions were clarified, working class people of all sexualities had of necessity often used public spaces for courting and more. Finally, the "masculine" presentation of many working class lesbians corresponded with their ability (or attempts) to claim "male" public space, though not without harassment.

Class was a significant factor among women, in fact, and again corresponded to disputes over gender presentation. Middle and upper class lesbians and bisexual women generally preferred more private venues for socializing—someone's house or apartment—and resisted the division into butch and femme (or fem) lesbians. For their part, working class women of all ethnicities often organized their public and private lives around this division, butches being those with "masculine" clothing, hair, behavior, etc., and femmes in traditionally "feminine" roles, appearance, and demeanor. They were equally disdainful of the lack of clear roles among privileged women, using terms like "bluff" ("butch" + "fluff") and "kiki." Both terms, according to Lillian Faderman, referred to "those who would not choose a role." While kiki women ridiculed the appearance of copying heterosexual roles, wrote Faderman, "Butches and femmes thought these 'kiki' women were the ones who were buckling under by dressing like conventional women. It was something of a class war."[25] Further explorations of roles include those of Joan Nestle and the work of Elizabeth Kennedy and Madeline Davis on Buffalo's lesbians, *Boots of Leather, Slippers of Gold* (1993). Kennedy and Davis include a thorough exploration of butch and fem (their spelling) and counter later lesbian feminist critiques with a defense of the roles. Butch/fem, they claim, were not merely copies of the larger sexist culture but instead played a crucial part in organizing public lives and in developing community. Significantly, *Boots* also traces some change from the older medical model, in which the only queers were the inverts (butch women and femme men), to the use of object choice to define sexuality (fem women and butch men could also be homosexual). Equally important, it was a change at the grassroots rather than one arising from the dictates of professionals. As for actual spaces, butch lesbians (often calling themselves dykes) could be found playing softball and other sports, and they frequented the bars that were so central to identity, community, and ultimately to the rise of a movement.

The key role played by bars in GLBT history has been suggested in Chapter 3 and the story continues to the present. In this era separate gay bars and lesbian bars, as opposed to those with mixed hetero/homo clientele, proliferated around the country and were important locales for forming and expressing identities. In this era too the generalized homophobia meant these bars, often run by organized crime, would retain the kind of underground status of bars during Prohibition. They were allowed to exist but perpetually subject to police raids, especially in elections seasons when public officials needed a quick way to prove their devotion to (heterosexual) law and order. As before, they were sites where a group consciousness formed but now existed as part and parcel of new organization around a minority identity. In San Francisco, for instance, the link between bars and a budding movement dates at least to 1951, when the California Supreme Court, in a case brought by the owner of the "bohemian" Black Cat, upheld the right of bars to serve homosexuals. The Black Cat also featured legendary drag queen José Sarria in the fifties and in turn he engaged in political work from that base. In 1960 he and others founded the League for Civil Education and the next year he ran for city supervisor. He lost, but as the first openly gay person in the United States to run for public office he paved the way for openly GLBT candidates at all levels of government. In 1962 San Francisco bar owners formed the Tavern Guild as a response to police harassment. By that time the Guild was one of several collective efforts that came to define the new activism of a homophile movement.

Postwar Organizations

In 1950 the idea of organizing homosexuals around their common sexual identity and their common oppression was not unprecedented. Neither was the goal of educating others through speaking, publishing, and soliciting help from legal and medical professionals. As early as 1924 Henry Gerber had founded the Society for Human Rights in Chicago to confront homophobia with education and in 1945 former soldiers formed the Veterans' Benevolent Association (see Chapter 3). The first survived less than a year, however, which limited its lasting impact or even the memory of it by anyone outside Chicago two decades later. The VBA continued to 1954, overlapping the early years of the homophile groups, but as a veterans' group was narrower in scope than ones devoted to homosexuals generally. Likewise, magazines aimed at lesbians and gay men were not unique to the new organizations. In mid-1947, "Lisa Ben" (an anagram for lesbian, now known to be Edythe Eyde) wrote the first of nine issues of the newsletter *Vice Versa*. It was aimed at other lesbians and she mailed out several copies in her home city of Los Angeles. *Vice Versa* folded before homophile groups got underway but other publications for male and female homosexuals would take its place. Paralleling those were the male bodybuilding magazines, among them the pioneering quarterly *Physique Pictorial,* produced by Bob Mizer for gay men and sold nationally in the early fifties. Through these means and many others, as seen above, some homosexual Americans gained a new pride as they gathered to discuss their status and secure their rights. When they did they adopted the term "homophile" ("loving the same") to emphasize a departure from the language and imagery of sick or criminal homosexuals.

The first homophile organization was Mattachine, which lasted ten years as a national entity, first as the Mattachine Foundation (1951–1953) and then as the Mattachine Society (1953–1961). After 1961 local chapters continued through the 1970s. The name derived from groups of masked performers in medieval France who sometimes protested injustice and fostered group solidarity. Harry Hay is credited as the principal founder, with a small group that included Chuck Rowland, Dale Jennings, and Bob Hull. Hay was schooled in Marxism and had belonged to the American Communist Party, factors which influenced the ideology and organization of the Foundation. When asked later why he conceived of Mattachine in the late forties, Hay recalled first the anti-communist investigations into Hollywood and the State Department purges:

> The country, it seemed to me, was beginning to move towards fascism and McCarthyism; the Jews wouldn't be used as a scapegoat this time—the painful example of Germany was still too clear to us. The Black organizations were already pretty successfully looking out for their interests. It was obvious McCarthy was setting up the pattern for a new scapegoat, and it was going to be us—Gays. We had to organize, we had to move, we had to get started.[26]

In 1951 they did get started in Los Angeles and within two years the organization had spread outside LA and into Northern California, with perhaps 2,000 lesbians and gay men involved. Mattachine adopted the secrecy and decentralized mode of communist cells, in which members knew only the identity of those in their own cell. Within the cells, though, the Foundation advocated a group consciousness based on common oppression, a view influenced by Marxist thought, and their stated goals were "to unify," "to educate," "to lead," and to promote "political action."[27]

Within the first few years there were at least three significant developments related to Mattachine: internal division; the founding of ONE, Inc., and the advent of *Mattachine Review.* Beginning a pattern that would be repeated throughout GLBT movement history, a struggle over leadership and direction emerged by 1953, resulting in the ousting of the founders and the election of new leaders, including Hal Call, Kenneth Burns, and Marilyn Rieger. The Mattachine Society was then formed in place of the Foundation, and the organization became more "conservative," at least in comparison to its radical origins and the assimilationist (or accommodationist) stance which came to characterize much of the homophile movement. (At the same time, it is difficult to call *any* group defending homosexuals "conservative" in the context of Cold War America.)

ONE, Inc. grew independently out of the Mattachine Foundation in 1952 and in January 1953 printed the first issue of *ONE* magazine, an important movement publication until 1968. Dorr Legg, *ONE*'s business manager, influenced the magazine's content and tone, and became "the movement's first fulltime worker." ONE, Inc. and *ONE* magazine maintained the more "militant spirit" of the Mattachine Foundation, and in 1958 the publication won a significant legal victory when the U.S. Supreme Court unanimously upheld the right of the magazine to exist and be sent through the mail.[28] In the meantime, the ONE Institute was founded, in 1955, to address ONE Inc.'s additional goals involving education, research, and social service. The next year it introduced the college-level course "homophile studies," the first of its kind, and in 1961 sponsored sessions on the subject of "A Homosexual Bill of Rights." Meanwhile the San Francisco chapter of the Mattachine Society began publishing its own journal in 1955, the *Mattachine Review. ONE* is considered the more "radical" of the two magazines but again the terms are relative and refer to tone as much as content. The *Mattachine Review* survived until 1966 and contributed to communication among lesbian and gay Americans and the promotion of gay culture and gay rights.

The national offices of Mattachine relocated to San Francisco in 1957 but four years later the Society was disbanded. By that time there were several chapters outside California in such cities as Boston, Denver, Detroit, New York City, and Philadelphia, and more were established in the mid and late sixties. In late 1961 Frank Kameny, Jack Nichols, and others founded the Mattachine Society of Washington with Kameny as its president. He had just emerged from a four-year legal battle with the U.S. government, a victim of its antigay purges. In 1957 he was fired from his job as astronomer with the Army Map Service in and began a process that culminated in the U.S. Supreme Court, who refused to hear his case. Significantly, he used the language and rationale of Constitutional rights and was in the forefront of establishing an increasingly "militant" arm of homophile activism. His messages and tactics predated Stonewall (1969) and even in the era of gay liberation that followed he continued his role as a recognized movement leader (see Chapters 5 and 6 also).

The third organization, after Mattachine and ONE, Inc., rounding out the main structure of early homophile activism was the DOB (Daughters of Bilitis). It began in 1955 when eight women in San Francisco gathered to discuss an association and from that came the country's first national lesbian group; they took the name from Pierre Louys' *Songs of Bilitis,* a literary reference to lesbianism. Phyllis Lyon and Del Martin

Frank Kameny has had a rare, fifty-year career as a gay activist. He is pictured here in 1971 amid the files of the Mattachine Society of Washington, DC, which he helped found ten years earlier. (Barbara Gittings and Kay Tobin Lahusen Gay History Papers and Photographs, Inc. of New York Records, Manuscripts and Archives Division, the New York Public Library, Astor, Lenox and Tilden)

were among those eight and emerged as leaders of the DOB and of homophile activism by the end of the decade. They soon expanded their purpose beyond socializing (though not without some dissent) and launched a small but key organization whose mission was both feminist and pro-homosexual. That is, maintaining DOB as strictly a lesbian organization reflected the conviction that the experiences and status of lesbians, though similar to those of gay men, also differed from those of any men. While homophobia united gay men and lesbians in a common oppression, and enforced gender roles stigmatized effeminate men as well as butch women, sexism uniquely affects females. The DOB adopted a mission that emphasized education and research, and sought the help of professionals in law, medicine, and religion. Like other mid-fifties homophile goals, theirs were a mixture of "conservative" and "radical" and cannot be categorized simply or in relation to later circumstances. On the one hand they believed that change would come by "advocating a mode of behavior and dress acceptable to society"; on the other, they referred to themselves as a "minority group" and promoted legal change and society's acceptance of homosexuality.[29] As time passed they and many of their male homophile counterparts came to seem overly optimistic and too "assimilationist," or too anxious to present themselves as "good Americans" in order to avoid persecution (see Debate, Chapter 6). They shared the conviction that U.S. society and institutions were basically good but people had been misinformed. Individuals, to the extent that their homosexuality became known, could act as ambassadors of sorts to change opinions.

During its fifteen-year existence the group also founded an important publication and added chapters throughout the nation. Only a year after their initial meetings the DOB launched the *Ladder* in San Francisco, a newsletter that became a significant literary journal and educational tool. Like *ONE* and *Mattachine Review* it reflected the faith in journalism and publication as a means of educating the public while creating community among far-flung individuals. The *Ladder* provided homophile news and solicited letters, poetry, and prose from its readers. Not only was it an outlet for aspiring lesbian writers—Rita Mae Brown and Valerie Taylor, for example—but it also helped to create the movement as a whole. The DOB was dissolved as a national entity in 1970 and at that point the *Ladder* became a lesbian feminist journal under the direction of Barbara Grier, ceasing publication in 1972. Between its founding and demise, the DOB spread to cities across the United States. In 1958 a Los Angeles chapter took shape, and the first chapter on the East Coast, the New York DOB, was founded by Barbara Gittings and others. By the sixties chapters existed in Boston, Chicago, Denver, and New Orleans and several other cities. The first national lesbian conference was a DOB-sponsored event held in San Francisco in 1960. The changes brought about by gay liberation and lesbian feminism coincided with the end of DOB, but its contribution in laying a foundation for pride and activism is profound.

On the East Coast a fourth organization arose and it was influential in the change of tone and tactics that occurred in the sixties. Like ONE, Inc. it can trace its lineage to Mattachine, but this time the decision for a separate organization arose from circumstances: a Mattachine chapter had been formed in Philadelphia just as the national group dissolved. In that way Janus Society of the Delaware Valley was born in 1962, and it thrived as a mixed sex group until disbanding in 1969. In its first two years, during which Mae Polakoff was president, Janus followed the patterns of the homophile movement: it embraced education, sponsored lectures by professionals, and encouraged gay men and lesbians to adhere to societal gender norms. In 1963, Clark Polak became president and brought about changes in Janus. He rejected the cautious tone of homophile accommodation and advocated the broader goal of sexual liberation. The group's newsletter became *Drum* magazine (1964–1969), a prominent addition to the literature of the early movement. As publisher and editor of *Drum* Polak exerted a powerful influence in East Coast activism, and the magazine's circulation grew to about 15,000, surpassing that of all other homophile publications combined. While heading Janus, Polak also founded the Homosexual Law Reform Society (1965–1969), a group involved in key legal cases in the later sixties (see Chapter 5).

A National Movement

In 1951, the same year that Harry Hay and a few like-minded men founded Mattachine a writer using the name Donald Webster Cory published *The Homosexual*

DEBATE: WHAT DID THE KINSEY STUDIES PROVE?

When Alfred Kinsey published *Sexual Behavior in the Human Male* (1948) and *Sexual Behavior in the Human Female* (1953) the books created a sensation, became best sellers, and laid the foundation for postwar sexology. They were the result of years of research involving over 11,000 in-depth interviews on a wide variety of sexual practices. Like some earlier sexologists, Kinsey regarded sex as a subject of scientific inquiry, separate from societal mores and judgments. He wrote, "This is first of all a report on what people do, which raises no question of what they should do, or what kinds of people do it."[30] Not everyone agreed, of course, and the works dubbed the Kinsey Reports did stimulate concern about the state of American society as reflected in sexual practices. They have generated debate also about the purpose, validity, and applications of their contents.

Kinsey's supporters and critics alike have questioned his intentions and his methods. His claims of objective research, conducted without preconception or bias, are challenged in two ways. One is from the perspective that *no* research, scientific or not, can completely eliminate the bias built into any human endeavor. The other is more specific to Kinsey and charges that he did have an agenda and that it rendered his findings suspect. In other words, Kinsey had some "shoulds" of his own, though they concerned opinions rather than behaviors: Americans should be aware of actual practices, should not experience guilt over those practices, and the result should be "nothing short of a revolution in Americans' attitudes toward sex."[31] Whether or not that revolution could occur rested partly on his methods as well. The size and especially the makeup of his sample raised doubts about it being representative of American men and women. Subjects were volunteers rather than randomly selected and such populations as college students or prison inmates may be overrepresented. Collecting oral data, although remarkably thorough in this case, always raises issues of subtle influences during the interview process (as it does in oral history).

Probably no portion of the reports has generated more discussion, interpretation, and adaptation than the data on bisexuality and homosexuality. By the time Kinsey published, the heterosexual/homosexual binary was becoming firmly entrenched in American thought, especially scientific thought; one was normal (hetero) or "deviant" (homo or bi) based variously on desires, behaviors, and gender presentation. What one did (or wanted to) had become a *type* of person, an idea embraced by self-described queers as much as those trying to cure them. Kinsey doubted the validity of such classifications, suspecting that at best they limited our understanding of actual human experience and, at worst, created secrecy and guilt when a sexual identity was virtually outlawed. To that end he included questions about same-sex activity and his findings shocked an America where queers had become largely invisible: 37 percent of the males interviewed reported same-sex activity to orgasm while 46 percent of the men had "reacted to" men as well as women sexually (the numbers for women were smaller and for a number of reasons created less concern by themselves, though the idea that women were sexual at all was still explosive).

From his data Kinsey developed his infamous seven-point scale of (male) sexuality, and plotted subjects on the scale according to their testimonies:

0—Exclusively heterosexual with no homosexual

1—Predominantly heterosexual, only incidentally homosexual

2—Predominantly heterosexual, but more than incidentally homosexual

3—Equally heterosexual and homosexual

4—Predominantly homosexual, but more than incidentally heterosexual

5—Predominantly homosexual, only incidentally heterosexual

6—Exclusively homosexual

"Males," he explained, "do not represent two discrete populations, heterosexual and homosexual. The world is not to be divided into sheep and goats. It is a fundamental of taxonomy that nature rarely deals with discrete categories.... The living world is a continuum in each and every one of its aspects." Further, he advocated a continuum of personal sexuality over time and therefore added, "An individual may be assigned a position on this scale, for each period in his life."[32] Finally, his data are reflected in the "ten percent" figure eventually adopted by gay/lesbian rights advocates; according to Kinsey, ten percent of the males were "predominantly homosexual" and eight percent "exclusively homosexual for at least three years" between ages sixteen and fifty-five; four percent "had been exclusively homosexual after the onset of adolescence up to the time of their interviews."[33]

One of the ironies of the debates over Kinsey is the certainty attached to the ten percent figure by GLBT activists as much as by their opponents. For the first group, it "proves" at least a fixed population that cannot be denied rights; for the other it is a group too small to be relevant in electoral politics. Bisexual activists have stayed closer to Kinsey's purposes, though they too want to claim a reality of identity based on numbers. However, they remind us that if the data suggest any majority identity, it is bisexuality, not heterosexuality, since overall the numbers suggest that *exclusive* heterosexuality is as small a minority as *exclusive* heterosexuality. What is even clearer is that what the Kinsey Reports prove is that humans will adapt information to fit their own times, places, and needs.

in America: A Subjective Approach. It was an unusual work and an influential one for soon-to-be homophile organizers, for in its pages he argued strongly that homosexuals shared a "minority" status with other groups and like other minorities were denied civil rights and social equality. From those basic ideas the outlines of a national movement were drawn, the substance to be added, changed, and disputed from that time to this. To claim that the sum of accomplishments of the movement to 1963 are meager, as some do, may reflect expectations born of a later era more than the possibilities of the fifties. It would be hard to imagine a more difficult climate in which to organize homosexuals to fight for respect and equality. As John D'Emilio put it, "...the movement took upon itself an impossible burden—appearing respectable to a society that defined homosexuality as beyond respectability."[34]

As the year 1963 began no one could know that events in the coming months would change the contours of U.S. history. In August 200,000 peaceful demonstrators would gather for the March on Washington for Jobs and Freedom and hear powerful voices speak for racial justice. Less than four months later, on November 22, President John F. Kennedy was killed while riding in a motorcade in Dallas. Looking back, the assassination seemed a turning point of one kind or another: either away from the confidence, prosperity, and youthful optimism symbolized by the Kennedys toward the darker days of war, protest, and dishonest government; or away from the façade of consensus and contentment toward a welcome era of heightened social consciousness and agitation towards justice "for all." In was in 1963 also that a new association was created by the homophile groups. That January in Philadelphia members of Mattachine's New York and DC chapters and DOB's New York group combined with Janus to form ECHO (East Coast Homophile Organizations) and met in September for its first conference. To many GLBT people this too signaled the end of one era and the beginning of another, in which blossomed the involvement and tactics that came to define "the sixties."

NOTES

1. Martin Duberman, *About Time: Exploring the Gay Past* (New York: Gay Presses of New York, 1986), 359, 344, 377; Martin Duberman, *Cures: A Gay Man's Odyssey* (New York: Dutton, 1991), 3.

2. John Morton Blum, *V Was for Victory: Politics and American Culture During World War II* (New York: Harcourt Brace Jovanovich, 1976); Franklin D. Roosevelt, "The Four Freedoms," Annual Message to Congress, January 6, 1941.

3. Godfrey Hodgson, *America In Our Time* (New York: Vintage Books, 1976), 75; also see his entire chap. 4, "The Ideology of the Liberal Consensus," 67–98.

4. Kinsey's data are available at http://www.kinseyinstitute.org/research/ak-data.html.

5. James T. Sears, "Race, Class, Gender, and Sexuality in Pre-Stonewall Charleston: Perspectives on the Gordon Langley Hall Affair," in *Carryin' On in the Lesbian and Gay South,* ed. John Howard (New York: New York University Press, 1997); quotes pp. 179 and 185.

6. Allan Bérubé, *Coming Out Under Fire: The History of Gay Men and Women in World War Two* (New York: The Free Press, 1990), 259.

7. Eric Marcus, *Making Gay History: The Half-Century Fight for Lesbian and Gay Equal Rights* (New York: Harper Perennial, 2002), 58–59.

8. Richard R. Lingeman, "There Was Another Fifties," *New York Times Magazine,* June 17, 1973, 27.

9. "Special Message to the Congress on Urgent National Needs," May 25, 1961, at http://www.jfklibrary.org/Historical+Resources/Archives/Reference+Desk/Speeches/JFK/Urgent+National+Needs+Page+4.htm.

10. "Inaugural Address of President John F. Kennedy," January 20, 1961, at http://www.jfklibrary.org/Historical+Resources/Archives/Reference+Desk/Speeches/JFK/003POF03Inaugural01201961.htm.

11. Section 2, paragraph 11, at http://www.rosenbergtrial.org/docmcaran.html.

12. David K. Johnson, *The Lavender Scare: The Cold War Persecution of Gays and Lesbians in the Federal Government* (Chicago: University of Chicago Press, 2004), 2.

13. George Chauncey, Jr., "The Postwar Sex Crime Panic," in *True Stories from the American Past,* ed. William Graebner (New York: McGraw-Hill, 1993), 163.

14. Seth Randal and Alan Virta, "Idaho's Original Same-Sex Scandal," *The New York Times,* September 2, 2007, at http://www.nytimes.com/2007/09/02/opinion/02randal.html.

15. Barry Werth, *The Scarlet Professor: Newton Arvin: A Literary Life Shattered by Scandal* (New York: Anchor Books, 2002). Information on the film can be found at http://www.pbs.org/independentlens/greatpinkscare.

16. James A. Schnur, "Closet Crusaders: The Johns Committee and Homophobia, 1956–1965," in *Carryin' On in the Lesbian and Gay South,* ed. John Howard (New York: New York University Press, 1997), 156.

17. Tab Hunter, with Eddie Muller, *Tab Hunter Confidential: The Making of a Movie Star* (Chapel Hill, NC: Algonquin Books, 2005).

18. Hunter, *Tab Hunter Confidential,* 107.

19. Ibid., 125.

20. Caryn E. Neumann, "Foster, Jeannette Howard," *glbtq: An Encyclopedia of Gay, Lesbian, Bisexual, Transgender, and Queer Culture,* 2003, http://www.glbtq.com/literature/foster_jh.html.

21. See Jane de Hart Mathews, "Art and Politics in Cold War America," *American Historical Review* 81, no. 4 (October 1976): 762–87.

22. John D'Emilio, *Sexual Politics, Sexual Communities: The Making of a Homosexual Minority in the United States, 1940–1970* (Chicago: University of Chicago Press, 1983; 1998), xiii.

23. John Howard, "The Library, the Park, and the Pervert: Public Space and Homosexual Encounter in Post-World War II Atlanta," in *Carryin' On in the Lesbian and Gay South,* ed. John Howard (New York: New York University Press, 1997), 122.

24. Howard, "The Library, the Park, and the Pervert," 118.

25. Lillian Faderman, *Odd Girls and Twilight Lovers: A History of Lesbian Life in Twentieth-Century America* (New York: Penguin Books, 1992), quotes pp. 168, 181; also see chap. 7, "Butches, Femmes, and Kikis: Creating Lesbian Subcultures in the 1950s and '60s."

26. Quoted in Jonathan Ned Katz, *Gay American History: Lesbians and Gay Men in the U.S.A.,* rev. ed. (New York: Penguin Meridian, 1992), 408.

27. Katz, *Gay American History,* 412.

28. Phrases quoted from D'Emilio, *Sexual Politics,* 88, 87.

29. Katz, *Gay American History,* 426.

30. Kinsey et al., *Sexual Behavior in the Human Male* (Philadelphia: W.B. Saunders Company, 1948), 7.

31. http://www.pbs.org/wgbh/amex/kinsey/peopleevents/.

32. Kinsey et al., *Sexual Behavior in the Human Male,* 639; quoted at http://www.kinseyinstitute.org/research/ak-hhscale.html.

33. Ibid., 651; quoted at http://www.kinseyinstitute.org/research/ak-data.html. For a good summary see the Web site accompanying the PBS production of the documentary, *Kinsey* (2005): http://www.pbs.org/wgbh/amex/kinsey/. Also, in 2004 the feature film *Kinsey* was released, starring Liam Neeson in the title role.

34. D'Emilio, *Sexual Politics,* 125.

SUGGESTED RESOURCES

General

Bronski, M. (2003). *Pulp friction: Uncovering the golden age of gay male pulps.* New York: St. Martin's Press.

Chadwick, W., & de Courtivron, I. (Eds.). (1993). *Significant others: Creativity and intimate partnership.* London: Thames and Hudson.

Corber, R.J. (1997). *Homosexuality in Cold War America: Resistance and the crisis of masculinity.* Durham: Duke University Press.

Cory, D.W. [E. Sagarin]. (1951). *The homosexual in America: A subjective approach.* New York: Greenberg Press.

Forrest, K.V. (2005). *Lesbian pulp fiction: The sexually intrepid world of lesbian paperback novels 1950–1965.* San Francisco: Cleis Press.

Foster, J. (1956). *Sex variant women in literature: A historical and quantitative survey.* New York: Vantage Press.

Freeman, C. (2001). Something they did in the dark: Lesbian and gay novels in the United States, 1948–1973. In A. Black (Ed.), *Modern American queer history* (pp. 131–151). Philadelphia: Temple University Press.

Gerassi, J. (1966/2001). *The Boys of Boise: Furor, vice, and folly in an American city.* New York: Macmillan; Seattle: University of Washington Press.

Gladney, M.R. (2001). Paula Snelling: A significant other. In A. Black (Ed.), *Modern American queer history* (pp. 69–78). Philadelphia: Temple University Press.

Gorman, M.R. (1998). *The empress is a man: Stories from the life and times of Jose Sarria.* Binghamton, NY: Haworth Press.

Irvine, J.M. (1990). *Disorders of desire: Sex and gender in modern American sexology.* Philadelphia: Temple University Press.

Johnson, D.K. (2004). *The Lavender Scare: The Cold War persecution of gays and lesbians in the Federal Government.* Chicago: University of Chicago Press.

Jorgensen, C. (with a new introduction by Stryker, S.) (2000). *Christine Jorgensen: A personal autobiography* (2nd ed.). San Francisco: Cleis Press.

Kepner, J. (1998). *Rough news, daring views: 1950'S pioneer gay press journalism.* Binghamton, NY: Haworth Press.

Meyer, R. (2002). *Outlaw representation: Censorship and homosexuality in twentieth-century American art.* New York: Oxford University Press.

Miller, N. (2002). *Sex-crime panic: A journey to the paranoid heart of the 1950s.* Boston: Alyson Publications.

Stryker, S. (2001). *Queer pulp: Perverted passions from the golden age of the paperback.* San Francisco: Chronicle Books.

Community and Subculture Formation

Armstrong, E. (2002). *Forging gay identities: Organizing sexuality in San Francisco, 1950–1994.* Chicago: University of Chicago Press.

Atkins, G.L. (2003). *Gay Seattle: Stories of exile and belonging.* Seattle: University of Washington Press.

Beemyn, B. (Ed.). (1997). *Creating a place for ourselves: Lesbian, gay, and bisexual community histories.* New York: Routledge.

Boyd, N.A. (2003). *Wide open town: A history of queer San Francisco to 1965.* Berkeley: University of California Press.

Buring, D. (1997). Softball and alcohol: The limits of lesbian community in Memphis from the 1940s through the 1960s. In J. Howard (Ed.), *Carryin' on in the lesbian and gay south* (pp. 203–223). New York: New York University Press.

D'Emilio, J. (1989). Gay politics and community in San Francisco since World War II. In M. Duberman, M. Vicinus, & G. Chauncey, Jr. (Eds.), *Hidden from history: Reclaiming the gay and lesbian past* (pp. 456–473). New York: New American Library.

Faderman, L., & Timmons, S. (2006). *Gay L. A.: A history of sexual outlaws, power politics, and lipstick lesbians.* New York: Basic Books.

Howard, J. (1999). *Men like that: A southern queer history.* Chicago: University of Chicago Press.

Kaiser, C. (1997). *The gay metropolis, 1940–1996.* Boston: Houghton Mifflin.

Kennedy, E., & Davis, M. (1993). *Boots of leather, slippers of gold: The history of a lesbian community.* New York: Routledge.

Meeker, M. (2006). *Contacts desired: Gay and lesbian communications and community, 1940s–1970s.* Chicago: University of Chicago.

Newton, E. (1993). *Cherry Grove, Fire Island: Sixty years in America's first gay and lesbian town.* Boston: Beacon Press.

Stein, M. (2004). *City of sisterly and brotherly loves: Lesbian and gay Philadelphia, 1945–1972.* Philadelphia: Temple University Press.

Stryker, S., & Van Buskirk, J. (1996). *Gay by the bay: A history of queer culture in the San Francisco bay area.* San Francisco: Chronicle Books.

Zipter, Y. (1988). *Diamonds are a dyke's best friend: Reflections, reminiscences, and reports from the field on the lesbian national pastime.* Ithaca, NY: Firebrand Books.

Homosexual/Homophile Organizing

Boag, P. (2004, Spring). 'Does Portland Need a Homophile Society?' Gay culture and activism in the Rose City between World War II and Stonewall. *Oregon Historical Quarterly, 105,* 6–39.

Gallo, M.M. (2006). *Different daughters: A history of the Daughters of Bilitis and the rise of the lesbian rights movement.* New York: Carroll & Graf.

Legg, W.D. (1994). *Homophile studies in theory and practice.* San Francisco: GLB Publishers and ONE Institute Press.

Marcus, E. (2002). *Making gay history: The half-century fight for lesbian and gay equal rights.* New York: Harper Perennial.

Poling, J.D. (2005, Spring). Standing up for gay rights. *Chicago History, 33,* 4–17.

Rimmerman, C.A. (2002). *From identity to politics: The lesbian and gay movements in the United States.* Philadelphia: Temple University Press.

Sears, J.T. (2007). *Behind the Mask of the Mattachine: The Hal Call chronicles and the early movement for homosexual emancipation.* Binghamton, NY: Haworth Press.

Timmons, S. (1990). *The trouble with Harry Hay: Founder of the modern gay movement.* Boston: Alyson Publications.

5 THE SIXTIES

Philadelphia, July 4, 1965. Forty-four homosexuals march at Independence Hall on the nation's birthday. "It was the proudest moment of my life," Lilli Vincenz said decades later, "...to be walking there and to not be afraid and hold up that picket sign and to say 'this is who I am and this is what I stand for and...what's being said about homosexuals is a lie.'" They are marching, Barbara Gittings recalled, "to remind the public that a large group of citizens is denied the rights and equality promised by the Declaration of Independence." Indeed, some picketers carry signs at this and similar demonstrations that make the points explicit: "Homosexuals Ask For Equality Before the Law," "Homosexual Americans Demand Their Civil Rights," and the lengthy "The Pursuit of Happiness an Inalienable Right for Homosexuals Also."

The well-dressed men and women circling quietly with signs upraised represented something of a transition between the "homophile" movement of the 1950s and the more visible and often "militant" activism of the 1970s. Some had already marched a half-dozen times since the previous fall, at such sites as Manhattan's U.S. Army induction center, the White House, and the Civil Service Commission. In each case, the picketers sought to raise public awareness about government-sanctioned discrimination against homosexual Americans, and in doing so offer visible proof that gay men and lesbians were not half-crazed, child-molesting monsters. Later activists sometimes ridiculed the picketers' strict dress and conduct codes ("men will wear suits, white shirts, and ties, women will wear dresses; picketers will be well groomed; signs will be neatly and clearly lettered; signs will always be carried in the designated order," etc.) but the goals were to highlight the messages over the people carrying them and, said Vincenz, "to make us look normal."

The timing was significant; 1965, said Frank Kameny, was "our picketing year" with at least nine marches, and the demonstration at Independence Hall became the Annual Reminder for four more years. The picketers were able to build on both previous homophile actions and models offered by the civil rights, student, and antiwar movements of that turbulent decade. By the last Annual Reminder in 1969, the Stonewall riot was only days old, and according to most accounts the era of gay liberation had begun. However, Kameny emphasized continuity between eras of GLBT history: "Those demonstrations led directly into Stonewall in '69." Picketer Randolfe Wicker agreed, in more vivid language: "We built the airplane and those queens from Stonewall just climbed into it and flew off with it."[1]

When the homophile picketers selected July 4 as a day of protest they followed the lead, knowingly or not, of radical abolitionists before the Civil War. To those earlier reformers, July 4 was the ideal day to draw attention to the nation's promises celebrated in the Declaration of Independence and to the gap between those promises and the reality lived by enslaved Americans. More than a century later, activists for the civil rights of African Americans, women, and homosexuals, among others, revived the fervor and tactics of their forebears who shared their outrage over inequalities in the "land of the free."

A continuation of civil rights agitation, whether from the fifties or the entire century since the Civil War, was only one of the factors that have come to define the era. Also significant were a new wave of feminism and a rebellion of youth that took many forms, including a "counterculture" that challenged American society at its core. The key event, however, was the Vietnam War, without which there may have been no "sixties" as we now understand the term. In retrospect, it is hardly surprising that people targeted in previous years for sexual nonconformity would draw upon their own experiences as well as those of other groups to fight back with words and actions. As they did so they inaugurated a new phase of activism known as "gay (and lesbian, eventually) liberation."

DREAMS OF CHANGE

The African American civil rights movement through the fifties provided important models of thought and action for other activists of the era and after (see Chapter 4). Not surprisingly, the racial basis of discrimination in the United States was increasingly intolerable in a country that held itself up as the beacon of freedom in the postwar world. Although members of other groups also rejected the enforced conformity and inequalities of the time they were silenced, ignored, or they directed their rebellion into poetry and music. That would all change in the watershed year of 1963.

Marching on Washington

On August 28, 1963, in front of more than 200,000 marchers gathered at the Lincoln Memorial, Rev. Martin Luther King, Jr. said that African Americans were still waiting for the fulfillment of the promise of "Life, Liberty, and the pursuit of Happiness," outlined in the Declaration of Independence. However, he urged his listeners against bitterness and violence and continued, more famously, with a list of dreams. Among them were the desires that the United States eventually would be a nation of equality—a nation in which race would have nothing to do with assumptions about a person's integrity and abilities.[2] At that event, the March on Washington for Jobs and Freedom, King was one of ten speakers on a full program that included music, prayer, and a "Tribute to Negro Women Fighters for Freedom." Despite other eloquent statements it was King's words that inspired Americans throughout the country to reject injustice and to strive peacefully for their goals. Many would do just that in the next few years, for a variety of causes.

Homophile activists picketed the White House, the United Nations, and government offices in the 1960s to protest discrimination against homosexuals. In Philadelphia Annual Reminders began in 1965 at Independence Hall and were observed through 1969. In this photo pioneer gay and lesbian rights advocate Barbara Gittings (in striped dress) marches at Independence Hall in 1966. (Barbara Gittings and Kay Tobin Lahusen Gay History Papers and Photographs, Inc. of New York Records, Manuscripts and Archives Division, the New York Public Library, Astor, Lenox and Tilden)

If King was the "star" of the day and the movement, Bayard Rustin, organizer of the March, was producer and director in important ways. Rustin did gain national attention at the time but his homosexuality placed him in largely unseen roles before and after the march, due to the homophobia inside and outside the civil rights movement. Rustin had a long history in Christian pacifism and African American civil rights, seeking to join the two in the forties. He had joined the Fellowship of Reconciliation in 1941, the next year was a founding member of CORE (Congress of Racial Equality), and worked for desegregation through the war years and after. He met King in Montgomery, Alabama, during the bus boycott protesting segregation and became, in biographer John D'Emilio's words, the minister's "closest adviser." As such, wrote D'Emilio, "Rustin initiated the process that transformed King into the most illustrious proponent of nonviolence in the world" and he formulated the plans for SCLC (Southern Christian Leadership Conference).[3] However, his 1953 conviction of "public lewdness" hung like a cloud over his accomplishments in an era with no tolerance for "perverts." He offered to resign as King's assistant in 1960 amid threats of exposure from rival African American leader Adam Clayton Powell, and King accepted. Only recently has Rustin been restored to his rightful place in this story, a story with many dimensions. D'Emilio concluded, in 1995, "Rustin's move from margin to

Bayard Rustin was a pacifist who profoundly influenced Dr. Martin Luther King, Jr., and who organized the 1963 March on Washington. Knowledge among movement leaders that Rustin was gay led to his resignation as King's closest advisor and his disappearance from movement history until recently. Rustin is shown here on August 27, 1963, in the Statler Hotel, at a news briefing concerning the March on Washington. (Courtesy Library of Congress)

center—and then back again—is a tale of gay oppression whose consequences have reverberated loudly in American politics from then until now."[4]

Since 1963 a march on Washington has become a primary strategy for any movement wishing to have a voice. It was significant not only in what was said there or the number of people gathered, but in joining the cause of civil rights with mass media. The march was followed by some of the most important legislation in U.S. history: the Civil Rights Act of 1964, the 24th Amendment abolishing the poll tax (1964), and the Voting Rights Act of 1965. However, it was not the simple case of cause and effect that it appears to be (hold a march, change occurs). The legislation signed by President Lyndon Johnson had been well underway in the Kennedy administration (1961–1963) and the march was as much a celebration of the impending Civil Rights Act as a demand for it. Other movements, including those of GLBT Americans, have used the strategy of demonstrating in the nation's capital. The "results" are difficult to measure since often the events are important for providing much-needed moral support and sense of community as for the political statements they make.

Feminism Reborn

The year 1963, important for civil rights and the end of the Kennedy era, was key to women's rights also: in that year *The Feminine Mystique* was published and helped launch another phase of the U.S. women's movement. The "rebirth" of feminism, like other movements, was rooted in the conditions of postwar America and in ideas even older. Defined variously, "feminism" in the United States usually has been linked to the movement for women's rights as compared to men's rights. As early as 1776, Abigail Adams and others argued that women (or "ladies") be included as the colonies declared independence by drawing upon the natural "rights of man." As it turned out, those rights were applied selectively and an American brand of feminism arose before the Civil War that noted the political, economic, and educational opportunities (among other) available to men but not women. When women and men met at Seneca Falls in 1948, their Declaration included such demands as access to higher education and professions, married women's property rights and, famously, the right to vote. By the end of the 19th century this "first wave" of American feminism had accomplished some of its goals, though national women's suffrage was still two decades away.

The 19th Amendment (prohibiting the denial of voting rights on the basis of sex), ratified in 1920, did not grant full equality, nor ban all discrimination on the basis of sex. To that end, an Equal Rights Amendment was introduced in 1923 and repeatedly thereafter. Certainly feminism did not die in the twenties but seems to have been directed away from overtly political ends, perhaps because of the energy expended on the suffrage. The relative freedom of young privileged women in the 1920s, the economic crisis of the thirties, and some easing of gender roles during World War II (allowing white married women to work for wages and wear pants) all may have made feminism seem less relevant. After 1945, though, the United States experienced a new Victorianism that included all the old ideas of passivity and domesticity for middle-class women and a revised version of obsession with (controlling) sex and gender (see Chapters 3 and 4).

By the early 1960s, many women had become disillusioned with their prescribed role in postwar America. Out of their discontent came a "second wave" of feminism, or a movement with elements of both continuity and change—espousing the older ideals of women's equality and self-determination but responding to new circumstances, often with new language. When Betty Friedan published *The Feminine Mystique* (1963) she tapped into unhappiness that had been simmering for years and in a now famous phrase she set out to identify the "problem with no name." The problem was a sense of emptiness despite having everything materially a woman could (or was supposed to) want: husband, children, ample food, shelter, and even leisure time. Although the book later would be criticized for its narrow white, middle-class perspective, it helped revive a serious critique of all women's status that went beyond individual unhappiness to questioning structures that promoted sexism. In mid-1966 Friedan and more than twenty others founded the National Organization for Women to fight sex discrimination on many fronts and it became the largest feminist organization in the country. Friedan became a household name, as did Gloria Steinem, who cofounded other feminist groups and, most famously, *Ms.* magazine (1972).

Legal and social changes affecting women developed in conjunction with a newly organized movement. Congress passed the Equal Pay Act in 1963, an important step against economic sex discrimination, as was the agreement of some newspaper editors to stop classifying job advertisements by sex. In the courts, laws limiting women's reproductive freedom were challenged, leading to landmark decisions. In *Griswold v. Connecticut* (1965) the U.S. Supreme Court upheld a married couple's right to use contraception and eight years later, in *Roe v. Wade,* placed restrictions on government interference with a woman's right to decide to end a pregnancy (see Chapter 6). Socially, women's demand for control over their bodies acted as both cause and effect of a "sexual revolution," as did feminist efforts to eliminate the "double standard" of sexual behavior (wherein men could be more sexually free than women without censure or name-calling). Scientists aided these efforts further with the development of the first birth control pill for women.

There were limits to the sexual revolution and the women's movement, however. For example, both theoretically encouraged sexual freedom and variety, but the double standard persisted well beyond the sixties. Also, revolutionaries and feminists occasionally revealed as much homophobia as middle America when "experimentation" was with same-sex partners (rather than multiple opposite-sex ones) and/or became a commitment to a nonstraight identity. The women's movement faced not only sexism from conservatives but also charges from within that the voices and needs of women outside the straight, white middle class were ignored. Among those inside critics were radical feminists who by the early seventies felt that the moderate goal of women's equality to men was not enough; to them a true "women's liberation" could be accomplished only by questioning—and destroying—patriarchy (the system of men's power over women and children, seen as both the cause and justification of sexism). Importantly, lesbian and bisexual women were in the forefront of all varieties of American feminism (as they always had been). In particular they developed some of the most insightful and groundbreaking ideas of women's liberation, and planted the seeds of lesbian theory and lesbian feminism that blossomed in the seventies (see Chapter 6).

CULTURE AND COUNTERCULTURE

At the height of sixties Theodore Roszak observed that "...it would hardly seem an exaggeration to call what we see arising among the young a 'counter culture.' Meaning: a culture so radically disaffiliated from the mainstream assumptions of our society that it scarcely looks to many as a culture at all, but takes on the alarming appearance of a barbaric intrusion."[5] The questions of who and what should be included as counter-culture, or even if there really was such a thing, are still debated. What does seem clear is that traditional institutions and values were seriously challenged on more fronts than ever, and in new forms if not new movements. As noted above, civil rights and feminism helped create the "the sixties" in their organized resistance to racism and sexism. A general concern with saving the planet was channeled, for example, into ecology and environmentalism, and into organized antinuclear and antiwar demonstration. Young people—baby boomers reaching maturity—were at the heart of the new spirit and their various approaches were seen in the politics of the New Left and in the styles and messages of the hippies. Prejudices remained even within the newer groups, though: sexism was apparent among men working for civil rights and the New Left; racism plagued youth and feminist causes; and at times homophobia pervaded even the most "radical" countercultural groups.

Cold and Hot Wars

Historians generally agree that U.S. foreign policy of the 1960s—a central factor of "the sixties"—can be best understood in the context of the ongoing Cold War with the Soviet Union (see Chapter 4). Baby boomers (born 1946 and after) had been raised on vague fears of both "Commies" and nuclear war and understood equally vaguely that the two were related. Above all, it was America's duty to defeat communism everywhere and in every form. To that end the Truman, Eisenhower, and Kennedy administrations were willing to rebuild Europe, send aid to Greece and Turkey, intervene in the Middle East and Latin America, and provide the majority of troops in the Korean War. The arms race was well underway and the parallel contest in space-age technology was accelerated by the time JFK tragically died in 1963, the victim of assassination. Astronaut Alan Shepard, part of NASA's Mercury program, was the first American in space in 1961 and John Glenn orbited the earth the next year. The Gemini and Apollo programs continued the quest through the sixties and after. On July 20, 1969, the goal of putting an American on the moon as a show of superior technology was fulfilled by the crew of Apollo 11.

The moon landing was a welcome relief and chance for patriotism for many Americans who saw the country divided during the sixties. The catalyst to upheaval, though by no means its only focus, was American involvement in Vietnam. Although few Americans were aware of it that involvement did not begin in the sixties but instead in the aftermath of World War II. Vietnam had been part of French Indochina when the world war erupted and once the Allies won the French faced Vietnamese nationalist forces, the Vietminh. France sought to reclaim its colonial territory, and the United States hoped to strengthen alliances in the fight against communism. Between 1950 and 1954, U.S. aid to the French in Indochina rose from 15 percent to 80 percent of all funds designated for that conflict. France withdrew after a significant defeat in 1954, however, and soon the Geneva Accords divided the nation into North and South Vietnam. U.S. involvement increased on all levels and included support of the unpopular Ngo Dinh Diem as Vietnamese president. A civil war in South Vietnam between noncommunists and communists (Vietcong) further complicated affairs on the region, as did nationalist (but not necessarily communist) resistance to foreign interference. By the time JFK was killed in 1963 the number of American troops had increased from the 900 stationed there in 1960 to more than 16,000; by 1968 few Americans could claim to have never heard of Vietnam.

A turning point was the news that a U.S. ship was attacked in the Gulf of Tonkin in August, 1964. Although Congress never passed a declaration of war, the Tonkin Gulf Resolution served essentially the same purpose. President Lyndon Johnson, already in the office after JFK's death, was running in that year's election against Republican Barry Goldwater and won with 61 percent of the vote. The following year the process of "Americanizing" the war was fully underway, with more than 180,000 combat troops in Vietnam by the end of 1965, as was the air war on North Vietnam. The war escalated on both sides over the next three years and casualties mounted: by 1968 nearly 20,000 Americans and many more Vietnamese soldiers and civilians had died in a conflict whose purpose was still unclear to many citizens. As early as 1966 hearings revealed mixed opinion within the government over this application of containment policy, and as more Americans died opposition to the war crystallized into organized actions. The Tet Offensive launched against South Vietnamese cities in early 1968 was another turning point, this time in widening the "credibility gap" between a government predicting victory and the mass of people who could no longer believe victory was possible. America's most trusted figure, TV news anchor Walter Cronkite, told viewers he thought the war was "unwinnable," and Johnson's approval fell to 35 percent. It was only the beginning of a momentous year inside and outside the United States. At elections that fall Americans elected as president former vice president Richard Nixon, who had promised "peace with honor" through negotiation and "Vietnamization" (training South Vietnamese troops and withdrawing U.S. forces). Nixon hoped that his policies would quell domestic unrest, but there was to be no lasting respite through his time in power.

Liberalism under Attack

Equal in importance to the Vietnam War in understanding the sixties were the collection of programs under Johnson called the Great Society. The concept and its implementation were similar to those of the New Deal, indicating a continuation of the New Deal's legacy among Democrats. In particular, they shared the conviction that social and economic programs, including aid to the disadvantaged, fell within the government's responsibility to "promote the general welfare" of the American people.

The Great Society consisted of federal action and support in several areas, with racial equality in the forefront. Progress toward civil rights included the Civil Rights Act, the Equal Employment Opportunity Commission, the 24th Amendment (abolishing the poll tax), and the Voting Rights Act, all in 1964–1965. In 1967 the Supreme Court ruled that laws banning interracial marriage are unconstitutional in the case *Loving v. Virginia,* a decision with implications for not only racial equality but also in linking marriage with civil rights (and later cited as precedent by same-sex marriage advocates). Finally, a second Civil Rights Act in 1968 added protections and means of enforcing the Act of 1964. Each Great Society blow for civil rights was significant, but likely none would have occurred without the organized grassroots movement acting in tandem with Congress, the president, and the courts for well over a decade by then.

Other areas of the Great Society included a "War on Poverty," education, the environment, immigration reform, and attention to the nation's cultural resources. The Economic Opportunity Act, Job Corps, and VISTA, for example, all from 1964, were part of the "War on Poverty" and the next year Medicare and Medicaid were added to ensure some affordable health care for older and lower income Americans. Also in 1965 came Head Start and Upward Bound programs for underprivileged children and teens, the Air and Water Quality Acts, a new Immigration and Nationality Act, and the creation of the National Endowments, for the Arts and for the Humanities. Much of the Great Society is still in place but the momentum of the train setting out to end poverty and racism in the United States and establish equal opportunities was derailed, in a sense, by the escalation of the Vietnam War.

Like the New Deal of the 1930s, the Great Society also spawned political challenges from both the right and the left, and signaled the beginning of the end of the "liberal consensus" (see Chapter 4). At one end were the neoconservatives, or "neocons," a group of former political liberals who saw Great Society programs as moving the nation too far to the left, creating too large a government bureaucracy, and diverting attention from an aggressive, or "hawkish" foreign policy. Even before the Great Society was fully launched their influence was apparent in the candidacy of Republican Barry Goldwater for president in 1964; the next year the journal *The Public Interest* was founded as an outlet for neoconservative views. They laid the foundation for what evolved into the New Right of the 1980s, in which political and economic conservatism merged with evangelical Christian views of morality and resulted in a powerful backlash against gains made by women, nonwhites, and GLBT people by then (see Chapter 7).

Another factor in the rise of the neoconservatives was an increasingly vocal New Left. Like their counterparts in the Old Left observing the New Deal, New Left critics viewed the Great Society as a beginning but fundamentally flawed in its commitment to industrial capitalism and to reform over revolution. The New Left, like the new conservatism, originated years earlier but the events and policies of the mid-sixties and after spurred its growth. Its origins are usually dated from 1962, when white student activists met in Michigan and founded SDS (Students for a Democratic Society). They decried the poverty, racism, and violence they saw in their society (for which they were considered "subversive") and called for a genuine democracy of the American people. Two years later New Left activism was further defined in the Free Speech Movement at the University of California at Berkeley, in which students protested restrictions on the kinds of political activities allowed on campus. By the end of the decade the New Left was a significant political presence, although somewhat diffuse in its collection of ideologies and causes. Radicalized students were an effective voice in transforming life on campuses, for example demanding student government and curricular reform, and the New Left played a central role in organizing opposition to American involvement in Vietnam.

The relationship of the New Left to queer people and movements was something like that of siblings in a larger "family" of sixties activism: they coexisted, often at odds but ultimately interdependent, each important to the other's development. The actual number of GLB people (transsexualism was not yet part of the dialogue) in the New Left is difficult to determine due to the homophobia it shared with mainstream society. However some, like Carl Wittman and bisexual Greg Calvert, are known for their contributions and for the antigay harassment they experienced from fellow radicals. Calvert directed his energies into the antiwar and antinuclear movements and Wittman went on to write the key gay liberation tract, "Refugees from Amerika: A Gay Manifesto" (see below). For lesbians in the movement, their status as women was as problematic as their sexuality. Many women grew disillusioned with the sexism of their male comrades and gravitated toward the new wave of feminism gaining ground in the late sixties. Lesbians found that initially they were no more welcome there than women and gay men were in the New Left, however. Therefore, while radical student and antiwar protest provided some training and theory for a new generation of queers, most GLB radicals would have to take their energies elsewhere, to movements in which their interests were uppermost.

Peace and Violence

To some participants and observers the "true" counterculture lay not in the overt political activism of the New Left, the civil rights movement, or other causes. Instead it was the more subtle politics of the hippies who opposed the mainstream with messages of peace and love, "sex, drugs, and rock 'n' roll." Whether they were only one counterculture group or the only one, though, they clearly presented a challenge to the economic, militarist, consumerist, sexual, and gender assumptions deeply embedded in U.S. culture. They were mostly young, white, and privileged men and women in the tradition of the Beats who adopted alternative styles of dress, music, drug use, personal philosophy as their mode of rebelling against what they saw as corruption. Many participated in nonviolent actions of the time while others "dropped out" and flocked to communes as well as to areas like the Haight-Ashbury district of San Francisco. They advocated "free love" and men especially violated gender rules in wearing long hair and "feminine" jewelry like beads and earrings. While homophobia was not unheard of in hippie culture there seemed to be less stake in maintaining masculine modes of competitive behavior and sexuality than in the New Left. By 1967 mass media outlets were referring to them as hippies and "Flower Children," sometimes derisively, but still providing the coverage that drew ever-larger numbers to the movement. That year alone began with a Human Be-In in San Francisco and by midyear the Monterey Pop Festival and the "Summer of Love" drew hundreds of thousands of people to the area. The peak of the movement likely came in August, 1969, with the Woodstock Music and Art Festival in upstate New York. More than a half-million people gathered over the long weekend to listen to the top rock performers of the time and celebrate values of peace and harmony.

Messages of peace and nonviolence, and the tactic of civil disobedience continued as parts of the civil rights movement also, of course. Unity (if it ever exists) is difficult for any group to maintain, though, and especially so in the midst of a decade seemingly defined by violent acts. Although 1963 was the year of the March on Washington it was also the year of police brutality in Alabama and the church bombing there that killed four young African American girls, the murder of Medgar Evers in Mississippi, and the assassination of JFK. The next year three young men registering African American voters in Mississippi were found murdered, victims of the white racist terrorist group, the Ku Klux Klan. Black nationalist leader Malcolm X was killed in 1965, by which time civil rights activists were divided over goals and methods; in 1966 the Black Panthers were founded in Oakland, California, and Stokely Carmichael (Kwame Ture) and many others used the phrases "Black Power" and "Black is Beautiful" in the late sixties as slogans for a more militant stance toward racism. Early in 1968 LBJ famously announced he would not seek reelection and the Democratic race became a referendum on Vietnam. The life of frontrunner Robert F. Kennedy ended in June at the hands of an assassin after winning the California primary, and only two months after Martin Luther King, Jr. was shot to death in Memphis, sparking riots throughout the nation. When the Democrats met in Chicago that summer to select their candidate,

Chicago police were primed for more trouble, and attempts at peaceful protest there ended in more violence. In Martin Duberman's words:

> When the police rioted at the Democratic National Convention that summer in Chicago, the drift toward militancy became a stampede. By the fall of 1968, there were at least a third again as many SDS chapters as before the convention; black students took over administration buildings at Cornell while boldly brandishing their rifles in front of the television cameras; the Black Panthers and the Oakland police had a shoot-out; a contingent of feminists invaded the hitherto sacrosanct Miss America pageant; and incidents of arson and bombings became commonplace.[6]

Also in that fall's election Democrat Hubert Humphrey, a moderate who had served as LBJ's vice president, could not beat Richard Nixon. Nixon began his term on a note of hope, promising a policy of negotiation and withdrawal from Vietnam. His terms were among the most turbulent yet, though, ending in the first and only resignation of an American president.

"GAY IS GOOD"

In 2007, 82-year-old Frank Kameny was interviewed at the national convention of American Veterans for Equal Rights, where he was scheduled to give the keynote address. The year also marked the 50th anniversary of his discharge from government service as part of the Cold War purge of homosexuals (Kameny sued the government and lost). Subsequently he was a founder and first president of the Mattachine Society of Washington, he participated in pickets, and has been a tireless organizer and speaker. Further, he was in the lead in changing the way mental health professionals thought about homosexuality (see Chapters 4 and 6). However, he said at that interview, "If I'm not remembered for anything else, I want to be remembered for coining the slogan, 'Gay is Good.'" He acknowledged the influence "Black is Beautiful" and the attitude of pride it represented. "We needed a slogan," he told Eric Resnick, "and we needed to be proactive. It wasn't good enough to say 'gay isn't bad.'"[7] The year was 1968 when Kameny gave the movement a rallying cry. By then it had been five years since organizers formed ECHO (East Coast Homophile Organizations) and held its first conference in Philadelphia, an event one historian has called "the culmination of the homophile strategy of heterosocial respectability."[8] In the interim much had happened from the West Coast to the East to make the 1960s as crucial a time in GLBT history as it was for U.S. history as a whole.

A Public Presence

In the West, it is logical to begin in San Francisco, not for its later fame as a gay mecca but because so many strains of culture and subculture met there. In the fifties there were the Beats, whose rebellion against establishment mores paved the way for hippie expression. These elements combined with an already long-standing queer presence that had flourished during and after World War II. A queer subculture, as represented by bars like the Black Cat, fostered queer political action, a relationship seen in other cities but not always to the same degree. By the end of 1962 drag queen José Sarria had organized the League for Civil Education and had run for city supervisor, and local bar owners had founded the Tavern Guild as a response to repeated police harassment of bars serving homosexuals. Two years later a group of gay men that included William Beardemphl, Mark Forrester, Jim Foster, and Bill Plath founded SIR (Society for Individual Rights). SIR was broadly conceived as a social, educational, and political organization and, significantly, "took for granted the 'worth of the homosexual...and [his] right to his own sexual orientation.'"[9] The group published the monthly magazine *Vector* beginning in 1965 and the next year founded the nation's first gay community center.

San Francisco is notable also for at least two additional milestones prior to the seventies: the CRH (Council on Religion and the Homosexual) and the riot at Compton's Cafeteria. The first originated from discussions between local homophile leaders and Protestant ministers that began in May 1964. At the end of the year, they formed the CRH and sponsored a New Year's ball, at which police arrived and engaged in harassing the partygoers, taking their pictures and trying to force entry with no cause or warrant. Although such treatment by police was familiar to the queer people in attendance, their straight supporters were educated in real-life discrimination that night. Four people were arrested during attempts to block police entry—also not unusual—but this time an organization existed able to respond. On January 2 CRH members, including straight ministers, held a press conference in which they protested the actions of the police, and the four people arrested were found not guilty at their trial the next month at the direction of the judge. While the CRH actions were firmly in the tradition of both homophile organizing and nonviolent resistance, another type of action occurred in August 1966, at Compton's Cafeteria. One evening when police staged a raid on Compton's, a popular spot in the Tenderloin district for drag queens and others, the patrons fought back. The event is considered a turning point in transgender activism and, perhaps for that reason, was long neglected by GLB historians who emphasized the later Stonewall riot as a movement watershed (see below, and the Debate). A documentary film, *Screaming Queens: The Riot at Compton's Cafeteria* (2005), has helped restore the event's place in this story.

Outside San Francisco organizing also continued in cities to the north and the south. In Seattle the situation between city officials and bars serving gay men and lesbians was similar to that of San Francisco and other cities with significant gay and lesbian population. Bar owners and patrons were subjected to periodic police harassment, which served several purposes: intimidation of bar owners and their homosexual customers; providing city officials the appearance of a dedication to law and morality; and creating conditions in which brought payoffs to the police from bar owners hoping to avoid raids and closings. In this climate Mattachine Society efforts began in Seattle in 1965 and two years later organizers formed ASK/US (Association for Social Knowledge of the United States), a name soon changed to the Dorian Society. Dorian members achieved impressive visibility when a member appeared on the cover of *Seattle* magazine (November 1967), and the group created Dorian House in 1969 to serve homosexuals and transgender people. Similar attempts at organizing failed in Portland, though, which historian Peter Boag attributes to a more tolerant atmosphere. "Because police did not constantly harass bar patrons, there was little immediate incentive to protest," he wrote, reinforcing the idea that the relationship between politics and social venues like bars and baths is not predictable.[10] A flourishing bar culture could serve as the seedbed of political action, blossoming in response to oppression. It also could exist as an alternative to politics and, in the absence of obvious discrimination, contribute to a sense of security and undermine a more political consciousness.

Los Angeles, of course, was the birthplace of Mattachine and continued to serve as an important center of GLBT life. In their recent book on the city, *Gay L. A.,* Lillian

Faderman and Stuart Timmons explained that their goals, in part, were "to find out how Angelenos were able to establish the biggest, wealthiest, longest-lived gay and lesbian international church, community center, and national magazine" and "how they became major players in city and state politics and in the movie industry that influences the world;..."[11] The institutions to which they refer are the Metropolitan Community Church, the Los Angeles Gay Community Services Center, and *The Advocate,* all established between 1967 and 1972 (see Chapter 6). Gay bars in L.A. were also subjected to police harassment and in 1967 protests occurred in response to a raid on the Black Cat bar in Silver Lake. The sixties, in other words, were a time of important developments in "gay L.A." and those developments came to be central to a national GLBT community.

In the middle and southern parts of the country there was a smaller visible presence and comparatively less political action in the sixties, except in Chicago. A Mattachine chapter was organized there as early as 1953, but its membership remained small. However, by 1964 the level of harassment and discrimination grew intolerable to many of Chicago's queers, and new organizing was sparked by a raid on the Fun Lounge, a West Side gay club. The result was Mattachine Midwest, which became a vital center for homophile communication and organizing through the rest of the decade. Members produced and circulated a newsletter, started a telephone help line, and worked within the court system to address discrimination. Denver was another small beacon between the coasts. Local homophile activists organized a Mattachine chapter in 1956 and in 1959 hosted Mattachine's yearly national meeting. Results were mixed, though, since the local press covered the event favorably but in so doing drew the attention of antigay forces, including the police. Mattachine members' homes were raided and one was arrested, actions that effectively stalled the movement in Denver for years.

In the South, there were small homophile groups in places like New Orleans but organizing generally did not become more visible until the 1970s. In Mississippi and Texas the homophile group Wicker Research Studies (named after organizer Randy Wicker) began meeting in 1959. As John Howard has noted, the southern movement had the additional history of intense racism and civil rights agitation, which created unique circumstances. There was both community and organized activity in the South before the mid-sixties (which is usually ignored by GLBT historians), Howard explained, but this was not a story of linear "progress":

> As civil rights activism took Mississippi by storm in the 1960s, police targeted homosexuals in and outside the movement. Queer organizing all but ceased. On occasion, a coalition of leftists—not specifically gay-identified—protested anti-homosexual initiatives, utilizing broader calls for free speech and freedom of expression. Queer writing found outlets in late-sixties, left-wing, counterculture publications such as the underground newspaper *Kudzu,* printed in Jackson and distributed on high school and college campuses throughout the state. But [homophile activist Eddie] Sandifer remembers it as a time of retrenchment, a time of great repression as compared to the forties and fifties.[12]

If other regions of the country suffered from a lack of supportive environments, less homophile activity, and/or initial neglect by GLBT historians, such is not the case with the East Coast. Something of a coastal rivalry has characterized the stories of movement development, in fact, with later historians challenging the sometimes exclusive attention paid to the "East Coast militancy" first outlined in detail by John D'Emilio. Those arguments aside, the eastern arm of the movement can boast an impressive history of homophile workers' adoption of direct action—marches, demonstrations, or other immediate responses to a situation, often involving civil disobedience.

Key cities here are Philadelphia, Washington, DC, and New York, where organizing included not only Mattachine and Daughters of Bilitis chapters but also, in Philadelphia, the Janus Society (f. 1962), the Homosexual Law Reform Society (f. 1965), and the Homophile Action League (f. 1967). Each would publish the magazines and newsletters so crucial to community building: *Drum,* the *Homophile Action League Newsletter* and the *Eastern Mattachine Review.* At Columbia University in New York an openly bisexual student founded a Student Homophile League in 1966 and it became the first such group recognized by the administration of an American college. In Washington national homosexual rights took a hit when the U.S. Supreme Court upheld the deportation of a Canadian gay man under the Immigration and Nationality Act (McCarran-Walter Act) of 1952. The context and significance of the case, *Boutilier v. Immigration Service* (1967), have received thorough analysis in Marc Stein's award-winning article on the topic.[13]

The Earliest Gay Pickets: When, Where, Why

Preface
"The indefatigable Randolfe Wicker has proposed a picketing of the White House 'to highlight not only the homosexual movement but also discriminatory governmental policies in a variety of areas.'"
—*The Ladder,* **national lesbian magazine published by Daughters of Bilitis, August 1963, p. 20**

September 19, 1964. The first gay picket! 10 women and men (4 gay and 6 straight supporters) picket at the U.S. Army induction center on Whitehall Street in lower Manhattan to protest Arn1Y rejection of gays and issuance of 1ess-than-honorable discharges. ("We Don't Dodge the Draft—The Draft Dodges Us")

December 2, 1964. 4 gay men and women picket a psychoanalyst lecturing on "Homosexuality: A Disease" at Cooper Union in New York City. They demanded and got 10 minutes' rebuttal time for their spokesman.

April 17 and 18, 1965. Pickets spurred by news that Fidel Castro was going to put Cuban homosexuals in labor camps. 10 picketers at the White House on April 17; 29 picketers at the United Nations on April 18. ("Cuba's Government Persecutes Homosexuals; U.S. Government Beat Them To It") Brief article in *Washington Afro-American,* April 20, 1965. Reporters present from *NY Times* and WTOP-TV.

May 29, 1965. 13 people picket at the White House. ("Government Should Combat Prejudice, Not Submit to It and Promote It") Coverage either on the scene or by prior interview by AP, UPI, Reuters, Agence France Presse, *NY*

World-Telegram & Sun, TV networks and White House Press Corps. Stories reportedly appeared in *NY Times, NY News, Washington Star, Orlando Sentinel,* and *Chicago Sun-Times.*

June 26, 1965. 18 men and 7 women picket at the Civil Service Commission over ban on employment of gays. ("The American Way: Employment Based Upon Competence, Ability, Training—NOT Upon Private Life") Brief mention next day in *Washington Post.*

July 4, 1965. 44 take part in the first of five annual July Fourth pickets (Annual Reminder Day) at Independence Hall in Philadelphia, to remind the public that a large group of citizens is denied the rights and equality promised by the Declaration of Independence, including "life, liberty and the pursuit of happiness." Demonstration shown on late-night TV in Philadelphia and given a brief front-page mention in next day's *Philadelphia Inquirer.*

July 31, 1965. 16 picket at the Pentagon over anti-gay policies of armed services. ("Homosexuals Died for Their Country Too") Covered on scene by CBS-TV; shown on evening TV in Washington.

August 28, 1965. 14 picket at the State Department on employment and security clearance issues. ("Government Policy Creates Security Risks") Story in *Washington Post,* August 29. Reporters on hand also from CBS-TV, Agence France Presse, *Kansas City Star.*

September 26, 1965. 30 people picket at San Francisco's Grace Cathedral to protest discrimination against a minister who was a straight ally. ("A True Christian") Stories next day in *SF Chronicle* and *SF Examiner.*

October 23, 1965. 45 picket at the White House. ("Denial of Equality of Opportunity Is Immoral")

July 4, 1966, 1967, 1968, and 1969. Second, third, fourth, and fifth Annual Reminder Day pickets at Independence Hall. Almost 150 picketers in 1969, a week after the Stonewall rebellion in New York City. Coverage in *NY Times,* July 5, 1967 (only 4 column inches under "Pickets Aid Homosexuals"); in Rose DeWolf's column in *Philadelphia Inquirer* on July 6, 1967, "Another Minority Bids for Equality"; in *Philadelphia Tribune* on July 12, 1969, "150 Homosexuals Parade Before Independence Hall to Protest Maltreatment"; photo in *NY Times Magazine,* November 12, 1967, with article by Webster Schott, "Civil Rights and the Homosexual: A 4-Million Minority Asks for Equal Rights."

(Notes: Published accounts vary on the exact number of picketers at these events. Information on mainstream news coverage is incomplete. Additional info is welcome.)

List prepared January 2005 by Barbara Gittings, gay activist since 1958.

Especially important are the direct actions conducted in the eastern cities. In 2005 Stein, drawing upon his extensive research also on Philadelphia's GLBT history, wrote a piece commemorating a little-known event:

> Forty years ago, three teen-agers in Philadelphia took an extraordinary step by refusing to take a step. Their sit-in began on Sunday, April 25, 1965, at Dewey's restaurant near Rittenhouse Square in Center City. According to an account provided several months later by Clark Polak, a gay-rights leader in Philadelphia, "the action was a result of Dewey's refusal to serve a large number of homosexuals and persons wearing non-conformist clothing."[14]

That sit-in took place amid the better-known pickets that began in the early sixties and remain key moments in GLBT history. Sources disagree about the year of the first picket, at the U.S. Army induction center in New York, in which a handful of men and women protested the draft board's violation of privacy in releasing sexual identity information to employers. Whether it was in 1962, '63, or '64, though, it remains the first and Randy Wicker is acknowledged as a key organizer. Other demonstrations in New York were held at the Cooper Union and the United Nations, but most picketing shifted to DC and Philadelphia, especially in 1965. That year homophile rights activists marched at the White House three times, in April, May, and October, and staged quiet demonstrations at the Civil Service Commission (June), the Pentagon (July), and the State Department (August). It was the pickets begun on July 4, 1965, at Independence Hall in Philadelphia, though, that have captured the most attention (see the opening story). The main reason is the decision to make it a yearly event, and the Annual Reminder was born. The Reminders were held every year through 1969, the last one occurring only days after a fracas in New York at an Inn in Greenwich Village.

Stonewall

In August of 1968 NACHO (North American Conference of Homophile Organizations) held their convention in Chicago. Since first meeting in Kansas City three years earlier the number of groups represented had grown from fifteen to twenty-six, but retained the structure of a confederation without a central authority. In addition to drafting a "Homosexual Bill of Rights" that year, the attendees also adopted Frank Kameny's slogan "Gay Is Good." The conference came weeks after the fourth Annual Reminder at Independence Hall, and a fifth, held on July 4, 1969, drew about 150 demonstrators. By the time ERCHO (Eastern Regional Conference of Homophile Organizations) met the following November 1969, in Philadelphia, New Yorker Craig Rodwell and others proposed a resolution to move the Reminder to New York and rename it as Christopher Street Liberation Day. The resolution passed.

The change from Reminder to Parade was one of many influenced by the fight that occurred Friday night, June 27, 1969 (and technically not underway until early morning on the 28th) at the Stonewall Inn on Christopher Street in Greenwich Village. The Stonewall was a popular gay bar with a mostly male clientele that included a cross-section of class, age, and gender (drag queens as well as "male" men); sources vary as to whether nonwhites were welcome, though they did patronize the bar. At about 1:20 a.m. police began one of their frequent raids on the place and expected the patrons either to slink off guiltily in the night or come along in the paddy wagons. However, none of it followed previous experience. In their recent summary and analysis of events, two sociologists have provided a terse account based on multiple sources:

> As [police] started checking identification, kicking people out, and making a few arrests, a crowd of ejected patrons, nearby residents, and passers-by gathered outside. This was unusual;...As they loaded the van with arrestees, the crowd grew angry and started throwing pennies, bottles, and bricks. With no backup, the police barricaded themselves inside the bar. The crown escalated its attacks, trapping the police inside. when backup arrived, the police began loading the wagon again.
>
> Riot police arrived around then, and tried for hours to disperse the crowd.... rioters [were able] to block the street and halt traffic in front of the Inn, and go around the block to taunt police from behind. Violence continued until the streets were finally cleared, at about 3:30 a. m. Papers reported nearly a thousand rioters and several hundred police. Four policemen were hurt and thirteen people were arrested.[15]

The violence on the rioters side included using a parking meter and a trash can against the door and window and throwing lighter fluid and matches inside, starting a fire; on their side, the police beat rioters, inciting more anger. Local press, TV, and radio reported the fight and Saturday night the Stonewall was mobbed. Police arrive and the riot was again underway; acts of resistance now included not only throwing objects but also public displays of affection between same-sex people, and a chorus line of drag queens. Battles with police occurred through the following Wednesday night, July 2. In the meantime, a division was widening between advocates of "Gay Power" (shouted and written on walls through the rebellion) and homophile activists of Mattachine in New York. Within the month radicals formed the GLF (Gay Liberation Front).

The five-day rebellion often simply called "Stonewall" has not suffered from historical neglect. That alone makes it unusual in the chronicle of GLBT history and thus raises a number of questions. There are arguments over who started it (drag queen? a lesbian?), for example, not to place blame but to claim pride of place in a historic action. Also disputed is the event's significance, addressed in this chapter's Debate. Beyond those probably the most common question is "Why then?" It is the fundamental historical question, really, since to address it forces us to consider how and why *anything* happens. Probably the most accurate answer, too, is something like Craig Rodwell's: "just everything came together at that one moment."[16]

From a broad historical view what came together that night were elements of American culture, sixties counterculture, and multiple subcultures. Briefly, elements of the dominant culture include the power of media generally, the postwar crusade against homosexuality, and the "law and order" posturing of government officials at all levels. The rise of a counterculture contributed radical politics among the young— an inclusive view of oppression that critiqued capitalism and imperialism while advocating pride and resistance to authorities. Subcultures included at least two old ones in U.S. history: a culture of organized crime, ready to capitalize on marginalized people (prostitutes, drug addicts, queers) and doing so in their control of gay bars, and of course the GLBT subcultures long in existence. Finally, it is hard to imagine Stonewall happening without the sub-subculture of militant homophile activists, already defiant, proud, and willing to show their faces in public as lesbian and gay. They would soon be dismissed as "dinosaurs," though, as an admittedly new phase of GLBT history began.

Gay Liberation

In July of 1969 activists met in New York and formed the Gay Liberation Front and soon additional chapters were founded in larger towns and cities. The name was adapted from South Vietnam's National Liberation Front and was meant to signal the radical politics of the new group. They aimed to address a variety of oppressions which they saw as rooted in the same basic institution, and so espoused a politics of coalition with such populations as (straight) women, nonwhites in the United States, and colonized people around the world. In addition, they emphasized coming out (declaring oneself gay, lesbian, or bisexual to others) as a political as well as a personal act, one that placed a person within a movement and signaled her/his identification with the oppression of GLB people. Within the year after Stonewall one of the most important tracts of the new phase of GLBT activism was published and circulated, Carl Wittman's "Refugees from Amerika: A Gay Manifesto." It began:

> San Francisco is a refugee camp for homosexuals. We have fled here from every part of the nation, and like refugees elsewhere, we came not because it is so great here, but because it was so bad there. By the tens of thousands, we fled small towns where to be ourselves would endanger our jobs and any hope of a decent life; we have fled from blackmailing cops, from families who disowned or 'tolerated' us; we have been drummed out of the armed services, thrown out of schools, fired from jobs, beaten by punks and policemen.

DEBATE: HOW IMPORTANT WAS THE STONEWALL RIOT?

"Everything changed after Stonewall." This brief sentence can be heard in the narration of the documentary *After Stonewall* (1999) and sums up a popular version of 20th-century GLBT history in the United States.[17] In fact, the very title, with that of the earlier film *Before Stonewall* (1984), positions the riot as a dividing line, much as terms like *antebellum* and *postbellum* reinforce the centrality of the Civil War in changing American life. Terms like "turning point" and "watershed" are commonly used in descriptions and assessments of the events of June 1969, and if any one piece of the GLBT past makes it into the U.S. history survey text used in schools and colleges, it is Stonewall. For most historians of GLBT movements and for many involved in postwar homophile activism, though, the notoriety of Stonewall may be just that: an event increasingly famous for being famous, but one whose star power has obscured as much as it has revealed. Perhaps more than any other debate in this book, this one raises the most fundamental questions of "doing" history: change versus continuity, the reconstruction of the past from memory and records; and the politics of historical interpretation.

The question of change is at the core of arguments over Stonewall—not so much *whether* anything changed, but *what* and *to what degree*. There is now too much evidence of previous resistance to consider Stonewall a genuine *first* but this is slightly different from calling it a *beginning*, a claim which does generate controversy. Beginning of what? The unique attention devoted to the riot (as in U.S. history texts, for example) contributes to the impression that no GLBT people existed before 1969, much less communities and an organized movement.

Suddenly there they are, shouting in the streets of the Village and throwing things at the police. The power of this image, of coming out of nowhere, is reflected in the disclaimers of homophile activists and GLBT historians. In a 1974 interview, for example, longtime protester Barbara Gittings said, "...the changes, all these consciousness changes were definitely fomenting in the sixties, well before Stonewall. The one thing that Stonewall represents, in my view, is a sudden burgeoning of grass-roots activity.... The militancy—the 'we are the experts, not these non-Gays'—all that developed well before Stonewall, thanks largely to Frank Kameny..."[18] Also, as recently as 1999 the claim of an anthology "that contemporary lesbian and gay culture did not begin in June 1969 with the Stonewall riots" could be called "a bold premise," and the authors of *Gay L. A.* (2006) still felt the need to assert that "Long before the 1969 Stonewall Rebellion, gay men were fantasizing about the possibility of banding together to fight for their rights."[19] Still, the language of gay (and soon, lesbian) liberation and new organizations devoted to new agendas and tactics can be traced to Stonewall.

To ask why anyone argues about a version of the past is also to ask what stake they have in their version. To some extent the debate over Stonewall has tapped into other cultural tensions and GLBT rivalries. There was a noticeable generation gap—a simple matter of age and experience—between homophile militants and gay/lesbian liberationists, for example, with the latter emphasizing the revolutionary nature of their actions. "What better way for post-Stonewall activists to represent themselves as having broken with the past," wrote Marc Stein, "than to deny that lesbian and gay politics even had a past?"[20] In addition, there already was an East/West rivalry brewing among GLBT activists before the riot. The attention devoted to the East after Stonewall only heightened the sense of an unappreciated West Coast movement, an invisible history inside a barely visible history.

Finally, there is the question of notoriety. If other events occurred, and they did, how did this one become the source of myth and legend as well as a historical staple in the GLBT story? In attempting to answer this Elizabeth A. Armstrong and Suzanna M. Crage compared Stonewall with four other similar events, three before 1969 (in San Francisco and Los Angeles) and one after (also in New York). The key, they asserted, was in the commemoration of Stonewall with what became an annual parade, and spread to the rest of the country. Not every event is commemorable, however, and they showed the way elements of shared memories and identity and community formation affected the ability to commemorate the event. Also, "Timing mattered...Stonewall activists were the first to claim to be first."[21]

Certainly commemoration has continued. Observing the last days in June as Pride days has grown into Pride Month and beyond in many places. The 25th anniversary of Stonewall in 1994 spawned an exhibit at the New York Public Library, and new controversy surrounding the parade in New York (see Chapter 8).[22] In 2000 a new chapter was added when the Stonewall Inn became a National Historic Landmark. Despite this official recognition the debate undoubtedly will continue, and as it does the significance of Stonewall, as before, will be inherent in the fact that it is worth the trouble.

Police attempt to hold back a crowd while arresting patrons of the Stonewall Inn on Christopher Street in Greenwich Village the night of June 27, 1969. The rioting that accompanied the raid marked the birth, to many, of a new era of "gay liberation." (N.Y. Daily News. Copyright Daily News L.P.)

Wittman continued by outlining in some detail seven areas of consideration: orientation, women, roles; oppression; sex; "our ghetto"; and coalition. In his conclusion was "AN OUTLINE OF IMPERATIVES FOR GAY LIBERATION":

1. Free ourselves: come out, everywhere; initiate self-defense and political activity; initiate community institutions; think.
2. Turn other gay people on: talk all the time; understand, accept, forgive.
3. Free the homosexual in everyone: we'll be getting a lot of shit from threatened latents: be gentle, and keep talking and acting free.
4. We've been playing an act for a long time: we're consummate actors. Now we can begin TO BE, and it'll be a good show![23]

GLF adopted consciousness raising as a goal and strategy (a method also used by women's liberation) and sought consensus in meetings that some considered refreshingly egalitarian and exciting. Others, however, felt that the specific needs of GLB people were in danger of getting lost amid too many causes and too diffuse an agenda.

In keeping with an already established pattern of homophile/GLB organizing (and all movement organizing, for that matter), there was a division before the end of 1969, out of which the Gay Activists Alliance was born. A group that included Jim Owles and Marty Robinson grew frustrated with the all-encompassing theory, the dominance of talk over action, and the chaos they felt dominated GLF and organized GAA along more traditional lines, at least in procedure. They held elections, operated according to *Robert's Rules of Order,* and held to majority rule rather than consensus. Their cause was exclusively gay rights (in the language of the time) and they were willing to work within the political system (voting, lobbying) to gain those rights. It would be a mistake to label GAA "conservative" and GLF "radical," though, since both were liberationist in philosophy. In addition, it was GAA that became known for the "zap" a New Left tactic in which campaigning politicians or other officials were confronted publicly and forced to address the topic of gay rights.

When thousands of queer men and women showed up for the Christopher Street Liberation Day Parade and "gay-in" following on June 28, 1970, it marked the nation's largest lesbian and gay rally in its history to that point. Only weeks earlier a gay couple in Minneapolis, Jack Baker and Michael McConnell, applied for a marriage license and were denied. In some ways these two events represent both the convergence of gay liberationist attitudes and the eventual divergence in movement goals. Both adopted an "in-your-face" action and both came from a core of pride and self-respect. The way in which gay and lesbian liberation developed further, and splintered further, is treated in the remaining chapters.

NOTES

1. Quotes from film, *Gay Pioneers* (2004). Produced and directed by Glenn Holsten. Malcolm Lazin, Executive Producer.

2. See http://www.stanford.edu/group/King/publications/speeches/address_at_march_on_washington.pdf.

3. John D'Emilio, "Homophobia and the Trajectory of Postwar American Radicalism: The Career of Bayard Rustin," in *Modern American Queer History,* ed. Allida Black (Philadelphia: Temple University Press, 2001), 86–87.

4. D'Emilio, "Homophobia," 94. See also John D'Emilio, *Lost Prophet: The Life and Times of Bayard Rustin* (Chicago: University of Chicago Press), 2004, and the documentary film on Rustin, *Brother Outsider* (2003).

5. Theodore Roszak, *The Making of a Counter Culture: Reflections on the Technocratic Society and Its Youthful Opposition,* new ed. (Berkeley: University of California Press, 1995), 42.

6. Martin Duberman, *Stonewall* (New York: Plume, 1993), 169–70.

7. Eric Resnick, "When the Army Fired Frank Kameny 50 Years Ago, He Began an Era," *Gay People's Chronicle,* April 27, 2007. http://www.gaypeopleschronicle.com/stories07/april/0427073.htm.

8. Marc Stein, *City of Sisterly and Brotherly Loves: Lesbian and Gay Philadelphia, 1945–1972* (Philadelphia: Temple University Press, 2004), 200.

9. John D'Emilio, *Sexual Politics, Sexual Communities: The Making of a Homosexual Minority in the United States, 1940–1970* (Chicago: University of Chicago Press, 1983; 1998), 190.

10. Peter Boag, "'Does Portland Need a Homophile Society?' Gay Culture and Activism in the Rose City Between World War II and Stonewall," *Oregon Historical Quarterly* 105 (Spring 2004): 34.

11. Lillian Faderman and Stuart Timmons, *Gay L. A.: A History of Sexual Outlaws, Power Politics, and Lipstick Lesbians* (New York: Basic Books, 2006), 5.

12. John Howard, "Protest and Protestantism: Early Lesbian and Gay Institution Building in Mississippi," in *Modern American Queer History,* ed. Allida Black (Philadelphia: Temple University Press, 2001), 200.

13. Marc Stein, "*Boutilier* and the U.S. Supreme Court's Sexual Revolution," *Law and History Review* 23, no. 3 (Fall 2005): 491–536. The facts of the case can be found at http://laws.findlaw.com/us/387/118.html.

14. Marc Stein, "The First Gay Sit-In," at http://hnn.us/articles/11652.html.

15. Elizabeth A. Armstrong and Suzanna M. Crage, "Movements and Memory: The Making of the Stonewall Myth," *American Sociological Review* 71, no. 5 (October 2006): 737.

16. Rodwell interview in the film *Before Stonewall: The Making of a Gay and Lesbian Community* (1984). Produced by Robert Rosenberg, John Scagliotti, and Greta Schiller. Directed by Greta Schiller, codirected by Robert Rosenberg.

17. *After Stonewall* (1999). Produced by John Scagliotti, Janet Baus, and Dan Hunt. Directed by John Scagliotti.

18. Quoted in Jonathan Ned Katz, *Gay American History: Lesbians and Gay Men in the U.S.A.,* rev. ed. (New York: Penguin Meridian, 1992), 427.

19. *Publisher's Weekly,* about Patricia Juliana Smith, ed., *The Queer Sixties* (New York: Routledge, 1999), at http://www.amazon.com/Queer-Sixties-Patricia-Juliana- Smith/dp/0415921694/ref=sr_1_1/105-0134905-2806064?ie=UTF8&s=books&qid=1191186119&sr=8-1; Faderman and Timmons, *Gay L .A.,* 108.

20. Stein, *City of Sisterly and Brotherly Loves,* 289.

21. Armstrong and Crage, "Movements and Memory," 725.

22. The exhibit was *Becoming Visible: The Legacy of Stonewall,* curated by Fred Wasserman, Molly McGarry, and Mimi Bowling. A book resulted from the exhibit by Molly McGarry and Fred Wasserman, *Becoming Visible: An Illustrated History of Lesbian and Gay Life in Twentieth-Century America* (New York: Penguin Studio, 1998).

23. Carl Wittman, "Refugees from Amerika: A Gay Manifesto," in *The Homosexual Dialectic,* ed. Joseph A. McCaffrey (Englewood Cliffs, NJ: Prentice-Hall, 1972), 157–71; quotes pp. 157, 170–71.

SUGGESTED RESOURCES

Armstrong, E. (2002). *Forging gay identities: Organizing sexuality in San Francisco, 1950–1994.* Chicago: University of Chicago Press.

Boag, P. (2004, Spring). 'Does Portland Need a Homophile Society?' Gay culture and activism in the Rose City between World War II and Stonewall. *Oregon Historical Quarterly, 105,* 6–39.

D'Emilio, J. (2004). *Lost prophet: The life and times of Bayard Rustin.* Chicago: University of Chicago Press.

Faderman, L. (1992). *Odd girls and twilight lovers: A history of lesbian life in twentieth-century America.* New York: Penguin Books.

Howard, J. (1999). *Men like that: A southern queer history.* Chicago: University of Chicago Press.

Kissack, T. (1995, Spring). Freaking fag revolutionaries: New York's Gay Liberation Front, 1969–1971. *Radical History Review, 62,* 104–134.

Lekus, I. (2003). Losing our kids: Queer perspectives on the Chicago Seven Conspiracy Trial. In J. McMillian & P. Buhle (Eds.), *The New Left revisited* (pp. 199–213). Philadelphia: Temple University Press.

Lekus, I. (2004, Spring). Queer harvests: Homosexuality, the U.S. New Left, and the Venceremos brigades to Cuba. *Radical History Review, 89,* 57–91.

Marcus, E. (2002). *Making gay history: The half-century fight for lesbian and gay equal rights.* New York: Harper Perennial.

Meeker, M. (2006). *Contacts desired: Gay and lesbian communications and community, 1940s–1970s.* Chicago: University of Chicago.

Newton, E. *Cherry Grove, Fire Island: Sixty years in America's first gay and lesbian town.* Boston: Beacon Press.

Poling, J.D. (2005, Spring). Standing up for gay rights. *Chicago History, 33,* 4–17.

Stein, M. (2005, Fall). *Boutilier* and the U.S. Supreme Court's sexual revolution. *Law and History Review, 23*(3), 491–536.

Stonewall

Armstrong, E.A., & Crage, S.M. (2006, October). Movements and memory: The making of the Stonewall myth. *American Sociological Review, 71*(5), 724–751.

Avila-Saavedra, G. (2006, August). *The construction of queer memory: Media coverage of Stonewall 25.* Unpublished paper delivered at the Association for Education in Journalism and Mass Communication, San Francisco. Accessed at http://list.msu.edu/cgi-bin/wa?A2=ind0610d&L=aejmc&P=2281.

Carter, D. (2004). *Stonewall: The riots that sparked the gay revolution.* New York: St. Martin's Press.

Duberman, M. (1993). *Stonewall.* New York: Plume.

Smith, P.J. (Ed.). (1999). *The queer sixties.* New York: Routledge.

6   CULTURES AND POLITICS AFTER STONEWALL

San Francisco, 1974. Armistead Maupin spends a Wednesday evening in a Safeway grocery story interviewing patrons about "singles night." Maupin, a North Carolina native and Vietnam veteran, had moved to San Francisco a few years earlier as he pursued a career in journalism. The singles at Safeway inspired Tales of the City, *a serial column that grew into a book series in which Cleveland-born Mary Ann Singleton seeks love and friendship among the quirky characters of 28 Barbary Lane. Mary Ann, Michael, Brian, Mona, and numerous others come and go through six volumes that are considered among the best depictions of a special time and place.*

In a scene from the final book of the series, Sure of You, *Michael's lover Thack, and former San Francisco resident Burke have a tense exchange when Burke brings up the sixties:*

> *"Anyway, it [the sixties] was a great time. Things happened. People cared enough to make them happen. I mean, look at the seventies. What a great big blank that was."*
>
> *"I don't know about that," Thack said.*
>
> *"O.K. What happened?"*
>
> *"Well," said Thack, "gay liberation for one thing."*
>
> *"In what form? Discos and bathhouses?"*
>
> *"Yeah," answered Thack, clearly beginning to bristle. "Among other things."*
>
> *"For instance?"*
>
> *"For instance...marches and political action, a new literature, marching bands, choruses...a whole new culture. You guys [journalists] didn't cover it, of course, but that doesn't mean it didn't happen.... I just think you should know that something happened in the seventies. It may not have been part of your experience, but something happened."*
>
> *[Michael added], "The seventies were our sixties, so to speak."*[1]

Although fictional, Thack and his anger ring true for many people who actually lived through the sixties and seventies, particularly feminists and gay/lesbian activists who felt their movements were first ridiculed and then quickly forgotten by the "public." Intentional or not, the sense that the social ferment of the sixties ended by the mid-seventies contributed to eliminating ongoing movements from both public memory and historical record. This notion was popularized by novelist Tom Wolfe when he called the 1970s the "Me Decade" in order to distinguish it from the focus on "Us" perceived in the sixties.[2] No doubt the question of when—or whether—the spirit of the sixties died will continue to be debated, but for GLBT Americans of the early seventies the "sixties" had indeed just begun.

The momentum to which the Stonewall riot contributed pervaded the 1970s. "Gay liberation" may not have been a brand new idea but it was able to blossom at this time in soil well prepared by both the social ferment of the sixties and the solid history of GLBT organizing and political action. By the time a new conservatism emerged nationally and elected Ronald Reagan in 1980, gay liberationists and lesbian feminists alongside older moderates and others had created or enlarged rich subcultures, complete with marches, festivals, magazines, and sophisticated theoretical offerings. They organized nationally as never before, scored a significant victory among medical professionals, and even dreamed of a federal law banning discrimination against them. If in retrospect this seems overly optimistic, it does indicate the sense of movement and growing pride made possible by brave people in a new context.

COMMUNITIES AND CULTURAL EXPRESSIONS

The era of gay and lesbian liberation witnessed an expansion of cultural expression in every conceivable form. Some of this built on familiar models while other forms were recent and a result of the newer climate. Above all, those still called homosexuals were now much more visible to each other and used that visibility to create networks through formal and informal modes. One reason for that visibility was the importance attached to coming out, or telling others that one is not completely straight. In postwar America the "closet" from which GLBT were stepping was a vivid emblem of the confinement and darkness so many had felt living secret lives and fearing loss of loved ones, livelihood, and even their lives. As demonstrated throughout this history, coming out had something at either end: coming *from* a closet and also coming *to* or *into* a group. By the seventies that group might be not only a community or a subculture as before, but now a movement as well. For that reason coming out was now viewed as much a *political* act as an individual or social one, since to identify as a sexual minority aligned one with the legal status of that minority and with those fighting for better treatment.

As before, subcultures provided a breeding ground for political work but it was never quite that simple. Sometimes the social and political, when they could be separated at all, were in conflict: thriving communities could foster the unity needed for activism *or* make that activism seem unnecessary. Historians continue to try to untangle the relationships among personal identity (of all kinds), community formation, and political movements. The seventies may not clarify the lines of influence ("which came first?") buy they do provide plenty of evidence that community, identity, and political action are certainly interconnected.

Towns and Neighborhoods

Settling in a particular geographic area is perhaps the most literal expression of community. Anthropologist Esther Newton has documented the rise of Cherry Grove on Fire Island as "America's first gay and lesbian town." Like some other gay/lesbian towns, it first drew professional people, often in theater and the arts, and features oceanside living. Both men and women retreated to Cherry Grove in growing numbers after World War II and it continued to have a lesbian population, while the newer development in Pines has been predominately male.[3] Also in the East, Key West, Florida, and other beach communities arose from roots similar to Cherry Grove's, and Provincetown, Massachusetts, grew to be one of the largest gay/lesbian towns in this period. Provincetown has a high percentage of gay- and lesbian-owned businesses and a population that became politically active by 1980. The town of Northampton, Massachusetts (home to Smith College) is known for the visibility of lesbians and lesbian-owned or lesbian-friendly businesses, as is the tiny village of New Hope, Pennsylvania. The emergence of the smaller town of Rehoboth Beach, Delaware, parallels that of the other resorts, while on the other coast West Hollywood and other Southern California communities became more "gay" in the seventies.

Many people might think of San Francisco as a, or *the* "gay city" due to its prominence as such in the media since the sixties. The growth of gay neighborhoods is hardly unique to San Francisco, though, but instead part of a larger pattern in postwar America. Other industrial cities with water access—Los Angeles, New Orleans, Philadelphia, Portland, Seattle—became gay (and sometimes lesbian) meccas after World War II. In these and other cities new neighborhoods often built on older traditions of nonconformity (as in Chicago or Manhattan) and followed patterns already long established by ethnic communities of settling (or being consigned to) in particular areas. What set San Francisco's Castro and other districts apart, probably, was not only media coverage but especially politics: gay men and lesbians used their voices and votes in the 1970s and created awareness of queers as a potential political bloc. Currently large cities throughout the country, including Washington, DC, Minneapolis, Denver, and Atlanta, have areas that might be called lesbian/gay neighborhoods that feature lesbian/gay residents and/or businesses.[4]

Institutions

Among the many businesses that defined a "gay ghetto" probably the bars, baths, and bookstores have been most central. Bars and baths had long been established, of course, and were a crucial institution throughout the century. They were not just places to meet and party but also could be arenas for politicization—for thinking of oneself as part of a political community based on identity or common experience. At the same time, they were also links to the larger culture, and provided American culture with styles, icons, and music, as seen especially in the rise of the discotheque and "disco" music. Disco is another in the long line of music designed for a dancing crowd. Also typical of American popular music (blues, jazz, rock and roll), it is rooted in African American styles, especially the sounds of rhythm and blues. In the 1970s disco was the music of gay bars, peaking around 1975 but dominating the decade. Popular artists and songs included Donna Summer ("Love To Love You Baby," "Hot Stuff," "On the Radio"), Sister Sledge ("We Are Family") and, of course, the Village People, whose costumes and songs "Macho Man" and "YMCA" were references to gay culture (see "Images, Types, and Stereotypes," below). Songs like "I Will Survive" and "I Am What I Am" (both recorded by Gloria Gaynor) became anthems of pride in this setting. Casablanca Records (1973–1984) became the biggest disco label while the film *Saturday Night Fever* (1977), and the Bee Gees' sound track, indicated the more general popularity of disco. The brief heyday of disco is also part of an older pattern of the "mainstream" co-opting gay—and white co-opting African American—culture for

The Village People were very popular among gay patrons of discos. The band dressed as characters associated with "macho" masculinity, clockwise from the top center: Cop, Military Man, Biker, Native American, Construction Worker, and Cowboy. (Photofest)

broader consumption (much like "voguing," popularized by the 1990 Madonna hit but taken from Harlem drag balls of the early century).

Gay baths, as shown in Chapter 3, are important to the GLBT story of the 20th century. Despite the crackdowns on gay bars and baths in the 1950s and 1960s they survived in some form and experienced a new phase with gay liberation. Beginning in the late 1960s, according to historian Allan Bérubé, the baths underwent "dramatic changes" and after Stonewall a "new generation of bathhouses established themselves as a major gay institution." Among the changes Bérubé details were a national chain, Club Baths, and many additions, from "orgy rooms," video rooms, and "fantasy environments" to parties, movie nights, snack bars, and dance floors. Live entertainment was added in some places like the Continental Baths in New York City, where Bette Midler and others performed for gay crowds. Baths grew into centers for political and health activism also, and in San Francisco survived a legal challenge in 1978 when it was determined that California's Consenting Adult Sex Bill included the baths.[5] In the next decade the baths would be the focus of serious debates regarding the politics of health in the age of AIDS.

Bookstores are another community institution that symbolize the blossoming of lesbian/gay culture. Craig Rodwell opened the Oscar Wilde Memorial Bookstore in Greenwich Village in 1967 and before long dozens of stores in cities across America catered to GLBT patrons. Among them were A Different Light (San Francisco and Los Angeles), Giovanni's Room (Philadelphia), Lambda Rising (Washington, DC), and Left Bank Books (St. Louis). Feminist/lesbian bookstores also proliferated at this time, often serving an important function as informal women-only space: Amazon Bookstore Cooperative (the first, founded in 1970 in Minneapolis), Antigone Books (Tucson, AZ), Charis Books and More (Atlanta, GA), New Words Bookstore (Cambridge, MA), and Silkwood Books (Rochester, NY). The importance of the bookstore as more than a print vendor cannot be exaggerated, since they have been significant sites for gathering, posting and sharing information, sometimes doubling as coffeehouses or other alternatives to bars. By the mid-1990s more than forty lesbian/gay bookstores had opened across the country but not all survived. Some GLBT/feminist bookstores still exist but others went the way of many independent bookstores in the 1990s, unable to compete with chains and internet booksellers.

GLBT institutions came in temporary or periodic as well as fixed forms. Annual public events that came to include GLBT people (or always had but less overtly) were Halloween, Mardi Gras, and St. Patrick's Day, though GLBT participation in the last two has been a source of friction. If "Gay Pride" was the hallmark of the new era the Pride parade or rally was its clearest expression. The June anniversary of Stonewall quickly became an occasion for yearly demonstration, as seen in the 1970 Christopher Street Liberation Day march in New York (see Chapter 5). The last few days of June were designated Pride days and eventually all of June became Pride Month across the country. In the largest cities annual events might draw thousands, while a few hundred or less turned out in smaller urban centers. Parades were/are held not only in New York, Los Angeles, and San Francisco but in midwestern, western, and southern cities as well. Rallies and speeches often accompanied parades or were held in place of them.

As might be expected, one issue that arose in public gatherings was representation. Who would be "allowed" to be the face of the community? Who had the right to define that community and include or exclude others? There were controversies, for example, about the most "flamboyant" or "outrageous" expressions, which usually meant crossdressing, leather (signifying sadomasochistic practices), or few clothes at all. Another twist was costumes, such as those of the Sisters of Perpetual Indulgence, men dressed as nuns, who debuted in the Castro in 1979. The convergence of publicity and politics at this time intensified old debates about the "face" of "the movement." Throughout the century among some middle class, moderate (and often closeted) GLB people, drag performance had been an embarrassment that perpetuated negative stereotypes, and in the seventies radical feminists added their own objections (see below). Also controversial, and also drawing feminist criticism since its 1978 inception has been NAMBLA (North American Man/Boy Love Association). NAMBLA members officially condemn sexual abuse and coercion but also oppose society's ageism and antisex attitudes. The organization seeks "to end the extreme oppression of men and boys in mutually consensual relationships" and to that end has worked for changes in law. Some feminists have feared that legal reform would only increase the male power that defines patriarchy and, rather than liberating children, place both girls and boys even more firmly under adult male control.

Less controversial, and possibly also lesser known, are the lesbian and gay musical groups that appeared in the seventies and served to build community and pride. Singers and instrumentalists began forming all-women's groups in the 1970s. These were often predominately but not exclusively lesbian, and included the Victoria Woodhull All-Women's Marching Band in New York (f. 1973), the Anna Crusis Women's Choir in Philadelphia (f . 1975), and the Los Angeles Community Women's Chorus (f. 1976). Since that time many more lesbians/feminists formed many more groups, including the Artemis Singers in Chicago and Amasong, billed as "Champaign-Urbana's premier lesbian/feminist chorus."

Gay men's ensembles, beginning with the Gotham Male Chorus in New York (1977) and the San Francisco Gay Men's Chorus (1978) gained popularity and similar groups were formed in most cities. As more groups emerged so did organization in the form of the Sister Singers Network and GALA (the Gay and Lesbian Association of choruses), both in 1981. New York hosted the first national GALA Festival in 1983 and twenty years later the association boasted 8,000 members in 170 choirs worldwide. Mixed-sex groups and instrumental groups are not as common, though they were also a part of this era; the San Francisco Gay Freedom Day Marching Band and Twirling Corps, begun in 1978, was the first of several bands that, like the other groups, combined joy in music with pride in openness.

For GLBT people wanting religious community there were an increasing number of possibilities, both within older and newer congregations. Dignity had its origins in a Southern California Catholic support group convened by a priest in 1969 and within four years was a national entity. Integrity, a similar gathering for Episcopalians, began in Georgia in 1974 and also grew rapidly. In 1972 the first (and world's oldest) gay synagogue opened in Los Angeles, Beth Chayim Chadashim. The United Church of Christ and the Unitarian Universalist Association also took significant steps toward inclusive policies, the former ordaining the first openly gay person, Reverend William Johnson, as a Christian minister in 1972. The Unitarian General Assembly of 1970 passed a resolution "[Urging] all peoples immediately to bring an end to all discrimination against homosexuals, homosexuality, bisexuals, and bisexuality,. . . ." and opened an Office of Gay Affairs in 1975. By then Unitarian ministers had already performed at least three "celebrations of love" for lesbian couples (in 1984 the UUA General Assembly adopted a resolution supporting same-sex unions).

Another option for GLBT people seeking a spiritual community was the Metropolitan Community Church, founded by Pentecostal minister Reverend Troy Perry. The origin of what became a worldwide institution was a small meeting in Perry's living room in 1968. In just over two years congregations had formed in at least four more large cities and their ministers held a General Conference; by early 1971 a "Mother Church" was dedicated in Los Angeles. The denomination represents a mixture of conservative Christian doctrine with liberal views on homosexuality, transgenderism, ordaining women as ministers, and performing same-sex unions. The church also was met with extreme homophobia, acted out violently. The method was arson and the targets were MCC structures in San Francisco, Los Angeles, Nashville, and New Orleans, all in 1973, and at least a dozen more fires in the next twenty years. In January of 1973 the Mother Church burned to the ground with no injuries. When that June an arsonist set a fire in the UpStairs bar (that doubled as the MCC church) in New Orleans, however, its patrons/congregants were not as fortunate. That horrific event resulted in thirty-two deaths and later was called "the first great tragedy of the modern gay rights movement" by two chroniclers. They added that it was possibly "the last major national news event in the gay community to go almost completely

Rev. Troy Perry, founder of the Metropolitan Community Church, stands in the ashes of the first church building after it burned to the ground on January 27, 1973. The Los Angeles church was one of several of the denomination's buildings targeted by arsonists over the years. (Photo by Anthony Enton Friedkin, courtesy of Anthony Enton Friedkin. © Anthony Enton Friedkin)

unreported."[6] Despite the hatred leveled at it, the Metropolitan Community Churches expanded to a worldwide network over the next decades.

Images, Types, and Stereotypes

The post-Stonewall years fostered an amazing array of symbols and images of all kinds. Some drew upon previous knowledge and events while much was a product of the effort to celebrate pride and to be recognized, if only by others "in the know." Personal presentation as gay or lesbian included the hair, clothing, and accessories one chose with an eye to the "messages" sent by them. It all fostered recognition within communities and also created or perpetuated several types and stereotypes that lasted well beyond those years, types that were cherished or ridiculed, depending upon the way they were viewed then and later. As always, mainstream media aided this process, with TV and film among the most powerful image-makers.

Gay men, lesbians, and bisexuals created or adopted a number of symbols and significant colors to show pride or otherwise signal their sexuality and/or politics. The pink and black triangles that the Nazis forced upon gay men and lesbians, respectively, are a good example of "co-opting" negative symbols and claiming them for the communities. The pink triangle reappeared as a sign of gay pride soon after Stonewall, and eventually was associated with the AIDS activist group ACT-UP in the 1980s; the black triangle was adopted in the eighties as part of a more general trend of promoting a separate visibility for lesbians. Eventually bisexual and transgender groups designed triangles specific to their identities as well. The Greek letter lambda, the labrys, and various combinations of the male (Mars) and female (Venus) symbols also now appeared and became lasting signs of GLBT pride. Lambda is an "all-purpose" sign while the labrys, the double-headed axe associated especially with Amazons, was adopted by lesbians (often lesbian feminists). The color lavender also signified lesbian while pink was more specific to gay men. The colors of the rainbow were put on a flag by the end of the decade to represent pride and later other flag designs for bisexuals and such subgroups as leather and bear communities developed.

In the 1970s gay men and lesbians adopted a number of symbols to claim their identities and celebrate a new sense of pride. Among them, clockwise from top left, were the Greek letter lambda, linked female (Venus) symbols, linked male (Mars) symbols, and the labrys (a double-headed axe associated with the legendary Amazons). (Author's collection)

Men in some areas—the Castro in San Francisco, for example—developed a look known as the "clone": a hypermasculine image that emphasized youth and fitness. Men cultivated muscles, wore short hair and trimmed mustaches and donned jeans and boots to be "macho men." Leather men were a variation of this (or vice versa), with the obvious addition of leather clothing. In some areas they added an elaborate system of color-coded hankies worn in one rear pants pocket or the other. They acted as signals for the wearer's preferences in sexual activity and/or type of partner. More generally, a stud through a pierced ear, often the right one, also signaled that the wearer was gay.

Not everyone fit the clone look or wanted to, and alternatives were also cultivated and celebrated. "Bears" were/are men who were bigger or "chubby," wore beards or had more body hair than the idealized clone, and generally did not fit the developing stereotype. Bear culture eventually evolved into a more formal movement, with organizations and publications in the eighties and nineties, beginning with Girth and Mirth in 1976. Another way of being gay was less about presentation and more rooted in a comprehensive philosophy: the Radical Faeries. The Faeries, reclaiming the name used for effeminate men while referring to the supernatural, grew out of informal gatherings with ideas akin to the hippie movement. Longtime activist Harry Hay founded the group in 1979 and envisioned it as a spiritual expression of the ways gay men were different (in contrast to the efforts of some gay rights advocates to show "we're just like everyone else"). The Faeries, still active today, draw upon older traditions that emphasize the sacredness of bodies and sex as well as nature and see themselves as part of an ancient history of queerness, often underground and usually expressed by gender nonconformity (a similar view of queerness is explored in Judy Grahn's 1984 book, *Another Mother Tongue*).

Some lesbians also adopted a kind of clone look, and ironically one similar to that of the men (minus the moustache). Lesbian feminists, for example, rebelled against the restricting and uncomfortable clothing society demanded of the feminine ideal, and also against the butch/femme gender dichotomy of the previous years. The look was androgynous, favoring short hair, jeans, flannel shirts, and boots or sandals, all in rejection of the narrow beauty standards and ways to be female (that were seen as emphasizing sexuality—or sexiness—over any other human attribute). Many proudly claimed the term "dyke" and used clothing to signify not sexual interests but class and/or other activities, sometimes humorously: "Blazer dyke" (professionals); "sweatshirt dyke" (athletes); "belle dyke" (traditionally feminine with makeup, big hair, dresses, heels), and so on. Women might wear jewelry with the labrys, lambda, or linked Venus symbols both in pride and to signal one another in public (before those symbols were more commonly recognized).

If lesbians and gay men themselves helped created types and stereotypes, mass media were never far behind. Typically TV and movies, though sometimes enlightening forces, also drew upon the most obvious images for news or portraying gay/lesbian people. Prior to the seventies a few documentaries, talk shows, and dramas had addressed the topic of homosexuality but rarely in a positive light; typical of postwar attitudes, for example, was *Confidential File*'s 1954 feature on "Homosexuals and the Problems They Present."[7] Ten years later Randy Wicker became the first openly gay guest on a talk show when he appeared on *The Les Crane Show,* broadcast in New York. (Wicker had also been instrumental in persuading New York City radio station WBAI to air a favorable discussion of homosexuality among several gay people in 1962; six years later the same station broadcast a weekly show that included positive treatment of lesbians and gay men.) Another landmark, though largely critical in content, came in 1967 when CBS aired a special with Mike Wallace entitled, "The Homosexuals." Gay/lesbian liberation did receive more sympathetic TV coverage when gay activists appeared on *The Dick Cavett Show* in 1970 and David Susskind featured movement figures on his televised talk show twice—in 1971 and 1974.

Comedy and drama programming in early TV, like films under the Hays Code (see Chapters 3 and 4), included characters or dynamics that some gay and lesbian viewers could claim were "coded" or possessing a "gay sensibility," from Miss Hatheway in *The Beverly Hillbillies* or Felix Unger in *The Odd Couple* to the entire show *Bewitched*. In 1971 the already controversial *All in the Family* became the first sitcom (situation comedy) to present a homosexual character in a sympathetic light, and the next year *That Certain Summer* became a landmark TV-movie for its story line of a gay father with a teenage son that avoided stereotypes. Gay male and lesbian characters appeared here and there in 1970s TV, often as killers or the butt of jokes, but in ways reflecting both the greater general visibility of post-Stonewall homosexuals and activism that targeted media. Soon after its own founding the Gay Activists Alliance had formed a Publicity Committee, and the Gay Media Task Force was consulting on scripts by the mid-seventies. In 1977 the sitcom *Soap* introduced recurring character Jodie Dallas (played by Billy Crystal), termed in Stephen Tropiano's exhaustive study of programming, "certainly the most memorable gay character of the pre-Ellen era."[8] In the same year, perhaps the most memorable pretending-to-be-gay character also appeared: John Ritter as Jack Tripper, posing as gay in order to share an apartment with two women and offering up repeated opportunities for antigay jokes at his expense.

On film, the lifting of the ban on portraying homosexuality (see Chapters 3 and 4) resulted in a mixed picture before and after Stonewall. A few movies explored gay, lesbian, and transsexual life, but often in ways perpetuating narrow stereotypes and behaviors. For the most part, once they were visible, queer people on film were violent, mentally unstable, unhappy, or doomed to die. (Film historian Vito Russo includes a "Necrology" in *The Celluloid Closet,* listing thirty-nine films, the GLBT characters, and their cause of death.[9]) Examples include *The Fox* and *The Sergeant,* both released in 1968, and in both of which a homosexual commits suicide. In the same year, however, moviegoers could see *The Killing of Sister George,* one of the two films, with 1970's *The Boys in the Band,* called "the two most important Hollywood films of the era to deal with homosexuality."[10] Both were adaptations of Broadway plays and both present several facets of lesbian and gay life, respectively. Opinions vary about the films, some seeing them as basically negative—self-hating and/or violence and conflict prevail. Trans people on screen included a transvestite killer in *Caprice* (1967) and transsexuals, one fictional, one real: *Myra Breckinridge* (1970), from the novel by Gore Vidal, and *The Christine Jorgensen Story* (1970). In 1975 trans themes were explored in wildly different ways in the cult film *The Rocky Horror Picture Show* and the fact-based drama *Dog Day Afternoon.* Outside the Hollywood mainstream the era is significant for the films of John Waters, featuring drag queen Divine (Harris Glenn Milstead), the documentaries *Word Is Out* (1977) and *Gay USA* (1978), and the emergence of lesbian feminist filmmakers, as represented by Barbara Hammer.

In Print

As we have seen, print culture has always been important in the United States as a means of conveying information and shaping opinion, whether in the larger culture or in specific communities. As before, mainstream coverage of homosexuality and gay liberation varied in tone, but did increase overall. The venerable *Life* magazine included a story on "Homosexuality in America" in its June 26, 1964 issue, which lured the uninformed reader to the article with a picture taken in a leather bar accompanied by this text:

> These brawny young men in their leather caps, shirts, jackets and pants are practicing homosexuals, men who turn to other men for affection and sexual satisfaction. They are part of what they call the "gay world," which is actually a sad and often sordid world. On these pages, LIFE reports on homosexuality in America, on its locale and habits and sums up what science knows and seeks to know about it.

In the two years following Stonewall, stories in *Time* and *Harper's* magazines drew fire from activists for their negative commentary. However, in the same period *The New York Times* published a somewhat more balanced front-page treatment, *The New York Times Magazine* published Merle Miller's essay, "What It Means to Be a Homosexual," and *Look* magazine included gay couple Jack Baker and Michael McConnell (who had applied for a marriage license—see below) in its issue on "The American Family."[11] *Time* ran its first cover story on an openly gay man on September 8, 1975, when it profiled Air Force Sgt. Leonard Matlovich, who had been discharged for being gay (see Chapter 8). Years after 1969 homosexuality was far from accepted, though, and the new visibility combined with older associations with immorality and disgrace to provide tabloids with a rich source of revenue. As one observer noted, even by 1990 the topic was still shocking but because of activism it had become "acceptably scandalous" rather than "unprintably scandalous."[12]

Building on a solid foundation of communicating in print, gay and lesbian liberationists started magazines and papers that reflected the changes occurring and were a vital part of the rich culture rapidly developing. *The Advocate,* founded in 1967, was distributed nationally beginning in 1969. In 1974 a wealthy San Franciscan, David Goodstein bought it and transformed it into a magazine with broad coverage of news and the arts. The first gay weekly paper, *GAY,* began its run in 1969 (to 1973), as did the Gay Liberation Front's *Come Out!* "A Newspaper by and for the Gay Community." After 1970, numerous local magazines and papers joined those already in print; they ranged from Boston's *Fag Rag* and *Gay Community News* to the *Washington Blade* in the nation's capital and *RFD,* "A Country Journal By Gay Men" published in various locations in the Midwest, West, and South. In New York City *Christopher Street* and the *Native* soon became important organs, but New York's oldest gay and lesbian paper still in print, *The Empty Closet* (f. 1971) came from upstate, in Rochester. Early publications by and for lesbians included *Lesbian Tide* (f. 1971), *Lesbian Connection* (f. 1974), and *Sinister Wisdom* (f. 1976), picking up where *The Ladder* left off after folding in 1972. African American periodicals like *Blacklight* and *Onyx,* for gay men and lesbians, respectively, began to appear in the late seventies. On the scholarly front, the *Journal of Homosexuality* was founded in 1974 and continues as a venue for important work, and *Gay Literature* began publication in 1976.

Gay- and lesbian-owned presses have been vital to the development of GLBT culture as well. Two lesbian presses, Daughters, Inc. and Naiad Press, were founded in 1973. Daughters Inc. published five works a year, including groundbreaking theory, through 1978 while Naiad, disbanded in 2004, became known for fiction, including lesbian romances. Winston Leyland, who started the *Gay Sunshine Journal* in 1971, formed the Gay Sunshine Press a few years later. In 1977 Felice Picano founded SeaHorse Press in New York City and Sasha Alyson started Alyson Press in Boston;

in Binghamton, New York the Haworth Press began publishing in 1978 and its list now includes significant academic journals as well as books in GLBT studies.

Lesbian and gay fiction also reflected the sense of pride and the greater ability to express it in many forms. Isabel Miller (Alma Routsong) wrote *A Place for Us* in the late sixties and it was commercially published under the title *Patience and Sarah* in 1972. A love story based on an actual female couple of the 1820s, it soon became a lesbian classic, a status enhanced since then by its adaptation into a chamber opera that debuted at the Lincoln Center Festival in 1998.[13] Surpassing even *Patience and Sarah* in popularity was Rita Mae Brown's 1973 autobiographical novel *Rubyfruit Jungle,* a coming-out-while-coming-of-age story that traces the adventures of Molly Bolt from her girlhood in the South to her trek to New York City to study filmmaking. Gay men and their relationships were treated sensitively in the 1974 landmark, *The Front Runner* by Patricia Nell Warren. Essentially a love story between a closeted coach and an openly gay runner, the novel also treats the (still) taboo subject of gay athletes. Warren followed up with other gay-themes works while gay fiction by gay men blossomed. A number of important works appeared in the later seventies: Andrew Holleran's *Dancer from the Dance* (1978); Larry Kramer's satire *Faggots* (1978) and the popular *Tales of the City* series by Armistead Maupin (1978–1989) that began in serial form in the *San Francisco Chronicle* in 1976 (and from which the opening story to this chapter is taken). Also at this time Jack Fritscher embarked on a long career of publishing in both academic and popular genres (including the early 'zine *MAN2MAN*); his 1990 "memoir novel" of gay liberation in San Francisco, *Some Dance to Remember,* became widely known as "the gay *Gone with the Wind.*" By the turn of the eighties an informal group of gay writers known as the Violet (also Lavender) Quill were meeting in Manhattan. Among them were writers whose works came to be among the most significant expressions of urban life in the years from liberation through AIDS: Christopher Cox, Robert Ferro, Michael Grumley, Andrew Holleran, Felice Picano, Edmund White, and George Whitmore.[14] (Also see below, "In the Academy," for additional books of the era.)

WOMEN, FEMINISTS, LESBIANS

Success and Limits of the Second Wave

As described in Chapter 5, a revitalized women's movement arose out of the conditions of the fifties and the discontents of the sixties while reviving the concerns and unfinished business of 19th-century feminists. In the ten years between *The Feminine Mystique* and *Roe v. Wade* a fully developed movement emerged, complete with a variety of goals, approaches, and organizations. Even with the divisions that emerged, it accomplished an impressive amount of change for women, and with remarkable speed.

Feminists of the reborn movement addressed a broad range of issues. A focus on reproductive rights, for example, was but part of a larger analysis of the ways that social, medical, and legal institutions controlled women's bodies and women's health. Those who started the public protests of the Miss America Pageant in 1968, for example, objected not just to the narrow images of beauty ("the Degrading Mindless-Boob-Girlie Symbol") but to other aspects of the contest. Among the ten points of protest:

> *Racism with Roses.* Since its inception in 1921, the Pageant has not had one Black finalist, and this has not been for a lack of test-case contestants. There has never been a Puerto Rican, Alaskan, Hawaiian, or Mexican-American winner. Nor has there ever been a *true* Miss America—an American Indian.

The Irrelevant Crown on the Throne of Mediocrity. Miss America represents what women are supposed to be: inoffensive, bland, apolitical. If you are tall, short, over or under what weight The Man prescribes you should be, forget it. Personality, articulateness, intelligence, and commitment—unwise. Conformity is the key to the crown—and, by extension, to success in our Society.

Miss America as Dream Equivalent To—? In this reputedly democratic society, where every little boy supposedly can grow up to be president, what can every little girl hope to grow to be? Miss America. That's where it's at. Real power to control our own lives is restricted to men, while women get patronizing pseudo-power, an ermine clock and a bunch of flowers; men are judged by their actions, women by appearance.[15]

A few years later control over female bodies and women's health were more firmly linked when the Boston Women's Health Book Collective published *Our Bodies Ourselves* in its first commercial edition in 1973. It offered women information towards regaining some of that control, and has been republished in updated editions since that time. In the same year, the U.S. Supreme Court ruled in *Roe v. Wade* that the decision to end a pregnancy is a fundamental right—part of the "right of privacy" as guaranteed by the 14th Amendment. This decision is significant not only for women's reproductive rights, but for GLBT movements as well, since it establishes the "privacy" rationale that has since been used to argue for some GLBT rights.

Work, family, and education were also included in the revived feminism agenda. Economic concerns included not just "equal pay for equal work" but included more fundamental analyses of such issues as sex discrimination, the "gendering" of occupations, and the lack of support systems for working women. In these critiques, African American feminists were particularly important. In groups such as the Third World Women's Alliance (f. 1968) and in works like *The Black Woman,* they raised economic and other issues they felt were ignored by white, middle-class women.[16] African American feminists also formed the Combahee River Collective in Roxbury, Massachusetts in 1974; in a significant 1977 statement they expressed their position:

We are a collective of Black feminists who have been meeting together since 1974. During that time we have been involved in the process of defining and clarifying our politics, while at the same time doing political work within our own group and in coalition with other progressive organizations and movements. . . . we are actively committed to struggling against racial, sexual, heterosexual, and class oppression and see as our particular task the development of integrated analysis and practice based upon the fact that the major systems of oppression are interlocking. . . . As Black women we see Black feminism as the logical political movement to combat the manifold and simultaneous oppressions that all women of color face.[17]

Working mothers of all ethnicities especially felt the crunch of society's expectation, and suffered from the wage gap (in which women's overall earnings have varied from 59 percent to 70 percent of men's overall earnings). Gender training began young, it was noted, with girls and boys encouraged toward different interests deemed appropriate to being masculine or feminine, a process that continued through their college and even graduate training (with "male" disciplines usually paying more salary). The new field of Women's Studies was introduced into college curricula by second wave feminists and eventually became established in institutions throughout the country.

A temporary victory for postwar feminism was congressional approval in 1972 of a proposed ERA (Equal Rights Amendment). A similar constitutional amendment had been proposed in 1923 but it failed repeatedly in Congress through the years. Finally in

1972 a version passed the Senate and, having passed the House the previous year, the ERA was sent to the states. Within the first year twenty-two states ratified it and hopes ran high for its eventual adoption. However, conservatives quickly mobilized an effective opposition and only thirteen more states ratified between 1973 and 1978, totaling thirty-five of the thirty-eight required. Newly formed antifeminist groups like Phyllis Schlafly's Eagle Forum/STOP ERA were able to raise enough questions and fears about the application of "women's equality" that the ERA never passed, despite a three-year extension on the original seven-year limit.

The ERA typified liberal or moderate feminism as opposed to radical feminism. The liberal/radical division is common to movements for change and is expressed in the language used to define goals, language like "rights" (liberal) versus "liberation" (radical). Liberal feminism, like the liberal arm of the civil rights movement, seeks equality of citizenship and equal opportunities in the economic and social realms. In this worldview discrimination based on sexism is the barrier to equality. Liberal feminists have addressed both the discrimination and the sexism causing it; the first through legal reform and the second through educational efforts. Beneath this and any liberal perspective is a basic faith in the validity of America's political and economic systems, but a belief that fallible human beings and their prejudices do not allow the systems to work perfectly. Reform through the system's channels—equal pay and access to all professions, laws allowing women to control their property and their bodies—will chip away at sexism until it disappears.

In contrast radical feminists have proposed that sexism, like discrimination, is also an effect rather than a cause, and that both are rooted in patriarchy (to be "radical" in fact, is to seek the "root" of a problem). Patriarchy is a system of power in which men dominate women (and children) and can enforce that domination using society's institutions. In theory all women are subject to all men, giving rise to the concept of sisterhood based on the category "Woman" (a combination of one's given sex and the sex roles, or gender, assigned because of biology). In order for Woman to achieve true freedom and equality, said radical feminists, women must achieve sisterhood (a sense that they have subjugation to men in common) and unite to destroy patriarchy. An important contribution of radical feminists—notably the Redstockings (f. 1969 and still active)—was the "consciousness-raising" session in which many women were allowed to explore many of their emotions, including anger, for the first time in their lives. These sessions also verified a key idea adopted since then by other movements, that "the personal is political." Radicals also recognized that many barriers existed between women, such as race, class, and religion, causing them to identify more with "their" men. As a result radicals, especially women of color, were in the forefront of analyzing intersecting systems of oppression. Capitalism also came under attack, though there was debate regarding its relationship—was is cause or effect?—to patriarchy. From this perspective, a goal like equal pay for equal work would be like a coat of paint on a house full of termites: it might make the structure look better and those looking at it feel better, but does not address the problem at its core.

If radicals felt there were limits to the women's movement as it reemerged in the sixties, lesbians and bisexual women, whether liberal or radical, had plenty of reason to agree. Betty Friedan and the National Organization for Women were openly hostile to lesbians, Friedan herself referring to them as the "lavender menace" and their issues as a "lavender herring" and a "diversion" from the real business of NOW. Friedan apparently feared that to embrace lesbianism would destroy the women's movement and even suspected the open lesbians to be CIA operative sent to do just that. In late

1970 Friedan engineered the expulsion of lesbians, including local president Ivy Bottini, from NOW's New York chapter. Lesbians in the movements were not inclined to give up and continued to press for inclusion in NOW and in the movement at large (which was often equated with NOW). Within a year of the New York purge, members of NOW's national convention passed a resolution stating in part, "NOW recognizes the double oppression of women who are lesbians…NOW acknowledges the oppression of lesbians as a legitimate concern of feminism."[18]

Lesbian Feminism as Theory and Practice

"What is a lesbian?" So began the tract, "The Woman Identified Woman" produced by lesbians of the Gay Liberation Front who, under the names Lavender Menace, Lesbian Liberation, and Radicalesbians, were fed up with the sexism of gay liberation and the homophobia of mainstream feminism. The tract's authors then answered the question and stated now-famous positions:

> A lesbian is the rage of all women condensed to the point of explosion…. Lesbian is a label invented by the Man to throw at any woman who dares to be his equal, who dares to challenge his prerogatives…who dares to assert the primacy of her own needs. To have the label applied to people active in women's liberation is just the most recent instance of a long history;…For in this sexist society, for a woman to be independent means she can't be a woman—she must be a dyke…. It is the primacy of women relating to women, of women creating a new consciousness of and with each other, which is at the heart of women's liberation, and the basis for the cultural revolution. Together we must find, reinforce, and validate our authentic selves. As we do this, we confirm in each other that struggling, incipient sense of pride and strength, the divisive barriers begin to melt, we feel this growing solidarity with our sisters. We see ourselves as prime, find our centers inside of ourselves. We find receding the sense of alienation, of being cut off, of being behind a locked window, of being unable to get out what we know is inside. We feel a real-ness, feel at last we are coinciding with ourselves. With that real self, with that consciousness, we begin a revolution to end the imposition of all coercive identifications, and to achieve maximum autonomy in human expression.[19]

The manifesto was distributed during the Lavender Menace takeover of the Second Congress to Unite Women in New York City on May 1, 1970: seventeen women clad in lavender T-shirts with "Lavender Menace" written on them disrupted the conference to demand attention to lesbian issues. They were successful in many ways, and the work of these and many other lesbians created the lesbian feminism of the seventies that made a lasting impact.

The context was significant: lesbian feminists were active in gay liberation and/or second wave feminism but found both movements lacking in sensitivity to lesbians, and as willing as the larger culture to silence or marginalize them. In response they founded collectives and developed groundbreaking theory. A notable example, though short lived, was the Furies collective in Washington, DC, whose members married ideas to action (and vice versa) in their communal arrangement and through *The Furies* newspaper. Lesbian feminist books appeared as well: Kate Millett's *Sexual Politics* (1970); *Sappho Was a Right-On Woman* by Sidney Abbott and Barbara Love, and *Lesbian/Woman* by Del Martin and Phyllis Lyon (both in 1972); and Jill Johnston's *Lesbian Nation: The Feminist Solution* (1973). The scholarly journal *Signs* was launched in 1975 and although it was not exclusively lesbian its first issue featured an article that helped pave the way for lesbian history, Carroll Smith-Rosenberg's

"The Female World of Love and Ritual: Relations Between Women in Nineteenth-Century America." (See also the Suggested Resources for this chapter under "Lesbians/Feminism/Lesbian Feminism.")

At the end of the decade *Signs* made a major contribution to lesbian feminist theory by publishing a piece by Adrienne Rich entitled, "Compulsory Heterosexuality and Lesbian Existence" (1980). In its pages Rich added at least two elements to the radical critique of patriarchy. First is an analysis of the ways heterosexuality, because it is required by society ("compulsory"), acts as both product and prop of patriarchy by forcing would-be lesbians (and gay men) into heterosexual relations. For women especially, the limits placed on their economic and social choices further make hetero-sexual marriage necessary in many cases. This suggests a hidden history of lesbians who would live as such given the choice and opportunities. Second is Rich's presentation of a "lesbian continuum," challenging the largely accepted "either/or" model of hetero-homo sexualities (with bi in an uneasy position as another identity rather than a fluid condition). A continuum, or line, of lesbian possibilities would allow many more women on it than in the older category "lesbian" and include love and desire, as well as sexual activity——the romantic friends of the 19th century, for example, would be claimed for the continuum.

Lesbian feminists thus took controversial stands and raised thorny issues, even within lesbian/gay liberation, generating heated debate. For example, they saw the butch/femme roles adopted by postwar working-class lesbians (see Chapter 4) as the re-creation of patriarchy through gender, and instead promoted a more androgynous look and behavior. They investigated sexual identity itself and the role of choice in determining sexuality. Out of this came the concept of the political lesbian (as outlined above in "The Woman Identified Woman") and promoting the term "sexual preference" just at the time rights activists were insisting on "sexual orientation." Many lesbian feminists felt (and still do) that social conditioning combines with inborn sex to make "Womyn" and "Men" distinct categories. This resulted in lesbian separatism, which included the insistence on womyn-only spaces to include only "womyn-born-womyn" (that is, no MTF trans people allowed—see "Music and Festivals," below). Conflicts between lesbian feminists and trans people erupted: Jean O'Leary and others refused to let trans activist Sylvia Rivera speak at the 1973 New York City Gay Pride rally while in the same year transsexual lesbian Beth Elliot was expelled from the West Coast Women's Conference. Disputes also occurred among lesbians and lesbian feminists, over the inclusion of nonwhite, nonprivileged voices and, by the early 1980s, over pornography and sadomasochisim (S&M) in the so-called "sex wars." This latter coincided with the declaration of a "third wave" of feminism and reflected a kind of generation gap also present between the waves. Lesbian (and other) feminists by now were older and the position some took against porn and S&M seemed to younger women more "antisex" than "antipatriarchy." When Catharine MacKinnon and Andrea Dworkin attempted to institute legal bans on pornography their actions were likened to those of earlier moralistic censors and the emerging New Right (neither of whom were friends of feminists and queers). The debates have continued in publications and in women spaces that are among the legacies of 1970s lesbian feminism.

Music and Festivals

Lesbians and lesbian feminist philosophy were driving forces in what is generally called women's music and the annual festivals that celebrate women's creativity.

Aside from residential and publishing collectives they are among the rare instances of applied theory in any movement. Among pioneering lesbian musicians Holly Near, Alix Dobkin, Meg Christian, and Cris Williamson take center stage—all singer-songwriters that added melodic expressions of pride and community. Holly Near founded Redwood Records in 1972, a few years before she came out as a lesbian. The next year openly lesbian feminist Alix Dobkin formed the label Women's Wax Works and with Kay Gardner produced *Lavender Jane Loves Women.* The album made history as the first completely produced by lesbians, from financing to performance. Also in 1973 a group including Ginny Berson, Meg Christian, Judy Dlugacz, Cris Williamson, and Jennifer Woodul founded the collective Olivia Records and released a 45 rpm recording. Their first album was Meg Christian's *I Know You Know* and in 1975 they released perhaps the most popular album in the genre, Cris Williamson's *The Changer and the Changed,* also one of the best-selling independent albums of all time. Margie Adam, Therese Edell, Ferron, Sue Fink, Robin Flower, Betsy Rose, Linda Tillery, Teresa Trull, and Cathy Winter were among those who performed and recorded women's music in its early years. By injected humor into their songs many singers also defied the stereotype of the stern (lesbian) feminist, as did the laughter evoked by lesbian stand-up comedians like Robin Tyler and Kate Clinton as the decade closed.

Women's music became an important outlet for feminist and lesbian feminist expression begin-ning in the 1970s, and festivals were organized around the country as celebrations of female strength and spirit. Pictured here is a 1980s concert at the Michigan Womyn's Music Festival, which draws thousands of women each year. (© 2007 JEB (Joan E. Biren) No reproduction without permission.)

An important venue for performance and for celebrating women generally has been the music festival. The first was the National Women's Music Festival, begun in Champaign-Urbana, Illinois in 1974 and held since then at varying midwest locations. The same year festivals were mounted in California and Maryland and in 1976 came the event that soon defined the institution, the Michigan Womyn's Music Festival. Michfest, as it is known, became the largest festival, attracting thousands of women for a week of camping with music, comedy, craft sales, workshops, and other events. It is famous as "safe space" for women and controversial for its policy excluding all but "womyn-born-womyn." Trans women and boys over five are thus not allowed on the land, though the latter can attend a nearby camp. The few national festivals gave rise to local and regional events throughout the country, from Alaska and Hawai'i to New Mexico and Texas to several on the eastern seaboard. Lesbians have been important in documenting the festivals (and GLBT history overall), as in photographs and publications by Toni Armstrong Jr. and Joan E. Biren (JEB), and the book by historian Bonnie Morris, *Eden Built by Eves.*

A BURST OF ORGANIZING

In the Academy

Within a year after Stonewall, professionals in higher education began forming groups within their professional organizations to address issues specific to the lives and scholarship of lesbians and gay men. First were librarians, who in 1970 formed a Task Force on Gay Liberation (now the GLBT Round Table) within the American Library Association. Caucuses within the Modern Language Association and American Psychological Association followed in 1973, as did the broader Gay Academic Union. The GAU began in New York City to create a network in colleges and universities that would support activism on the one hand and research and teaching on the other. Until it ended in 1984 it sponsored national conferences and regional meetings and was instrumental in laying the foundation for Gay and Lesbian Studies and in working against discrimination. Members also bridged the traditional gap between "academic" and "real" worlds, as in the case of Gregory Sprague, a national director of the GAU who founded the Chicago Gay History Project in 1978 (later the Gerber/Hart Library). By mid-decade professionals formed groups within a half-dozen more disciplines, including sociology (Sociologists' Lesbian and Gay Caucus) and history (Committee on Lesbian and Gay History). Over the next twenty years GLBT members started subgroups in the majority of professional and academic organizations. Importantly, from the beginning these groups held meetings at their larger conventions and published newsletters that enhanced communication among caucus members, with the "parent" organization, and with other caucuses (by exchanging newsletters and, later, e-mail news).

Out of the academic ferment came courses in gay studies, lesbian studies, or both. The first such class is thought to be that of Louis Crompton, taught at the University of Nebraska in 1970. A survey of gay and lesbian literature at San Francisco City College and a course taught by Madeline Davis on "Lesbianism" at SUNY Buffalo were among the first courses to appear anywhere in the early 1970s. Sociology, psychology, and more literature courses soon were offered in a few institutions in such states as California (San Jose State University, UCLA), Connecticut (Yale), and Oregon (Southern Oregon State University); instructors began teaching gay history in a few departments in the 1980s. The first gay studies program is attributed to California State University,

Sacramento, in 1972 but the first separate department granting a degree in the field was nearly twenty years in the future.

Corresponding with new courses and the new climate generally, documenting GL life began in earnest. Within three years of Stonewall a handful of books were available, including *Out of the Closets: Voices of Gay Liberation* (1972), edited by Karla Jay and Allen Young; Merle Miller's *On Being Different: What It Means to Be Homosexual* (1971); *The Gay Militants* (1971), edited by Donn Teal; Kay Tobin's and Randy Wicker's, *The Gay Crusaders* (1972); and *Homosexuals and the Military: A Study of Less Than Honorable Discharge* (1971) by Colin J. Williams and Martin S. Weinberg. In 1973 *The Gay Liberation Book* appeared, edited by Len Richmond and Gary Noguera, and Jonathan Ned Katz published his landmark collection of primary sources, *Gay American History,* in 1976.

The Task Force and Lambda Legal

The fall of 1973 was significant for organizing around law and policy. In October of that year a handful of frustrated Gay Activists Alliance members met in New York City and sought to create "an American Civil Liberties Union for gays, a voice for the 'ordinary' homosexual." The result was the National Gay Task Force. The founders included Bruce Voeller, Nathalie Rockhill, and Tom Smith, and they agreed that part of its general mission would be encouraging people to come out while working on the legal and social barriers to that process. Similar to many in the homophile movement after the mid-1950s, they hoped to replace public stereotypes of "mannish women or Nellie men" with images of well-dressed, middle-class gay men and lesbians and to work within the legal and medical systems to enact change.[20] Their plan was for a national civil rights organization with paid staff and a board of directors, a structure in line with their relatively mainstream goals.

Under Voeller's leadership the Task Force soon created a broad agenda that included fighting for local and national antidiscrimination laws, for better media portrayals of homosexuals, and against psychiatry's designation of homosexuality as an illness (see below). In 1976 Jean O'Leary became coexecutive director alongside Voeller, partly in response to the desire for representation of women's concerns in a national forum (a decade later, in a pattern duplicated throughout the rights movements, the word "Lesbian" was added to the name, making it the National Gay and Lesbian Task Force). One goal to the end of the decade was to foster better relations with the Democratic Party and work with the Party against the antigay backlash then gaining momentum (see Chapter 7). The NGTF was instrumental in arranging a historic 1977 meeting—the first ever—between lesbian and gay movement leaders and White House staff for a briefing on a broad range of issues (President Carter did not attend, however, and no sitting president would meet with GLBT activists until Clinton did so in 1993).

Virginia Apuzzo was named director in 1982 and in her three years the Task Force was energized, particularly in addressing the new crisis of AIDS. Jeff Levi was hired to lobby in Washington, and he went on to direct the NGLTF, moving its headquarters to DC. This allowed better access and potentially more collaboration with other activists, though at times there seemed as much competition as cooperation for national leadership (such as that between NGLTF and the Human Rights Campaign Fund, founded in DC in 1980). A Policy Institute was added in 1995 and it continues to be an important educational and political arm of the movements as a whole. In a recent account of the NGLTF historian John D'Emilio fittingly summarized that "...no account of the changes in the laws and public policies that shape gay and lesbian life in the United States would be complete without attention to the Task Force."[21]

The LLDEF (Lambda Legal Defense and Education Fund) also had its beginnings in October 1973, when it was incorporated. The following year it was granted federal tax-exempt status, a first for any gay rights group. Almost immediately LLDEF took up the cause of a gay student group at the New Hampshire, and by the end of the decade its lawyers had helped lesbian and gay parents gain visitation or custody rights and successfully sued to restore a gay professor's position when he was fired due to his orientation. In the early eighties Lambda Legal took on the federal government in the form of the Immigration and Naturalization Service, the Defense Department, and the prison system, winning significant victories and paving the way for further actions. In New York, Lambda Legal won a case that struck down the state's sodomy law in 1980 and the organization has since been at the center of cases related to AIDS, domestic partnership, and other rights issues.

The APA Victory

The "first great victory of the movement" came not in the realm of law but in medicine.[22] The designation of homosexuality as a mental illness was rooted in late-19th-century sexology and blossomed side-by-side with postwar homophile organizing. This was not coincidental: psychology and psychiatry enjoyed increasing popularity in an era obsessed with secrecy, ulterior motives, and eliminating "subversives." Any "difference"—foreign birth, Jewish faith, advocating civil rights—was equated with the communist threat, with homosexuality second only to Communist Party membership on the "top dangers to the American way" list. Thus in 1952 the APA (American Psychiatric Association) listed homosexuality as a "sociopathic personality disturbance" in its first *DSM* (*Diagnostic and Statistical Manual of Mental Disorders*) while early homophile groups sought professionals in medicine as well as law and religion to legitimize them and their efforts (see Chapter 4). Even when the *Manual* was revised in 1968 homosexuality remained, now as a "nonpsychotic mental disorder."

Although some lesbians and gay men had internalized the prevalent view that they were ill and needed treatment, not everyone did. According to pioneer activist Barbara Gittings a turning point came in the early sixties when Frank Kameny first formulated not only "a complete, coherent philosophy for the Gay movement," but one that also included the message, "we are not sick."[23] Through the sixties Gittings and Kameny remained in the forefront of conveying this to professional and lay people, straight and GLBT, and gay liberation enlivened the debate with new tactics and less patience. In the early seventies liberationists were willing to confront psychiatrists at their meetings and disrupt panel discussions while also seeking to present their own case. In a now-famous event a five-member panel addressed "Psychiatry: Friend or Foe to Homosexuals? A Dialogue" at the 1972 APA convention; the panelists were Gittings, Kameny, Dr. Judd Marmor, Dr. Robert Seidenberg, and "Dr. H. Anonymous." The last was a gay psychiatrist, who agreed to speak, but only with a mask and wig obscuring his identity (Dr. John Fryer "came out" as that panelist years later). Activists continued to work with psychiatrists and against psychiatry to change the official mental health view. In December of 1973 the APA Board of Trustees voted to revise its statement on homosexuality in *DSM-II* with this new category and explanation:

302.0 Sexual orientation disturbance (Homosexuality)

This category is for individuals whose sexual interests are directed primarily toward people of the same sex and who are either disturbed by, in conflict with, or wish to change their sexual orientation. This diagnostic category is distinguished from homosexuality, which by itself does not constitute a psychiatric disorder. Homosexuality per se is one form of sexual behavior and, like other forms of sexual behavior which are not by themselves psychiatric disorders, is not listed in this nomenclature of mental disorders.[24]

The change may seem mild from the distance of thirty years, but to those who spent their lives struggling to accept themselves it was monumental. As Barbara Gittings loved to recount about the power of that vote, "We went to bed sick and we woke up cured!"[25]

Outsiders among Outsiders

Effective organization, with results like the APA victory, appeared to be key for gay/lesbian liberation as for other movements in the past. However, as lesbians had found among both gay men and straight women, there will still be blind spots among the most dedicated activists. People who were older, nonwhite, and/or (ironically) neither straight nor lesbian/gay often felt invisible within movements supposedly developing an understanding of oppression. Not surprisingly, their reaction was further organizing around identity markers. Age and ethnicity issues caused some to desire better representation. Older lesbians and gay men and their allies founded SAGE (Senior Action in a Gay Environment) in 1977. It survives and serves as an advocacy, informational, and social group for GLBT senior citizens, whose numbers will only increase as GLBT baby boomers grow as old as their straight cohorts.

Race (and class) could be divisive among GLBT people, especially when white privilege was ignored or dismissed by whites. Nonwhite or non-Anglo people first formed caucuses within larger organizations and/or local groups. Lesbian and gay Chicanos in Los Angeles, for example, met in *Unidos,* founded in 1970. In San Francisco Randy Burns and Barbara Cameron, with ten others, formed Gay American Indians in 1975 and the network grew quickly to include nations all over the country. African Americans met in caucuses in New York, Detroit, and many other cities in the seventies. Reverend Dolores Jackson and others founded the Salsa Soul Sisters for Black and Latina lesbians in New York in 1974, the first such organization in the country; the name, and to some degree the focus, was changed later to African Ancestral Lesbians United for Societal Change. Lesbians of Color in Los Angeles (f. 1978) also represented a broader approach since it included women of Asian, African, Latina, and Native American descent. By the end of the decade the National Coalition of Black Lesbians and Gays existed in Washington, DC and had organized a National Third World Lesbian and Gay Conference to coincide with the first National March on Washington for Lesbian and Gay Rights (see Chapter 7).

If people of color saw gay and lesbian liberationist as a white-dominated movement, bisexuals and transgendered people felt it welcomed the theory of their sexualities more than the living representatives of that theory. The very term "liberation" suggested not only the right to one's body and to engage in consensual sexuality activity, but diverse and fluid identities as well. In practice, however, the politics of liberation often was more exclusive, or at least focused primarily on homophobia as the problem and therefore homosexuals as its main target. As seen above, lesbian feminists had issues of their own with bisexual women and MTF and cross-dressing men while other gay men and lesbians adopted a kind of "one-cause-at-a-time" politics very familiar in the United States.

One result was the beginning of bisexual and trans organizing in the 1970s. In New York bi activists formed the National Bisexual Liberation Group (1972) and the Bisexual Forum (1975), across the country they launched the San Francisco Bisexual Center in 1976, and local groups also formed in many "heartland" cities—Chicago, Detroit, and Minneapolis. Similarly, both straight and gay cross-dressers developed various groups and theories—the very term "transgender" is credited to heterosexual cross-dresser Virginia (Charles) Prince, founder of the Society for the Second Self (Tri-Ess, f. 1976). Gay drag queens were in the forefront of most trans activism, though. As early as 1970 Sylvia Rivera and Marsha P. Johnson formed STAR (Street Transvestite Action Revolutionaries) in New York and in Los Angeles Angela Douglas founded TAO (Transsexual/Transvestite Action Organization); in Philadelphia activists organized the Radical Queens Collective in the early seventies. Pioneering transsexuality expert Harry Benjamin retired at this time and in his honor a number of medical professionals created the Harry Benjamin International Gender Dysphoria Association (1979). Male-to-female transsexual surgery gained national attention when tennis player Richard Raskind became Renée Richards. She competed professionally as a woman, but only after a successful lawsuit against the U.S. Tennis Association. Her story was dramatized in a 1986 TV movie, *Second Serve,* starring Vanessa Redgrave.

Finally, a group (loosely speaking) whose status as insiders or outsiders within GLBT culture is unclear consists of straight women who cultivate close friendships with gay men. The origin of the term "fag hag" to describe these women is unclear—there are claims that it came out of Berkeley, California specifically in 1963 while other sources place it sometime between 1965 and 1970. Also vague is whether it was used initially in a positive or an demeaning way, and by whom. As with "fag" itself and other loaded terms (dyke, pansy, queer, and a host of ethnic slang words) the expression's power as an endearment versus an insult lay partially in who uses it and in what circumstances. Often "insiders" adopt the language used against them to deflect or redirect the potency of the words. "Fag hag" is therefore an interesting case, since it appears to have been used by gay men as both a compliment, to include the women, and dismissive, to exclude or ridicule them. The true insider is the straight woman seeking the company of one or more gay men, and some have proudly claimed the term. As a cultural phenomenon, the gay man/straight woman is revealing, especially in the desire of straight women for environments both "safe" and containing a male presence and the belief that safety and friendship with men is possible only if sexual tension is removed.

POLITICAL ARENAS

Change was in the air, and the time for organizing in all directions clearly was ripe. Differences over strategy would continue and the successes on all fronts led to further action. One of those fronts was traditional politics, where new organizations from national to local levels produced results. The Gay Activists Alliance in New York, coupled with the second-ever campaign of an openly gay candidate, fostered the new Gay Activists Alliance in the U.S. capital (like the NGTF, the group added "Lesbian" to its name in 1986). The Alliance continues to exist, making it the nation's oldest gay rights operation. On the West coast the Municipal Elections Committee of Los Angeles became something of a model after its inception in 1977. To critics of later political action, though, it also represented the model of the dominance of white, privileged gay men since its founders fit that description.

The Democratic Party

Gay men and lesbians seeking inclusion felt the Democrats rather than the Republicans were their best hope for working within the system. On one hand, lesbian and gay Democrats had formed clubs in a few cities by the time the '72 elections rolled around, and began to influence the party. That year was historic, in fact: Madeline Davis and Jim Foster, both out, addressed the Democratic National Convention and their speeches were televised. On the other hand, a gay rights plank was not adopted; according to insider Steve Endean, "the lesbian and gay rights issue was still too young and emerging to successfully become a part of the agenda" of progressives in the party, who had nominated George McGovern for president. Four years later the situation was mixed. NGTF members were "literally locked out of the Democratic National Platform deliberations" Endean recalled, but after Jimmy Carter won election he took more positive steps while serving as president.[26] Carter appointed openly lesbian Margaret (Midge) Costanza as his assistant for Public Liaison and she in turn convened the 1977 White House meeting with movement leaders (see above, under "The Task Force and Lambda Legal").

Running for Office

Although the first openly gay person had run for office in 1961, his bid was unsuccessful (see Chapter 4). It was another ten years before the second foray into politics of someone out, and not until 1974 did openly gay people win their first elections. Frank Kameny ran for Congress in 1971 in Washington, DC, to fill a House nonvoting seat recently created for the District. Although he came in fourth in a field of six, he was accurate in 1994 when he recalled, "My groundbreaking campaign created an ongoing gay political effort that has continued to the present."[27] Certainly the seventies were a turning point in this area as with so many others in lesbian and gay life, and the momentum, and victories, only increased to the end of the century. While gay men and lesbians began to win elections, a distinction is necessary among those who were out when they ran and those who came out at some point during or after their service. In addition, not everyone who later came out did so completely voluntarily. The seventies offer examples of all these cases.

The early seventies were significant in GLBT political history, but in ways that would not be apparent immediately. In 1972, Allan Spear and Barney Frank were elected to the Minnesota state senate and Massachusetts house, respectively, and Gerry Studds (D-MA) won a seat in the U.S. House of Representatives; the following year Robert Bauman (R-MD) was also elected to Congress as a representative. None were out at that time, but in 1974 Allan Spear came out and became one of the first three open homosexuals serving in government. He went on to a long career in Minnesota politics, eventually becoming Senate president and was, by the time he retired in 2000, "The Longest-Serving Openly Gay Elected Official in America."[28] Frank, still closeted, went on to the U.S. House in 1981 but did come out six years later and continued to win reelection. Preceding Frank in publicly acknowledging being gay was Studds, who in 1983 was the first member of Congress to do so, and won reelection until retiring in

1996. Finally, around the time Studds was publicly acknowledging his sexuality, Bob Bauman was at last accepting his. Bauman was notorious among many gay activists, not only for his antigay votes in Congress but for his secret gay life, while carrying on a public life as a married father and conservative spokesperson. News of his soliciting male prostitutes hit the media in 1980, and he lost reelection that year. At the time, he linked his behavior to alcoholism, which not only offended more proudly out gay men and lesbians but also may have contributed to his ability to deny his homosexuality to himself for a few more years. Once he came out to himself, however, he tried to work against homophobia among his fellow conservatives (see Chapter 7).

Interestingly, the first two out people to run and also win were both lesbians, and both won in 1974: Kathy Kozachenko was elected to the Ann Arbor (MI) City Council and Elaine Noble was elected to the Massachusetts state house. By 1980 at least four other gay/lesbian people had been elected or appointed to local posts in Massachusetts, New Jersey, and California, with one was coming out after he was in office (and winning reelection).

Probably the person best known as an openly gay public servant was elected to a local post, and his short tenure ended in tragedy. Harvey Milk, elected in 1977 to the San Francisco Board of Supervisors was assassinated, along with Mayor George Moscone, a year later (see Chapter 7). Milk was a relative newcomer, and his Castro Camera shop and political aspirations were not universally welcomed by more

Harvey Milk was among the first openly gay or lesbian people to run for office and win. Milk was elected to the San Francisco Board of Supervisors in 1977 and is pictured here at his inaugural walk to City Hall from the Castro neighborhood on January 9, 1978. Later that year Milk and Mayor George Moscone were assassinated. (© Dan Nicoletta.)

established residents, gay or straight. He had run unsuccessfully in the previous two elections but by '77 he had solidified a wider base of support and received the most votes out of the seventeen candidates running. In a tape of his political will, Milk expressed views that to many reflected both his career and reasons for running for office as openly gay:

> I ask for the movement to continue, for the movement to grow because last week, I got the phone call from Altoona, Pennsylvania and my election gave somebody else, one more person, hope. And after all it's what this is all about. It's not about personal gain, not about ego, not about power—it's about giving those young people out there in the Altoona, Pennsylvania's hope. You gotta give them hope.[29]

Legislating against Discrimination

Electing sympathetic people to office was one avenue to equality. Once there, officials and lobbyists worked to convince enough lawmakers that sexuality should not be used as a tool of discrimination. Efforts were largely twofold and involved passing some laws and repealing others. Thanks to political activists cities across the country began to include "sexual orientation" in statues prohibiting discrimination ("sexual preference" was a term also in use but deemed less effective in law since it suggests choosing a sexuality—or behavior—that most lawmakers already felt did not deserve any protection). Seattle, Washington, DC, Minneapolis, St. Paul, and tiny Alfred, New York, led the way, passing antidiscrimination ordinances in 1973–1974, and more than thirty followed by the end of 1977. Among them were Austin, Texas, Tucson, Arizona, Wichita, Kansas, Eugene, Oregon, Champaign-Urbana, Illinois, and Aspen, Colorado. At the county level Miami-Dade in Florida adopted an ordinance in early 1977 that soon would focus the nation's attention on the issue. In the states no similar efforts were yet successful, though Minnesota was again out in front with the Gay Rights Legislative Committee, (renamed the Minnesota Committee for Gay Rights in 1974), the nation's first such group. The other legal avenue, repeal, was focused on sodomy statutes: by 1986 those laws were rescinded in more than half of the states.

Legal challenges also included the proposed right of same-sex couples to marry. This had been raised before, in the 1950s, but in the early phase of gay liberation it likely seemed more possible (though certainly not all activists favored pressing for this right). A few couples brought cases forward to test the law, beginning in 1970, when Michael McConnell and Jack Baker applied for a license in Minneapolis. As expected, they were denied and they sued, losing their case. On appeal, the state Supreme Court ruled against their claim of constitutional protection under the 14th Amendment, and the U.S. Supreme Court dismissed their appeal to that body. Couples in Washington state and Kentucky also sued to marry with similar results, and a few others applied for licenses but did not file lawsuits. What was lost in terms of legal precedent (and employment, in two instances) the movement gained in exposure to the discrepancies in treatment between heterosexuals and homosexuals. The rights of lesbians and gay men in life partnerships would continue to be on the agendas of several organizations, with some success in all but legal marriage until the early 21st century.

A National Bill

The optimism resulting from successes with the APA and legislation on the local and state levels carried over into the national arena, as did the mentality of civil rights legislation from the 1960s. Riding these waves, Congresswoman Bella Abzug (D-NY) introduced the "Equality Act of 1974" in May of that year. The bill prohibited discrimination based on sexual orientation as well as sex and marital status. The next year a bill concerning only "affectional or sexual preference" was introduced as the Civil Rights Amendments of 1975 (to 1964 Civil Rights Act). From the beginning of this effort, at least three issues remained controversial inside and outside gay/lesbian communities. The first was whether legislation was the proper strategy at all. Second, if it was, should a national bill include other categories or stand alone? Finally, beneath it all was whether homosexuals should be defined as a "class" or "minority." The last point many movement activists had taken as a given while both opponents and supporters of gay rights and/or gay liberation had questioned that approach (though for very different reasons). When Moral Majority founder Jerry Falwell reacted to the bill, he warned that "...our government seems determined to legalize homosexuals as a legitimate 'minority.'"[30] While many activists would have celebrated such a goal (had it been true of Congress) others felt that truly liberationist aims would be sacrificed for a short-term legal "stamp of approval."

The bill continued to be reintroduced throughout the seventies and eighties, with a general pattern of changing principal sponsors and an increasingly longer list of cosponsors. In 1977 Ed Koch (D-NY) reintroduced the bill in the House, and the following year Ted Weiss (D-NY) and Henry Waxman (D-CA) did the same. The two national gay rights organizations, the National Gay Task Force and the Gay Rights National Lobby, were working closely with selected congressmen, and once Steve Endean arrived in 1978 he made the bill a top priority.

For a national gay rights bill ever to get past committee, Endean and others knew that three goals must be met: more sponsors, Republican support, and a Senate bill. All three were accomplished to some degree as early as 1980, in spite of (or perhaps because of) a growing backlash against gay and lesbian visibility and rights. In 1979, when the number of cosponsors exceeded forty, the list included three Republicans. Two of those Republicans, Pete McCloskey (CA) and William Green (NY) penned a "Dear Colleagues" letter to encourage other party supporters, and its wording reveals something of the strategy and debates of the time. It read, in part:

> The 1976 Republican Platform states that: "The Government must protect your constitutional rights. The government must assure equal opportunity."
>
> Support of this legislation does not condone homosexuality per se.... attempts to regulate the private lives of citizens run directly counter to the Republican commitment to lessen the role of government in the lives of the citizens of the U.S.[31]

At the end of that year Paul Tsongas (D-MA), with Lowell Weicker (R-CT) and Daniel Moynihan (D-NY), introduced a Senate version and in October of 1980 a historic congressional field hearing was held in San Francisco—the first ever on a federal gay civil rights bill. Less than two years later, a similar hearing was held in DC, but by then a New Right and a new disease had emerged that, separately and together, were able to stall the remarkable momentum of the seventies (see Chapter 7).[32]

ONE STEP FORWARD...

To many lesbian and gay Americans who were there and later had the opportunity to look back on them the seventies were a kind of Golden Age. Although the early nineties came to be called the "gay moment" by observers, the years after Stonewall and before

"Gay Liberation," a sculpture by George Segal, was commissioned in 1979 as a commemoration of the Stonewall riot. It was completed in 1980 but not installed at Sheridan Square in New York City until 1992. (© Lee Snider/The Image Works)

AIDS deserve special attention as a mini-era. Certainly the seeds of gay/lesbian pride and gay/lesbian liberation had been sown long before Stonewall, and in fact had bloomed into different forms throughout the century. "Homosexuals"—at least those who violated their assigned gender—had even been highly visible early in the century in some urban settings, had formed communities and had devised signals for mutual recognition in a hostile society. A great deal of change and significance is simply timing, though; if the early nineties would become the "gay moment" the seventies were (to paraphrase a motto of Reconstruction) "the lesbians' and gays' hour." During that decade political theories of gay liberation and lesbian feminism developed rapidly and would have lasting influence. Political action of all kinds arose from the grassroots and reached into the halls of Congress. Organizing encompassed every sex, gender, and color. As before, GLBT expression used every medium from print to music but now had larger audiences inside and outside "the family." Truly, gay, lesbian, bisexual, and transgendered cultures that survived unbroken are a major legacy of the so-called "Me Decade."

The United States did not suddenly abandon its deeply rooted homophobia as a result, of course. (Tellingly, the term "homophobia" was coined in the 1970s, and by an American psychologist, George Weinberg.) Every movement involving difference and translated into a greater share of collective power has been met with ridicule, resistance, and violence. The temptation is often to "blame the victim": if only "they" (slaves, women, workers, opponents of war, and so on) would just be quiet and accept their place others would not be "provoked" into drastic measures to silence them. A number of GLBT people had never been silent despite the risks and after 1970 that

DEBATE: ASSIMILATION OR LIBERATION?

Gay and lesbian liberationists intensified an older debate within GLBT activism, perhaps clarifying it without resolving it. Resolution, though, may not be possible: all movements for social change have divided and usually one of the first splits is over assimilation. Also called accommodation, it implies just that: bending to the needs or wishes of others, making them comfortable. On one side is an emphasis on how similar the group is to those in the "mainstream"; their goals are political equality, economic opportunities, and "tolerance" of any differences they embody. On the other side are nonassimilationists, or nonaccommodationists, who *may* have the same goals but believe that toleration is not enough—differences should be accepted or even celebrated. The latter view is usually considered "radical," and in the context of the sixties it was associated also with "liberationist" politics. Like radical feminism, radical politics of any kind represents fundamental change and are liberationist when they link that change to the idea of interdependent oppressions—to attack one is to attack all. The issue of difference in the United States has been sticky, mired in the problem of balancing personal freedom with national unity and conferring more rights on those who conform to a cultural ideal than on those who do not. Which differences matter and why? How similar to people need to be to a "norm" to gain equality in a capitalist democracy? As Native Americans, selected immigrants, African Americans, and women found, the right to be different (from a Protestant, English/Western European, male, middle-class, standard) has often clashed with the fear that too much difference will destroy the country, resulting in the demand to assimilate.

As already shown, as soon as there was a sustained GLBT movement there were arguments over assimilation. Even before that the issue was always lurking beneath the actions of publicly "flamboyant" men and "masculine" women on the one hand and the closeted people who sought distance from the public queers on the other. After World War II the twin impulses towards asserting rights *and* conforming were at a peak and affected the new homophile movement (see Chapter 4). After only a few years the Mattachine Society adopted a "conservative" line—we (homosexuals) are just like you (heterosexuals) except for the minor difference of our sexuality—and the Daughters of Bilitis followed suit. As the groups grew larger and new organizations arose the basic division between assimilation/moderate and liberation/radical would deepen accordingly, but not always along a neat fault line. Moderate theory might combine with radical actions (or vice versa). For example, the organizers of the pickets in DC and Philadelphia adopted strict assimilationist dress codes and were seeking government employment; at the same time, many of them already believed the radical view that "Gay is Good," and to picket for rights at a time when homosexuality was still unspeakable was a radical strategy toward a moderate goal.

All these differences were well developed by the time gay liberation was more formally declared in 1969. The context had changed, though, and among many young people there was less tolerance for tolerance—less patience with accommodating to a society already under attack for its toleration of poverty amid plenty and of racism, sexism, and war. Like the militants before them gay liberationists rejected the idea that only those willing to be straight, act straight, or say they were straight deserved to be treated decently. Philosophically gay liberation, sexual liberation, and political liberation were part and parcel of each other, and building coalitions with other movements was one strategy. When they began organizing, though, they also confronted old dilemmas in attempting to unify theory, practice, goals, and actions. How should meetings be conducted? Who, if anyone is "in charge" and by what process? Should decisions be by consensus or simple majority? Should the goal be a powerful organization eventually working within the system to undermine it or will its very existence automatically undermine more radical goals? In other words, how is change accomplished in the United States? Historian Martin Duberman participated in the early liberationist groups and summarized many of these issues at the time. The night the formation of the National Gay Task Force was announced he wrote in his diary that

> NGTF clearly wants to pattern itself on the ACLU [American Civil Liberties Union] or NAACP [National Association for the Advancement of Colored People]—which means it can make a valuable contribution, but in the liberal, reformist mode: "let us in" rather than "let us show you new possibilities."

The following month he spoke at the Gay Academic Union and later reflected on the situation:

> ...we were in the ambivalent position of being products of the same set of cultural values that we were organizing to protest against—"values that confuse maleness with machismo, femaleness with docility, bisexuality with indecision, and sexuality with orgasm."... Indeed by 1974 the gay movement in general was heading into the same set of interlocking dilemmas that have characterized protest movements throughout our history. How to prevent a radical impulse from degenerating into reformist tinkering?"[33]

GLBT people would continue to confront these issues as they enjoyed greater public visibility and gained political power. With power and success comes the ability to define and exclude, however, and an irony of liberation has been an impulse to require conformity among its adherents.

number grew exponentially. By mid-decade a social and political backlash against the perceived "excesses" of the previous dozen years was forming among conservatives, for whom the gay/lesbian and pro-choice movements were symbols of all that had gone wrong. Public condemnations of GLBT people only fueled less civilized expressions of disapproval: the harassment, arson, assaults (by police and citizens alike) and murders also a part of the era seem almost predictable consequences of visibility and inching towards equality. When the Arkansas legislature first repealed its sodomy laws in 1975 and then rescinded the repeal two years later (that is, recriminalizing sodomy) it was the first in a series of more famous reversals to come.

Something of the mixed nature of "progress" toward visibility and acceptance is perfectly embodied in the circuitous route the statue "Gay Liberation" took to arrive at its current site. In 1979 a private organization commissioned sculptor George Segal to create a work commemorating the Stonewall riot. He fashioned two castings (one for New York and one for Los Angeles) of two groupings out of bronze—two men and two women—that were painted white. In his own words, "The sculpture concentrates on tenderness, gentleness and sensitivity as expressed in gesture. It makes the delicate point that gay people are as feeling as anyone else."[34] Once it came time to install the sculptures in its proposed, however, a variety of objections arose, and enough of them to halt the project in both cities. One was installed at Stanford University in 1984, where it was repeatedly vandalized, removed, and repaired. The other casting was placed in Madison, Wisconsin and finally moved to the originally intended site of Sheridan Square, near the site of the riot. It was dedicated there in June of 1992, the same year that Democratic presidential candidate (and eventual winner) Bill Clinton raised the hopes of GLBT people after a harrowing decade of disease, death, rage, and reorganization.

NOTES

1. Armistead Maupin, *Sure of You* (New York: Harper & Row, 1989), 91–92. Additional information from Brad L. Graham, "For Armistead Maupin, There Are Still *Tales* To Tell," http://www.bradlands.com/words/post/maupin-writethru.html.

2. Tom Wolfe, "The Me Decade and The Third Great Awakening," in *Mauve Gloves & Madmen, Clutter & Vine and Other Stories, Sketches, and Essays* (New York: Farrar, Straus and Giroux, 1976), 117–56.

3. Esther Newton, *Cherry Grove, Fire Island: Sixty Years in America's First Gay and Lesbian Town* (Boston: Beacon Press, 1993).

4. See "Cities/States" under Suggested Resources for studies of towns and neighborhoods.

5. Allan Bérubé, "The History of Gay Bathhouses," in *Policing Public Sex: Queer Politics and the Future of AIDS Activism,* ed. Dangerous Bedfellows (Boston: South End Press, 1996), 200–203; quotes p. 200.

6. Dudley Clendinen and Adam Nagourney, *Out for Good: The Struggle to Build a Gay Rights Movement in America* (New York: Simon & Schuster, 1999), 182.

7. Stephen Tropiano, *The Prime Time Closet: A History of Gays and Lesbians on TV* (New York: Applause Books, 2002), ix, 269. Also see Appendix, 261–311, for a GLBT TV Episode Guide, and his lists of "bests," 313–17.

8. Tropiano, *Prime Time Closet,* 240.

9. Vito Russo, *The Celluloid Closet: Homosexuality in the Movies,* rev. ed. (New York: Harper & Row, 1987), 347–49.

10. Harry M. Benshoff and Sean Griffin, *Queer Images: A History of Gay and Lesbian Film in America* (Lanham, MD: Rowman & Littlefield, 2006), 137.

11. *Time*'s "The Homosexual in America" cover feature consisted of "The Homosexual: Newly Visible, Newly Understood," "Four Lives in the Gay World," and "A Discussion: Are Homosexuals Sick?" October 31, 1969; "Homo/Hetero: The Struggle for Sexual Identity," *Harper's,* October 27, 1970; "Homosexuals in Revolt," *The New York Times,* August 24, 1970; Merle Miller, "What it Means to Be a Homosexual," *The New York Times Magazine,* January 17, 1971; "The Homosexual Couple," *Look,* January 26, 1971.

12. Michelangelo Signorile, *Queer in America: Sex, the Media, and the Closets of Power* (New York: Random House, 1993), 291.

13. *Patience & Sarah: A Pioneering Love Story,* music by Paula M. Kimper, libretto by Wende Persons.

14. See David Bergman, *The Violet Quill Reader* (New York: St. Martin's Press, 1994).

15. "No More Miss America!" in *Sisterhood in Powerful: An Anthology of Writings from the Women's Liberation Movement,* ed. Robin Morgan (New York: Vintage Books, 1970), 584–88; also available at http://www.cwluherstory.org/classic-feminist-writings/no-more-miss-america-2.html.

16. Toni Cade Bambara, ed., *The Black Woman* (New York: New American Library, 1970).

17. "A Black Feminist Statement," in *This Bridge Called My Back: Writings by Radical Women of Color,* ed. Cherríe Moraga and Gloria Anzaldúa (New York: Kitchen Table Press, 1981), 210.

18. Quotations from Clendinen and Nagourney, *Out for Good,* 98–102.

19. Radicalesbians, "The Woman Identified Woman," The Digital Scriptorium, Special Collections Library, Duke University, http://scriptorium.lib.duke.edu/wlm/womid/.

20. Quotations from Clendinen and Nagourney, *Out for Good,* 191–92.

21. John D'Emilio, "Organizational Tales: Interpreting the NGLTF Story," in *Creating Change™: Sexuality, Public Policy, and Civil Rights,* ed. John D'Emilio, William B. Turner, and Urvashi Vaid (New York: St. Martin's Press, 2000), 469.

22. Clendinen and Nagourney, *Out for Good,* 199.

23. Quoted from a 1974 interview with Gittings, in Jonathan Ned Katz, *Gay American History: Lesbians and Gay Men in the U.S.A.,* rev. ed. (New York: Penguin Meridian, 1992), 427.

24. American Psychiatric Association, "Homosexuality and Sexual Orientation Disturbance: Proposed Change in DSM-II," APA Document Reference No. 730008, available at http://www.psych.org/edu/other_res/lib_archives/archives/197308.pdf.

25. Conversation between Barbara Gittings and the author, March 7, 2003.

26. Quotations from Steve Endean, *Bringing Lesbian and Gay Rights into the Mainstream,* ed. Vicki L. Eaklor (Binghamton, NY: Haworth Press, 2006), 59.

27. Kathleen DeBold, ed., *Out for Office: Campaigning in the Gay Nineties* (Washington, DC: Gay and Lesbian Victory Fund, 1994), 13.

28. Title of a profile of Spear in Ken Yeager, *Trailblazers: Profiles of America's Gay and Lesbian Elected Officials* (Binghamton, NY: Haworth Press, 1999), 13–28. Although Barney Frank has been in office longer than Spear was, it will be 2013 before he matches Spear's record of serving twenty-six years as an *openly* gay person.

29. Quoted in Randy Shilts, *The Mayor of Castro Street: The Life & Times of Harvey Milk* (New York: St. Martin's Press, 1982), 375.

30. Jerry Falwell, *Listen, America!* (New York: Doubleday, 1980), 253.

31. Quoted in Endean, *Mainstream,* 215.

32. Also see Appendix B, "Cosponsors of the National Lesbian and Gay Civil Rights Bill [1975–1992]," in Endean, *Mainstream,* 301–6.

33. Martin Duberman, *Cures: A Gay Man's Odyssey* (New York: Dutton, 1991), 291, 296, and 297–98.

34. Art on File, at http://www.artonfile.com/html/projectnotes.lasso?id=1193.

SUGGESTED RESOURCES

General

Clendinen, D., & Nagourney, A. (1999). *Out for good: The struggle to build a gay rights movement in America.* New York: Simon & Schuster.

Feldblum, C.R. (2000). The Federal gay rights bill: From Bella to ENDA. In J. D'Emilio, W.B. Turner, & U. Vaid (Eds.), *Creating Change™: Sexuality, public policy, and civil rights* (pp. 149–187). New York: St. Martin's Press.

Shilts, R. (1982). *The mayor of Castro Street: The life & times of Harvey Milk.* New York: St. Martin's Press.

Cities/States

Armstrong, E. (2002). *Forging gay identities: Organizing sexuality in San Francisco, 1950–1994.* Chicago: University of Chicago Press.

Boag, P. (2004, Spring). 'Does Portland Need a Homophile Society?' Gay culture and activism in the Rose City between World War II and Stonewall. *Oregon Historical Quarterly, 105,* 6–39.

Boyd, N.A. (2003). *Wide open town: A history of Queer San Francisco to 1965.* Berkeley: University of California Press.

D'Emilio, J. (1989). Gay politics and community in San Francisco since World War II. In M. Duberman, M. Vicinus, & G. Chauncey, Jr. (Eds.), *Hidden from history: Reclaiming the gay and lesbian past* (pp. 456–473). New York: New American Library.

Faderman, L., & Timmons, S. (2006). *Gay L.A.: A history of sexual outlaws, power politics, and lipstick lesbians.* New York: Basic Books.

Howard, J. (2001). Protest and protestantism: Early lesbian and gay institution building in Mississippi. In A. Black (Ed.), *Modern American queer history* (pp. 198–223). Philadelphia: Temple University Press.

Kaiser, C. (1997). *The gay metropolis, 1940–1996.* Boston: Houghton Mifflin.

Krahulik, K.C. (2005). *Provincetown: From pilgrim landing to gay resort.* New York: New York University Press.

Stein, M. (2004). *City of sisterly and brotherly loves: Lesbian and gay Philadelphia, 1945–1972.* Philadelphia: Temple University Press.

Lesbians/Feminism/Lesbian Feminism

Abbott, S., & Love, B. (1972). *Sappho was a right-on woman: A liberated view of lesbianism.* New York: Scarborough House.

Atkinson, T.-G. (1974). *Amazon odyssey.* New York: Links Books.

Daly, M. (1973). *Beyond God the Father: Toward a philosophy of women's liberation.* Boston: Beacon Press.

Daly, M. (1978). *Gyn/ecology: The metaethics of radical feminism.* Boston: Beacon Press.

Duggan, L., & Hunter, N.D. (1995). *Sex wars: Sexual dissent and political culture.* New York: Routledge.

Firestone, S. (1970). *The dialectic of sex: The case for feminist revolution.* New York: William Morrow and Company.

hooks, b. (1981). *Ain't I a woman: Black women and feminism.* Boston: South End Press.

Jay, K. (2000). *Tales of the Lavender Menace: A memoir of liberation.* New York: Basic Books.

Johnston, J. (1973). *Lesbian nation: The feminist solution.* New York: Simon & Schuster.

Martin, D., & Lyon, P. (1983). *Lesbian/woman,* rev. ed. New York: Bantam Books.

Millett, K. (1970). *Sexual politics.* New York: Doubleday.

Morgan, R. (Ed.). (1970). *Sisterhood in powerful: An anthology of writings from the Women's Liberation Movement.* New York: Vintage Books.

Morris, B.J. (1999). *Eden built by Eves: The culture of women's music festivals.* Boston: Alyson Publications.

Rich, A. (1980, Summer). Compulsory heterosexuality and lesbian existence. *Signs: Journal of Women in Culture and Society, 5,* 631–660.

Smith, B. (Ed.). (1983). *Home girls: A black feminist anthology.* New York: Kitchen Table Women of Color Press.

Smith-Rosenberg, C. (1975). The female world of love and ritual: Relations between women in nineteenth-century America. *Signs, 1,* 1–29.

Springer, K. (2001). Black feminist organizations and the emergence of interstitial politics. In A. Black (Ed.), *Modern American queer history* (pp. 181–197). Philadelphia: Temple University Press.

Primary Sources, 1970s

Bell, A. (1971). *Dancing the gay lib blues: A year in the homosexual liberation movement.* New York: Simon & Schuster.

Humphreys, L. (1972). *Out of the closets: The sociology of homosexual liberation.* Englewood Cliffs, NJ: Prentice Hall.

Jay, K., & Young, A. (Eds.). (1972; 1992). *Out of the closets: Voices of gay liberation.* New York: New York University Press.

Knutson, D.C. (Ed.). (1979). *Homosexuality and the law.* Binghamton, NY: Haworth Press.

McCaffrey, J.A. (Ed.). (1972). *The homosexual dialectic.* Englewood Cliffs, NJ: Prentice-Hall.

Miller, M. (1971). *On being different: What it means to be homosexual.* New York: Random House.

Murphy, J. (1971). *Homosexual liberation: A personal view.* New York: Praeger Publishers.

Richmond, L., & Noguera, G. (Eds.). (1973). *The gay liberation book.* San Francisco: Ramparts Press.

Teal, D. (Ed.). (1971). *The gay militants.* New York: Stein and Day.

Tobin, K., & Wicker, R. (1972). *The gay crusaders.* New York: Paperback Library.

Williams, C.J., & Weinberg, M.S. (1971). *Homosexuals and the military: A study of less than honorable discharge.* New York: Harper & Row.

7 BACKLASH AND REGROUPING

Washington, DC, 1978. Minnesota native Steve Endean arrives in the nation's capital in September to head the Gay Rights National Lobby. He had just turned 30 years old the previous month, but already was one of the most seasoned activists of the era. Shortly after coming out in 1971, he founded Minnesota's first lesbian/gay political organization, the Gay Rights Legislative Committee, beginning a career as a political activist for lesbian and gay rights that lasted until his death in 1993.

By the mid-1970s Endean was one of the few gay and lesbian rights lobbyists in the country, seeing victory when in 1974 Minneapolis became the third major city to pass legislation barring discrimination against gay men and lesbians. His activism, like that of so many people at the time, was not narrowly defined: he picketed against employment discrimination and talked rights to the patrons of the gay bar where he checked coats. He served as board cochair of America's first national gay rights organization, the National Gay Task Force and would go on to found the Human Rights Campaign Fund and pioneer various efforts towards GLBT equality, including a national gay and lesbian civil rights bill.

In 1978, though, Endean had just come off the unsuccessful efforts to defeat antigay initiatives in Miami-Dade County, Florida and St. Paul, Minnesota, and no one could predict the gains of the next 20 years. When he arrived in Washington to assume his duties with GRNL he found an office without a working phone and a bank account of only nine dollars. Even before these discoveries, he had a sense that all was not well when he explained his move to his host:

> *Exhausted from a long flight, coping with tons of luggage and very nervous about such a big move, I mustered the energy to explain earnestly that I'd been hired to be the first director and lobbyist for the Gay Rights National Lobby. To my shock, this distinguished gentleman doubled up with laughter and, in his charming Southern drawl, told me the Gay Rights National Lobby was dead as a doornail. He went on to suggest if that is what really brought me to Washington, D.C., I might not want to haul all those boxes upstairs and perhaps I should just pack up and catch a return flight to Minnesota.*

That was my welcome to Washington, D.C. Cold, white Minnesota never looked so appealing.[1]

The 1980s were years of multiple challenges for GLBT people and a decade of tremendous growth, change, and regrouping for the movements that had taken root previously. While GLBT movements were celebrating their new visibility and the occasional victory, a general backlash against liberal reforms and radical activism had also emerged and gained momentum as the seventies waned. By 1980 a New Right had taken shape that would continue to influence electoral politics into the next century. More immediately, a conservative shift was apparent in the election to the presidency of Ronald Reagan (1980 and 1984), and George H. W. Bush (1988). Encouraged by their own victories, proponents of "family values" sought to reverse those of not only the lesbian and gay movements but those of women and other minorities as well. Conservatives portrayed feminists as antifamily and sought to overturn the *Roe v. Wade* decision, attacked Affirmative Action programs designed to force employers and schools to seriously consider as candidates women and nonwhite men, and demonized gay men and lesbians as dangerous to children. And then there was AIDS.

The timing of the first known AIDS cases could not have been worse. To many Americans, the United States had been in a downward spiral since the mid-1960s, and especially to blame were protesters, whether against war or for the rights of women, nonwhites, and homosexuals. Much like their predecessors in the 1930s, some

Longtime activist Steve Endean began his political career in his native Minnesota and founded the state's first lesbian/gay political organization. Best known as the controversial founder of the Human Rights Campaign (Fund), he also served on the board of the National Gay Task Force, directed the Gay Rights National Lobby, and pioneered the use of mailgrams for grassroots pressure on Congress for lesbian and gay rights. (© Human Rights Campaign)

on the political right saw moral judgment behind national calamity. In the thirties, there were those who practically welcomed the Great Depression as punishment for the sinfulness of the "Roaring 20s"; in the eighties some on the New Right depicted AIDS as predictable retribution for the "permissive" society allowed since the sixties. In turn GLBT activists not only responded effectively to the crisis but also took their movements in new and important directions. By 1992 those movements, though tragically depleted by death and disease, produced impressive results: lasting nationwide organizations; hundreds of sponsors for a federal gay and lesbian civil rights bill; and two marches on Washington with a third in the works.

FROM CARTER TO REAGAN

When President Jimmy Carter took the oath of office in 1977 he faced a country experiencing an identity crisis. To the World War II generation, the government was trustworthy, standards of living only got higher, resources never ran out, and the military always won wars (if one ignored the undeclared war in Korea). Now, faith in those basic tenets was tested on all fronts. News of withdrawal from Vietnam without a clear victory and the Watergate break-in and cover-up was compounded with a discouraging economic situation: the first U.S. trade deficit in history, the first "energy crisis" related to reliance on imported oil, inflation, and a general recession lasting through the Ford administration (1974–1977). True, there were valiant efforts to celebrate the U.S. bicentennial in the 1976 election year, but the effects of unprecedented political, diplomatic, and economic failures were not easily overcome by TV specials and readings of the Declaration of Independence. In the fall elections, only about half of eligible voters went to the polls. Even though many baby boomers (and their elders) had anticipated some of the crises as predictable results of American arrogance, there was no glory in being right. By the time Carter left office, fifty-two Americans were being held hostage in Iran and observers from a variety of perspectives would soon use terms like "dismal" and "malaise" to describe most of the decade.

As indicated in Chapter 7, lesbian and gay activists had many reasons for celebration despite the national crises, however. Not only were they rapidly developing a visible presence and cultural institutions, they were making inroads as well into national politics through the Democratic Party. True, previous attempts in the 1970s to get the Democrats to adopt a gay rights plank failed, but in 1980 the platform committee cautiously wrote an antidiscrimination statement to include "sexual orientation" but without the words "gay," "lesbian," or "homosexual." The battle to get even that much had divided activists over strategy and reflected similar divisions in the Party but as Steve Endean later recalled, "By the time the actual convention in New York arrived, the real drama was over."[2] Still, a bit more history was made (if not covered by media) at that year's Democratic convention. The gay and lesbian caucus was able to collect enough signatures to nominate Mel Boozer, an openly gay African American man, for vice president, and Boozer delivered a speech linking racial and antigay bigotry. That same concern for human rights had characterized Carter as person and president, explaining in part the "peculiar position" of lesbian/gay rights during his tenure.[3] Like Reagan after him, Carter was generally silent on the subject, but his administration did work to oppose antigay discrimination, particularly through the Office of Public Liaison. One of his more public endorsements was support of proposed immigration reform removing the ban on homosexual immigrants (see Chapter 4). Since leaving the presidency, Carter has further explained his past and current views on numerous topics, most recently in

Our Endangered Values: America's Moral Crisis. In it, homosexuality is placed in the broader contexts of Christian morality on the one hand and church-state relations on the other. Seemingly consistent with his positions while he was president, he reiterated a concern for human rights and dignity and especially encouraged the removal of moralizing from government when he addressed gay marriage:

> Rather than letting the controversial issue remain so divisive among our citizens, perhaps we should separate the two basic approaches, by letting governments define and protect equal rights for citizens, including those of "civil unions," and letting church congregations define "holy matrimony."[4]

Indeed to Carter, America after 2000 is facing a "moral crisis" not because of the GLBT movements but due to a religious right wing worming its way into politics. "The most important factor" in the crisis, he wrote,

> is that fundamentalists have become increasingly influential in both religion and government, and have managed to change the nuances and subtleties of historical debate into black-and-white rigidities and the personal derogation of those who dare to disagree. At the same time, these religious and political conservatives have melded their efforts, bridging the formerly respected separation of church and state. This has empowered a group of influential "neoconservatives," who have been able to implement their long-frustrated philosophy in both domestic and foreign policy.[5]

As he knew, these changes were well under way during Carter's own presidency.

A New Right

If historians share the more general sense of disillusionment of the late seventies, they agree also, with Carter, that the United States was experiencing a "turn to the right" politically at this time. There had been people defined as "liberal" and "conservative" since the nation's very beginnings, but the meanings of those terms shifted repeatedly as new movements disrupted entrenched positions. As noted in Chapter 5, a New Left emerged in the 1960s that challenged not only self-defined moderates and conservatives—supporters of the United States in Vietnam and/or opponents of integration, for example—but its proponents also confronted those on the "Old Left" that came of age in the middle of the century. In the late 1970s, a New Right coalesced and eventually became one of the most powerful political forces of the late 20th century.

"Political" is the key word, in fact. Since the country's beginnings, there had been a "Left" and "Right," distinguished by differing emphases on issues specifically related to civic, and often economic, life. In the early republic, for example, "leftists" like Thomas Jefferson were suspicious of centralized authority and advocated vigilance against claims on individual and states' rights. Those more conservative, led by Alexander Hamilton, were equally wary of the divisive potential of those individuals and states, and perhaps of human nature itself. Since their era, many new issues and situations arose to continually redefine political "sides." By the third quarter of the 20th century, debates over the role and size of government distinguished those to the left and right of "center." The former—more accurately termed liberal than Leftist—supported New Deal and Great Society programs aimed at relieving poverty and injustice, while the latter believed those programs undermined older American values of hard work and individualism. True Leftists in both the 1930s and 1960s would distance themselves from liberals, whom they viewed as merely co-opting the discontented with gradual reforms rather than significantly changing systems that they felt denied people civil and economic equality (see Chapters 3 and 5). Until the 1970s, though, there seemed to be some agreement on all sides that moral and/or religious views should remain separate from party politics. Government protection of the freedom to profess and practice a variety of faiths was essential, but its role did not extend to advancing one specific view over another and enforcing it through legislation.

What was new about the New Right, then, was the attempt of conservative Christians to influence American political life at all levels. Perhaps dating from as early as the mid-1960s, the New Right rapidly coalesced in the late seventies, with organizations like the American Family Association (1977), Concerned Women for America (1979), Focus on the Family (1977), and the Moral Majority Coalition (1979) joining the earlier Eagle Forum (1972) in the conviction that a return to "family values" was a legitimate goal of electoral politics. By 1980 the landslide that brought Ronald Reagan to the White House and sent packing some key liberal Democratic senators was as much result as cause of the New Right, though it certainly further emboldened its adherents to pursue their agenda. Reagan himself, a movie and TV actor-turned-politician and New Deal Democrat-turned-Republican, actually had a mixed and relatively moderate record during his two terms as governor of California (1967–1975). Conservative Christian thought and action eventually dominated his presidential administrations, however, as its proponents successfully moved the Republican Party further to the right and cast liberals as dangerous radicals as they did so. Landmarks of New Right politics include not only the presidencies of Reagan and George H.W. Bush (1989–1993), but also the 1988 bid for the Republican presidential nomination of TV evangelist Pat Robertson and, most recently, the administrations of George W. Bush (2001–2009).

Prime examples of New Right goals and strategies are the ill-fated history of the ERA (Equal Rights Amendment, 1972–1982) and repeated efforts to undermine or overturn *Roe v. Wade*. An ERA that would prohibit discrimination on the basis of sex was proposed as early as 1923, only to languish for decades until Congress passed a slightly different version in 1972. Now, in the midst of second wave feminism, a possible 27th Amendment was ratified in the first year by twenty-two of the required thirty-eight states. A well-organized opposition was able to slow the process and finally bring it to a halt in 1977, the year Indiana became the thirty-fifth (and last) state to ratify. Despite a three-year extension (to the original 1979 deadline), no more states ratified the ERA before 1982 and it has yet to become an amendment. In the same years, antiabortion conservatives in government were mobilizing in the wake of *Roe v. Wade* (1973) and by 1976 had succeeded in limiting Medicaid patients' access to abortions through the Hyde Amendment. Legal and extralegal challenges continued through the 1980s and 1990s, during which time the Supreme Court upheld state restrictions on abortions and more radical antiabortionists used pickets, blockades, harassment, and occasional violence aimed at either clinics or their staff.

Antigay Legislation and Violence

The proposed ERA and legalized abortion were not the only targets of the New Right, however. Rev. Jerry Falwell summarized the program of both the Moral Majority and much of New Right mentality when he wrote, "We must stand against the Equal Rights Amendment, the feminist revolution, and the homosexual revolution."[6] To Christian conservatives, the legal and social changes associated with feminism and lesbian/gay activism threatened the stability of the traditional family. They believed (and continue to believe), in turn, that the nuclear, two-heterosexual-parent, male-headed family was the foundation of America's strength. Like their forbears in the tradition of American exceptionalism, then (see Chapter 2), New Right activists interpret violations of their moral code as dangerous to the nation and therefore the legitimate business of politics. Of all the tenets of that moral code, hostility to homo-sexuality has been as central as opposition to abortion, though it is not always clear if that hostility is sincerely doctrinal or moral or if it is opportunism on the part of politi-cians. In either case, conservatives have been able to demonize the lesbian/gay rights movements in ways similar to those used against feminism, and convince voters that both movements are nothing less than conspiracies against the American family and traditional American values. In particular, they warn of a "homosexual agenda" that seeks not merely tolerance but full acceptance of GLBT "lifestyles." Although this might in fact be the goal of many GLBT activists, conservatives have cast this as equal only to a Communist or, more recently, radical Muslim takeover of the country in its consequences for U.S. identity.

Using these reasons, extreme conservatives targeted legislation that prohibited discrimination based on sexual orientation. Probably the most famous attack on the modest gains of the post-Stonewall lesbian/gay rights movement came in 1977 in Florida. In January that year Miami-Dade County had passed an ordinance prohibiting discrimination based on sexual orientation. In response, former beauty queen and Christian right representative Anita Bryant mounted the "Save Our Children" cam-paign, perpetuating the stereotype that gay men and lesbians are especially dangerous to young people. Because homosexuals cannot reproduce (at least as a result of same-sex activity), the reasoning goes, they need to recruit others to their cause (much like the abstinence-preaching Shakers, apparently). This was added to older fears of homo-sexuals as sexual predators unable to control their impulses (see Chapter 4) and the general view that youth are more easily influenced to create a powerful if irrational basis to question antidiscrimination law. The ordinance was repealed by referendum six months after it passed. Though a devastating blow, the reversal also became a "turning point" from which many gay men and lesbians "later would trace their own coming out or interest in gay politics."[7] In a frightening pattern, within the following year voters in St. Paul, Minnesota, Eugene, Oregon, and Wichita, Kansas, overturned similar ordinances as a result of effective organizing around the supposed immorality of homosexuality. A St. Paul minister heading that city's effort, for example, expressed his desire not "to live in a community that gives respect to homosexuals."[8]

Amid these obvious setbacks were signs of hope for lesbian/gay politics. In San Francisco, openly gay Harvey Milk was elected in 1977 to the Board of Supervisors after having served as an appointed commissioner (see Chapter 6). Also on the West coast, the following year efforts to repeal Seattle's gay rights ordinance failed by nearly 2-1 and voters in California rejected Proposition 6, also known as the Briggs initiative, for the state senator sponsoring the bill. The Proposition was based on arguments like those of Bryant's "Save Our Children" campaign and designed to remove from the state's classrooms not only homosexual teachers but anyone presenting homosexuality in a positive way. In these cases, opponents of the antigay measures were able to fight fear of homosexuals with fear of government intervention into everyone's personal lives. More specifically, reproductive rights advocates by now had introduced the concept of a basic right to privacy, and the Supreme Court had concurred, interpreting the 14th Amendment as including protection of such a right. Just where the limits of that protection lay, however, would be seen later in the decade when the Court ruled in *Bowers v. Hardwick* (see below).

Gay men and lesbians in California were able to celebrate the Briggs defeat only a few weeks before events began that caused despair and rage, but that also led to further mobilization for national visibility and action. On November 27, former San Francisco supervisor Dan White entered city hall and used a handgun to murder Mayor George Moscone and Supervisor Harvey Milk. White had resigned earlier that month, soon asked Moscone to reappoint him, and was denied his request. News of the murders sparked a candle-light vigil at City Hall but mourning turned to anger when the verdict in White's trial was announced the following May: manslaughter and a sentence of less than eight years in prison (five of which White served). For years gay and lesbian San Franciscans, like their brothers and sisters throughout the nation, had endured antigay prejudice, from harassment and physical attacks to bombs, arson, and murder. They were at a breaking point. The night of the verdict, thousands of lesbians and gay men rioted and police unleashed their own fury, attacking gay bars and their patrons. In the wake of these reactions, lesbian/gay politics became more deeply entrenched into the city's workings, and more lesbian and gay people sought and won positions in the government.

In the nation's capital, legislation increasingly reflected the moralistic politics of Miami more than the practical adjustments of San Francisco. During Carter's administration Republicans already had brought to Congress the McDonald amendment to the Legal Assistance Act (1977) and the Family Protection Act (1979), both of which included denial of federal funds for any person, group, or action construed (in McDonald's terms) as "promoting, protecting and defending homosexuality." The McDonald amendment passed the House but was rejected in the Senate and the Family Protection Act, though reintroduced in 1980 and 1981, also failed to pass. Reactionary forces did prevail in 1981, however, when Congress, holding veto power over municipal actions, overturned the DC reform act that included decriminalizing consensual sodomy. (In frustration, one activist said to a *Washington Post* reporter, "Not only will two-thirds of the Members of the House who voted to overturn D.C. sodomy and fornication laws violate those laws, but half will do so by midnight tonight!"[9]).

National Lobbying, Lesbian and Gay Rights

Even before events in Miami, San Francisco, and elsewhere seemed to demand more effective national action *The Advocate* publisher David Goodstein called for a conference to discuss the form of that action. Convened in 1976, it was dubbed *The Advocate* International Conference and was seen by many, then and since, as a political move to wrest control of the movement by creating an organization to compete with the NGTF (National Gay Task Force), formed in 1973 (see Chapter 6). Whatever Goodstein's motives, the move reflected the dissention all too typical of this and other progressive movements, but was successful in its immediate goal; conferees left the meeting with a commitment to organize the GRNL (Gay Rights National Lobby).

By 1978, supporters of the lobby had tapped Steve Endean to move to Washington, DC to direct, in his words, the "basically dysfunctional national lobby." Endean was a natural choice for the job, having lobbied for gay rights in his native Minnesota, and being a self-described "control freak" who insisted on lists of goals, objectives, and strategies. His "top priorities," he later wrote, "were to put GRNL's financial house in good enough order to keep the doors open and to figure out how to advance the national non-discrimination bill, thereby giving the lesbian and gay community something to rally around nationally."[10]

Almost immediately GRNL went on the offensive, seeking more sponsors for the national bill and founding a Right to Privacy Foundation to demonstrate the need for a bill by documenting the job and housing discrimination faced by lesbians and gay men. Lesbian/gay voter registration drives were organized and for the first time legislators were rated on lesbian/gay issues to aid constituents' decisions. The group found itself constantly on the defensive as well, though, with the flurry of antigay acts coming from the New Right demanding responses and counterattacks. Eventually a number of factors combined to force Endean from leadership of GRNL (and from the Human Rights Campaign Fund, below) in 1983 and two years later the organization merged with HRCF. These factors included infighting, due to philosophical, political, and personality conflicts reminiscent of Mattachine in the 1950s; questions about the group's financial affairs (possibly part of the infighting) and charges that GRNL was not responding adequately to the AIDS crisis. Although largely ignored at the time, GRNL also sponsored a landmark study, "Does Support for Gay Rights Spell Political Suicide?" in an attempt to convince incumbents to remove a perceived barrier to sponsorship of the national bill. The lack of attention the report received, in fact, contributed to the growing conviction that a PAC (Political Action Committee) was the logical next step in DC, a step taken in 1980.

Additional organizations were underway before 1980, though, and they reflect the vitality of the concept of rights in the United States. Two, in fact, indicate this focus in their names and both had their beginnings in San Francisco. Donald C. Knutson and Richard Rouilard cofounded the NGRA (National Gay Rights Advocates) in the late seventies. In its role as a nonprofit public interest law firm it eventually grew from local offices to a genuinely national entity, though it lasted only until 1991. In 1985 the AIDS Civil Rights Project was added and NGRA won important legal battles on this and other issues. At about the same time Donna J. Hitchens formed a similar group—also a public interest and nonprofit law firm—first called the Lesbian Rights Project. It became the National Center for Lesbian Rights and eventually took on a variety of legal causes, including those of marriage/family, youth and elders, and transgendered people. On the other coast the Gay and Lesbian Advocates and Defenders was launched in Boston in 1978 and soon represented clients throughout New England. Within a few years it provided legal aid and such resources as the "National Lesbian and Gay Attorney's Referral Directory" and a "Rights Card" for referral in case of arrest.

The National Lesbian and Gay Health Foundation (f. 1977) and the International Lesbian and Gay Association (f. 1978) also took shape at this time. The Health Foundation later merged with Alliance of Lesbian and Gay Health Clinics (f. 1992) to become the National Lesbian and Gay Health Association. All three groups have been significant not only through the AIDS crisis but in their education and advocacy in all areas of health care and research. The ILGA, as the name implies, was formed as a worldwide network in the interest of GLBT civil rights and remains the only such organization—nonprofit, nongovernment, and community based—working on a global level.

The First March on Washington

Formal organizations were one kind of response to the growing backlash against lesbian/gay rights—and lesbian/gay people—and another was the gathering of tens of thousands of marchers in Washington, DC, on October 14, 1979, rallying to the motto, "Break the Chains."[11] They assembled at the Washington Monument after filing past the White House from the Capitol, demonstrating the numbers and visibility considered key to the movement's politics. While some spent the day listening to speeches, music, and comedy, others worked with GRNL to seek the support of their senators and representatives for the national gay rights bill. To Lucia Valeska, then codirector of the NGTF, the march signaled "the birth of a national gay movement."[12]

By some accounts, the idea of a march arose as early as 1973 in Illinois, to be repeated in 1978, among Minneapolis activists and by Harvey Milk that summer and again in the fall as he and others celebrated the defeat of Proposition 6.[13] Marches were nothing new in this era, of course; thousands had descended on Washington to demonstrate for such causes as peace, the environment, and women's rights, all undoubtedly taking their cue from the 1963 March on Washington for Jobs and Freedom. Given the climate of the late seventies, and the desire of many activists to forge a national movement out of scattered goals and actions, a National March on Washington for Lesbian and Gay Rights seemed the obvious next step. Once Milk was assassinated it seemed essential. March coordinators Steve Ault and Joyce Hunter saw the event as "a tribute to Harvey Milk and to the countless others who have suffered and perished at the hands of bigots."[14] The 10th anniversary of Stonewall also provided a movement milestone, and organization for the march was underway by the winter of 1979.

If leaders felt the need for more unity and national action, organizing a centralized movement around rights remained controversial (and remains so to the present). Legal protections were then at the forefront, though, and the demands circulated that October reflect those concerns. They included a national lesbian/gay rights bill as well as the repeal of all antigay/lesbian legislation, for example, and also addressed protection of lesbian and gay youth and of lesbian and gay parents seeking child custody. Less contentious was the call to come out, an act seen, especially after Stonewall, in a political as well as personal or social contexts. Like the three marches that have followed, in fact, the first one may have accomplished little in the way of changing hearts and minds—and laws—in Washington. As a mass celebration of Gay Pride, however, the march offered a sense of belonging to formerly isolated individuals and a counter to the negative images of homosexuality of the previous decades. "If Stonewall marked the beginning of the modern gay movement," one activist wrote, "the first national queer march in 1979 was its coming-out party."[15]

Human Rights Campaign Fund

If 1980 was a key year for conservatives it was no less one to those in the lesbian and gay movements who sought greater political clout in Washington. That summer the HRCF was founded as the first national PAC devoted to lesbian/gay issues. The name and purpose grew out of the plans of a small group—Larry Bye, Steve Endean, Jim Foster, and James Hormel—for a mechanism to support candidates friendly to the cause, and to more effectively gain sponsors for a national gay and lesbian rights bill.

The new organization, with Steve Endean as executive director, had some early successes with the 1980 reelection of the congressional candidate that received its first contribution and a 1982 black-tie fund-raising dinner at New York's Waldorf-Astoria that featured a speech from former vice president Walter Mondale. Supporters of HRCF strategy would come to see this dinner and many more like it in cities throughout the United States over the years as signs of progress. To other activists, however, the expensive dinners, organized by committees dominated by wealthy white (and often closeted) men, were symbolic of a disturbing elitism, too similar to that of the national power structure generally (by the mid-1980s, critics would dub the group the "Human Rights Champagne Fund").

Despite ongoing conflicts surrounding it, HRCF would become the nation's largest national GBLT rights organization, claiming a membership of 25,000 in 1989 and nearly 600,000 by 2006. In 1983, Endean resigned from leadership of HRCF as well as GRNL, but would return in 1987 to operate his grassroots mobilization project, Fairness Fund (renamed Speak Out). By that time, HRCF had absorbed GRNL and hired its own lobbyists, leading some to praise its expansion and others to bemoan its apparent attempts to dominate movement activities. Through the eighties and into the nineties goals of HRCF included building coalitions with feminist and African American groups, changing its elitist reputation while modernizing its functioning and image ("Fund" was dropped from the name and a new "equal sign" logo was created), fighting against the military's discriminatory policy on homosexuals and for AIDS research funding and Hate Crimes legislation, and further consolidating its influence in DC. In 1986 civil rights figure Coretta Scott King announced her "solidarity with the gay and lesbian community" at the 5th annual New York City dinner.

THE CHALLENGE OF AIDS

The discovery of a new deadly disease quickly linked in the public mind to homosexuality could not have come at a worse time for gay men and lesbians in the United States. Just as they were fending off attacks from the New Right and attempting to move forward with various approaches—from grassroots organizing to lobbying and legislation—the condition eventually called AIDS (Acquired Immune Deficiency Syndrome) created a unique situation demanding action.

From "Gay Cancer" to HIV

On June 6, 1981, *The San Francisco Chronicle* ran a column (p. 4) entitled "A Pneumonia That Strikes Gay Males." Researchers in San Francisco and at the National Centers for Disease Control (CDC), the brief story reported, were puzzled by cases arising in several large U.S. cities of a pneumonia usually seen in cancer patients or others with weak immune systems, not "generally healthy young men." "But," it continued, quoting the CDC report issued the day before, " 'the fact that those patients were all homosexuals suggests an association between some aspect of a homosexual lifestyle or disease acquired through sexual contact and the pneumonia.' " Less than a month later, *The New York Times* ran a similar story, this time focusing on reports of Kaposi's Sarcoma in men unusually young and otherwise healthy for its appearance, under the heading, "Rare Cancer Seen in 41 Homosexuals." This column reported theories by investigating physicians that included a link to viral infections as well as some connection to gay men who had frequent sex with multiple partners. A CDC spokesman, in fact, was quoted as saying, "there was no apparent danger to non-homosexuals from contagion. 'The best evidence against contagion,' he said, 'is that no cases have been reported to date outside the homosexual community or in women.' "[16]

Responding to such coverage, and terms like "gay cancer," "gay plague," and the more official GRID (Gay-Related Immune Deficiency), gay activists quickly organized to change the perception that the deadly disease was related only to gay men or a "homosexual lifestyle." It would be another year, however, before the name "Acquired Immunodeficiency Syndrome" (AIDS) was created, coupled with the news that infection rather than contagion likely accounted for the spread of AIDS; casual contact, in other words, was not a factor. Despite the new name and information, though, by then the public association between the condition and homosexuality was pretty much fixed. Even when AIDS was initially diagnosed in nongay patients, they also had the misfortune of being relative outsiders in American society: intravenous drug users, hemophiliacs, and Haitians. The concept of group membership dominated public discussions of the epidemic and affected the way many Americans perceived both the disease and its victims. As historian Jennifer Brier summarized:

> Almost immediately, the emerging public face of AIDS was linked to certain kinds of people instead of to certain kinds of behaviors. Public health officials regularly talked about the likelihood that a member of a risk group would be infected with AIDS, but rarely seemed interested in detailing how a person's behavior, whether sexual or not, made him or her more likely to become infected. This construction had major implications for how the epidemic would be reported and understood from then on.[17]

Scientists in both the United States and France discovered the virus responsible for AIDS in 1984, and that it was a virus not spread through casual contact. Eventually the information was clearer on high-risk behaviors—"exchange of bodily fluids" from sexual activity and sharing needles among drug users—as was the possibility of receiving infected blood via transfusions. By 1986, health officials, who had used various terms for the virus, finally settled on HIV—human immunodeficiency virus—and had developed a test for HIV antibodies in the blood. The idea of testing for HIV would further illustrate the complexities of treating a deadly virus as a public health concern within a climate of fear and the antigay backlash, however. Only in 1985, when popular movie actor Rock Hudson revealed he had AIDS, did President Reagan first mention the disease publicly. By the time Hudson succumbed to the illness later that year, he was one of nearly 7,000 Americans who died of AIDS in 1985 and one of more than 12,000 deaths from the disease since 1981. The number of deaths would increase each year for the next decade, but Hudson's death did contribute to some change in the public perception of both AIDS and gay men.[18] At the same time, gay and lesbian activists were gearing up for more radical approaches to raise public awareness.

Responses

Any history of the first decade of AIDS in the United States is incomplete if it tracks only the progress of the disease and the people affected, whether as famous individuals or as groups likely to be infected. A key issue is the variety of ways in which the "public" (usually perceived as nongay), the government, and gay men and lesbians themselves shaped that history in the nature of their responses—or silence.

The dynamics of the U.S. AIDS crisis, in fact, not only offer a case study in 1980s culture but also serve to highlight key aspects of American society up to that point. Discovery of HIV/AIDS brought together, in ways tragic though revealing, generally unforgiving American attitudes in at least three areas: victims of circumstance, illness and disease, and sex and sexuality. The result was a number of dilemmas for those seeking or planning solutions to the situation.

First, a "blame the victim" mentality seemed to help define an American consciousness since the nation's origins. The ethic of "self-made men" and belief in individual initiative of the 19th century often left little room for compassion for the poor and homeless. This had devastating results during the Great Depression, for example, when so many men suddenly could no longer support their families. After all, if one's economic success was due to his hard work and living right, then the opposite traits accounted for his failure. Similarly, victims of violence, especially females enduring sexual assaults, have been all too familiar with the notion that somehow they brought in on themselves. Americans often are critical of misfortune, it seems, with the brunt of the hostility aimed at the unfortunate.

Second, Americans have complex attitudes toward illness, infirmity, and disease that also reflect cultural biases. By the late 20th century, Americans' cult-like worship of youth and health was well known, as was the tendency to segregate the ill and elderly from family and friends, whether in hospitals, nursing homes, or simply retirement communities. When this is coupled with Americans' faith in science, especially medicine, literally to cure all ills, disease and death become "unnatural." Just as there is no excuse for poverty, there is little tolerance for illness in general, and little patience with pain and suffering. Often elimination of symptoms takes precedence over cure or prevention, a situation further complicated by the status of American medicine as a group of for-profit industries. In many ways, then, views of HIV/AIDS and those afflicted were but exaggerations of pervasive attitudes.

Finally, HIV/AIDS pushed the hottest buttons in American culture: sex and sexuality. As we have seen, public discourse of these topics was not that old by the eighties. As Alfred Kinsey (and responses to his studies) had shown (see Chapter 4), by mid-century honest sex talk remained taboo. Even after the "sexual revolution" of the sixties public discourse still seemed adolescent and voyeuristic, a situation likely encouraged by the place of sex as just another commodity in consumer culture.

Given all this, and the timing of the crisis amid the backlash against the "permissive" and "anti-family" sixties and seventies, homophobia reached a level not seen since the Cold War, and perhaps never expressed quite so openly. Harassment and violence directed at gay people continued (and more than doubled from 1985 to 1986), but now seemed justified. Anyone appearing stereotypically gay could be either targeted or shunned while people actually with HIV were refused treatment. Quarantine seemed a legitimate option, as did mandatory testing for the virus. Visible right-wing leaders encouraged a witch-hunt mentality with statements calling AIDS "the judgment of God" against those who "declared war upon nature," and popularized a distinction between the (evil, self-indulgent homosexual) carriers of the virus and their "innocent" (heterosexual) victims eventually infected.[19]

In these same early years that AIDS generated a variety of public reactions, the federal government was noticeably silent and inactive. Besides the alliance between Republicans and the Christian right, Reagan also was a fiscal conservative, encouraging a "New Federalism" that basically meant less spending on the federal level and more responsibility placed on state and local treasuries. This was especially true of social programs, including those concerning public health. Therefore in the early eighties it was city governments that initially bore the economic burden in the absence of federal funds. Municipal responses, in turn, were directly related to the presence, size, and especially organization of lesbian and gay communities within them.

As gay men and lesbians mobilized against both AIDS and homophobia, they were faced with dilemmas that sometimes divided them and always complicated any response. To say that AIDS research was inadequate because of bias against the gay victims of the disease was to feed the "gay plague" mentality, for example, while to insist that nongays could also be infected aided those who saw gay men as typhoid Marys. In a homophobia environment, there was no winning argument. Similarly, while quick and effective organizing was crucial, it was not always clear if limited energies and resources should be directed at government bureaucracies or toward building voluntary action and care; the more effective the latter, the less necessary the former would seem, or so some feared.

Despite many divisions over goals and tactics, gay men and lesbians did indeed take action, both through existing organizations and the creation of many new ones specific to the situation. The GMHC (Gay Men's Health Crisis) was formed in New York City as 1982 began, and became a model for ASOs (AIDS service organizations) in urban areas across the nation. ASOs were notable in offering information and support while working on both treatment and prevention of the disease. The People with AIDS Coalition became a national group by 1985 and the term PWAs (People with AIDS) came to signify a rejection of a victim mentality as well as a demand for better treatment. By the later eighties the AIDS Action Council had joined the list of organizations and a new coalition had emerged, National Organizations Responding to AIDS. Meanwhile, of the three national organizations, the NGTF under Virginia Apuzzo's leadership was and is perceived as the most proactive at the time. GRNL and the HRCF were criticized for a lack of focus on the issue, a perception that contributed further to Steve Endean's expulsion as director of both groups. By the mid-eighties and after, however, NGTF and HRCF were both working, together and separately, on pressuring Congress for legislation to increase AIDS-related appropriations. In 1990, among the acts signed into law by President George H.W. Bush were the Ryan White CARE (Comprehensive AIDS Resources Emergency) Act and the Americans with Disabilities Act (which included protection of people with AIDS and HIV from discrimination). By that time, however, more radical measures had joined with traditional lobbying efforts to render ignoring the crisis impossible if not irresponsible.

Among direct action groups in GLBT history, perhaps none is better known than ACT UP (AIDS Coalition to Unleash Power), formed in March of 1987. One of ACT UP's cofounders was writer Larry Kramer, who had also helped form the GMHC. Kramer was an outspoken critic of inaction, whether by governments or by gay community members; many of his views are represented in his play *The Normal Heart* (1985), still considered a theatrical landmark. ACT UP became known for the slogan "Silence = Death" and direct-action demonstrations in the late eighties and early nineties that called attention to the crisis in ways impossible to ignore. Among institutions targeted for shutdown or dramatic interruption were Wall Street, the FDA (Food and Drug Administration), the NIH (National Institutes of Health), the CDC (Centers for Disease Control), and New York's St. Patrick's Cathedral ("Stop the Church"). Members of ACT UP were instrumental in reclaiming the term "queer" from its negative associations of the earlier 20th century, and in 1990 contributed to the founding of a splinter group, Queer Nation, who formed to protest increasing violence against GLBT people and advocate sexual freedom.

Yet another approach to the crisis came in 1987 when "a small group of strangers gathered in a San Francisco storefront to document the lives they feared history would neglect."[20] Their idea was to memorialize those who had died and their means were quilt panels, and idea conceived earlier, in the form of placards with names, by Cleve Jones. In this way, the NAMES Project AIDS Memorial Quilt took shape. By October that same year it contained 1,920 panels (3′ × 6′ each) and was first displayed on the

The NAMES Project AIDS Memorial Quilt stands as one of the most creative and moving reminders of the devastation caused by AIDS. The Quilt is shown here in a display at the Washington Monument in 1992, one of several showings at the nation's capital since 1987. (Smithsonian)

National Mall during the second March on Washington (see below); only a year later the quilt comprised over 8,000 panels and was again displayed in Washington, this time with names of the deceased read aloud. The reading of the names has since become a tradition, while the quilt continues to grow, exceeding 45,000 panels by 2006.

The quilt was but one of many artistic avenues used for expressing emotions and raising awareness. People in visual and performing arts, many of them personally affected by the disease, created works and images that transcended the time and topic. In the visual arts the murals and graphic designs of Keith Haring raised public aware-ness, as did Gran Fury (1988–1994), a group founded out of ACT UP who ultimately received funding from art institutions for production of their images aimed at a broad public. Choreographers Alvin Ailey and Bill T. Jones documented the epidemic's effects through dance while others, like Marlon Riggs and David Wojnarowicz, did the same using film. To document the history of the relationship between the epidemic and the arts in the United States is one of the goals of the Estate Project (f. 1991), which preserves and presents works in all media. In an initiative that became ongoing, in 1989 hundreds of groups organized the first Day Without Art, observed on December 1. Deemed a "national day of action and mourning" to raise public awareness of the effects of AIDS, the day's activities ranged from closing museums and galleries to sponsoring exhibits of artworks specifically about AIDS.

Unity and Division

As the above examples reveal, the apparent public and government apathy over AIDS acted as a catalyst to unite people identifying as gay, lesbian, or bisexual.

At the same time, more deeply rooted rifts continued, and new ones appeared specific to AIDS and the issues it raised. Among the older divisions were those between men and women, and those caused by philosophical differences over the proper goals and "position" relative to mainstream America that activists should adopt. In addition, there were those who argued for setting aside ideology (and principle, to some) in favor of pragmatism: what would save gay men's lives?

The debates that emerged over proposals on both coasts to close bathhouses—sites for sex with multiple partners—perfectly represent the various strains of thought, and strain on a movement well into its fourth decade. To some policy makers and activists alike, closing bathhouses seemed a common-sense stopgap to the spread of AIDS. Others, however, saw the move to close the baths less as an effort to save (gay) lives and more as a political act consistent with previous actions against gay gathering spots; intended or not, said the opponents, closing the baths simply continued the history of government antigay harassment and discrimination. In their view, the focus should be more on safe sex practices (later called "safer sex"), including distribution and use of condoms, and less on cooperating with legislation perceived as essentially antigay. As Allan Bérubé wrote in his important 1984 defense of the baths:

> For the gay community, gay bathhouses represent a major success in a century-long struggle to overcome isolation and develop a sense of community and pride in their sexuality, to gain their right to sexual privacy, to win their right to associate with each other in public, and to create "safety zones" where gay men could be sexual and affectionate with each other with a minimal threat of violence, blackmail, loss of employment, arrest, imprisonment, and humiliation.[21]

Despite such arguments, in the mid-eighties public health officials ordered the baths closed in the key cities in the debate, San Francisco and New York, a move reinforced by a Congressional Act passed in 1985 authorizing the U.S. Surgeon General to close the baths.

The larger issue surrounding the baths concerned the actions gay men should take, and gay authors stimulated lively debate in books of the time. In 1983 Michael Callen and Richard Berkowitz published *How to Have Sex in an Epidemic: One Approach*, which was among the earliest works to promote safe sex as part of the general argument for changes in gay men's behavior. Such authors as Larry Kramer, Gabriel Rotello, and Michelangelo Signorile also called for gay men to take responsibility and reconsider the sexual practices born in the wake of gay liberation. Journalist Randy Shilts contributed to the debate when he wrote what remains probably the best-known history of the epidemic, *And the Band Played On* (published 1987 and adapted into a TV movie in 1993). In it Shilts, gay and HIV-positive himself, cited the failings of gay men as well as the government, and for that was criticized within gay communities.

This debate and others also heightened some tensions present for decades between gay men and lesbians. Certainly there had been significant cooperation between the sexes, but the recent advent of lesbian feminism offered a firmer theoretical grounding for solidarity by sex rather than sexuality. To many lesbians, gay men were still men and had revealed their sexism in organizational efforts from local to national levels; their reactions already ranged from abandoning politics to advocating lesbian separatism (see Chapter 6). To those already critical of anonymous, public sex—associated with "male" modes of sexual expression—it was galling to be equally linked with AIDS in the public mind, especially in light of the lack, in the eighties, of AIDS cases involving lesbians.

Despite some misgivings, however, lesbians also distanced themselves from those who saw the fate of gay men with AIDS as deserved, and many joined in radical AIDS activism and/or became caretakers of ill men (another typically "women's role" to some). From the beginning lesbians were participating in the more radical direct actions and were staffing hot lines and community programs providing food and other services. Also, the baths debate intersected with larger questions about sexual freedom that many lesbians saw as relevant to their lives, further encouraging solidarity with men. Eventually, as the awareness grew that women also were contracting HIV/AIDS, lesbians were in the forefront of raising awareness of safer sex practices for women as well as for men; by 1992 the GMHC had a separate Lesbian AIDS Project.

At the same time, lesbians also were important advocates in the eighties on issues specific to women, concerning especially health and violence. Women's health advocacy included both health problems treated in men but often ignored in women (like heart disease) and illnesses affecting women uniquely or disproportionately (cervical, ovarian, and breast cancers). The landmark book *Our Bodies, Ourselves* continued to address these issues, becoming a best seller with its third edition in 1979; in 1984 it was revised into a fourth edition, *The New Our Bodies, Ourselves.* Within the women's health movement, lesbians argued that not only do all women face sexism in health care but lesbians often face homophobia as well if they reveal themselves to their providers, a situation discouraging many to even seek medical care. As a result, activists formed organizations to serve lesbians' distinct concerns and needs. In 1990, after Mary-Helen Mautner died of breast cancer, her partner founded the Mautner Project (the National Lesbian Health Organization) to provide a variety of services for lesbians with life-threatening conditions. In the same year, Congress passed the Breast and Cervical Cancer Mortality Prevention Act, establishing the Early Detection Program as part of the CDC. The program included screening exams and an effort to reach out women traditionally having less access to health care.

Similarly, potential and actual violence against all women had been a concern of Second Wave feminists long before AIDS-related homophobia made lesbians even more vulnerable. Feminist theorists had described U.S. society as a "rape culture" in which the romanticized notion of "normal" male aggression and female passivity encouraged and protected men who abused women verbally, emotionally, and physically. The murder of women, they proposed, was at once more common (as in serial killings) and less acknowledged, at least as an issue rooted in gender. As with all areas of feminist thought, lesbians were important in raising awareness of this violence, and had been particular targets of those hostile to both homosexuals *and* women. A graphic example of this came in 1988 when Claudia Brenner and her lover Rebecca Wight were hiking the Appalachian Trail in Pennsylvania, unaware they were being followed by a gunman. He opened fire on them, killing Wight and wounding Brenner with five shots to her head and neck. Brenner survived and wrote about the experience in *Eight Bullets: One Woman's Story of Surviving Anti-Gay Violence.* The gunman was sentenced to life in prison without parole after his conviction for first-degree murder, a result celebrated by those more used to indifference on the part of police and courts to attacks on gay men and all women.

In sum, lesbian visibility was a testament to the success of lesbian advocates and continued to increase through the eighties despite dissension among women (see Chapter 6) and between men and women. National organizations responded to concerns of women: the National Gay Task Force became the National Gay and Lesbian Task Force in 1986 and the HRCF continued to build a coalition with women's rights groups. In 1991, a National Lesbian Conference convened in Atlanta and drew 2,500 women.

Raising awareness of privilege derived from race and class as well as sex also reemerged with greater force out of AIDS activism. Philadelphia ACT UP member Kiyoshi Kuromiya, for example (born in a Japanese-American internment camp during World War II), was a pioneer in forming coalitions across class and race during the eighties and nineties. African Americans like Marlon Riggs sought to break the silence about homosexuality and HIV/AIDS among nonwhites, as in his film *Tongues Untied.* Others criticized mainstream media for the race and class bias involved in distinguishing between "innocent" (white, privileged) AIDS sufferers from those (nonwhite, lower-class sex workers and drug users) portrayed as more deserving of their plight.

Intersecting with other perennial split among activists were those differences over basic philosophy. Apparent in debates over baths and over AIDS strategy generally are the same fundamental issues that had repeatedly divided the homophile/homosexual/ gay and lesbian movements (and every other movement) in the United States: more "radical" versus more "moderate" approaches. While the former advocates less cooperation with the larger culture, more celebration of difference, and expects more rapid changes, the latter usually works within existing systems (government, medicine) to accomplish more gradual and "accommodationist" goals, all the while stressing the values shared between the minority and majority (and see Chapter 7 Debate). In part, AIDS activism not only heightened these differences but also allowed a resurgence of earlier radicalism. Writing of his personal experiences of that time and since, historian Les Wright recalled,

> I had become deeply disaffected...by the dramatic recasting of the (radical) gay liberation movement of the early 1970s into the (assimilationist) gay rights movement of the 1980s. As my generation's hippies transformed into 1980s yuppies, so too my gay-radical compatriots just as quickly became respectable "good gays." It was but a logical progression when queer national activists gave way to queer-conformist consumers, and the corporate media began touting "metrosexuality."[22]

As Wright noted, older differences and patterns were apparent even as new dynamics were emerging. Some of these concerned not only class, race, and sex (especially as they intersected when consumerism was associated with privileged white males) but the emerging voices of bisexual and transgendered people.

The place of bisexuals in the post-Stonewall movements had often been tenuous, but by the end of the 1980s there were single-sex and/or mixed-sex organizations for bisexuals in several large cities, including Boston, Chicago, Philadelphia, and San Francisco. A movement specifically for bisexuals is usually dated from the 1987 March on Washington for Lesbian and Gay Rights (see below), where activists' meetings led to the formation of a national organization, the North American Bisexual Network (later BiNet U.S.A.), and the first national conference for bisexuals in 1990.

Transgender activism included the goal of educating people inside and outside lesbian and gay communities and followed much the same pattern at the same time. In the early eighties, transgender politics was rapidly developing and claiming a place in the movements traditionally centered on homosexuals/gays/lesbians. While a MFT (male-to-female) community had coalesced earlier, only now did FTM (female-to-male) people, led by such pioneers as Lou Sullivan, begin significant organizing. Based in San Francisco, Sullivan founded what would become the largest FTM group, FTM International, in 1986. Within a half-dozen years additional organizations appeared, including the IFGE (International Foundation for Gender Education) and Transgender Nation, and Leslie Feinberg published the important work, *Transgender Liberation: A Movement Whose Time Has Come.*

LAW AND POLITICS

Although not everyone agreed on the strategy of working through the legal, judicial, and political systems, many activists have consistently felt that those arenas could not be ignored. Further, they advocated an increasingly professional approach, in effect "fighting fire with fire," and of necessity used a three-pronged method: promoting legislation that would protect gays and lesbians from discrimination, countering efforts to pass antigay acts, and repealing sodomy laws. In addition, lesbians and gay men would continue to seek political office, often successfully, further challenging destructive stereotypes of homosexuals.

Bills meant to ensure that gay men and lesbians received equal treatment took several forms. Most basic were the acts banning discrimination on the basis on sexual orientation, with a few states now joining the increasing number of localities with measures prohibiting antigay legal bias. Wisconsin legislators passed the first such bill at the state level in 1982, and six more states followed suit in some fashion in the next ten years (Massachusetts, Hawai'i, Connecticut, New Jersey, Vermont, California). In 1986 New York City joined the forty-plus communities around the country that had added nondiscrimination ordinances of some kind by then, as had about a dozen counties. While the push for a national bill continued less successfully (see below) "sexual orientation" did enter federal law for the first time with passage of the Hate Crimes Statistics Act. When President George H.W. Bush signed the act into law in 1990, in fact, it marked the first such ceremony to include openly lesbian and gay activists.

Movement members also found themselves fighting overtly antigay measures through the eighties, many of them in Congress and instigated by Senator Jesse Helms. Among the measures the North Carolina Republican sponsored were (with the earlier Family Protection Act) those intended to restrict federal AIDS funds only to educational materials that promoted monogamous (heterosexual) marriage (passed 1988), and place similar limits on works and artists receiving National Endowment for the Arts. In the latter case, the 1990 Appropriations Bill denied grants to projects that "promote, disseminate or produce materials which...may be considered obscene, including but not limited to, depictions of sadomasochism, homoeroticism, the sexual exploitation of children, or individuals engaged in sex acts and which, taken as a whole, do not have serious literary, artistic, political or scientific value."[23]

Gay and lesbian rights advocates saw clearer victories in bills that included protection of the rights of people with AIDS and successful immigration reform sponsored by Alan Simpson (R-WY) and Romano Mazzoli (D-KY), with significant help from Barney Frank. The former included the Civil Rights Restoration Act and Fair Housing Amendments Act, both passed in 1988; the Simpson-Mazzoli Act (1986) removed the "sexual deviation" clause that had been used to exclude homosexual immigrants since the Lavender Scare days of the fifties (see Chapter 4).

Running for Office

As noted in Chapter 6, when lesbians and gay men have run for public office, their sexual orientation may or may not have been public knowledge when initially elected.

Before 1980, fewer than a dozen homosexuals had been elected to office, and at least one of those—the only congressman, in fact—was not yet out. The last two decades of the century witnessed a marked and steady increase in the numbers of gay and lesbian people running for and winning office, and most of them eventually did so openly. From 1980 through 1991, at least fifty-one lesbians or gay men were newly elected or appointed to government posts. By 1991 there were at least fifty-two openly gay/lesbian people serving terms, a significant increase from twenty only four years previously. Not surprisingly, the breakdown among government levels is basically proportional to the number of potential offices in each: the majority of officials (40) served in city or county government and eight won seats in their state houses or senates. Only three gay congressmen served in the eighties, but because none were out when elected only their "post-out" careers can—and do—offer any indication of developments at the federal level.

Geographic patterns and general record-keeping also fall along predictable lines. California, New England, and New York are well represented among the fifty-one officials, as are traditionally liberal areas of Minnesota and Wisconsin. Small towns and villages are less represented—perhaps less documented—but it is worth noting that openly gay Gene Ulrich served as mayor of the tiny town of Bunceton, Missouri, from 1980 until his retirement in 2006. Beyond the West Coast and Northeast, local and state candidates in Arizona, Florida, Iowa, North Carolina, and Texas were successful in this period, though not all were out at the time they won. On the state level acceptance appears to have come more slowly, since all but one of the state officers were elected in 1988 through 1991. As with treatments of GLBT people in general, it is likely that many more GLBT people have served in office than official lists indicate. A central issue, though, is serving openly as a nonstraight person, whether one is out before or after taking office; only those out, of course, are known and thus appear on the lists. Also not counted here are people first elected earlier and serving into the 1980s or even 1990s (like Allan Spear, who retired from Minnesota state government only in 2000).

Tellingly, it is on the national level that the story is much more brief, but more complicated. Congressman Gerry Studds (D-MA), first elected in 1972, became the first openly gay member of Congress in 1983 (see Chapter 6), but no nonincumbent was voted into congressional office as an out gay person until 1998. Rather, while the early 1980s saw the initial election of Steve Gunderson (R-WI, 1980), Barney Frank (D-MA, 1981), and Jim Kolbe (R-AZ, 1984), none had run as an openly gay man. Of the three, only Barney Frank came out completely voluntarily (in 1987), and preceded the others in doing so by at least seven years. Despite predictions that he was endangering his career, he won reelection in every subsequent cycle and as of 2006 he continued to represent the Massachusetts 4th District.

The reluctance of gay government officials in DC to reveal themselves is reflected in the efforts of a handful of gay conservatives to start an organization called CAIR (Concerned Americans for Individual Rights) in 1985. As recalled by former congressman Bob Bauman (see Chapter 6) they were concerned about the antigay attitudes touted by "the Jesse Helms and William Dannemeyer types" in Congress and wanted to oppose them with more positive views of homosexuality. "CAIR never got off the ground," however, said Bauman, because not only would no gay Republicans come out,

They wouldn't even write checks. They would give cash, so there was no traceable evidence. CAIR could fill a suburban Washington home for a cocktail party with nearly a hundred gay men who worked everywhere from the White House to the offices of the most conservative Republican senators and congressmen, the Republican National Committee, and all parts of the Reagan administration. But they wouldn't publicly acknowledge their role in the group.[24]

This situation, and in the midst of the AIDS crisis, would fuel the controversy over "outing," or revealing someone's homosexuality without their permission (see Debate). In the meantime, hopes of putting a more conservative face on gay and lesbian people would not be fulfilled until the founding of the Log Cabin Republicans in 1993.

The National Bill in the Eighties

The climate in Washington, along with energy spent in the battle against AIDS, also affected the momentum of the drive to achieve federal antidiscrimination legislation. While hearings for a national lesbian and gay rights bill in San Francisco in 1980 and in Washington in 1982 were landmarks in the effort, movement attention shifted largely to organizing around HIV/AIDS and addressing government inaction. Even at the 1982 hearing, Jean O'Leary was careful to address ongoing concerns that to support homosexual rights was to sanction what many believed was immoral behavior. "H.R. 1454," she insisted, "will not condone homosexuality."[25] Advocates of the bill did make modest gains in the eighties: all candidates for the Democratic presidential nomination in 1984 endorsed the bill, and the House and Senate measures were reintroduced throughout the decade. At the same time, national lesbian/gay rights groups were building valuable coalitions with labor organizations and other civil rights workers—LCCR (Leadership Conference on Civil Rights) admitted both the NGTF and HRCF—and homosexuals with HIV/AIDS benefited from more general legislation prohibiting discrimination against people with disabilities. By the time the bill was introduced once again in 1991 it was with a record 110 cosponsors, nearly double the number it had a decade earlier.[26] Just as HIV/AIDS determined much of the focus and strategy of eighties activism, however, the ban on homosexuals serving in the U.S. military had a similar effect on lesbian/gay rights efforts of the early nineties. Ultimately a national bill was shelved in favor of other means to the same end.

Families, Relationships, and Work

In many ways GLBT movements of the eighties were similar to those of previous decades, even as specific issues changed. Just as activists had divided over accommodating to mainstream (or heterosexual) culture and values since the 1950s, they continued to do so as the rhetoric of "family values" became part of the political landscape. As organizations mobilized to recognize GLBT families and family members, and advocate legal rights for same-sex partners and parents, they were attacked alternately for violating family values and for succumbing to and promoting those same values. At the same time, there was an element of the purely practical among the more ideological stances (just as there was, for example, in debates over responses to AIDS). To some, matters of principles like equality and justice were both motivation and end goal, while others focused more on issues related to day-to-day survival, literally in the short term and economically in the long term.

GLBT families and family members were not a new phenomenon in the 1980s, of course. As outlined thus far, same-sex relationships, and people with same-sex emotional and/or sexual attractions, have been a constant in American—and human— life, though they have been variously defined over time. What was new was the level of visibility of self-defined GLBT people coupled with the conservative rhetoric of the traditional "fifties-style" American family, as represented by such groups as Focus on the Family (f. 1977) and the Family Research Council (f. 1983). The time was right, it seemed, to use a variety of approaches responding the narrow definition of family and a seeming cultural acceptance of families "discarding" their GLBT members.

A significant turn came when in 1982 of Parents and Friends of Lesbians and Gays (now Parents, Families, and Friends of Lesbians and Gays) was incorporated. Jeanne Manford, whose son had been a victim of gay-bashers, founded the organization from a small discussion group ten years earlier. In effect, it asks straight people to "come out" in support of their GLBT kin and friends, a process as difficult for some as it was for the nonstraight people who came out to them. It recognized that a crucial difference between youth (especially) identifying with a sexual minority and those of racial/ethnic minorities is the family support available *based on their identity.* Non-white families usually share the minority status and can offer support to each other, but parents often rejected, even literally disowned, their nonstraight children. Recognizing this, PFLAG organizers sought to provide support and education on a family level, and worked to organize chapters in rural as well as urban areas. The organization hired an executive director and moved to Washington, DC in 1990, gaining attention by seeking and receiving the support of First Lady Barbara Bush.

Related to older debates on the politics of relationships and the newer crisis of AIDS were renewed discussions of monogamy and alternatives to it. Radical feminists had long questioned the "double standard" by which women but not men were expected to limit themselves to one lifetime sexual partner. Many gay/lesbian liberationists also saw monogamy as more an institution for control rooted in notions of property and selectively applied to some people and not others. In light of a deadly sexually transmitted disease, however, many gay men and lesbians now promoted monogamy as practical, while others pointed out that serial monogamy—multiple monogamous relationships over a lifetime—was a valid alternative and already established, especially in lesbian circles (and straight ones, too, when divorce and remarriage are considered).

Regardless of disputes over ideal arrangements, innumerable lesbians and gay men had formed partnerships in same-sex couples, and devised their own public ceremonies to celebrate their unions and commitments. While gay and lesbian couples found emotional support in these rituals, many others sought recognition through their churches and synagogues. A few of the most liberal denominations—Quaker and Unitarian Universalist—offered commitment ceremonies to same-sex couples in the 1980s and earlier, and the momentum of acceptance of GLBT people and blessing lesbian and gay unions would increase in the next decades (see Chapters 8 and 9).

With or without a spiritual component, though, marriage always included legal and economic benefits to the couple with a license, as most committed same-sex duos were all too aware. The inequities involved between the rights of homosexual partners and heterosexual couples (who could marry legally) gained national attention through the experiences of Minnesota couple Sharon Kowalski and Karen Thompson. In 1983 Kowalski was seriously injured in a car accident that left her disabled, though eventually able to communicate by typing messages. Kowalski's family objected to her lesbian relationship and legally was able to move her to a distant facility and deny Karen any access to her partner. Karen's court battle to take Sharon home (a goal that Sharon also expressed repeatedly through her keyboard) continued until 1991, when she finally was awarded guardianship. Their lengthy ordeal publicized the lack of legal protections for both the disabled and for lesbians and gay men in chosen families—issues already related through the AIDS crisis—while encouraging the use of means potentially available to them (such as living wills, health care proxies, and durable powers of attorney).[27] Although controversial within gay and lesbian communities as well as outside them, the right to marry legally was raised again as a possible movement goal. In 1991 the case of *Baehr v. Lewin,* in which three same-sex couples sued for the right to marry, began to work its way through Hawai'i's court system, and the issue increasingly came to the forefront as the century closed.

Expecting domestic partnership benefits, much less legal marriage, likely seemed extremely optimistic to gay men and lesbians excluded or fired from jobs simply on the basis of their sexuality. Since the 1970s, employment discrimination against homosexuals had been a key issue for rights advocates, and national organizations continued to work through the 1980s to persuade governments and businesses that homosexuality and job performance are unrelated. The issue gained national attention in 1991 when Cheryl Summerville, a cook at a Cracker Barrel Old Country Store in Georgia was one of several employees fired for being gay/lesbian, or specifically, "failing to demonstrate normal heterosexual values."[28] By that time, national organizations had been raising awareness of the ability of employers to discriminate against their gay and lesbian workers, and were therefore prepared to mobilize both publicity and protest. The case received coverage in the national press and on TV (including *20/20* and *The Oprah Winfrey Show*), and helped expose the fact that in nearly all U.S. states Cracker Barrel's actions were perfectly legal. As with partnership rights and same-sex marriage, the movement for rights of nonheterosexual workers gained momentum in the next decade, even reaching the national level. Not until 2002, however, did Cracker Barrel add sexual orientation to its written nondiscrimination policy.

Sodomy Law and *Bowers v. Hardwick*

As late as 1960, all U.S. states and Washington, DC had laws prohibiting sodomy. These laws, prohibiting anal sex between any two people (and sometimes defined more broadly to include oral sex), originated in the colonial era and were used then to punish behavior considered sinful and threatening (see Chapter 2). By the later 20th century sodomy was associated more specifically with the relatively new identity of homosexuality and laws against it were used to penalize homosexuals especially. For that reason, the laws had also become one of the targets of the movement, from its homophile days through the liberationist years.

The slow process of removing the laws from state codes began in 1961, when Illinois repealed its sodomy statute. By the mid-1980s twenty-five more states followed suit, leaving sodomy laws in twenty-four states and DC. Another legal avenue presented itself in the 1960s when "privacy," at least within a heterosexual marriage, was deemed a right by the U.S. Supreme Court in *Griswold v. Connecticut* (1965). The same concept was used in the landmark *Roe v. Wade* (1973) decision as well and suggested the possibility of extending the right to privacy to any adult over his or her own body, to engage in any consensual sexual activity.

The chance to test state sodomy laws in the Supreme Court came in 1986. Four years earlier, Michael Hardwick had been arrested under Georgia's sodomy law when police entered his home, and his bedroom, to find him and another man sexually engaged. Charges against him were dropped, but Hardwick decided to participate in a suit designed to test the law, and won in the U.S. Court of Appeals on the basis of a right to privacy. Upon Georgia's appeal to the U.S. Supreme Court, however, the Justices voted 5-4 to uphold the Georgia law. In his opinion concurring with the majority, Chief Justice Warren Burger wrote, "...I write separately to underscore my view that in constitutional terms there is no such thing as a fundamental right to commit homosexual sodomy."[29] Predictably, GLB activists saw the decision as a devastating blow amid other setbacks of the decade, evoking "the deepest response among gay men and lesbians since the Dade County referendum nine years before."[30] Also predictable by now was that disappointment and anger would foster a renewed commitment to fighting back.

VISIBILITY, MEDIA, AND CULTURE

The quest for greater visibility went hand-in-hand with ongoing divisions among activists over the best strategies and the ultimate goals of their activities. Who should receive attention, and what kind of attention? To what degree could the movements control that attention, and who within the movements should exert that control? To many, the rights of nonstraight people were becoming increasingly commercialized and more easily co-opted by those whose goals were more moderate than radical. Such arguments intensified as the possibilities for visibility expanded and as some within the movements pushed for a sharper focus on their economics, professionalism, and relation to the media.

The Second March and National Coming Out Day

The first march on Washington for lesbian and gay rights in 1979 had arisen out of the conditions of the time—a lively gay/lesbian liberation movement, adopting strategies from the civil rights movement to address a homophobic backlash. The second time around, the 1987 National March on Washington for Lesbian and Gay Rights was a response to similar conditions, with the addition of two factors: the ongoing AIDS epidemic and the *Bowers* decision of the previous year (see above).

The march, held October 11, 1987, was one of many actions seeking to publicize the AIDS tragedy and government inaction (ACT UP had been founded in March of that year and had launched a series of protests). More than half a million people attended the march and had the opportunity to witness the first viewing of the NAMES Project AIDS Memorial Quilt. Other actions the same weekend reflected the variety of strategies utilized at this time: Rev. Troy Perry presided over "The Wedding" ceremony of thousands of same-sex couples outside the Internal Revenue Building on October 10; 600–800 demonstrators were arrested outside the Supreme Court on October 13 as they protested the *Bowers* decision; and the HRCF used the occasion to hold one of the largest GLBT political fundraisers.

Even as they planned the march, organizers saw it essentially as a rally of "believers"; Dudley Clendinen and Adam Nagourney recorded in *Out for Good* that Steve Ault (a 1979 march organizer also) said then, "A march is needed for ourselves. We need to say that we're not going back into the closet, and we need an event that will be a self-affirmation."[31] That it served exactly that purpose, especially for those outside urban areas with resources for sexual minorities, was suggested by Nadine Smith: "For those who traveled from the smaller towns, the march was a life-affirming revelation. Every conceivable segment of the community was there...And," she added, "in the aftermath of the 1987 march, grassroots organizations proliferated around the country, spreading far beyond major urban areas."[32] Not only did participants return to organize locally throughout the country, but at least two new national organizations resulted as well: BiNet U.S.A., to serve the needs of bisexual people, and the National Latina/o Lesbian and Gay Activists (NLLGA), soon renamed the National Latina/o Lesbian, Gay, Bisexual, and Transgender Organization (LLEGÓ). Importantly, the March and related events of that landmark October weekend were documented in a film entitled *For Love and For Life: The 1987 March on Washington For Lesbian and Gay Rights.*

One reason for the upswing in organizing was the "media blackout" of this march: major news outlets either ignored it or, as Barbara Raab recalled, offered less than a minute of dismissive coverage.[33] One response was a campaign focusing on the economics (if not the injustice) of ignoring the GLBT communities and involved writing "no march, no money" on the subscription cards that inevitably fall out of every *Time* or *Newsweek* magazine and mailing them in, at the publishers' expense. Another result of the October 11 march was the designation of that date in 1988 and after as NCOD (National Coming Out Day). Importantly, this not only acknowledged the date as significant but used the energy from the rally—often dissipated once people return to their "real" lives—to create an ongoing series of "actions" that join the personal and the political. Organizing the first NCOD was the National Gay Rights Advocates, who worked with producers of *The Oprah Winfrey Show* to provide a panel for her

Keith Haring's graphic of a person dancing out of a closet is one of the most enduring images of GLBT pride. It is the logo for National Coming Out Day, first held on October 11, 1988, and sometimes appears with the caption, "Come out, come out, wherever you are!" (© The Estate of Keith Haring)

broadcast that day. Panelist Greg Brock recalled the effect of that show, and the day, on his own thinking, saying, "One of the things being on *Oprah* helped convince me of was that coming out is key to the movement and to our lives. I don't think it will solve all of our problems or answer all the questions, but I think it's a major part of the solution."[34] In 1993 NCOD became the NCOP (National Coming Out Project) under the auspices of the HRCF and worked with celebrity spokespersons to enhance the movement's visibility while encouraging others to come out.

As Seen on TV (and Other Media)

Although network news may have been reluctant to give GLBT people air time, entertainment programming was changing significantly in the 1980s. Following typical trends in American culture, the portrayal of sexual minorities, like that of all minorities in popular media, developed generally from absence to negative stereotypes to more fully realized treatments. Along the way were efforts to treat the topic and people with more sensitivity, and to move from the family member, neighbor, or best friend whose function was to be "the gay one" to those who "happened to be gay" in addition to other attributes. Not surprisingly, the AIDS crisis affected what kind of television programming, plays, and films audiences could see at that time, while the more general visibility of sexual minorities would flow, ebb, and eventually flow again.

As Steven Capsuto has noted, TV seemed to take a turn toward being "a gay-friendly medium" in the late 1970s but that development did not continue along a straight line; he adds that the shows of that time featuring gay characters and story lines "were an oasis in the desert."[35] The turn of the eighties saw a mix of old and new: cross-dressing men played for laughs on *Bosom Buddies* (1980–1982) and Tony Randall starring two seasons (1981–1983) as a lonely gay man in *Love, Sidney* (but one whose sexuality is all but absent except to the most alert viewer). Also at this time the nighttime soap *Dynasty* made history with a bisexual main character, Steven Carrington. Over the next dozen years, and especially after the mid-eighties, GLBT characters multiplied: *Brothers* debuted on Showtime in 1984 with a gay brother, *thirtysomething* showed two men in bed in 1989, and two women kissed on *L. A. Law* in 1991. Hit sitcoms *The Golden Girls* (1985–1992) and *Designing Women* (1986–1993) treated gay- and lesbian-related topics in a generally sympathetic way in several episodes between them; *Golden Girl* Blanche's gay brother, for example, made two appearances, first coming out and later marrying his lover. Adding to the total media picture, ABC even ran an After School Special entitled *What If I'm Gay?* (1987) and network talk shows like *Donahue* featured real GLBT people several times and in ways more sympathetic than similar shows before 1970. Charles Kaiser, in fact, has claimed that Phil Donahue was "the person who played the largest role in ending the invisibility of gay life in America."[36]

Not surprisingly, AIDS was a topic on 1980s TV. A few regular dramas, beginning with *St. Elsewhere* in 1983, ran AIDS episodes, and even a sitcom, *Designing Women* featured a standout episode in the subject (1987). Other notable broadcasts were the made-for-TV movies *An Early Frost* (1985) and the PBS presentation of playwright Terrence McNally's *Andre's Mother* (1990). TV viewers also saw the story of MTF transsexual Renee Richards in 1986 in *Second Serve*. Activism that combined AIDS, gay/lesbian themes, and the media emerged in this decade with the founding of GLAAD (Gay and Lesbian Alliance Against Defamation) in New York City in 1985. Three years later a branch in Los Angeles was organized, and in 1994 the coastal offices combined to form a national organization. General visibility and type/tone of attention, especially news coverage, were original concerns, but monitoring quickly expanded to include all media and types of programming.

Film, for example, came under GLAAD's purview within a few years. Had it existed in 1980 undoubtedly it would have joined the protests of 1980's *Cruising,* starring Al Pacino as an undercover cop seeking a killer of gay men in S&M bars and clubs. Activists felt the movie portrayed gayness itself as inherently dangerous, violent (and deserving of violence against it), and contagious (Pacino's character begins to question his sexuality). Two years later came a more sympathetic Hollywood treatment, *Making Love* (1982), about a married man falling in love with another man. Films featuring lesbian relationships included *Personal Best* (1982), *Lianna* (1983), and the now-classic lesbian romance, *Desert Hearts* (1985). Independent films, often focusing on AIDS, included *Buddies* (1985), *Parting Glances* (1986), and *Longtime Companion* (1990), and several landmark documentaries were available to art-house audiences: *Before Stonewall* (1984), *The Times of Harvey Milk* (1984), and *Paris Is Burning* (1990), among others. It was in this decade also that Vito Russo's *The Celluloid Closet* was first published and then revised. Russo, a longtime activist, had been a member of Gay Activists Alliance and a founding member of GLAAD; tragically, in 1990 he was added to the lengthening list of talented men who died of complications from AIDS.

Perhaps more than other media, it was the theatre that confronted gay themes effectively and in ways far removed from 1968s *The Boys in the Band* (see Chapter 6). In 1982 *Torch Song Trilogy* by Harvey Fierstein began its three-year run in New York, winning the 1983 Tony Awards for Best Actor (Fierstein) and Best Play; it was adapted into a film version in 1988. AIDS in particular received attention from playwrights, notably in Larry Kramer's *The Normal Heart* (1985) and what is, to one critic, "the one unrivaled theatrical masterpiece of the AIDS era" *Angels in America* (1991) by Tony Kushner.[37] Subtitled, *A Gay Fantasia on National Themes,* the play won multiple awards, including the 1991 Pulitzer Prize for drama.

The eighties were especially significant years for the development of gay/lesbian studies—and gay/lesbian history in particular—as an academic field. In 1980, Michel Foucault published his *History of Sexuality* and this small volume, with other of his works, helped launch new ways of thinking about the past (see Debate, Chapter 9). The next year Randy Shilts' study of Harvey Milk, *The Mayor of Castro Street,* appeared, while Lillian Faderman brought out her pioneering work in lesbian history, *Surpassing the Love of Men.* John D'Emilio's landmark political history, *Sexual Politics, Sexual Communities* followed in 1983, as did Jonathan Ned Katz's second volume of primary sources, the *Gay/Lesbian Almanac.* By the decade's end Martin Duberman had published a series of essays in *About Time* (1986) and, with coeditors George Chauncey and Martha Vicinus, the volume *Hidden From History* (1989), a collection of then-cutting-edge articles on homosexuality in the United States and the world.

The close relationship between "the movement" and its stories continued through the eighties, with women and nonwhites claiming a clearer and self-determined place in both. Lesbian writers Judy Grahn, Joan Nestle, Adrienne Rich made important contributions to the new areas of lesbian history/lesbian studies through their poetry and prose, as did Margaret Cruikshank, with *Lesbian Studies* (1982). The specific issues surrounding gay African Americans were explored in Joseph Beam's collection, *In the Life: A Black Gay Anthology* (1986) while studies of Native Americans helped illustrate the limited nature of thinking only in terms of homosexual/heterosexual. Walter Williams published *Spirit and the Flesh: Sexual Diversity in American Indian Culture* in 1986 and Will Roscoe followed with *Living the Spirit: A Gay American Indian Anthology* in 1988. Lesbians in nonwhite cultures received attention in such books as *This Bridge Called My Back* (1981), *The Sacred Hoop* (1986), and the works of African American writer Audre Lorde. Describing herself as a "Black lesbian, mother, warrior, poet," Lorde was also a teacher, publisher, and activist for justice around the world. Among her many distinctions, she was a featured speaker at the 1979 March on Washington and a founder of Kitchen Table: Women of Color Press and Sisterhood in Support of Sisters in South Africa. At the time of her death from cancer in 1992 she was Poet Laureate of New York State, and had published poetry and prose whose influence continues to the present; these include *Zami: A New Spelling of My Name* (1982) and *Sister Outsider* (1984).

"Culture Wars"

The maturing in the eighties of Gay and Lesbian Studies, including development and debates surrounding theory, literature, and history, amplified rather than resolved the same dispute over values with which the decade had begun. Now termed "culture wars," they were fought especially over social and educational policies from the local to the national level. Fueling New Right concern was the increase in resources available to students, parents, and educators seeking to promote tolerance. In 1989 Lesléa Newman's *Heather Has Two Mommies* was published, followed by *Daddy's Roommate*. Within a few years controversy surrounded both books and others like them, about and for children with lesbian or gay parents. Librarians around the country defended such books (and replaced them as they disappeared), for example, while in New York City their inclusion in a proposed "Rainbow Curriculum" in 1992 crystallized sentiment on both sides. Ultimately the curriculum was adopted, but without the suggested books concerning lesbian and gay families. At the same time, educators sought other avenues to support nonstraight students and studies in secondary and higher education. The Hetrick-Martin Institute, founded in 1979 to address the needs of lesbian and gay youth, created a public high school in 1984 as a safe option for those youth. Located in New York City, it is fittingly named the Harvey Milk High School. In higher education, the first Gay and Lesbian Studies Department was formed at San Francisco City College in 1989, a landmark in the effort to legitimize the field.

As the country approached the 1992 election year, life for GLBT Americans was typically mixed. The eighties had begun with unprecedented strength and activity of organized lesbian and gay activists of all stripes, and they persevered amid political backlash and medical disaster. Many GLBT people rejoiced when in July of 1992 the Democratic Party selected Bill Clinton as its presidential candidate, a person who had promised some support of lesbian/gay rights. A month later, though, Patrick Buchanan reiterated the sentiments of his party's right wing when he spoke at the Republican National Convention. "The American people are not going to buy back into the failed liberalism of the 1960s and '70s—no matter how slick the package in 1992," he said, and went on to use GLBT support of Clinton, and (limited) Democratic support of lesbian/gay rights, against him:

> ...a militant leader of the homosexual rights movement could rise at [the Democratic National] convention and exult: "Bill Clinton and Al Gore represent the most pro-lesbian and pro-gay ticket in history." And so they do....

DEBATE: SHOULD PUBLIC FIGURES BE "OUTED"?

As the 1980s drew to a close a heated argument emerged that sparked discussion well outside GLBT communities. The timing was not surprising, since it reflected general issues of the decade—government inaction, the role of media in shaping public opinion—as well as divisions already present in GLBT politics. "Coming out of the closet," or revealing that oneself is gay or lesbian, has been seen as an important political act especially in the post-Stonewall era (for example, the slogan of the 1987 National March on Washington for Lesbian and Gay Rights was "Come Out for Freedom"). Both before and after Stonewall, though, an unwritten code dictated that one gay/lesbian person never revealed the identity of another to a nongay person, a code taken very seriously in the climate of postwar America (see Chapter 4).

It was not just a community code of silence but also one among journalists that began to rankle AIDS-era activists. When famous gay people died of AIDS-related illnesses, both the cause of death and their sexuality were treated as literally unmentionable; in obituaries, surviving same-sex partners often became "longtime companions" (hence the title of the 1990 film). For the living, too, the code held sway: media gossip's obsession with who among the rich and powerful was dating/marrying/cheating clearly was reserved for heterosexual activities only. Some insisted that the code was a simple matter of respecting the privacy of public figures while to its opponents it was noticeably selective, since it seemed to apply only to nonstraight people. Perhaps more important, said the critics of "inning," journalists in mainstream and GL media alike not only reflected both homophobia and hypocrisy in their silence but also perpetuated them. In particular, the proponents of outing were concerned with those in "the closets of power" as Michelangelo Signorile termed the centers of government and media influence of Hollywood, New York, and Washington, DC in his 1993 book, *Queer in America.*

Signorile was a key figure in the controversy over outing, a term coined in 1990 in *Time* magazine. By then members of the national GL rights organizations had suggested outing as a political strategy in light of antigay measures in Congress through the decade. For them, the threat of outing might be used to wield power against closeted congressmen who voted for antigay measures, but it was still under discussion when others took the idea beyond the conference rooms. Also by 1990 the new GL magazine *OutWeek* was featuring a "Gossip Watch" by Signorile, who used it to attack the enforced silence of the traditional gossip columns on the topic of homosexuality; eventually lists of names also appeared. As Larry Gross noted in his detailed account of the controversy, Signorile's "disillusionment with the ethics of gossip journalists, fueled by his newly militant gay politics and AIDS activism, turned to anger, which he unleashed in his 'Gossip Watch' column."[38]

In March of 1990 *OutWeek* ran a story on "The Secret Gay Life of Malcolm Forbes," the multimillionaire publisher who had died the month before, and soon both GL and mainstream media were arguing the pros and cons of outing. Noted gay author Armistead Maupin, for example, joined those naming names, saying, "'If the gay press has any function at all it's to tweak the conscience of famous people who are in the closet;...I'm taking the hard line on it and saying homophobia is homophobia.'"[39] C. Carr also saw homophobia in action, but from a different source, explaining "Why Outing Must Stop" in a 1991 issue of the *Village Voice.* "Born in rage and hatred, directed exclusively at gay people, outing is gay bashing at its sickest," she insisted. "Ostensibly, outers want closeted homosexuals to come out for the common good—consequences to their individual lives be damned. That's totalitarian thinking, a regime I can't live in. . . . I don't want to be told how to be gay."[40] For others it was the more general image of GL people turning their anger on each other, coupled with the apparent violation of the very privacy rights on which many were basing defenses of GL rights (as in the furor over the *Bowers* decision, above). Still others were torn, supporting the outing of the worst offenders (gay congressmen voting against gay rights) but worried over it as a more generally applied strategy. In a piece entitled, "Malcolm Forbes, Malcolm X and Me," in 1990, for example, Andrew Miller asked, "Since when did telling the truth become taboo?" He also stated, "There is no constitutional right to stay in the closet. . . . ," but then outlined his reservations: "Nevertheless, I'm uncomfortable with the idea of a revolution by any means necessary," worrying that the tactic could be more divisive than its results justified.[41]

Ironically, outing, centered on the way media operated, became a media event itself, and typical of such events it had a relatively short public life span. Older issues never completely went away, but as the nation geared up for the presidential race of 1992 many of even the most jaded activists may have felt a glimmer of hope. As attention was directed toward candidates and their promises, the topic of outing seemed to fade quickly. It was taken up in another form by academics, though, and continues to the present in debates over how, why, and in what terms to present the sexuality of people of the past.

The agenda Clinton & Clinton would impose on America—abortion on demand, a litmus test for the Supreme Court, homosexual rights, discrimination against religious schools, women in combat—that's change, all right. But it is not the kind of change America wants. It is not the kind of change America needs. And it is not the kind of change we can tolerate in a nation that we still call God's country. . . .

Yes, we disagreed with President Bush, but we stand with him for freedom to choice religious schools, and we stand with him against the amoral idea that gay and lesbian couples should have the same standing in law as married men and women. . . .

My friends, this election is about much more than who gets what. It is about who we are. It is about what we believe. It is about what we stand for as Americans. There is a religious war going on in our country for the soul of America. It is a cultural war, as critical to the kind of nation we will one day be as was the Cold War itself. And in that struggle for the soul of America, Clinton & Clinton are on the other side, and George Bush is on our side. . . .

. . .we must take back our cities, and take back our culture, and take back our country.[42]

Yes, GLBT people had won a few battles but the wars, cultural or otherwise, were hardly over.

NOTES

1. Steve Endean, *Bringing Lesbian and Gay Rights into the Mainstream,* ed. Vicki L. Eaklor (Binghamton, NY: Haworth Press, 2006), 36, 72.

2. Endean, *Mainstream,* 64.

3. William B. Turner, "Mirror Images: Lesbian/Gay Civil Rights in the Carter and Reagan Administrations," in *Creating Change™: Sexuality, Public Policy, and Civil Rights,* ed. John D'Emilio, William B. Turner, and Urvashi Vaid (New York: St. Martin's Press, 2000), 17.

4. Jimmy Carter, *Our Endangered Values: America's Moral Crisis* (New York: Simon & Schuster, 2005), 69.

5. Carter, *Our Endangered Values,* 3.

6. Jerry Falwell, *Listen, America!* (New York: Doubleday, 1980), 19.

7. Dudley Clendinen and Adam Nagourney, *Out for Good: The Struggle to Build a Gay Rights Movement in America* (New York: Simon & Schuster, 1999), 310.

8. Quoted in Clendinen and Nagourney, *Out for Good,* 324.

9. Endean, *Mainstream,* 256.

10. Ibid., 35, 214.

11. Estimates of numbers of participants range from 25,000 to as many as 125,000. This pattern of varying numbers continued for all GLBT marches in the capital, stirring controversy over the politics of the way the marches were represented.

12. Quoted in Mark Thompson, "18 Years Ago," *Advocate,* no. 745 (October 28, 1997): 10.

13. Amin Ghaziani, "Breakthrough: The 1979 National March," *The Gay & Lesbian Review Worldwide* 12, no. 2 (March–April 2005): 31–32; Nadine Smith, "Three Marches, Many Lessons," in *Creating Change™: Sexuality, Public Policy, and Civil Rights,* ed. John D'Emilio, William B. Turner, and Urvashi Vaid (New York: St. Martin's Press, 2000), 441; Clendinen and Nagourney, *Out for Good,* 398, 403.

14. Quoted in Ghaziani, "Breakthrough," 32.

15. Smith, "Three Marches," 442.

16. Lawrence K. Altman, "Rare Cancer Seen in 41 Homosexuals," *The New York Times,* July 3, 1981, A20.

17. Jennifer Brier, "AIDS and People with AIDS," *Encyclopedia of Lesbian, Gay, Bisexual and Transgendered History in America,* ed. Marc Stein (Detroit: Gale Publishing Group, 2004), 27.

18. For statistics on AIDS diagnoses and deaths see http://www.avert.org/usastaty.htm.

19. For statistics on violence see note of Clendinen and Nagourney, *Out for Good,* 548; quotes also in *Out for Good,* 488, 484.

20. http://www.aidsquilt.org/history.htm.

21. Allan Bérubé, "The History of Gay Bathhouses," in *Policing Public Sex: Queer Politics and the Future of AIDS Activism,* ed. Dangerous Bedfellows (Boston: South End Press, 1996), 188.

22. Les Wright, "Tangled Memories of a Wounded Storyteller: Notes on Bear History and Cultural Memory," *torquere: Journal of the Canadian Lesbian and Gay Studies Association* 6 (2004): 72.

23. http://www.publiceye.org/theocrat/Mapplethorpe_Chrono.html.

24. Quoted in Eric Marcus, *Making Gay History: The Half-Century Fight for Lesbian and Gay Equal Rights* (New York: Harper Perennial, 2002), 284.

25. Quoted in Chai R. Feldblum, "The Federal Gay Rights Bill: From Bella to ENDA," in *Creating Change™: Sexuality, Public Policy, and Civil Rights,* ed. John D'Emilio, William B. Turner, and Urvashi Vaid (New York: St. Martin's Press, 2000), 164.

26. See Appendix B, "Cosponsors of the National Lesbian and Gay Civil Rights Bill [1975–1992]," in Endean, *Mainstream,* 301–6.

27. See Karen Thompson and Julie Andrzejewski, *Why Can't Sharon Kowalski Come Home?* (San Francisco, CA: Aunt Lute Books, 1989); their story is also treated in the film, *Lifetime Commitment: A Portrait of Karen Thompson* (Kiki Zeldes, 1993), and inspired the play, *Standing in the Shadows* by Rosemary McLaughlin.

28. Quoted in advertisement for the film *Out at Work* (1996). The film profiles three people, including Summerville, who fought employment discrimination against lesbian and gay workers.

29. Quoted in Kevin Jennings, ed., *Becoming Visible: A Reader in Gay & Lesbian History for High School & College Students* (Boston: Alyson Publications, 1994), 232, from his very useful chapter on the case that offers a summary and document selections.

30. Clendinen and Nagourney, *Out for Good,* 528.

31. Quoted in Clendinen and Nagourney, *Out for Good,* 538.

32. Smith, "Three Marches," 443.

33. Barbara Raab, "Gays, Lesbians, and the Media: the Slow Road to Acceptance," *USA Today,* July, 1996, 56–59.

34. Quoted in Marcus, *Making Gay History,* 318.

35. Steven Capsuto, *Alternate Channels: The Uncensored Story of Gay and Lesbian Images on Radio and Television* (New York: Ballantine Books, 2000), xi, xii.

36. Charles Kaiser, *The Gay Metropolis, 1940–1996* (Boston: Houghton Mifflin, 1997), 206.

37. Steven Winn, "AIDS AT 25," *San Francisco Chronicle,* June 7, 2006, http://www.sfgate.com/cgi-bin/article.cgi?f=/c/a/2006/06/07/DDG4PJ9AN224.DTL.

38. Larry Gross, *Contested Closets: The Politics and Ethics of Outing* (Minneapolis: University of Minnesota Press, 1993), 58.

39. Quoted in Gross, *Contested Closets,* 61.

40. Ibid., 274.

41. Ibid., 253–54.

42. Patrick J. Buchanan, "1992 Republican National Convention Speech," August 17, 1992, as posted on http://www.buchanan.org/pa-92-0817-rnc.html.

SUGGESTED RESOURCES

General/Politics

Brenner, C. (with Ashley, H.) (1995). *Eight bullets: One woman's story of surviving anti-gay violence.* Ithaca, NY: Firebrand Books.

Charles, C. (2003). *The Sharon Kowalski case: Lesbian and gay rights on trial.* Lawrence: University Press of Kansas.

D'Emilio, J. (1989). Gay politics and community in San Francisco since World War II. In M. Duberman, M. Vicinus, & G. Chauncey, Jr. (Eds.), *Hidden from history: Reclaiming the gay and lesbian past* (pp. 456–473). New York: New American Library.

Feinberg, L. (1992). *Transgender liberation: A movement whose time has come.* New York: World View Forum.

Pohlman, H.L. (1999). *The whole truth: A case of murder on the Appalachian trail.* Amherst, MA: University of Massachusetts Press.

Schulman, S. (1994). *My American history: Lesbian and gay life during the Reagan/Bush years.* New York: Routledge.

Yeager, K. (1999). *Trailblazers: Profiles of America's gay and lesbian elected officials.* Binghamton, NY: Haworth Press.

AIDS

AP (1981, June 6). A pneumonia that strikes gay males. *The San Francisco Chronicle,* p. 4.

Cohen, C.J. (2000). Contested membership: Black gay identities and the politics of AIDS. In J. D'Emilio, W.B. Turner, & U. Vaid (Eds.), *Creating Change™: Sexuality, public policy, and civil rights* (pp. 382–406). New York: St. Martin's Press.

Shilts, R. (1987). *And the band played on: Politics, people, and the AIDS epidemic.* New York: St. Martin's Press.

Woods, W.J., & Binson, D. (Eds.). (2003). *Gay bathhouses and public health policy.* Binghamton, NY: Harrington Park Press.

Media

Bad Object-Choices (Ed.). (1991). *How do I look? Queer film and video.* Seattle, WA: Bay Press.

Benshoff, H.M., & Griffin, S. (2006). *Queer images: A history of gay and lesbian film in America.* Lanham, MD: Rowman & Littlefield.

Russo, V. (1981; 1987). *The celluloid closet: Homosexuality in the movies.* New York: Harper & Row.

Signorile, M. (1993). *Queer in America: Sex, the media, and the closets of power.* New York: Random House.

8   THE GLBT NINETIES

New York City, 1994. On the 25th Anniversary of the Stonewall riot (June 1969), Sylvia Rivera leads a march down Fifth Avenue. This was not the "official" Stonewall 25 celebration—touted as a "Gay, Lesbian, and Bisexual Event"—but a countermarch to continue AIDS activism and protest the exclusion of transgendered people and politics from the main event. Soon after the watershed moment of Stonewall an arm of the movement had espoused gay liberation. In the following decades lesbians and bisexuals fought for and won a measure of visibility within the movements, but transgendered people continued as outsiders. Only in the mid-nineties did their status begin to change more rapidly.

Rivera was the obvious choice to lead the protest of a march some saw as too mainstream itself. Born Ray Rivera Mendosa in 1951, Sylvia was a biological male who became an important voice for youth like herself, whose gender and bodies did not match as society dictated. During a childhood of abuse from relatives and peers, Sylvia began living on the streets of New York City, surviving as a prostitute and with the help of other "street queens." When the police raided the Stonewall Inn on that historical June night Sylvia was not only present, but also among those who fought back: a friend suggested they leave for a while and she responded, "Are you nuts? I'm not missing a minute of this—it's the revolution!*" In 1970 she and another transgendered sex worker, Marsha P. Johnson, launched STAR (Street Transvestite Action Revolutionaries) to organize aid and support and to infuse that aid with politics that linked other oppressions (of, sex, race, class, etc.) with homophobia and transphobia.*

By the time she died in 2002 Rivera had endured periods of drug addiction and homelessness, and had engaged in an ongoing struggle with the ever-evolving GLB movement for inclusion. She had worked for peace and was active in Latino/a communities and in the Metropolitan Community Church. Also in 2002 the Sylvia Rivera Law Project was founded to address discrimination grounded in both poverty and gender identity, and three years later a corner near the Stonewall Inn was renamed Rivera Way in her honor. Something of her spirit is evident in her encounter with police while petitioning for gay rights on New York's Forty-second Street in 1970:

Police: "Move on, and make it snappy."
Sylvia: "I'm only getting signatures to stop the discrimination against homo-
sexuals."
Police: "You have to move."
Sylvia: "Well, I'm not moving. I got my constitutional rights, just like everybody
else. I got the right to stand here and petition to change the laws just like anybody
else."[1]

Sylvia Rivera is a perfect symbol for the way "the more things change, the more they stay the same," a phrase descriptive of the nineties as much as for any previous decade for GLBT Americans. She was an old-fashioned drag queen growing up in the pre-Stonewall era, who proudly claimed both that identity and newer terms as politics and issues shifted. She was a revolutionary and remained so, seeming ever more radical as the mainstream movement, according to its inside critics, grew increasingly concerned with money, image, and respectability. By the century's end, the paradoxes of GLBT life in the United States seemed especially pronounced: on the one hand an appearance of rapid progress toward full citizenship, accompanied by unprecedented visibility, on the other the same old antigay myths and rhetoric to counter, with activists continuing their arguments over responses and initiatives.

NEW REGIME, OLD STRUGGLES

The rights of openly gay and lesbian people, along with those of all women and minority men, had been used politically through the eighties to unite a more radical New Right, who sought to stop or turn back those rights in the name of "family values." Indeed, Patrick Buchanan clearly sought to discredit the Democrats generally and their 1992 candidate (and spouse) specifically when he raised the specters of "abortion on demand,...homosexual rights, discrimination against religious schools, women in combat" as the agenda of "Clinton & Clinton" (see Chapter 7).[2] The "culture wars" were on in full force, which might have discouraged activists already battle-scarred from the politics of AIDS. Instead, GLBT people thought they had greater reason for hope than ever; though soon they would be disillusioned, the momentum of visibility already gained would indeed continue to the next century.

The '92 Elections

President George H. W. Bush was running for reelection amid a mixed national mood. The United States had fought a brief and apparently successful Persian Gulf War in early 1991, which raised the president's popularity, only to have it wane due to a recession through the rest of his term. Benefiting from the economic downturn were the relative unknowns in the race, Arkansas governor William Jefferson Clinton and Independent Party candidate billionaire Ross Perot.

For GLBT people inclined toward party politics 1992 was a red-letter year. Although the Democrats had generally supported (if not embraced) many tenets of GLBT rights, never before had a serious presidential candidate so openly sought (or even conceived of) a "gay vote." In the spring, while campaigning in Los Angeles, Clinton addressed a GLBT fundraising event for his campaign. Introduced by his friend David Mixner (a longtime activist and openly gay advisor on the campaign) Clinton spoke for an America that included lesbians and gay men, and against discrimination, promising to end the ban against homosexuals in the military once he became president. As a result, GLBT people contributed three million dollars to his campaign and likely voted as a bloc for the first time, contributing to Clinton's victory. Now both Congress and the presidency would be controlled by Democrats, the latter for the first time in a dozen years.

For those who believed there was change in the air, early signs looked good nationally. In the April following his inauguration Clinton was the first president to hold a meeting in the Oval Office with community leaders, including the heads of the Human Rights Campaign Fund, the National Lesbian and Gay Task Force, the Gay and Lesbian Victory Fund, and the recently formed Campaign for Military Service. In addition, he appointed Roberta Achtenberg to the post of assistant secretary of Housing and Urban Development. Upon her Senate confirmation she made history as the first openly lesbian/gay person to go through that process at that level.

In the states the outcome of the 1992 elections was as mixed as the national picture would soon be. Notably, voters in Oregon rejected Proposition 9, created by the right-wing Oregon Citizens Alliance and prohibiting the public schools or the state from any action that would "promote, encourage, or facilitate homosexuality, pedophilia, sadism, or masochism." At the same time, though, just over 53 percent of Coloradoans voted in favor of antigay Amendment 2, which was presented to voters as insurance against "special rights" demanded by GLB people. It stated, in notably comprehensive language:

> No Protected Status Based on Homosexual, Lesbian, or Bisexual Orientation. Neither the State of Colorado, through any of its branches or departments, nor any of its agencies, political subdivisions, municipalities or school districts, shall enact, adopt or enforce any statute, regulation, ordinance or policy whereby homosexual, lesbian or bisexual orientation, conduct, practices or relationships shall constitute or otherwise be the basis of or entitle any person or class of persons to have or claim any minority status, quota preferences, protected status or claim of discrimination.[3]

One effect of Amendment 2 would be to nullify laws already in effect in Denver, Boulder, and Aspen that protected GLB people from discrimination on the basis of their sexual identity. Opponents of the Amendment soon began a legal challenge that was not resolved until 1996 (see below, *Romer v. Evans,* under "In the States").

Don't Ask, Don't Tell

The vote in Colorado was discouraging enough, but the failed attempt to end discrimination against lesbians and gay men in the military demonstrated the breadth and depth of obstacles to full equality on the federal as well as the state level. Certainly "gays in the military" (as the short version goes) was not a new phenomenon any more than the fact that obvious discrimination existed against them. As noted in Chapter 4, homosexuals became a category of person subject to removal during World War II, as the relatively new psychiatric profession worked in tandem with the military to define those "fit" for service. From the 1940s to the 1980s, tens of thousands of men and women were denied benefits due to being discharged dishonorably; only in the early eighties were honorable discharges more available. To serve as openly gay or lesbian, however, remained a goal unrealized through the nineties and beyond.

Beginning in the seventies challenges to the policy increased in both number and, seemingly, the chances of overturning it. Two notable cases were those of Air Force Sgt. Leonard Matlovich and Army Sgt. Miriam Ben-Shalom. Matlovich was a twelve-year veteran with multiple medals when he came out to the Air Force Secretary in a 1975 letter. Upon an investigation (during which Matlovich was asked to "prove" his homosexuality), the government concluded that he was unfit for further service and recommended that he be discharged. Amid his challenge to the finding, *Time* magazine placed his picture on the cover (September 8, 1975), making him the first openly gay man to appear there. After rulings in his favor the Air Force, rather than reinstating him as ordered, arrived at an agreement with Matlovich in 1980 that included a monetary settlement and an honorable discharge. Only eight years later, he died of complications from AIDS; his tombstone reads, "When I was in the military, they gave me a medal for killing two men, and a discharge for loving one."

Just a year after Matlovich began his action the army discharged Miriam Ben-Shalom for her admission to being a lesbian. She sued to be reinstated and a U.S. District judge found in her favor in 1980. The fight dragged on for years, though, because of the army's persistent refusal to comply with court orders to reinstate Ben-Shalom, only relenting in 1988. Within a year of her reenlistment the decision was reversed and she appealed to the U.S. Supreme Court, who in 1990 declined the case. No longer a service member, Ben-Shalom became a founding member of the Gay, Lesbian and Bisexual Veterans of America, Inc. (1990), now called American Veterans for Equal Rights, Inc. (AVER).

The consequences of Matlovich's case in particular were mixed. After Steve Estes conducted an oral history of gay veterans he concluded, "As a result of the Matlovich case, the federal government clarified and hardened its opposition to gays in the military, at the same time that more gays in uniform began coming out to challenge this discrimination in court."[4] Indeed, the 1981 revision (Directive 1332.14) not only restated the conviction that "homosexuality is incompatible with military service" but also added phrases (in italics, below) that outlawed the identity of *being* gay or lesbian; it stated:

> The presence in the military environment of persons who engage in homosexual conduct *or who, by their statements, demonstrate a propensity to engage in homosexual conduct,* seriously impairs the accomplishment of the military mission. The presence of such members adversely affects the ability of the Armed Forces to maintain discipline, good order, and morale;...Discharge for homosexuality can result from: 1) committing homosexual acts; 2) attempting to commit homosexual acts; 3) *stating the desire or intent to commit homosexual acts.*

A notable case resulting from the newer policy was that of Army Sgt. Perry Watkins, an African American drafted in 1968. Despite being openly gay, he served until 1982, when he was discharged for homosexuality. Watkins was reinstated in 1990, however, after the Supreme Court refused to hear the army's appeal, and he eventually retired with full honors.

Another factor bringing the question to a head was the presence of ROTC (Reserve Officers' Training Corps) programs on college and university campuses; as in the Vietnam era, these programs allowed opponents of military policy an opportunity for organized action on a national level. In 1989, the story of James M. Holobaugh, a student at Washington University in St. Louis, helped galvanize opposition to the antigay policy. The army not only had suspended him after he told a superior he was gay but also recommended that he pay back his entire ROTC scholarship ($25,000). The following spring, after members of Congress signed letters to the army and navy in support of Holobaugh and of two Massachusetts NROTC midshipmen, both branches dropped their demands that scholarship money be returned. To address the issues and possibilities surrounding the ROTC, Lesbian and Gay Rights Project of the ACLU (American Civil Liberties Union) organized the ABOUT FACE conference at the University of Minnesota in the fall of 1990 and featured Miriam Ben-Shalom, James Holobaugh, and Rep. Gerry Studds among its speakers. In the same academic year—a year that saw further service of lesbians and gay men in the Persian Gulf War (January–February 1991)—many campuses participated in the Day of National Coordinated Action (April 10, 1991). Activities included both national initiatives, including signing a petition objecting to Defense Department policy, and local initiatives to be determined by campus leaders. At the time, almost 1,400 schools had ROTC programs, and concerted action could seriously threaten their viability.[5] Statistics and other information circulated through the campuses were disturbing: between 1973 and 1992, more than 25,000 people had been "separated" from the service, with women especially vulnerable (their rate of discharge since 1983 was ten times the rate of their male peers). Activists also publicized the results of the government's 1988–89 Personnel Security Research and Education Center (PERSEREC) Reports, which, according to an ACLU summary, "were very favorable toward the integration of lesbians, bisexuals, and gay men into the military."

Higher education institutions across the country responded to the antigay policy with a variety of actions, the DoD countering with threats of suspending grants and other funds. At several University of California campuses and The Ohio State University students and others held protests, rallies, and sit-ins, and demanded meetings with administrators. Elsewhere faculty and administrators voluntarily released statements and wrote letters critical of the policy and even a few governing boards passed resolutions of opposition. At Rutgers, ROTC scholarships were abolished and recruiters barred from campus, and Yale simply refused to reinstate the program, banned from campus during the Vietnam War. At Alfred University in New York, faculty initiated a unique response: removing credit from all ROTC courses, a move approved by its board in 1992 and enacted for the class entering in 1997.

In the midst of this—and even a few years before—additional cases arose and, equally important, were publicized through national media outlets, including the *New York Times, U.S. News & World Report, The New Republic, The Washington Post, The Los Angeles Times,* and *The Phil Donahue Show.* One of Donahue's guests, for example, was Joseph Steffan. Just weeks before his graduation from the U.S. Naval Academy in 1987, model officer Steffan answered honestly when asked whether he was gay. He was allowed neither to graduate nor to accept his commission and sued, with aid from the Lambda Legal Defense and Education Fund. Although a panel ruled in Steffan's favor in 1993, the order to reinstate him was reversed on appeal the next year and Steffan did not take the case further. A similar fight awaited Navy Lt. Tracy Thorne after he appeared on ABC's *Nightline* in 1992 supporting efforts to end to the ban and coming out as gay (he was discharged in 1995, by now under the new "Don't Ask, Don't Tell" policy). More tragic was the fate of Petty Officer Allen R. Schindler, who was murdered in Japan in 1992 by two shipmates who discovered he was gay. Of the two assailants, one was sentenced to life imprisonment, while the other served less than three months. The former, according to a witness, had admitted that "he hated homosexuals" and had no remorse for the killing, reportedly saying, "I don't regret it. I'd do it again...He deserved it."

Real and potential violence, along with the apparent hypocrisy of demanding honesty and honor but forcing gay men and lesbians to lie in order to remain in the service, further turned much public opinion toward questioning the policy, as did the additional story of Margarethe Cammermeyer. Army Colonel Cammermeyer, a decorated Vietnam veteran and nurse in the Washington State National Guard, was ousted in 1992 after more than twenty-five years of service. She was the highest-ranking person yet dismissed solely for being homosexual and upon appeal won reinstatement in 1994 despite attempts to delay it by the Justice Department; her story was dramatized in a 1995 TV movie, *Serving in Silence,* starring Glenn Close.

Given what seemed a ground swell of opposition to a policy that seemed blatantly unfair, both President Clinton was as surprised as LBG leaders at resistance within the government. Tim McFeeley, then head of the Human Rights Campaign Fund, later described the environment of early 1993:

> As gay organizers we had never before had a president say a kind word about gay and lesbian Americans, and now we had the new president fighting Congress and the military establishment on our behalf. It was almost impossible to believe at that time that we could lose.... Not only had we failed to anticipate and combat the opposition to Clinton's initiative to lift the ban, but at that time we didn't recognize that we had already lost the debate.[6]

After hearings in which military officials severely resisted lifting the ban on homosexuals, Clinton agreed to a compromise in the summer of 1993 termed, "Don't Ask, Don't Tell, Don't Pursue, Don't Harass"—"Don't Ask, Don't Tell" for short (or "Lie and Hide" to GLB people feeling betrayed). Supposedly addressing the homosexual's dilemma over how to respond if questioned about sexual orientation (be honest and get discharged or lie and serve), in effect the new guidelines, by allowing only closeted GLB people to serve, represented no significant change in attitudes. For their part,

"This one's for not asking, and this one's for not telling."

The "Don't Ask, Don't Tell" policy, requiring gay and lesbian military personnel to be closeted, went into effect in early 1994. This cartoon by Christopher Weyant was one of many that lampooned the compromise. (© The New Yorker Collection 2000 Christopher Weyant from cartoonbank.com. All Rights Reserved.)

military officials were to stop their efforts to "weed out" gay men and lesbians. In September, Congress overwhelmingly voted the new policy into law and the next month the president signed the bill, to go into effect in February of 1994. The policy stands at this writing despite ongoing protest and mounting evidence that it has brought no real improvement to the lives of GLB service people.

Another March

The movement's third march, held April 25, 1993, occurred amid joy and, more typically, anger, both reactions to events surrounding the elections of 1992. There seemed more cause to celebrate this time with the change in administration, but that was tempered by new issues arising out of the same election cycle: several statewide antigay efforts in the '92 elections, including passage of Colorado's Amendment 2, and the ongoing struggle for equal treatment in the military (above). In addition, frustration over federal AIDS policies and homophobic legislation had motivated the original discussions for another march begun two years earlier, and continued through the planning process. The result, the "March on Washington for Lesbian, Gay and Bi Equal Rights and Liberation" was therefore as much a mix of older and newer concerns as the title suggests.

Notable was the addition of the word "Bi," for bisexuals, who had been pressing for inclusion since the eighties in much the same way lesbians had done in the seventies. Transgender advocates felt "Trans" should also be in the title, but compromised on that point in return for use of the term in march literature. The first of the seven demands, for example, begins, "We demand passage of a Lesbian, Gay, Bisexual, and Transgender civil rights bill..." Also significant are the goals implied in the phrase, "Rights and Liberation," which could be seen as evidence of either progress or confusion (or both). Movements for rights and liberation had certainly existed side by side for decades (see Chapter 6 Debate), but their adherents often were at odds over "moderate" versus "radical" goals. To liberationists, equal rights, born of liberal thinking, represented mere tolerance (and often grudging at that) instead of true acceptance of difference; they also had viewed homophobia as only one of society's many problems, all of which could be addressed better in coalitions and through more fundamental changes than "equal rights." The voice of liberation was even more clearly evident in the march platform, which began:

> The Lesbian, Gay, Bisexual and Transgender movement recognizes that our quest for social justice fundamentally links us to the struggles against racism and sexism, class bias, economic injustice and religious intolerance. We must realize if one of us is oppressed we all are oppressed. The diversity of our movement requires and compels us to stand in opposition to all forms of oppression that diminish the quality of life for all people. We will be vigilant in our determination to rid our movement and our society of all forms of oppression and exploitation, so that all of us can develop to our full human potential without regard to race, religion, sexual orientation/identification, identity, gender and gender expression, ability, age or class.[7]

Building coalitions with other civil rights groups had been a goal for years, in fact, and was realized in the unprecedented support of the NAACP (National Association for the Advancement of Colored People), whose board voted unanimously to endorse the march. Female visibility also got a boost when the recently founded Lesbian Avengers held the first Dyke March in a separate but corresponding action, and one that caught on in large U.S. cities as part of Pride festivities.

The March on Washington for Lesbian, Gay and Bi Equal Rights and Liberation was held on April 25, 1993. The main event of several days' activities, it was the movement's third march on Washington and possibly drew close to a million participants. (© Patsy Lynch)

Also new this time around was the level of coverage in the media, in stark contrast to the blackout of 1987 (see Chapter 7). The national and international press ran stories on the march, and it was televised live on C-SPAN. Perhaps one reason for the level of attention was the number of marchers. The usual controversy erupted over reporting the numbers, but now the stakes were higher, since organizers' claim of at least one million participants would render this the largest civil rights demonstration in U.S. history. Police and government estimates, well under a half million, seemed to be efforts to diminish the actual size and strength of the GLBT movements.

If the number of attendees and their visibility were greater than ever, in other ways the '93 march was like that of 1987. As before, the march was but one of many events—over 200 in this case—that occurred over several days, from political lobbying and protests to dances and celebrations. The AIDS Quilt was again displayed on the Mall and over at the Internal Revenue Service building Rev. Troy Perry repeated the wedding ceremony, now for 2,600 couples (including this author and her partner), introduced in the previous march. Speakers and performers included Melissa Etheridge, Rev. Jesse Jackson, Sir Ian McKellan, Martina Navratilova, Holly Near, and RuPaul. Filmmaker Joan E. Biren documented much of this, as she had in 1987, and produced a work that borrowed its title from the march slogan: *A Simple Matter of Justice.*

DEBATES AND DIVISION

Even as these actions helped to bring many GLBT people together, fighting the military ban and preparing for the march also raised questions over strategy and the direction the national movement was headed. As Nadine Smith wrote about those first months of the Clinton era, "leaders seemed not to know how to respond when they found the door ajar. Activists appeared either too enamored of the new level of access or far too disdainful of it."⁸ Among the "enamored" were those who remained optimistic despite the recent setback, and who continued to insist on working through the political system at all levels. To some in the latter group, though, the more money, power, and visibility movement groups acquired, the more the tendency to "sell out" goals of liberation and rethinking societal structures in favor of accommodation to the larger culture. Also, older fault lines of class, race, and sex still divided nonstraight people while individuals who identified as bisexual, transgendered, intersexed, and/or queer were organized around those concepts and entered the discussions more visibly. Finally, there was concern that a relatively few were speaking for the many among GLBT people (with the Human Rights Campaign Fund a particular target), and that buying a hat, button, or T-shirt threatened to replace grassroots organizing as "activism." For example, responding to the perceived commercialization of GLBT concerns, African American writer Barbara Smith saw the 1993 march as the "beginning of the end" of truly radical goals.⁹

The Mainstream and Its Critics

Those considered moderate or "mainstream" among GLBT advocates argued that inclusion in political life and "equality" should be the focus of activity. Many others resisted this, however, especially if it meant portraying all nonstraight people as "just like them" ("them" being straight, presumably middle-class, and usually white). This was neither a new debate, of course, nor one peculiar to GLBT movements (see Chapter 6 Debate). What changed were the issues that arose over the years and the growing income and power of the largest organizations. The latter aggravated tensions along typical American lines of race, class, and sex that had always intersected with economic power. As some saw it, rich white men (and a few women) still controlled everything, including GLBT agendas, and there seemed more attention to "selling" the movement (sometimes literally, with logo-bearing products) to and through a white middle class using corporate techniques than to maintaining a goal of liberation through coalitions among less privileged people. Adding to this perception were new books making the case for more assimilationist tactics, perhaps in response to radical AIDS activism: Marshall Kirk and Hunter Madsen's *After the Ball: How America Will Conquer Its Fear & Hatred of Gays in the 90s* (1990); *A Place at the Table: The Gay Individual in Society* (1993) by Bruce Bawer; and Andrew Sullivan's *Virtually Normal: An Argument about Homosexuality* (1995).

Not surprisingly, the failure to lift the military ban on homosexuals caused some finger-pointing and soul-searching (although the outcome likely was beyond any activists' control at that time). By September of 1993 the two most prominent organizations, the National Gay and Lesbian Task Force and the Human Rights Campaign Fund, were "Taking a Serious Look at Themselves" amid criticism from such quarters as Gay and Lesbian Americans. GLA, a group formed that summer by former Queer Nation leaders, brought a more radical, less accommodating perspective to debates over direction and called for more grassroots organizing over the "Washington insider" approach seemingly favored by HRCF especially. Among the important points radicals had always provided were the insistence on consensus-style decision making (rather than a "top-down" approach), inclusion of more nonwhite, nonelite voices, and a demand for a society accepting difference, not merely tolerating those who looked and acted like the mainstream image. That fall the executive director of the NGLTF resigned after only six months in the position while the HRCF conducted an internal reevaluation.[10] Within two years the leadership of HRCF passed to Elizabeth Birch, who directed efforts toward greater professionalism on the one hand (going online, hiring "experts" in law, lobbying, and marketing) and achieving more diversity in personnel and membership on the other.

Just as the national groups came under attack, a new political organization was born: the Log Cabin Republicans, founded in 1993. The group of lesbian and gay Republicans agree with their party on issues like limited government and a conservative fiscal policy, but oppose the antigay measures generated by their party's right wing. Taking the name "Log Cabin" as a reference to the party of Abraham Lincoln (now ironic, in light of recent claims that Lincoln was not straight—see Chapter 1) its founders sought to revise the view that one could not be a GLBT person and Republican. Working through state chapters with offices in Washington, DC, members added a research and education arm, the Log Cabin Education Fund in 1995 (later, the Liberty Education Forum). Despite their efforts, many Republican leaders continued to be ambivalent, when not openly hostile, toward GLBT rights.

While gay Republicans worked for change within their party GLBT Democrats sought greater organization within their national party. Over forty local GLBT Democratic Clubs existed by the late nineties, operating on the municipal and sometimes state level. In 1998 members formed the National Stonewall Democratic Federation in order to act more effectively within the national party structure. As in the general political scene by the end of the decade, disagreements resurfaced over whether any differences between Republicans and Democrats outweighed what some saw as the inherent limitations of *all* party politics.

A landmark for the mainstream movement was the night of November 8, 1997, when the Human Rights Campaign ("Fund" had been dropped) held its first National Dinner and Awards, featuring President Clinton as the keynote speaker. Now in his second term, Clinton was the first sitting president to address a GL organization, and he delighted attendees that night when he spoke of the inclusion of GL Americans in the "American dream." Further, he said that "...when we deny opportunity because of ancestry or religion, race or gender, disability or sexual orientation, we break the compact [of equal opportunity for all]. It is wrong. And it should be illegal." As before, while many GLBT people across the country marveled at the changes they felt the dinner represented, others saw it as yet another example of the dominance of wealthy white men (and some women) in national GLBT politics, resulting in goals and methods too narrowly defined and prone to compromise.

Sex, Gender, Identity

It seemed to many LBT women that their issues continued to be ignored or trivialized both within and beyond the movements. As noted in Chapter 7, lesbians and bisexual women had encountered sexism in the early years of gay liberation and were fighting homophobia within the feminist movement at the same time. By the early nineties, LBT women and their concerns were recognized as central to feminism while feminism itself entered a new phase, now called the "Third Wave." The term was coined by Rebecca Walker in a response to the national discussion on sexual harassment during and after the televised hearings in which Anita Hill testified to being sexually harassed by Supreme Court Justice nominee Clarence Thomas. Further, because both Hill and Thomas are African American, many feminists of color were divided in their opinions and support. Walker (also an African American) saw the eventual confirmation of Thomas as part of the ongoing backlash against all women and called upon her peers not just to be angry but to then "turn that outrage into political power." In declaring herself the Third Wave rather than "postfeminist" Walker helped revitalize feminism for a generation being told that feminism, as either a failure or a success, was no longer relevant. Avowed Third Wave feminists have tried to address concerns of race, class, and sexuality—and multiple oppressions—in ways they perceived their "mothers" had not done (or as thoroughly).[11]

Given the overall wage gap between men and women in the United States, economic concerns at times drove another wedge between GBT men and LBT women. In the larger culture, some advertisers (of cars, clothes, alcohol) came to see gay (white) men as a market niche with disposable income; within GLBT culture publications seemed focused primarily on (white) men. In the larger culture also the illusion of acceptance was symbolized by "lesbian chic" and attention to lesbian motherhood, both presented more as trendy and cool than as issues related to identity, civil rights, and discrimination (*Newsweek,* for example, ran a cover story on June 21, 1993 entitled, "Lesbians Coming Out Strong"). Despite this sort of visibility, women continued to feel marginalized. Also, LBT women struggled not just for more sensitive media treatment but for attention to serious issues like health and violence.

Several organizations were created in the nineties that illustrate the varied responses and concerns of lesbians. Just as the eighties ended, for example, older activists formed Old Lesbians Organizing for Change (OLOC, f. 1989), a group open to women over sixty who want to confront ageism both among GLBT people and in American society. In the early nineties activists using street theatre and direct action techniques founded Dyke Action Machine (f. 1991) and the Lesbian Avengers (f. 1992) in New York City. Both were similar to ACT UP and both sought to create lesbian visibility while raising awareness of societal problems. Dyke Action Machine utilized public art projects on city streets, many of them designed to blend in with mainstream advertising, and by the end of the decade their work was exhibited in "serious" art galleries and museums. Lesbian Avengers were (and are) dedicated to fighting multiple oppressions inside and outside lesbian communities. Activists in Atlanta formed a chapter in 1993 and many others followed. Each of the fifty-plus chapters remains independent and dedicated to lesbian visibility generally and a more inclusive movement.

Like women, people of color responded with their own groups and resources while working within the larger organizations. Also like women, there was a potential for dual (or more) identities in the content of U.S. politics. For GLBT African Americans a central question was the degree to which sexuality or race should be foremost in activism (with emphasis on race termed Afrocentrist). The group Black and White Men Together (f. 1980) is an example of promoting unity around the outsider status shared by gay men, a model deemed especially appropriate at the height of the AIDS crisis in the eighties. At the turn of the decade about two hundred groups for African American GLBT people had formed, the majority aimed at GL over BT concerns. Nationally, before 1990 a few groups existed, including the National Black Lesbian and Gay Leadership Forum (f. 1988) and the Salsa Soul Sisters (f. 1974), which became the African Ancestral Lesbians United for Societal Change at this time. More organizations, such as the Zuna Institute (for queer African American women) and the International Federation of Black Prides joined the older ones by 2000, as did several periodicals devoted to queer African American readers.

For other GLBT people of color the issues of identity and affiliation were similar, but further compounded by "white" Americans' ignorance of variety within larger ethnic or language groups. Latino/a Americans (GLBT or not) are often frustrated in being lumped together, when their families may have originated in Spain, Mexico, the Caribbean, or Central or South America (and in the last case may speak Portuguese rather than Spanish). People of "Asian" origin might be of East Asian, South Asian, or Pacific Island descent. Native Americans comprise the smallest group in the 20th century, but within it a large number of different nations and languages. When all this is combined, the task of forming organizations around yet another identity can be difficult. Still, many citywide groups appeared, often in response to AIDS, and a few national associations, such as LLEGÓ (National Latina/o Lesbian, Gay, Bisexual and Transgender Organization) and Asian/Pacific-Islander Lesbian and Bisexual Network were formed in the late eighties. International conferences have been an important method the groups use for connecting with those outside the United States, and gatherings have included also the *Encuentros de Lesbianas Feministas de Latinoamérica y el Caribe* (Latin American and Caribbean Feminist Lesbian Gatherings) begun in the late eighties. Native Americans uniquely had a long tradition of acceptance of and respect for GLBT people, but one interrupted by European colonization and then revived in the context of both gay liberation and the American Indian Movement. Though an ancient concept, the term "Two-Spirit" was adopted only in the 1990s and the organizations, meetings, and works of Two-Spirited People are a vital part of Native American and GLBT cultures.

If women sometimes felt the "G" outweighed the "L" in GLBT movements certainly those represented by "B" and "T" often thought their letters were added less sincerely and more politically by the end of the decade. As "gay and lesbian" groups became "gay-lesbian-bisexual-transgendered" groups, in other words, those in the latter categories sometimes remained skeptical of their genuine inclusion. As noted in Chapter 7, a distinctive bisexual movement emerged only in the late 1980s despite people who were identified, or self-identified, as such for decades. Like many women and nonwhites working for gay liberation, bisexuals had often felt like a less important, thus less visible, minority-within-a-minority. Many times bisexuals faced double discrimination—from straight people for their sexual nonconformity and from GL people who did not trust their commitment to nonstraight sexual freedom and rights. Also, there were men and women who had called themselves bisexual at some point before identifying as gay or lesbian (perhaps seeing it as "safer" at the time), causing a tendency to generalize that it was more a "phase" than a true sexuality. Politically, there was the persistent fear of "watering down" or confusing the message and focus of gay/lesbian rights with too many other issues, including this one.

By the early 1990s, however, bisexual organizing grew rapidly, with groups on both coasts and a national group, the North American Bisexual Network (now BiNet U.S.A.). In 1990 the first national conference for bisexuals convened, followed in 1991 by the first international bisexual conference, held biannually since. Local groups multiplied rapidly through the decade and numbered in the hundreds by the new millennium. In 1990 also the University of California-Berkeley offered the first academic course on bisexuality and the following year *Anything That Moves: Beyond the Myths of Bisexuality,* the first bisexual magazine in the United States, was published by the Bay Area Bisexual Network in San Francisco. Books followed rapidly, including *Bi Any Other Name: Bisexual People Speak Out* (1991), *Dual Attraction: Understanding Bisexuality* (1994), *Bisexual Politics: Theories, Queries, and Visions* (1995), and *Creating a Place for Ourselves: Lesbian, Gay, and Bisexual Community Histories* (1997). An academic periodical, the *Journal of Bisexuality,* made its debut in 2001. In general, the nineties witnessed greater visibility of bisexuals, including openly bisexual musicians and actors, in mainstream media and greater acceptance of bisexuality as a genuine identity both inside and outside sexual minority movements.

For transgendered people, however, the situation was more contradictory. That is, for some visibility was never the issue: those who performed as drag queens and kings, for example, had been a continual presence—often controversial—and even embodied the stereotype of the homosexual to many Americans. At the end of the century drag performances continued to draw large crowds in many cities, from smaller club venues (like those explored by Leila Rupp and Verta Taylor in *Drag Queens at the 801 Cabaret* or in the film study of drag kings, *Venus Boyz*) to elaborate drag balls (such as those profiled in the documentary *Paris is Burning*). However, literal visibility has not translated into equal attention within movements and trans people have found themselves fighting additional battles.

The term transgendered itself has been contested, some promoting it as an umbrella term (similar to queer) for anyone not conforming to societal gender rules, regardless of the person's sexuality. This usage would include all transvestites (cross-dressers), all transsexuals, and all intersexual people (formerly called hermaphrodites) as well as those whose sex and gender do not appear to "match," whether naturally or deliberately. This meaning is more recent and is intended, by authors like Leslie Feinberg, to be overtly political—it both represents and advocates common ground among gender nonconformists and calls for liberation of people from those gender rules and roles. Previously, the term transgender as coined in the eighties referred to cross-dressers, often heterosexual, who lived as the opposite sex. As Susan Stryker summarized (for glbtq.com), "The logic of the term [as first used] is that, while transvestites episodically change their clothes and transsexuals permanently change their genitals, transgenders make a sustained change of their social gender through non-surgical means." As Stryker has also noted, the term in its various meanings came into common use by the mid-nineties, joining "GLB" politically if not always equally.

As the opening story of Sylvia Rivera shows, acceptance does not necessarily follow from visibility, either inside or outside GLB communities. Many lesbian feminists had opposed varieties of MTF (male-to-female) transgender on political grounds and continued to do so (see Chapter 6). More conservative gays—who just wanted to pass unnoticed—were repelled by the stereotypes they saw as reinforced by MTF transgenders, both cross-dressers and transsexuals. (As in earlier decades, though, the public confusion of all trans forms with homosexuality also enabled gender-conforming gay men and lesbians to stay hidden if they wished.) Trans inclusion was an issue not only at Stonewall 25 but in the three national marches held so far and in countless local actions as well. By the late 1980s, after decades of invisible or unacknowledged activism for GLB causes, trans activists advocated more strongly for their place in the movements. Among them were Phyllis Randolph Frye, Jamison Green, Anne Osborne, Susan Stryker, Sharon Stuart, and Riki Wilchins.

Like gay men, lesbians, and bisexuals, trans people have sought legal protection against discrimination in such areas as employment and housing and prosecution of those who assaulted them. The first International Conference on Transgender Law and Employment Policy convened in 1992 and the next year adopted an International Bill of Gender Rights. It states, in part, "It is fundamental that individuals have the right to define, and to redefine as their lives unfold, their own gender identities, without regard to chromosomal sex, genitalia, assigned birth sex, or initial gender role."[12]

Trans activists have founded a number of organizations representing different interests, and other groups have adopted the cause. In 1990 Dallas Denny began the American Educational Gender Information Service (AEGIS; later, part of Gender Education and Advocacy). AEGIS has published *Chrysalis* since 1991 and oversees the National Transgender Library & Archive in Atlanta. Transgender Nation in San Francisco followed closely upon the appearance of Feinberg's *Transgender Liberation* (1992), both Transsexual Menace and Transgenders Against Discrimination and Defamation (TADD; later, Transgender Health Empowerment) appeared in 1994 and GenderPAC followed in 1996. Trans concerns were adopted by the NLGLA (National Lesbian and Gay Law Association), the GLBVA (Gay, Lesbian and Bisexual Veterans of America, Inc.), and the NGLTF (National Gay and Lesbian Task Force) by mid-decade; only at end of 1998 did the Human Rights Campaign add trans issues to their agenda, for which they were criticized. By the end of the century the ACLU also took up the cause while providing a concise explanation in its Lesbian and Gay Rights Project report for 2000:

> . . . transgender issues also challenge one of society's most closely held (though fluid) notions: what it is to be male, and what it is to be female. The hate and disgust that transgender people can provoke is a fear of people who do not fit stereotypes of appropriate sex roles. And that is the same fear that often fuels discrimination against lesbian and gay people.[13]

The nineties also saw the advent of the intersexual, at least as a new term. In general, the move away from such words as "hermaphrodite" and "transvestite" (and "homosexual") represented a rejection of the medical model within which those terms were coined and understood to mean "deviant" conditions in need of intervention. Like other sex and gender nonconformists, intersexuals claimed the identity and also the right of people, whether born sexually ambiguous or not, to choose their gender or to remain ambiguous. The Intersex Society of North America (f. 1993) represents the political aims, and individuals like Del LaGrace Volcano literally embody that politics. Del's Web sites include these statements:

> I am a gender variant visual artist. In a previous incarnation I was known as Della Grace, lesbian photographer. That lasted nearly twenty years and was a handle I was proud to grip. I kept pushing the parameters of what a lesbian could be (was permitted to be) until I broke through the cell wall and swam free into "the sea, the sea of possibilities" (Patty Smith, "Horses," an early influence).
>
> As a gender variant visual artist I access "technologies of gender" in order to amplify rather than erase the hermaphroditic traces of my body. *I name* myself. A gender abolitionist. A part time gender terrorist. An intentional mutation and intersex by design, (as opposed to diagnosis), in order to distinguish my journey from the thousands of intersex individuals who have had their "ambiguous" bodies mutilated and disfigured in a misguided attempt at "normalization". I believe in crossing the line as many times as it takes to build a bridge we can all walk across.[14]

Old and new terms came to exist side-by-side. "Queer" had been reclaimed by younger people as positive and all-encompassing while theorists began writing of the challenges to "heteronormativity" presented by the multiple identities now presented. In the meantime, the politics of the movement—and more so of the nation—often were perceived as lingering in the era when "queer" was still an insult.

"Del Boy, London, 2000," is a self-portrait of artist Del LaGrace Volcano and part of Del's "Gender Optional Series." Del is a self-defined intersex person, in this case one who challenges society's norms of only two sexes and two genders through both art and life. (Del LaGrace Volcano)

LAW AND POLITICS

During the nineties the wing of the movement working for political equality altered their strategies somewhat though not their eventual goals. As the decade opened the dream lingered of a National Gay Rights Bill (introduced in Congress in 1974 and 1980). It was brought before Congress once again in 1991, now with over one hundred sponsors. After Clinton's election, there was an effort to draft a new version, now with help from the LCCR (Leadership Conference on Civil Rights), an important coalition in Washington whose acceptance of GLB rights in 1982 was significant. Between the military debate and planning for the march, however, the energy for drafting a new bill was redirected into at least three avenues: toward those immediate issues; into the ongoing fight against state and local antigay initiatives; and into obtaining individual provisions of the bill in different ways. In addition, Steve Endean, whose vision of the bill helped sustain it and gain sponsors through the eighties, died in the summer of 1993.

The year 1993 represented a setback in the form of "Don't Ask, Don't Tell" and the following year conservatives scored a victory in the midterm elections of 1994. The Republican Party, seemingly controlled by its right wing for more than a decade, now dominated both houses of Congress for the first time in nearly fifty years and those in the House soon released an agenda entitled the "Contract with America" designed to reduce the spending and size of the federal government. Among the ten proposed bills of the Contract were measures not only to balance the budget and limit taxes but also acts entitled "Personal Responsibility" and "Family Reinforcement."[15] Overall liberals perceived the Contract as an attack upon the federal welfare system (and its recipients) that included efforts to legislate a narrow definition of "family." Although not mentioned specifically, GLBT people feared the results of federal law upholding only the "traditional" family (with heterosexual parents adhering to gender roles). Some of the aims of the Contract were realized in a welfare reform bill, passed in 1996 and signed by Clinton. In that election cycle Clinton became the first Democrat reelected since Franklin Roosevelt, while Republicans retained their control of Congress. Before fulfilling his second term Clinton faced articles of impeachment set in motion over accusations of sexual misconduct with a White House intern. At his trial in early 1999, however, the Senate votes fell far short of the two-thirds majority needed to convict and remove a president. After Clinton left office in 2001 GLBT Americans, like many others, continued to have mixed feelings about him and his legacy. He had publicly courted and supported GLBT groups more than any previous president, had appointed openly gay and lesbian people to federal positions, and had declared June 1999 (and again in 2000) Gay and Lesbian Pride Month; but he also had an uneven record delivering on this and other causes.

(Still) Running for Office

In 1991 a new political organization was founded to support openly gay and lesbian political candidates, the Gay and Lesbian Victory Fund. In the cycle ending in the '92 elections, forty candidates sought money from the fund. By 1996, that number increased nearly seven times, though only a fourth of those requesting funds received them. Considering the recently closeted history of candidates for office, the numbers of openly GL people running was impressive and has remained so to the present.

Through the nineties openly GL candidates not only sought office, but were elected as well, more than doubling their numbers from 1991 to 1997 (from 52 to 124). Following previous patterns, the largest number in 1997 were serving at the local level (74) and the fewest (3) at the national level. In between were the nineteen people elected to state offices through the decade, such as Liz Stefanics in New Mexico, Tim Van Zandt in Missouri, and Larry McKeon in Illinois. The nineties also saw the first openly transgender person in a state office, Althea Garrison, elected in 1992 but serving only one term in Massachusetts' House.

Of the twenty or so state officials newly elected in 1994 at least one gained national attention: Sheila Kuehl, voted into legislative office in California. After serving six years in the Assembly, where she was also the first female Speaker pro tempore, she was elected to the state Senate (and reelected in 2004). Kuehl had been in the public eye before, starring as Zelda Gilroy on the TV comedy *The Many Loves of Dobie Gillis* (1959–1963). She was not the first media personality to achieve public office in California, whose voters elected to the governorship Ronald Reagan (1967–1975) and more recently Arnold Schwarzenegger (2003–present), but she was the first openly lesbian or gay person to do so. A 1995 news item about her noted her groundbreaking role in politics and recounted a favorite story of Kuehl's:

> "Sheila is a true trailblazer. She's like a beacon for gay and lesbian people," says Eric Baumann, president of the Stonewall Democratic Club in Los Angeles. The surprising fact that her "star quality" has helped her make friends among conservatives, he added, "is just a huge bonus."
>
> It was one of those memorable moments on the campaign trail. Sitting in a Los Angeles restaurant, candidate Kuehl was approached by a constituent, who said that while he views most politicians as liars, he knew she could be trusted.

"I said, 'Me? Why me?'" Kuehl recalls with a grin. "He said, 'Well, you've already told us the worst thing about yourself. Why would you lie about anything else?' The worst thing, of course, was that I'm a lesbian."[16]

In the nineties Rep. Barney Frank, out since 1987, was joined in national government by two open lesbians and two fellow congressmen brought out as gay (Rep. Gerry Studds was also still serving as the nineties began, retiring in 1996). African American Sabrina Sojourner was elected to a term in the House representing Washington, DC in 1997 while the next year Tammy Baldwin culminated a series of personal "firsts" in her successful bid for a seat in the U.S. House. She had already been the first open lesbian on her Wisconsin county Board of Supervisors and had served three terms in the Wisconsin House; now she was the first female representative from Wisconsin as well as the first open lesbian *and* the first nonincumbent openly GLBT person elected to Congress (notably, other openly GL firsts in politics were also women: Kathy Kozachenko in local office and Elaine Noble on the state level—see Chapter 7).

The remaining two gay congressmen of the decade were Steve Gunderson (R-WI) and Jim Kolbe (R-AZ). In both cases, however, they came out after serving several terms, and neither did so completely voluntarily. Gunderson had been in office since 1981 but by 1994 faced threats of "outing" from both antigay party members and GLBT leaders—the former to "expose" him as gay, the latter to "expose" him as a gay representative voting against GLBT people. Once he had come out, Gunderson was the first openly gay Republican congressman, but serving only one term as such before retiring in 1996. Just as Gunderson was stepping down a similar series of events affected the career of Jim Kolbe, first elected in 1984. As the national gay magazine *The Advocate* prepared a 1996 article, it contacted Kolbe about his antigay voting record and his closeted identity, offering him the chance to come out before being outed in print (in particular, Kolbe had voted for the controversial Defense of Marriage Act—see below). Kolbe later described his feelings when a reporter told him the magazine was going ahead with the story on him, causing his decision to out himself:

> ...it was the closest thing I've ever had to a religious experience. It was absolutely amazing. An unbelievable sense of peace and calm descended over me. I could physically feel fifty years just go "phew!" up off my shoulders. And I said to myself, "It's over. It's done. I know what I have to do now." I would have to deal with it, but I didn't have to worry about hiding this thing anymore.[17]

Kolbe was reelected in 1996 and in every cycle after that, serving until his retirement in 2006.

In the States

The 1992 elections and after offered reason for optimism for GLBT people in the states as well as in the national elections. New Jersey, Vermont, and California enacted some form of gay rights legislation that year, following the lead of Wisconsin (1982), Massachusetts (1989), Hawai'i (1991), and Connecticut (1991). The next year Minnesota became the eighth state to pass an antidiscrimination law (in this case one that included transsexual and transgender people as well, and the only state law to do so before 2001), and similar laws in Rhode Island (1995), New Hampshire (1997), and Nevada (1999) brought the total to eleven by 2000. Dozens of communities, including Washington, DC, also adopted antidiscrimination statutes by the end of the decade.

Another positive sign to activists was the failure of a few antigay state initiatives: in 1994 voters defeated Proposition 1 in Idaho and Proposition 13 in Oregon and in Maine a similar measure was rejected the next year.

Even in Colorado, whose voters had approved the comprehensive antigay language of Amendment 2 in 1992 (see above), opponents of discrimination were able to mobilize and eventually win an important legal victory. In early 1993 a District Court injunction was granted that halted the process of adding Amendment 2 to the state constitution. When the state appealed to Colorado's Supreme Court, that court upheld the injunction against Amendment 2. It was returned to the District Court and there, in December 1993, was found unconstitutional due to a failure to prove the Amendment fulfilled a "compelling state interest." Eventually Colorado appealed to the U.S. Supreme Court and the case *Romer v. Evans* was argued in October of 1995. In a 6-3 decision of May 1996, the Court ruled Amendment 2 unconstitutional. The majority opinion, written by Justice Anthony Kennedy, denied that antidiscrimination laws afforded GL people "special rights." Rather, the opinion stated, Amendment 2

> imposes a special disability upon those persons alone. Homosexuals are forbidden the safeguards that others enjoy or may seek without constraint.... its sheer breadth is so discontinuous with the reasons offered for it that the amendment seems inexplicable by anything but animus toward the class that it affects; it lacks a rational relationship to legitimate state interests.... It identifies persons by a single trait and then denies them protection across the board. The resulting disqualification of a class of persons from the right to seek specific protection from the law is unprecedented in our jurisprudence.[18]

GLBT activists celebrated the decision, feeling it was a strike against discrimination, but recognized that most protections and benefits offered to heterosexuals continued to be denied to homosexuals, including those in committed relationships. As scores of incidents through the AIDS epidemic demonstrated, same-sex couples were especially vulnerable in health crises without legal protections, a fact underscored by the case of Sharon Kowalski and Karen Thompson (see Chapter 7). Partners of ill or injured people could be denied everything from access to their hospital rooms and decision-making power to denial of benefits, inheritance, or housing upon a partner's death (if a lease or mortgage was in the deceased's name, for example).

Same-sex couples, in fact, are barred from over 1,000 benefits available to legally married couples. Many are economic, such as tax breaks, insurance breaks, or the right to a deceased spouse's Social Security payments, and many concern families and children. Not only do married couples have the right to adopt children, for example, but as a rule do not face separation from their children because of the choice of a partner. The latter was the situation of Sharon Bottoms, whose custody case in Virginia gained national attention. While married to a man, Sharon gave birth to a son, and subsequently divorced the father. When she entered a lesbian relationship her mother sued for custody and won. Bottoms won on appeal in 1994, in a decision that stated, "The fact that a parent is homosexual does not per se render a parent unfit to have custody of his or her child." The next year, however, an appeal to the Virginia Supreme Court ruled in favor of the boy's grandmother, using Virginia's sodomy law that defined homosexuals as felons.[19]

Efforts to achieve rights and benefits equal to those of married couples took two basic forms: a series of piecemeal acts and documents on the one hand, and one single act or document on the other (as in a marriage license). Increasing numbers of employers and municipalities offered domestic partnership benefits to unmarried couples (often both same-sex and opposite-sex), though these could be limited according to a state's legal stance regarding antigay discrimination. Legal marriage, on the other hand, automatically conferred the benefits of domestic partner registrations and numerous other documents that had to be acquired individually (health care proxies, durable powers of attorney, etc.), and activism for same-sex marriage came to the forefront as never before in the nineties.

Marriage generally and legal marriage specifically were not new issues. Many religious communities were already performing marriage in their congregations (see below), and same-sex couples had attempted to marry legally in the seventies (see Chapter 6). Both the 1987 and 1993 marches on Washington had featured mass weddings not only as a statement of commitment but also a protest of political inequality. At the same time, activists had always disagreed over whether to advocate marriage at all and, if it was a goal, when to press for it.

Events in Hawai'i and Vermont created landmarks in the debates. First, the case of *Baehr v. Lewin* (1991) in Hawai'i provided an opportunity to test laws and public sentiment. Three couples sued for the right to marriage licenses and lost, but in 1993 the Hawai'i Supreme Court reversed the decision on the basis that denying marriage licenses to same-sex couples denied them equal protection under the law and constituted sex discrimination. The state legislature then passed a law the next year defining marriage as limited to one man and one woman. The case continued, though (as *Baehr v. Miike,* 1996), with a ruling again in favor of same-sex marriage and the state again appealed. In 1998, however, voters approved an amendment to their state constitution that affirmed the legislature's definition of marriage and the case (now *Baehr v. Anderson*) was dropped.

In Vermont it was also three couples that forced the issue, but with different results. In 1996 they applied for marriage licenses, were denied, sued, and lost on the grounds that same-sex marriage violated the link between marriage and procreation. The couples appealed to the state Supreme Court and in 1999, the Vermont court ruled unanimously in a historic decision that Vermont's denial of marriage rights to same-sex couples was unconstitutional. The following year a new term entered public and movement debates as Vermont's legislature voted to approve same-sex "civil unions" that conferred the rights of marriage, but only within the state of Vermont (federal benefits and protections remained unavailable).

The National Scene

The combination of an election year and the possibility that Hawai'i would eventually allow same-sex marriage generated a political response from Congress. As Chai Feldblum has noted, "Although final resolution of the [Hawai'i] case would be years away, congressional Republicans decided the fall of 1996...would be an excellent time to put Congress on record as opposing same-sex marriage."[20] The result was DOMA (Defense of Marriage Act), passed and signed that September, right before the elections. Essentially, the act defined federal marriage as between a man and a woman, and authorized states to refuse to recognize same-sex marriages performed in other states.

Even as DOMA was debated that summer in Congress GLBT strategists remained hopeful about gaining federal protection against discrimination at work. An increasing number of Americans opposed people being fired or banned from employment due to their sexual orientation, but while many private businesses and educational institutions adopted nondiscriminatory policies, progress was slower on the legal front. In addition to compiling statistics, the Human Rights Campaign Fund, for example, had begun lobbying members of Congress to sign a statement reading, "The sexual orientation of an individual is not a consideration in the hiring, promoting, or terminating of an employee in my Congressional office." By mid-June of 1994, 234 representatives and 71 senators had signed the statement. The groundwork was thus laid for the introduction in Congress of ENDA (Employment Non-Discrimination Act) in mid-1994. Hearings followed that summer but it would be more than two years before the bill came to a vote—simultaneously with discussion of DOMA and ultimately part of those negotiations. In the end the Senate defeated ENDA in a 50-49 vote on the same day it passed DOMA (September 10, 1996). Still, the margin of only one vote encouraged activists, as did the fact that ENDA was reintroduced early the next year (and has been repeatedly reintroduced since 1997, though a federal act barring employment discrimination due to sexual orientation has yet to pass at this writing, in 2007). Also heartening was the Executive Order signed by President Clinton in May 1998 that prohibited antigay discrimination within the federal government.

Another area of federal legislation was that of hate crimes. According to http://www.counterhate.org/Statistics.htm, a hate crime is defined as "a criminal act or attempted act against a person, institution, or property that is motivated in whole or in part by the offender's bias against someone's race, color, ethnicity, religion, gender or sexual orientation." In 1996 Congress renewed the Hate Crimes Statistics Act of 1990 and by that time also had passed the Hate Crimes Sentencing Enhancement Act (1994) as part of another bill. The latter bill continued to include gay bashing as a federal hate crime despite right-wing efforts to remove the category of sexual orientation. By the decade's end the White House had held the first Conference on Hate Crimes, in 1997, and the Hate Crimes Prevention Act was introduced in Congress in the same year.

Crimes against GLBT people simply because of their sexuality or gender identity had long been a problem, of course, but now statistics lent reality to the claim. According to Stop Hate 2000 (http://www.stophate.us/hcpa.html), the number of bias-related incidents based in homophobia reported through the nineties fluctuated between 767 in 1992, down to 685 in 1994, and up to 1,102 in 1997, with the majority in the latter year (760) directed at gay men. Generally, sexual orientation ranked third, after race and religion, as the reason behind bias-related incidents and accounted for about 11 percent to 13 percent of all hate crimes.

Crimes committed out of anti-GLBT bigotry received unprecedented attention as the nineties waned. In October, 1998 Matthew Shepard, an openly gay student at the University of Wyoming, was brutally beaten by two men posing as gay and left tied to a fence outside Laramie. Shepard died of his injuries on October 12 and the story received prominent coverage in *Time, The New York Times,* and other major national media. Hate was put on display, too, at Shepard's funeral when Kansas Reverend Fred Phelps and a few followers attended, bearing signs reading, "No Tears for Queers" and "Matt in Hell."

One of the assailants plea bargained for life imprisonment rather than the death penalty and the other stood trial and was found guilty. Shepard's parents, Dennis and Judy, made a statement to the court against a death sentence, and the second man received two consecutive life sentences without parole or appeal instead. In pleading for the tolerance not shown his son, Dennis Shepard said, "My son Matthew paid a terrible price to open the eyes of all of us who live in Wyoming, the United States, and the world to the unjust and unnecessary fears, discrimination, and intolerance that members of the gay community face every day." Both parents became spokespersons for GLBT causes, founding the Matthew Shepard Foundation late in 1998. Judy Shepard especially has been a vocal advocate for GLBT rights and services for GLBT youth and has been active in such organizations as PFLAG (Parents, Families, and Friends of Lesbians and Gays), GLSEN (Gay, Lesbian and Straight Education Network), and the Human Rights Campaign. The events surrounding the murder were dramatized in the TV movie *The Matthew Shepard Story* in 2002, and the same year HBO released a film version of *The Laramie Project,* originally a play based on the murder, actual news, and interviews conducted with residents of the city.

Documentary and fiction films contributed to greater awareness of violence against transgendered people also. Transgendered youth Brandon Teena, born female but living as a man in rural Nebraska, was raped and murdered in 1994 by "friends" who had discovered he was not biologically male. The crime scene was recounted vividly by author and Court TV contributor Katherine Ramsland (below Brandon is referred to as "she," though it is customary to use the pronoun matching the gender presented visibly):

> It was a cold morning on December 31 in Humboldt, Nebraska, the heart of the Midwest. While many households were rising to prepare to bring in 1994, one sat ominously silent.
>
> ...Lying on a leaking waterbed were two people in their early twenties, a blond woman and a baby-faced young man with brown hair. They both appeared to have been shot execution style. Looking around for a weapon, the deputy found none. He had no idea who they were.... When Richardson County Sheriff Charles Laux eventually entered to have a look, he recognized one of the women on the bed as Teena Brandon, 21, who'd reported that John Lotter and Tom Nissen had raped her a week earlier, after a Christmas party.... Lifting [Brandon's] sweatshirt, officers saw a jagged wound, apparently made by a knife. Further up, a small bullet hole was evident under her chin, surrounded by gunpowder residue. That meant she'd been shot at close range. A fracture on her skull indicated that she'd been hit with a blunt object. Of the three bodies, hers was the most ravaged, so it was possible that she had been the primary target.
>
> ...It didn't take long to find out that three people had needlessly died because two young men had been unable to deal with someone who was different.[21]

Lotter and Nissen were arrested, tried (1996), and convicted; Lotter received a death sentence and Nissen received life in prison. The story resulted in a book, *All She Wanted* (1996), and a 1998 documentary, *The Brandon Teena Story.* However, it was the independent film *Boys Don't Cry* (1999), starring Hilary Swank (who won the Best Actress Academy Award for portraying Teena), that brought the brutality of hate crime to more viewers. While GLBT activists welcomed the outrage expressed at both Shepard's and Teena's murders, they also observed that many nonwhite people, and many transgendered people before Teena, had met the same fate with no reaction from police, media, or public.

A Gay Ambassador

Controversy moved from the national to the international stage to some degree when President Clinton nominated James C. Hormel to be ambassador to Luxembourg in 1997. A descendant of the founder of Hormel Foods and a former dean at the

James C. Hormel (left) became the nation's first openly gay ambassador despite a lengthy controversy over his nomination. Here he is sworn in by Secretary of State Madeleine Albright on June 29, 1999 in Washington, DC, accompanied by his partner Timothy Wu. (Getty)

University of Chicago Law School, Hormel was by then an openly gay philanthropist and respected member of the U.S. United Nations delegation. He had married in the fifties and fathered five children but like many of his generation he acknowledged his sexual identity later in life. He and his wife eventually divorced and Hormel went on to become a founding member of the Human Rights Campaign (Fund) and sat on its first board of directors.

The Senate Foreign Relations Committee approved Clinton's nomination of Hormel to the ambassador post (with opposition from only two members, Jesse Helms and John Ashcroft), but a handful of antigay conservative in the Senate blocked the appointment for nearly two years. Among them was Majority Leader Trent Lott (R-MS), who repeatedly resisted efforts to bring the appointment to a full Senate vote; his obstruction and his public remarks on homosexuality embarrassed even other conservatives, in fact, most of whom supported the nomination. When the process remained stalled in mid-1999, Clinton renamed Hormel in a "recess appointment" to the position during the Senate's Memorial Day hiatus. Despite outrage from the few opponents and their threats to block other Clinton appointments, Hormel was finally sworn in on June 29, 1999 and served through the end of 2000. Since leaving his post, Hormel and his partner have been active philanthropists, supporting education and health-related research; in 1996 the James C. Hormel Gay and Lesbian Center at the San Francisco Public Library opened, an important collection made possible by their generosity.

CULTURAL ISSUES AND INSTITUTIONS

Education and health are but two areas that reflect ongoing concerns in both the larger culture and in GLBT communities. Education, already contested in so many ways, from public school curricula and content to the politics of college professors, only grew more so. Health care in the United States came under scrutiny early in Clinton's first term, though attempts at reform of the system floundered on political reefs. Related to these and contentious in its own right was religion—Christianity in particular—with its role in American life generally and its intersections with GLBT life increasingly at the vortex of heated debate.

Education

The "culture wars" of previous years did not wane in the nineties. One of its main battlegrounds remained education and GLBT people and issues remained among the primary targets. In higher education institutions created offices devoted to diversity generally and to GLBT students and concerns specifically. The number of these grew to more than one hundred throughout the country. The academic units—courses or programs devoted to GLBT studies—also increased in number since the first Gay and Lesbian Studies Department was created in 1989 at San Francisco City College but not at the same pace. By 2000 about twenty institutions offered minors in some form of GLBT studies, usually within Gay and Lesbian Studies or within a Women's and Gender Studies program. Several more added similar concentrations and certifications and a handful designed BA degree programs in some form of GLBT/gender/sexuality studies. The Center for Lesbian and Gay Studies of the City University of New York opened in 1991 and remains one of very few institutions where one can pursue graduate-level work in this area.

Paralleling new courses and programs was an outpouring of scholarship on GLBT topics covering many fields, with works in history and politics prominent among them. *The Lesbian and Gay Studies Reader* (1993) was followed by a general history geared to high school and college students, *Becoming Visible* (1994), and the reader *Bisexuality in the United States* (1999). Margaret Cruikshank provided a political overview in 1992 in *The Gay and Lesbian Liberation Movement* and before 2000 the movement received detailed treatment in *Out for Good* (1999) and analysis in Urvashi Vaid's *Virtual Equality* (1995) and works by Michael Warner. Pioneering gay historian Martin Duberman profiled six individuals in *Stonewall* (1993) in addition to writing the autobiographical *Cures* (1991) and *Midlife Queer* (1996). Keith Boykin and William G. Hawkeswood explored the experiences of African American gay men and John Howard did the same for queer people in the South. Important studies of lesbians appeared as well: Lillian Faderman's 20th-century survey *Odd Girls and Twilight Lovers* (1992), and *Boots of Leather, Slippers of Gold: The History of a Lesbian Community* (1993), a study of Buffalo by Elizabeth Kennedy and Madeline Davis. Anthropologist Esther Newton published *Cherry Grove, Fire Island: Sixty Years in America's First Gay and Lesbian Town* in 1993 and the next year came George Chauncey's groundbreaking history of *Gay New York*.

At the precollegiate levels there has been more resistance to acknowledging GLBT people, whether as students and staff or in course material (though in 1994, an antigay amendment attached to the Elementary and Secondary Education Act was defeated). Harassment of GLBT students continued to be a problem; GLSEN released a report in late 1999 documenting "systemic hostility being leveled upon lesbian, gay, bisexual and transgender youth in schools across the country." Among the disturbing results: over 90 percent of students surveyed heard homophobic remarks, over 60 percent had been verbally harassed, and a third reported that faculty and staff participated in verbal assaults on queer students.

Efforts to change the school climate ranged from those of GLSEN and PFLAG (Parents, Friends and Families of Lesbians and Gays, which pioneered Safe Schools legislation in Massachusetts and began the *From Our House to the School House* campaign) to resources like the film *It's Elementary: Talking About Gay Issues in School* (1996) to student-run gay-straight alliances formed across the country. An attempt at the latter which gained notoriety was that of Kelli Peterson and friends at a Salt Lake City high school. The controversy surrounding her efforts is effectively profiled alongside important events and people in GLBT history in the film *Out of the Past* (1998). Although not part of public education, the controversy surrounding the exclusion of gay people from the Boy Scouts of America is related to the general climate for GLBT youth and their role models. When openly gay James Dale was dismissed as a scoutmaster, he sued the Boy Scouts and won a 1999 appeal in New Jersey's Supreme Court. When the BSA appealed to the U.S. Supreme Court, however, the Court ruled 5-4 in *Boy Scouts of America v. Dale* (2000) that as a private organization the Scouts have a right to discriminate against homosexuals. Amid all this many others, including heterosexuals (such as Scoutmaster David Rice and Scout Steven Cozza, cofounders of Scouting for All) voiced their objections to the policy and/or withheld their usual contributions to the Boy Scouts.

Health

Activists continued to work on several fronts when it came to health issues confronting GLBT Americans. While health care reform was investigated during Clinton's first term representatives of national organizations testified in the House regarding the discrimination faced by nonstraight people. Homophobia affected whether HIV/AIDS patients presumed to be gay had access to treatment, for example, and discouraged lesbians and gay men from even routine checkups in many cases. Women had long complained of dismissive or demeaning encounters with sexist practitioners and lesbians felt especially vulnerable. By the end of the decade, though, the *Journal of the Gay and Lesbian Medical Association* was launched while both government and private entities devoted more time and money to GL-related concerns.

Through the decade awareness about HIV/AIDS increased to some degree as the nineties began but as people began surviving longer with HIV the urgency seemed to wane (a promising protocol, protease inhibitors, was introduced in 1996). In 1988 the first World AIDS Day was held December 1 and became an annual reminder of those lost to the disease and that much work remained in fighting it and the prejudices that accompanied it. AIDS had truly become a global crisis, and one affecting women disproportionately by the 21st century. According to a study of "The Feminization of AIDS," worldwide half of people living with HIV and a more than a third of those who had died from AIDS in 2002 were women, often women living in poverty and under extreme patriarchies.[22]

Activities surrounding HIV/AIDS maintained efforts begun in the eighties. In 1996 Congress reauthorized the Ryan White CARE Act, designed to improve services for people with HIV. The Quilt of the NAMES Project continued to be displayed in pieces around the country, having grown too large for any but periodic complete viewings. It is considered the largest community art project in the world, in fact, and is the subject of *Common Threads: Stories From The Quilt* (1989), a film receiving several awards including an Oscar for best feature-length documentary. The entire quilt was displayed in Washington, DC in 1992 and 1996, the last time covering the entire Mall (equal to forty-three football fields).

Lesbian health advocates addressed the myth that lesbians were not at risk for HIV while focusing also on issues specific to women/lesbians. In 1994 the first national Lesbian Health Roundtable convened to discuss strategies for education and funding, and two years later the Lesbian Research Network was founded by those who had conducted the first survey of lesbian health in the eighties. Also, with important funding from the CDC the Mautner Project (the National Lesbian Health Organization) initiated Removing the Barriers™ to Accessing Health Care for Lesbians and in 1999 the Institute of Medicine released a report on lesbian health. Breast cancer and other cancers continued as primary concerns, not because they affect lesbians or women alone, but because lesbians may be less likely to seek preventive measures due to bad experiences with health care providers. Also, the stresses of rejection from family, friends, and society (on top of sex and gender discrimination) are thought to be linked to possibly disproportionate use of alcohol, drugs, and tobacco among lesbians. That sexual orientation (when combined with societal attitudes) can affect health and access to treatment was acknowledged for the first time in 2000 in the "Healthy People 2010" plan of the U.S. Department of Health and Human Services.

Finally, mental health was also an area of concern to GLBT people, who were sometimes considered to be at greater than average risk for depression, substance abuse, and suicide due to hostile environments (including discrimination and harassment). Several studies on GLBT youth concurred that the risk of suicide (attempted or completed) was three to four times higher than that of their straight counterparts; rates were higher among African Americans than whites, and the highest for transsexual teens generally. Also, treatments for different conditions have varied, according to the training and biases of the professional. While homosexuality had ceased to be an official psychiatric disorder twenty years earlier (see Chapter 6) "gender identity disorder" is still included in the *Diagnostic and Statistical Manual of Mental Disorders*. Also, manual or not, there remained counselors and therapists convinced that "adjustment" or "happiness" rested on heterosexuality and/or gender conformity. As the decade came to a close, "Sexual Conversion Therapy" to make queer people straight made a small comeback in "ex-gay" ads. The idea was hardly new, of course, but reappeared in a climate very different from the 1890s or the 1950s: now it was not driven by mental health professionals (the APA officially questioned the therapy in 1997) but by the same conservative Christians so influential in the larger culture wars.

Religion

Amid campaigns like those touting the joys of being "ex-gay" it is not surprising that GLBT people would continue to question their relationship to Christianity (and other organized religions). As before, some chose to break completely from their religious traditions, some worked for acceptance from within those traditions, and other became members of GLBT-friendly religious groups. The Universal Fellowship of Metropolitan Community Churches had grown to be one of the largest GLBT organizations of any kind. An African American MCC minister and gospel singer, Rev. Carl Bean, had founded a small Bible study group in Los Angeles in 1985, and by 1990 it became the Unity Fellowship Church Movement. As described on its Web site (http://www.ufc-usa.org) the movement is for those "looking for a church home that is rooted in spirituality and not in religion, one that celebrates all of God's diverse creation. . . . At Unity Fellowship Church, we know that God created us just as we are: Black, White, Latino, Native American, Asian, gay, lesbian, bisexual, transgendered, intersexed, or straight."

While many GLBT people sought new spiritual paths, others recognized that the right wing represented a small minority of traditional religious communities. In fact, a growing number of them welcomed openly queer people. In the mid-1980s some Christian denominations—United Church of Christ, the United Methodists, the Evangelical Lutherans, and the Presbyterian Church USA—had taken steps to be more welcoming. This divided congregations at times, as did the newer questions of blessing same-sex unions (a separate issue from legal marriage) and ordaining openly gay or lesbian clergy. The Unitarian Universalist Association and the Quakers, historically liberal denominations, had pioneered in performing same-sex unions, and were joined in the 1990s by other Christian groups and by both Reform and Reconstructionist Judaism.

Reform and Reconstructionist Jews also accept gay men and lesbians as rabbis and cantors, as do a few Christian denominations. Like marriage, the place of openly gay and lesbian spiritual leaders has been a source of dissension. When Episcopal bishop John Shelby Spong ordained an openly gay man in 1989 he ignited controversy, for example, as did those few already ordained who came out through the decade. In 2003 the Episcopal Diocese of New Hampshire made history by electing as bishop an openly gay priest, V. Gene Robinson, but the move further divided the Episcopal Church within the United States and around the world.

MEDIA OLD AND NEW

Speaking Out

The year of the third March on Washington, 1993, was also the year that National Coming Out Day (October 11) became the National Coming Out Project, with celebrity spokespersons. Candace Gingrich was NCOP's first director and later a spokesperson with actor Dan Butler. Other familiar faces coming out as lesbian or gay and representing the Project were Chastity Bono, Sean Sasser (of MTV's *Real World III*) and actor Amanda Bearse (of *Married with Children*). They joined the few other entertainers already out, but in a less "official" capacity. In 1995, producers Bruce Cohen and Nina Jacobson cofounded Out There, an organization of openly gay and lesbian entertainment personnel.

Before the nineties, in fact, it was rare for musicians, actors, or sports figures to declare themselves gay, lesbian, or bisexual; more often rumors circulated and were printed in tabloids as sensational news. However, singer k.d. lang bucked this trend and bravely came out as lesbian in 1992, followed the next year by singer Melissa Etheridge. African American drag queen RuPaul gained popularity in the nineties, representing both an old entertainment tradition and the newer media attention to the transgendered. A few actors, like Cherry Jones and Leslie Jordan already were openly lesbian or gay, and a few others came out by 2000: Michael Jeter, Nathan Lane, and Danny Pintauro acknowledged they are gay men and comedian Margaret Cho included her bisexuality in her shows. At the same time, this news continued to be sensational and sensationalized, treated as tabloid fare even outside the tabloids.

The process was most difficult, perhaps, for athletes both male and female. Sports had long been an area of strict enforcement of gender, second only to the military. Gay was still confused with effeminate in the culture, reinforcing the idea that to be gay and a winning athlete were mutually exclusive. For women, the situation was similar but reversed. If sports were no place for the feminine then that especially included women; female athletes must *by definition* be lesbian (if lesbian denotes crossing gender lines). Already "tainted" with these assumptions, female athletes feared charges of lesbianism, making coming out as one taboo, not to mention a career-ending move. Despite all this, a few athletes took the plunge and made their sexuality public, beginning with football running back Dave Kopay as early as 1975. On his decision Kopay later told Eric Marcus, "I was at a time and place in my own coming out where I felt that if I was going to survive I had to speak out. It was do that or maybe go crazy."[23] Only two more football players have since come out: Roy Simmons, in 1992 and Esera Tuaolo in 2002. In baseball only three pro players have declared themselves to be gay, beginning with Glenn Burke in 1982. Burke had retired in 1979 and went on to compete in other sports in Gay Games in the eighties (an interesting career tidbit is his association with the first use of the "high five" in a 1977 game). Major league umpire Dave Pallone followed Burke out eight years later and Billy Bean came out in 1999 after retiring from the San Diego Padres. Former Mr. Universe Bob Paris made news not only coming out but also by marrying Rod Jackson in 1989, actions that challenged public perceptions of professional bodybuilding. Diving may be a less stereotyped sport, but when Olympic gold medalist Greg Louganis came out as gay and HIV positive at Gay Games IV in 1994 he made a media splash. Women athletes public about being lesbian or bisexual remain rare, with tennis great Martina Navratilova beginning to be open in the early eighties and fully out in the nineties. Billie Jean King had come out by 2000 but, understandably, very few others beyond the occasional golf, tennis, or basketball pro have yet confronted society's prejudices. The difficulties faced by professional athletes seeking to come out are shared by coaches and players in schools and colleges who, like military personnel, face harassment, discrimination, and loss of employment if they "tell."

Despite public taboos that lingered about gay and lesbian athletes they formed their own organizations and events that publicly challenged negative stereotypes. As mentioned above, both Glenn Burke and Greg Louganis competed in the Gay Games, an event introduced in 1982 by former Olympic athlete Tom Waddell. The Gay Games are held every four years in between Olympic games years and by 1998 drew nearly 15,000 participants; at Gay Games IV (1994), held in New York City in conjunction with Stonewall 25, 10,879 athletes competed. National and international member groups of the Games include those devoted to running, tennis, the martial artists, football, and bowling. Gay rodeo competition has even older roots (probably since rodeos began, actually), in the National Reno Gay Rodeo in 1976 and the formation of the International Gay Rodeo Association in the 1980s, and its sponsored events expanded through the nineties.

Ellen Comes Out

As the world of sports demonstrates, historic landmarks can be cultural rather than purely political. This was the case in the 1996–1997 television season when writers of the ABC sitcom *Ellen* began to drop hints that the title character, Ellen Morgan, played by Ellen DeGeneres, might come out as a lesbian. DeGeneres had been a successful stand-up comic and had been in a few films when her show, first called *These Friends of Mine,* premiered in 1994. It was soon retooled and renamed and survived into a fourth season, during which scripts included hints that Ellen Morgan might step out of the closet.

Viewers hoping that was true were more than rewarded by the hour-long "Puppy Episode" (code-named to keep its contents a secret) on April 30, 1997. That night

Ellen's character said, "I'm gay" on TV, an event preceded by the "Yep, I'm Gay" cover story on the real Ellen in the April 14 issue of *Time* magazine. The day of the airing Ellen and then-girlfriend Anne Heche appeared on *The Oprah Winfrey Show* and a segment on *20/20* soon followed. Positive and negative publicity continued through the next year: GLBT advocates hailed Ellen's courage while those on the right attacked both her and ABC's parent company Disney (responses included a boycott by the Southern Baptist Convention).

Two episodes followed to finish out the season and they continued the coming out theme with episodes centering on the reactions of family, friends, and coworkers. The show returned in the fall and controversy ensued in the form of a girlfriend for Ellen and the addition of a "parental advisory" preceding each episode. The last new episode of *Ellen* was broadcast on March 13, 1998, the show having been cancelled. In the meantime, DeGeneres' mother Betty also made history as the first non-GLBT spokesperson for the National Coming Out Project and continued in the role through 1999.

TV and Film

In terms of both diversity and number of GLBT portrayals—on more than fifty series during the decade according to one scholar—the nineties were "revolutionary."[24] Even before Ellen Morgan was out a few fictional GLBT people showed up on TV. Usually they appeared in single episodes and occasionally in recurring supporting roles but were not yet the stars. Some series, like *Picket Fences,* had the "gay/lesbian episode" along the lines of previous treatments (see Chapter 7) and others broke some new ground: an African American gay man on *Spin City* and same-sex weddings on *Northern Exposure* (TV's first, in 1994), *Roseanne,* and *Friends,* for examples. *The Simpsons* had hinted that Waylon Smithers was gay from the beginning (1989) and in 1994 long-running sitcom *Roseanne* made news with a lesbian kiss. Another landmark in sitcoms came in 1998 when soon-to-be hit *Will & Grace* premiered, with title character Will Truman written as an openly gay man.

Other genres added GLBT people as well. In daytime drama (often overlooked but just as often introducing controversial topics) *All My Children* and *As the World Turns* had paved the way in the eighties for the few gay or lesbian soap characters that showed up in the nineties. The first openly gay men on Spanish-language television appeared at the end of the decade on Telemundo's *Los Beltrán* (1999–2001). Movies shown on TV included the AIDS film *And the Band Played On* premiering on HBO in 1993. That year also *Tales of the City,* shown as a PBS miniseries, received the network's highest ratings yet. Two more installments followed on Showtime, also based on the popular books by Armistead Maupin: *More Tales of the City* in 1998 and *Further Tales of the City* in 2001.

In movie theatres, the decade began and ended in with serious if not downright depressing features. The subject of AIDS was dramatized in *Longtime Companion* (1990) and *Philadelphia* (1993) and in 1999 the murder of Brandon Teena provided the story for *Boys Don't Cry* (see above). But in between were at least forty additional films, including lighter fare like *The Wedding Banquet* (1993), *The Birdcage* (1996), and *In & Out* (1997) and adaptations from the stage: Paul Rudnick's play *Jeffrey* appeared in 1995 and Terrence McNally's *Love! Valour! Compassion!* (1997) two years later. Lesbians were the subject of such films as *Claire of the Moon*(1992), *Go Fish* (1994), *The Incredibly True Adventures of Two Girls in Love* (1995), and *Watermelon Woman* (1995; the first by and about African American lesbians). *Fried Green*

Tomatoes (1991) generated discussion about Ruth and Idgie's relationship (were they or weren't they?) while a bigger controversies erupted over *The Silence of the Lambs* (1991) and *Basic Instinct* (1992).[25] Both the latter films concerned queer people (transgendered, bisexual) whose sexuality came across as linked to their penchant for murder, at least to those who protested the films. The gay man/straight-woman pairing so popular in *Will & Grace* was featured in several films, such as *The Object of My Affection* (1998) and *The Next Best Thing* (2000). A few movies were made highlighting transgendered people, including *Ed Wood* (1994) and *Flawless* (1999).

About twenty notable documentaries were produced in the nineties, reflecting the variety of people and concerns in GLBT America. *Out at Work* (1996) and *It's Elementary: Talking About Gay Issues in School* (1996) treated issues surrounding work and education, respectively. Native Americans received rare attention in *Two-Spirit People* (1991) and *Gendernauts* (1999) profiled transgendered individuals. GLBT history was the subject of two book-based films—*Coming Out Under Fire* (1994) and *The Celluloid Closet* (1995), as well as *Out of the Past* (1998) and *After Stonewall* (1999). In 1998 the Bravo TV network aired the British documentary *The Real Ellen Story,* which chronicled the very recent history of Ellen DeGeneres' "Puppy Episode" and its aftermath.

Words and Music

It is apparent above and throughout this chapter that there was no lack of popular or scholarly attention to GLBT topics through the nineties. This was true also of journalism, fiction, humor, and music, all of which had long been central to specifically GLBT communities (see Chapter 6) and all of which now experienced significant "crossover" to mainstream culture. That is, not only did major newspapers cover "gay stories" better and more often, for example, but older queer publications were joined by hundreds of local papers, some zines and comics, and a few new national glossies (*Curve, Genre, Girlfriends, Out, POZ*). The National Lesbian and Gay Journalists Association was founded in 1990 to promote better coverage of relevant issues and grew to over a thousand members. Important new outlets for scholarship also appeared at this time: *Journal of the History of Sexuality* (1990); *GLQ: A Journal of Lesbian and Gay Studies* (1991); *Lesbian Review of Books* (1994–2002); *Journal of Gay, Lesbian, and Bisexual Identity* (1996); and *Journal of Lesbian Studies* (1997). Literary tastes paralleled those of all Americans and ran the gamut as always from "literary" poetry and prose to such popular genres as romance and detective novels, in this case featuring lesbian and gay protagonists.

Humor came in several forms, sometimes from the same person. David Sedaris and Bob Smith were (and are) among the few openly gay men known widely for their humor, both spoken and written. Lesbian comedians and humorists of this era fell into two main categories: those who had begun earlier as openly lesbian and were still touring—Kate Clinton, Lea DeLaria, Suzanne Westenhoefer, and others—and those who began in comedy and then came out (Ellen DeGeneres and Rosie O'Donnell as lesbian, Margaret Cho as bisexual). The same type of crossover occurred in women's music, flourishing continually since its beginnings in the seventies (see Chapter 6). Festivals remained important venues for openly lesbian and bisexual performers, while a few (Tracy Chapman, Ani DiFranco, Indigo Girls) had become known outside them as well. Among the dozens of newer acts joining older performers still popular at festivals were Bitch and Animal, God-Des and She, and Tribe 8. Music by and for GBT men existed but had no similar festival structure, and The Flirtations gained national prominence in the 1990s.

A SHORTLIST OF WEB SITES OF GLBT INTEREST

365Gay.com, daily online news	http://www.365gay.com
Gay.com	http://www.gay.com
Glbtq.com, an encyclopedia of glbtq culture	http://www.glbtq.com
LesbiaNation.com	http://www.lesbianation.com
OurGayborhood.com	http://www.ourgayborhood.com
PlanetOut.com	http://www.planetout.com
TechnoDyke.com	http://www.technodyke.com
AIDS Action Council	http://www.aidsaction.org
Bisexual Resource Center	http://www.biresource.org
BLK Publishing Company (BLK lists resources for African Americans)	http://www.blk.com/resources
Center for Lesbian and Gay Studies	http://web.gc.cuny.edu/clags
Committee on Lesbian and Gay History	http://www.clghistory.org
Deaf Queer Resource Center	http://www.deafqueer.org
Gay and Lesbian Alliance Against Defamation	http://www.glaad.org
Gay Asian Pacific Support Network	http://www.gapsn.org
Gay, Lesbian and Straight Education Network	http://www.glsen.org
Gender Education & Advocacy	http://www.gender.org
Gender Public Advocacy Coalition	http://www.gpac.org
Human Rights Campaign	http://www.hrc.org
International Gay & Lesbian Review	http://gaybookreviews.info
International Lesbian and Gay Association	http://www.ilga.org
Intersex Society of North America	http://www.isna.org
Lambda Legal	http://www.lambdalegal.org
National Center for Lesbian Rights	http://www.nclrights.org
National Gay and Lesbian Task Force	http://www.thetaskforce.org
National Transgender Advocacy Coalition	http://www.ntac.org
Old Lesbians Organizing for Change	http://www.oloc.org
OutProud, The National Coalition for GLBT Youth	http://www.outproud.org
Parents, Families and Friends of Lesbians and Gays	http://www.pflag.org
Servicemembers Legal Defense Network	http://www.sldn.org
South Asian Lesbian & Gay Association	http://www.salganyc.org
Universal Fellowship of Metropolitan Community Churches	http://www.mcchurch.org

On the Web

The information highway has millions of GLBT travelers, and Web sites were created as social and educational as well as political space. Gay.com and PlanetOut.com appeared mid-decade and since have been joined by educational,

DEBATE: IS THERE A "GAY GENE"?

The question of whether homosexuality is the product of nature or nurture was hardly original in the 1990s. At this time, though, a new element was added to the older argument, and there was a changing context in which to voice familiar political views. The new wrinkle consisted of a few well-publicized studies that claimed scientific evidence for a genetic basis to sexuality. The validity and significance of the findings were debated within and beyond scientific communities around the world. GLBT activists responded in a variety of ways, from enthusiasm to fear to serious questioning of the purpose of the studies and their potential political applications.

Three studies in particular drew media attention in the early nineties. In 1991, Simon LeVay, an openly gay neurobiologist, published, "A Difference in Hypothalamic Structure Between Heterosexual and Homosexual Men," in *Science* in which he claimed that differences in the size of cell nuclei in the hypothalmus of male brains corresponded to their sexual orientation. The same year a study of twins compared to nontwin and adopted siblings conducted by J. Michael Bailey and Richard Pillard appeared in the *Archives of General Psychiatry.* In "A Genetic Study of Male Sexual Orientation," they reported a higher rate of homosexuality among identical twins than occurred among other siblings, supposedly demonstrating a genetic factor. This was followed in 1993 by the often-cited study, directed by Dean Hamer at the National Institutes of Health and published in *Science* with the self-explanatory title, "A Linkage Between DNA Markers on the X Chromosome and Male Sexual Orientation."[26]

Controversies over these reports erupted immediately and in many quarters. LeVay's study, for example, was criticized on many grounds, including his small sample and his methods of selecting and classifying them. All three were deemed inconclusive by the Council for Responsible Genetics; about the high proportion of gay identical twins the Council suggested that

> The fact that fraternal twins of gay men were found to be roughly twice as likely to be gay as other biological brothers shows that environmental factors play a role, since fraternal twins are no more similar biologically than are other biological brothers. In light of these results, it does not seem surprising that an even larger proportion of identical twins would have similar behaviors since the world thinks of them as "the same" and treats them accordingly, and they often share such feelings of sameness.

Further, the Council reported that Dean Hamer's research was being investigated "for possible scientific misconduct, because one of the study collaborators alleges that Hamer suppressed data that would have reduced the statistical significance of the reported results."[27]

GLBT activists in the United States and elsewhere also weighed in and with various reactions. For those working for equal rights proof of a "gay gene" could bolster claims derived from the "identity" model of American politics. Ethnic minorities and women had built cases against discrimination by asserting that inborn traits should not be used to bar them from housing, education, employment, and so on. The "born that way" argument, as it was often called, had become a staple in the mainstream lesbian and gay movement and appealed to a sense of fairness thought ingrained in American culture. Also, many queer people reported "feeling different" from an early age—sometimes from the time of their earliest memories. Since Americans had a history of respecting science as truth (as well as a legacy of a science–law alliance) these studies might at last put to rest the question of whether GLBT people should, or could, be treated differently. In the hopeful climate of the early nineties (often called the "gay moment" by movement historians) a genetic link to homosexuality seemed the last and necessary ingredient in the recipe for full equality.

There were other voices, though, and they expressed more alarm than optimism. For decades liberationists had resisted the "please don't hate/exclude/fire/ evict/kill me, I can't help it" approach. It may evoke pity or sympathy and may even cause some lawmakers to relent, they would assert, but does nothing in the long run to encourage a truly diverse population—one celebrating difference rather than apologizing for it. Instead, these critics reject the idea that one must "earn" rights through conformity to a very narrow model of citizenship (white, male, straight, able-bodied) or else be "awarded" them through the generosity of those who conform. For them the freedom to choose one's sex, sexuality, and/or gender would be genuine liberation.

Finally, there are those who fear the potential uses of science for *any* political agendas: if the gay gene theory could serve gay rights, might it not also play into the hands of a homophobic society? If a gay gene was identified might it be altered, or used to identify and then abort gay fetuses? (The latter is a particularly ironic possibility in light of the correlation between antiabortion and anti-GLBT activism). Here the questions are not whether there exists a gay gene but whether we should even ask, why we need to know, and why we need to know at this particular "moment" in the GLBT story.

informational, and social sites like glbtq.com and 365gay.com. Local, regional, and national organizations moved quickly in 1990s to create Web sites and those of the largest groups quickly grew in content and sophistication (see Box: Web sites). GLAAD, HRC, NGLTF, and many other groups also adopted e-mail use for news and press releases, special alerts, and calling subscribers to action. The last is made easier than ever, since Web sites often provide ready-made lists or letters to "sign" and send on; writing letters and sending telegrams to Congress is now replaced by a few clicks of a mouse. In 1996 Walter L. Williams founded *The International Gay & Lesbian Review,* the first academic journal published exclusively online. That GLBT Americans use the internet effectively is not surprising in light of the historical pairing of computers and queers: computer companies were among the first with inclusive policies, probably due to the disproportionate number of GLBT employees (ten times as many as in the fashion industry even in the early nineties and characterized then as "visible, organized, and highly productive"[28]).

The internet was only one of many elements creating equal amounts of optimism and anxiety as the year 2000 drew closer. Dire predictions of computer-related "Y2K" disasters caused some Americans to prepare in ways not seen since Cold War Americans built and stocked bomb shelters. Historians looked to the ends of previous centuries and saw similar patterns of cultural stress while some Christians gazed ahead expecting the return of the Messiah. As it turned out, 2000 arrived with fanfare but minus massive shutdowns or religious Armageddon. All this applied equally to GLBT people, of course, and was further complicated by yet another "family" squabble as the 21st century opened.

NOTES

1. Sylvia's quotes from Martin Duberman, *Stonewall* (New York: Plume, 1993), 198, 263.

2. Patrick J. Buchanan, "1992 Republican National Convention Speech," August 17, 1992, as posted on http://www.buchanan.org/pa-92-0817-rnc.html.

3. http://supct.law.cornell.edu/supct/html/94-1039.ZO.html.

4. Steve Estes, "Ask and Tell: Gay Veterans, Identity, and Oral History on a Civil Rights Frontier," *Oral History Review* 32, no. 2 (2005): 38.

5. Number of schools cited in "ROTC Challenged Over Ban on Homosexuals,"*USA Today,* December 3, 1990, 3A.

6. Tim McFeeley, "Getting it Straight: A Review of the 'Gays in the Military' Debate," in *Creating Change™: Sexuality, Public Policy, and Civil Rights,* ed. John D'Emilio, William B. Turner, and Urvashi Vaid (New York: St. Martin's Press, 2000), 245, 246.

7. For the 1993 March on Washington demands and platform see Kevin Jennings, ed., *Becoming Visible: A Reader in Gay & Lesbian History for High School & College Students* (Boston: Alyson Publications, 1994), 224–25; or Craig A. Rimmerman, *From Identity to Politics: The Lesbian and Gay Movements in the United States* (Philadelphia: Temple University Press, 2002), 187–90.

8. Nadine Smith, "Three Marches, Many Lessons," in *Creating Change™: Sexuality, Public Policy, and Civil Rights,* ed. John D'Emilio, William B. Turner, and Urvashi Vaid (New York: St. Martin's Press, 2000), 446.

9. Quote from film, *After Stonewall* (1999).

10. "Serious Look" headline from unsigned article in *The Wisconsin Light,* September 29, 1993. Other coverage includes articles in the *Southern Voice* (September 30, 1993) and *The Washington Times* (September 8, 1993).

11. Rebecca Walker, "Becoming the Third Wave," *Ms.* (January/February, 1992): 39–41.

12. http://inquirer.gn.apc.org/GDRights.html.

13. Walter L. Williams and Yolanda Retter, eds., *Gay and Lesbian Rights in the United States: A Documentary History* (Westport, CT: Greenwood Press, 2003), 276.

14. Quotes from http://www.sexmutant.com/del.htm and http://www.dellagracevolcano.com /statement.html.

15. http://www.house.gov/house/Contract/CONTRACT.html.

16. Jenifer Warren, "Lesbian Legislator Wows Conservatives," *The Milwaukee Journal Sentinel,* September 17, 1995 (Available for a fee from http://www.jsonline.com/).

17. Quoted in Eric Marcus, *Making Gay History: The Half-Century Fight for Lesbian and Gay Equal Rights* (New York: Harper Perennial, 2002), 379.

18. http://laws.findlaw.com/us/000/u10179.html.

19. Williams and Retter, eds., *Documentary History,* 230–31.

20. Chai R. Feldblum, "The Federal Gay Rights Bill: From Bella to ENDA," in *Creating Change™: Sexuality, Public Policy, and Civil Rights,* ed. John D'Emilio, William B. Turner, and Urvashi Vaid (New York: St. Martin's Press, 2000), 184.

21. "A Grisly Find," at http://www.crimelibrary.com/motorious_murders/not_guilty/ brandon/1.html.

22. Marielena Zuniga, "The Feminization of AIDS," in *Women: Images and Realities,* ed. Amy Kesselman, Lily D. McNair, and Nancy Schniedewind, 4th ed. (Boston: McGraw-Hill, 2008), 331, citing a report by the United Nations (UN) and World Health Organization (WHO).

23. Eric Marcus, *Making Gay History,* 194.

24. Steven Capsuto, "Television," in *Encyclopedia of Lesbian, Gay, Bisexual, and Transgender History in America,* ed. Marc Stein, vol. 3 (Detroit, MI: Gale, 2004), 178.

25. For perceptions of *Fried Green Tomatoes* and *Basic Instinct* see Vicki L. Eaklor, "'Seeing' Lesbians in Film and History," *Historical Reflections/Réflexions Historiques* 20, no. 2 (Summer, 1994): 321–33.

26. Simon LeVay, "A Difference in Hypothalamic Structure Between Heterosexual and Homosexual Men," *Science,* New Series, 253, no. 5023 (August 30, 1991): 1034–37; J. Michael Bailey and Richard Pillard, "A Genetic Study of Male Sexual Orientation," *Archives of General Psychiatry* 48 (December 1991): 1089–96; Dean Hamer et al., "A Linkage Between DNA Markers on the X Chromosome and Male Sexual Orientation," *Science,* New Series, 261, no. 5119 (July 16, 1993): 321–27. I am indebted to Crystal Lehman for her research on this topic, which resulted in the outstanding paper, "Polemical Science: 'Gay Gene' Theory and the Subversion of Progressive Feminist Politics" (unpublished, 2007).

27. "Do Genes Determine Our Sexuality?" Council for Responsible Genetics. http://www.gene-watch.org/educational/genes_and_sexuality.pdf.

28. Michelangelo Signorile, *Queer in America: Sex, the Media, and the Closets of Power* (New York: Random House, 1993), 345.

SUGGESTED RESOURCES

General/Politics

Abelove, H. (Ed.). (1993). *The lesbian and gay studies reader.* New York: Routledge.

Bawer, B. (1993). *A place at the table: The gay individual in society.* New York: Poseidon.

Chambers, D.L. (2000). Couples: Marriage, civil union, and domestic partnership. In J. D'Emilio, W.B. Turner, & U. Vaid (Eds.), *Creating Change™: Sexuality, public policy, and civil rights* (pp. 281–304). New York: St. Martin's Press.

Chauncey, G. (1994). *Gay New York: Gender, urban culture, and the making of the gay male world 1890–1940.* New York: Basic Books.

Clendinen, D., & Nagourney, A. (1999). *Out for good: The struggle to build a gay rights movement in America.* New York: Simon & Schuster.

Cruikshank, M. (1992). *The gay and lesbian liberation movement.* New York: Routledge.

DeBold, K. (Ed.). (1994). *Out for office: Campaigning in the gay nineties.* Washington, DC: Gay and Lesbian Victory Fund.

Duberman, M. (1991). *Cures: A gay man's odyssey.* New York: Dutton.

Duberman, M. (1996). *Midlife queer: Autobiography of a decade 1971–1981.* Madison: University of Wisconsin Press.

Endean, S. (2006). *Bringing lesbian and gay rights into the mainstream* (V.L. Eaklor, Ed.). Binghamton, NY: Haworth Press.

Howard, J. (Ed.). (1997). *Carryin' on in the lesbian and gay south.* New York: New York University Press.

Howard, J. (1999). *Men like that: A southern queer history.* Chicago: University of Chicago Press.

Kirk, M., & Madsen, H. (1990). *After the ball: How America will conquer its fear & hatred of gays in the 90s.* New York: Plume.

LeVay, S. (1996). *Queer science: The use and abuse of research into homosexuality.* Cambridge, MA: MIT Press.

Newton, E. (1993). *Cherry Grove, Fire Island: Sixty years in America's first gay and lesbian town.* Boston: Beacon Press.

Sullivan, A. (1995). *Virtually normal: An argument about homosexuality.* New York: Alfred A. Knopf.

Vaid, U. (1995). *Virtual equality: The mainstreaming of gay & lesbian liberation.* New York: Doubleday.

Warner, M. (1993). *Fear of a queer planet: Queer politics and social theory.* Minneapolis: University of Minnesota Press.

Warner, M. (1999). *The trouble with normal: Sex, politics, and the ethics of queer life.* New York: The Free Press.

African Americans

Boykin, K. (1996). *One more river to cross: Black & gay in America.* New York: Doubleday.

Hawkeswood, W.G. (1996). *One of the children: Gay black men in Harlem* (A.W. Costley, Ed.). Berkeley: University of California Press.

Bisexual and Transgender

Beemyn, B. (Ed.). (1997). *Creating a place for ourselves: Lesbian, gay, and bisexual community histories.* New York: Routledge.

Feinberg, L. (1992). *Transgender liberation: A movement whose time has come.* New York: World View Forum.

Frye, P.R. (2000). Facing discrimination, organizing for freedom: The transgender community. In J. D'Emilio, W.B. Turner, & U. Vaid (Eds.), *Creating Change™: Sexuality, public policy, and civil rights* (pp. 451–468). New York: St. Martin's Press.

Hutchins, L., & Kaahumanu, L. (Eds.). (1991). *Bi any other name: Bisexual people speak out.* Boston: Alyson Publications.

Jones, A. (1996). *All she wanted.* New York: Pocket Books.

Rupp, L., & Taylor, V. (2003). *Drag queens at the 801 Cabaret.* Chicago: University of Chicago Press.

Rust, P.C.R. (Ed.). (1999). *Bisexuality in the United States: A social science reader.* New York: Columbia University Press.

Tucker, N. (Ed.). (1995). *Bisexual politics: Theories, queries, and visions.* Binghamton, NY: Harrington Park Press.

Weinberg, M.S., Williams, C.J., & Pryor, D.W. (Eds.). (1994). *Dual attraction: Understanding bisexuality.* New York: Oxford University Press.

Lesbian

Faderman, L. (1992). *Odd girls and twilight lovers: A history of lesbian life in twentieth-century America.* New York: Penguin Books.

Kennedy, E., & Davis, M. (1993). *Boots of leather, slippers of gold: The history of a lesbian community.* New York: Routledge.

Plumb, M. (2000). Advocating for lesbian health in the Clinton years. In J. D'Emilio, W.B. Turner, & U. Vaid (Eds.), *Creating Change™: Sexuality, public policy, and civil rights* (pp. 361–381). New York: St. Martin's Press.

Media

Benshoff, H.M., & Griffin, S. (2006). *Queer images: A history of gay and lesbian film in America.* Lanham, MD: Rowman & Littlefield.

Capsuto, S. (2000). *Alternate channels: The uncensored story of gay and lesbian images on radio and television.* New York: Ballantine Books.

Tropiano, S. (2002). *The prime time closet: A history of gays and lesbians on TV.* New York: Applause Books.

Military

Humphrey, M.A. (1990). *My country, my right to serve: Experiences of gay men and women in the military, World War II to the present.* New York: HarperCollins.

Shilts, R. (1993). *Conduct unbecoming: Gays and lesbians in the U.S. military*. New York: St. Martin's Press.

Steffan, J. (1992). *Honor bound: A gay naval midshipman fights to serve his country*. New York: Villard Books.

Sports

Bean, B. (2003). *Going the other way: Lessons from a life in and out of Major League Baseball*. New York: Marlowe & Company.

Burke, G., Sherman, E., & Sherman, M. (1995). *Home: The Glenn Burke story*. Manchester, UK: Excel Publishing.

Jackson, R., & Paris, B. (1994). *Straight from the heart: A love story*. New York: Warner Books.

Louganis, G. (with Marcus, E.) (1995). *Breaking the surface*. New York: Random House.

Pallone, D. (with Steinberg, A.) (1990). *Behind the mask: My double life in baseball*. New York: Viking Press.

Simmons, R., & DiMarco, D. (2005). *Out of bounds: Coming out of sexual abuse, addiction, and my life of lies in the NFL closet*. New York: Carroll & Graf.

9 INTO THE 21ST CENTURY

Rochester, New York, 2004. Anne Tischer and Bess Watts are married in Washington Square Park on April 29 by the Rev. Jim Mulcahy of the Open Arms Metropolitan Community Church. Two days before their ceremony they applied for a marriage license at City Hall. By this time, civil unions had been legal in Vermont for four years and Massachusetts' historic decision to legalize same-sex marriage would go into effect the next month. In New York, however, the legal and economic protections offered through civil marriage were not available (New Paltz mayor Jason West's attempts to legitimize same-sex unions that March resulted in criminal charges filed against him). When Tischer and Watts applied for a license, the first same-sex couple in Rochester to do so, they were politely turned down. At the time Watts said, "it was probably one of the most positive rejections you could hope for. We were treated with respect and dignity."

Like many same-sex couples Anne and Bess had not rushed into exchanging vows though they felt like "soul mates" from the beginning and had "known forever we'd be getting married." In fact, they had been together ten years before deciding to celebrate their commitment while challenging the law. Also like so many others, they would not have described themselves as activists, even now, but instead just average folks expecting the same justice offered to other hard-working, tax-paying, loyal citizens (Bess, in fact, is a U.S. Army veteran). As Bess said on the occasion, "We want to show support for marriage equality. And for Anne and me, it's the real thing. We are the same as any other couple that would get married on this day." Anne underscored her point, and the desire to separate politics from celebration, while acknowledging the role of both: "For me personally the wedding's statement is the ability of two hearts to love each other. That can't be ruled by a legislature. That's something that's given as a gift of God." "Today, legal and political issues don't matter a bit. We're celebrating our love and commitment. Tomorrow, however . . . "[1]

As the 20th became the 21st century, life for GLBT people in the United States was typically mixed. Couples like Bess and Anne celebrated their unions in ceremonies not yet legal while their counterparts in other states saw civil union and marriage options opening to them. Still others continued to object to merely hoping for equal

Rev. Jim Mulcahy (center), of the Metropolitan Community Church, officiates at the wedding of Bess Watts (L) and Anne Tischer (R) in Washington Square Park, Rochester, NY, on April 29, 2004. The ceremony is one of thousands of same-sex spiritual unions performed for decades, through which couples have celebrated publicly their love and commitment. (© Bess Watts)

treatment and fought for more radical change. Visibility in the popular culture seemed assured, and more teens than ever had gay-straight alliances and media role models available to them. "Gay" was still the schoolyard word of choice for anything unacceptable, though, and anti-GLBT prejudice in government not only continued but heightened in a time of crisis. When on September 11, 2001, terrorists attacked the nation at the World Trade Center and the Pentagon, some on the Radical Right saw an opportunity to once again create scapegoats. Shortly after the attack, for example, evangelists Jerry Falwell and Pat Robertson blamed their old cultural (and political) enemies; on the TV show *The 700 Club* Falwell said, "I really believe that the pagans, and the abortionists, and the feminists, and the gays and the lesbians who are actively trying to make that an alternative lifestyle,...I point the finger in their face and say 'you helped this happen.'"[2] Such remarks, though extreme, confirmed that GLBT people would continue as scapegoats whose rights could serve as political footballs when all else failed.

CONTROVERSY, VISIBILITY, DIVERSITY

The Millennium March

On April 30, 2000, about 200,000 people assembled for a fourth demonstration at the nation's capital, this one called the Millennium March on Washington for Equality.

Unlike the previous marches, however, this one was seen as competing with rather than originating from grassroots activism, especially on the state level. As a result, controversy surrounded both the planning and the aftermath of the march, probably leading to smaller attendance rates while certainly driving a wider wedge between moderate and radical activists.

Amid a grassroots initiative to march on all fifty state capitals in 1999 called Equality Begins at Home the idea of the Millennium March arose. This time, however, a "top down" approach replaced the usual "bottom-up" process of establishing goals and planning actions through consultation with many voices, including non-GLBT coalitions. In addition, those announcing the event represented the wealthiest (and most assimilationist) among GLBT organizers: Elizabeth Birch of the Human Rights Campaign, Rev. Troy Perry of the Universal Fellowship of Metropolitan Community Churches, and promoter Robin Tyler. (In addition, the HRC was already under fire for its endorsement of the antiabortionist Sen. Alfonse D'Amato as he ran for reelection in 1998, a move also made without consultation among a wider range of activists). To its critics, this march was shaping up as "more of an entertainment extravaganza than a serious political event," as a letter to the feminist paper, *Off Our Backs* asserted. The letter's author also explained clearly and eloquently the liberationist view:

> The assimilationist strategy underlying the "march" call has been tried before. Assimilation has never worked for a visibly identifiable and despised group. We have a concrete example of that within living memory. It is called the Holocaust.
>
> We will not be protected by looking "just like them." We will not be made safe by throwing overboard all the tacky, unacceptable queers who might offend the audience watching at home. Our only hope is a society in which all have the right to fair and decent treatment, even if we are obviously "different." This is a question of justice, not style.[3]

Despite a virtual boycott by many, the event occurred, using the theme, "Faith and Family" (a phrase that further alienated skeptics). At the same time, march supporters had consciously chosen "Equality" over "Rights" in the march title to send a less compromising message. When Lorri Jean spoke at the March she expressed this theme and the feelings of many:

> I marched here for our rights in 1979; I had just come out and I was afraid. I march again in 1987, without fear and full of pride. I marched again in 1993, filled with excitement about the promise of a new President. But now it's the year 2000, and I'm not afraid and I'm not excited. I'm tired. I'm tired of marching. And I'm MAD! I'm mad because we should not have to be here....
>
> From this point onward, let us adopt a policy of ZERO TOLERANCE. Zero tolerance of discrimination, zero tolerance of bigotry and ignorance, zero tolerance for elected officials who refuse to support our full and complete participation in this society—especially those politicians who take out money!...
> FULL EQUALITY AND NOTHING LESS![4]

Besides the actual march, the weekend featured a concert, Equality Rocks, that included Garth Brooks, Melissa Etheridge, Chaka Khan, k.d. lang, and the Pet Shop Boys, and stars Ellen DeGeneres, Anne Heche, Kathy Najimy, and Nathan Lane. There was a festival with vendors selling GLBT-themed products and once again a mass wedding, this time at the Lincoln Memorial. Once it was over, the march had lost rather than raised money, depriving local groups of promised revenues and prompting charges of theft and a subsequent investigation.

Whatever the drawbacks of the Millennium March, at least one aspect had changed: this time there was no lack of coverage by mainstream TV and print media. The March was broadcast on C-SPAN and was front-page news in such major city papers as *The Washington Post, The Washington Times, The Los Angeles Times,* and *The Atlanta Journal-Constitution.*

In the Media

The first few years of the 2000s continued the trend of increasing GLBT visibility on television. Ellen DeGeneres returned to the sitcom in 2001 with *The Ellen Show* on CBS, three years after the last episode of her now-controversial show aired in 1998. Although the new sitcom aired only thirteen episodes, in 2003 she went to a hugely successful daytime talk format, *The Ellen DeGeneres Show.* Sitcoms and animated series still seem the genres of choice for launching GLBT characters, though not always successfully. Three new "gaycoms" (*Normal, Ohio, Some of My Best Friends, It's All Relative*) tried to capitalize on the popularity of *Will and Grace* but none lasted more than one season.[5] However, *South Park, Family Guy,* and of course *The Simpsons* feature a number of cartoon queers and GLBT people have shown up on about thirty drama or reality-based shows from 2000 to 2005. Notably, *Queer as Folk* premiered in 2000 on Showtime, the same network airing *The L Word* since 2004, with *Queer Eye for the Straight Guy* beginning on Bravo in the interim, in 2003. Transgendered characters continue to be rare, though the single season of *The Education of Max Bickford* (2001–2002) initially featured a MTF transsexual college professor as a recurring character (and close friend of Max).

As in previous years, television was also the medium through which millions of Americans were able to see GLBT-themed films. In 1996 an HBO production, *If These Walls Could Talk,* premiered and concerned a house in which three generations of women faced questions of pregnancy and abortion; in 2000 a sequel aired that continued the theme of different generations, this time on lesbians, *If These Walls Could Talk, 2. The Truth About Jane,* a drama about a teenager coming out to herself and her family and starring Stockard Channing, also aired in 2000, and in 2003 HBO broadcast the film version of Tony Kushner's highly honored play *Angels in America,* which received five Golden Globes and eleven Emmys, among other awards. In *Holiday Heart* (2000) an African American gay drag queen rescues a drug-addicted woman and her daughter and helps raise the daughter, and *Normal* (2003) portrays a middle-aged, long-married man deciding to undergo sex-reassignment surgery. Probably the best sign that GLBT viewers were considered an economic market, though, was the launching of TV networks with programming aimed at that niche; by late 2005 here! TV broadcast to forty-five million homes and Q Television Network and MTV's LOGO channel reached about a half-million and eighteen million homes, respectively.

A growing number of films with GLBT characters and themes appeared in the early years of the 21st century. By 2005, a dozen documentaries were available, including studies of such individuals as Bayard Rustin in *Brother Outsider* (2003), Harry Hay in *Hope Along the Wind* (2001), and the homophile activists who marched at Philadelphia in the 1960s in *Gay Pioneers* (2004). *Trembling Before G-d* (2001) broke ground in its depiction of lesbian/gay Orthodox and Hasidic Jews, and the history of women's music was the subject of *Radical Harmonies* (2002); transgender people were highlighted in such films as *Venus Boyz* (2002) and *TransGeneration* (2005).

Commercial films after 1999 included *Brother to Brother* (2004), *Saving Face* (2004)—depicting African Americans and Asian Americans, respectively—and *Transamerica* (2005), featuring TV's *Desperate Housewives'* star Felicity Huffman as a pre-operative MTF transsexual. In 2005 two films were released whose numerous awards and nominations put GLBT topics continually before the public. *Capote* garnered title actor Philip Seymour Hoffman a Best Actor Academy Award and *Brokeback Mountain,* portraying two gay cowboys in the 1960s, received seventy-five awards internationally, including three Oscars (for director, original score, and adapted screenplay).

When Ellen DeGeneres came out in 1997 what followed was hardly a mass exodus of actors from the closet. Still, a few American entertainers have since gone public as gay, lesbian, or bisexual. People relatively newer to show business, like Chad Allen and B.D. Wong, were joined by a few venerable American actors in coming out after 2000: heartthrobs of their times Richard Chamberlain and Tab Hunter, and *Star Trek*'s Mr. Sulu, George Takei. Out lesbians by 2005 included popular talk show host Rosie O'Donnell, who came out in a *Primetime Thursday* interview in 2002, and Sara Gilbert ("Darlene" of *Roseanne*).

GLBT Plus Q Plus…

In Chapter 8, Del LaGrace Volcano is quoted expressing the desire to take control of self-description and presentation, in this case as "gender variant," "gender abolitionist," and "gender terrorist." To many people sharing Volcano's personal and political goals the term "queer" is appropriate and can replace the addition of identities signaled by GLBT. Debates continue about this, though, with others preferring the addition of terms (and letters in the acronym) in order to preserve a sense of separate identity. As the 20th century ended the words "queer, questioning, intersexed and interested" were added in some instances: GLBTQQII. Although it seems unwieldy (and has the potential to get longer), it reflects a political stance that categories with which individuals have come to identify need to be preserved within a coalition representing diversity. Also, because lesbians, bisexuals, and transgendered people felt they had to fight for decades for visibility within a "gay movement" many are not so eager to be lumped under one term (especially one as loaded, and often understood as male as queer).

Yet a new wrinkle arose in the nineties and was given a term in 2002: the metrosexual. In some ways he is both cutting-edge queer *and* simply another version of old-fashioned market-driven image. Mark Simpson's subhead to "Meet the Metrosexual" expressed this succinctly: "He's Well Dressed, Narcissistic and Obsessed with Butts. But Don't Call Him Gay." What is not clear is whether "gay" is rejected because it is too narrow and old fashioned, or because of old fashioned, American homophobia. Simpson described the supposedly new urban male as

> a young man with money to spend, living in or within easy reach of a metropolis— because that's where all the best shops, clubs, gyms and hairdressers are. He might be officially gay, straight or bisexual, but this is utterly immaterial because he has clearly taken himself as his own love object and pleasure as his sexual preference.

The real point, he suggested, was not queer politics but mainstream profits: "The stoic, self-denying, modest straight male didn't shop enough (his role was to earn money for his wife to spend), and so he had to be replaced by a new kind of man, one less certain of his identity and much more interested in his image—that's to say, one who was much more interested in being looked at…"[6]

LAW AND POLITICS

The political struggles of the early 21st century have continued in the same vein as earlier times but in a climate changed by both a contested election and a terrorist attack on U.S. soil. The first brought in a conservative regime reminiscent of the New Right of the eighties but more attuned to the far right wing of the Republic Party. The Bush administration, like those preceding the Clinton years, has indicated its intention to halt or reverse the progress of any "gay agenda" (as they see it). In the wake of 9/11 GLBT issues were visible once again and revealing of the state of attitudes and policies. The Gay and Lesbian Alliance Against Defamation reported that media coverage included the numerous GLBT victims and heroes of the attacks, and often sympathetically. A *Washington Post* article that October, for example, included the following paragraph:

> Gays are intimately, tragically part of this war: David Charlebois, a fixture of Dupont Circle's upper set, was a pilot on one of the doomed airliners Sept. 11. And there was the 6-foot-5 rugby player from San Francisco, Mark Bingham, who is thought to have helped fellow passengers confront terrorists in a plane over Pennsylvania. The list goes on—the beloved gay chaplain of the New York Fire Department, killed in the World Trade Center collapse; two men and their adopted toddler killed on one of the planes; the many who lost longtime partners and are now navigating an iffy situation of relief aid and death benefits for non-traditional couples.[7]

The "iffy situation" was reported elsewhere, and revealed that while charitable groups had treated GLBT survivors generally well, government resources depended on the state in which one lived. This highlighted once again the disparity in treatment under the law between those once called heterosexual and homosexual.

Therefore discrimination in various forms continued to occupy mainstream organizations. Between 2000 and 2005 five additional states passed laws barring discrimination due to sexual orientation, bringing the total to sixteen; gender expression and identity was now included in three of the new laws and added to five of the previous eleven state laws, and to the Washington, DC law. States also added hate crimes legislation that includes offenses based on real or perceived sexual orientation, for a total of twenty-nine states and the District of Columbia with such laws at the end of 2005. Eight of those states and DC also specify gender identity and expression in their laws.

In the military, the DADT ("Don't Ask, Don't Tell") policy had gone into effect in 1994 but did not drastically improve the situation of lesbians and gay men in the military. Organizations like the SLDN (Servicemembers Legal Defense Network) continue to track the treatment and expulsion of military personnel due to charges of homosexuality; SLDN includes on its Web site that a Defense Department report issued in 2000 documented the existence of "rampant anti-gay harassment throughout the services." From 1994 to 2005 over 9,800 people were dismissed, with increases every year to a peak at 1,273 in 2001, then decreasing to 668 in 2004, and a slight jump again to 742 in 2005. The costs of the policy to the U.S. government in the same period have been estimated at close to $200 million, according to the Government Accountability Office.

The pattern of treatment has been mixed since U.S. troops have been engaged, first in Afghanistan in 2001 ("Operation Enduring Freedom"), and in Iraq since 2003 ("Operation Iraqi Freedom"). On the one hand, discharges of gay men and lesbians decreased after the onset of both engagements. On the other hand, it continues even when personnel are desperately needed, both generally and for their specific skills. Nine linguists in the U.S. Army were discharged in 2002 under the DADT policy, for instance, six of them among the few trained in Arabic translation. Besides outright dismissals, SLDN indicates that antigay harassment, threats, and assaults continue with commanders reluctant to stop any of it.

Elections

Voters in the year 2000 witnessed one of the most contested presidential elections in U.S. history. Too close to call on election night, Democrat Al Gore finally conceded to Republican George W. Bush in December but a sense that the election had been "stolen" from him via disputed electoral votes from Florida lingered among many Democrats long after 2000. At the same time, the news was better then and after for openly queer candidates, whose numbers had been growing since 1996. Although he was not elected, for example, Vermont Democrat Ed Flanagan was the first out gay man to run for the Senate, in 2000. That same year representatives Tammy Baldwin, Barney Frank, and Jim Kolbe remained the only out lesbian or gay people in Congress (Gerry Studds had retired in 1996), but at least seven more candidates ran for the House, including the first transgendered person to do so (also from Vermont). In state elections in 2000 more than sixty openly queer people ran as either incumbents or challengers. Nationwide, the gains were impressive: between 1997 and 2003 the number of openly GLBT people in office nearly doubled, from 124 to 245. The 2002 ballots included 135 such candidates and the number rose to 160 or more in 2004. In 2004, incumbent President Bush defeated Democratic contender John Kerry. This result alone was discouraging to many GLBT people, and the assault in the states on same-sex marriage that year confirmed many queers' worst fears (see below).

Lawrence v. Texas and GLBT History

At the turn of the new millennium GLBT rights groups continued to fight the sodomy laws used for so long to police sexual behavior, especially that of gay men. In the 1986 *Bowers v. Hardwick* decision the U.S. Supreme Court had upheld Georgia's statute, declaring that the Constitution did not protect any "right to commit homosexual sodomy" (see Chapter 7).[8] Despite that antigay victory there remained only thirteen states with laws against sodomy in 2003, four of those prohibiting homosexual but not heterosexual sodomy. One of the four (with Kansas, Oklahoma, and Missouri) was Texas.

The facts of the case resembled that of 1986 in its outlines, but ended very differently. *Lawrence* originated when two Houston men, John G. Lawrence and Tyron Garner, were arrested for having sex in Lawrence's home. The case reached the state Court of Appeals, which relied upon *Bowers v. Hardwick* to uphold the Texas sodomy law, and so the case was then appealed to the U.S. Supreme Court. In June 2003, the Court rendered a 6-3 decision in favor of Lawrence, not only reversing the Court of Appeals verdict but adding, in its majority opinion, "*Bowers* was not correct when it was decided, and it is not correct today. It ought not to remain binding precedent. *Bowers v. Hardwick* should be and now is overruled." Citing the 14th Amendment's guarantees of due process and equal protection under the law, Justice Anthony M. Kennedy wrote:

> When sexuality finds overt expression in intimate conduct with another person, the conduct can be but one element in a personal bond that is more enduring. The liberty protected by the Constitution allows homosexual persons the right to make this choice.
>
> The petitioners are entitled to respect for their private lives. The State cannot demean their existence or control their destiny by making their private sexual conduct

a crime. Their right to liberty under the Due Process Clause gives them the full right to engage in their conduct without intervention of the government.[9]

The *Lawrence* decision is related to GLBT history in at least two ways. It is part of that history, certainly, and has been compared to such rulings as *Brown v. the Board of Education* (1954) and *Roe v. Wade* (1973). Less known is the impact of GLBT scholars and scholarship upon the outcome, an impact summarized at the time by Rick Perlstein in *The Washington Post*. In "What Gay Studies Taught the Court," Perlstein asked what had changed since 1986 to reverse the *Bowers* ruling and answered, "nothing less than the historical understanding of laws regarding sexual conduct." Perlstein explained that the Court's conclusions relied especially on three *amicus curiae* briefs, including one written by George Chauncey and nine other historians; at the time of *Bowers* gay studies, Perlstein rightly noted, "was still embryonic, marginal and distrusted even within the academy." Between the two decisions, though,

> the practitioners of what some called "queer history" were hard at work, undertaking one of the hardest and most valuable tasks that historians can do—examining a set of assumptions so taken for granted, so apparently timeless, that they didn't seem to have histories at all. And fortunately for the eventual plaintiffs in *Lawrence v. Texas,* they gave *Bowers* the strictest of scrutiny.

The arguments of the historians are clearly evident in Kennedy's ruling, wrote Perlstein, even to citing such works as Jonathan Ned Katz's *The Invention of Heterosexuality*.[10] GLBT history had achieved a new validity, it seemed, as had the notion of equal rights for the people of that history.

Defining Marriage

The November following the *Lawrence* decision another landmark in GLBT history occurred, but one that further divided not only U.S. conservatives and liberals but also GLBT liberationists from accommodationists. That month the Supreme Judicial Court of Massachusetts ruled (in *Goodridge v. Massachusetts Department of Public Health*) that the state had not demonstrated "any constitutionally adequate reason" for denying legal marriage to same-sex couples. Same-sex marriage became available in May 2004 and within six months about 6,500 couples took advantage of the new legal situation. As of the end of 2005 Connecticut joined Vermont in offering civil unions to gay and lesbian couples, but Massachusetts remained the only state to provide equal marriage rights.

Other states, however, moved in another direction: not towards civil union but of outlawing any kind of same-sex legal recognition. In the 2004 elections antigay-marriage amendments were passed in eleven states (Arkansas, Georgia, Kentucky, Michigan, Mississippi, Montana, North Dakota, Ohio, Oklahoma, Oregon, and Utah). Earlier in the year, President Bush had announced his support of a federal amendment with the same purpose but repeated attempts to get one through Congress have failed. Additional states passed laws or amendments by mid-2005, however, bringing the total to thirty-eight states banning legal recognition of same-sex couples.

For both liberal and radical GLBT activists marriage has been perhaps the ultimate symbol of the fundamental differences in their goals. For those seeking equality, marriage might very well be the "last frontier" both for GLBT people and for U.S. civil rights. When Bess Watts said, "We are the same as any other couple" in the story opening this chapter she expressed perfectly the desire to be treated equally under the law.

To many Americans, discrimination against any group was always a matter of fairness in a country where one was taught to expect fairness. For decades there had been other goals as well, and goals not represented by the right to marry. In his *Washington Post* article, "For Some, A Sanitized Movement" (March 31, 2004, p. A03), Michael Powell summarized the views of activists dismayed by the focus on marriage. "They wonder what happened," he wrote, "to championing sexual freedom and universal health care, and upending patriarchy?" Among those he quotes are Jim Eigo, who asked, "'What's the use of being queer if you can't be different?'" and William Dobbs, who told Powell, "'Our movement has become about lusting for weddings and lavender picket fences, . . . It's so embarrassing—I feel like turning in my gay card.'" These reactions have been channeled into fashioning a broader agenda, such as that described in "Beyond Same-Sex Marriage: A New Strategic Vision For All Our Families and Relationships" (http://www.beyondmarriage.org/index.html). "The time has come to reframe the narrow terms of the marriage debate in the United States," it begins, and states further:

> We must respond to the full scope of the conservative marriage agenda by building alliances across issues and constituencies. Our strategies must be visionary, creative, and practical to counter the right's powerful and effective use of marriage as a "wedge" issue that pits one group against another. The struggle for marriage rights should be part of a larger effort to strengthen the stability and security of diverse households and families.

Not surprisingly, the debate has also generated several books and much commentary. The collection edited by Andrew Sullivan, *Same-Sex Marriage, Pro and Con* was published in 1997 and then in 2004 three more books hit the market: *Why Marriage? The History Shaping Today's Debate Over Gay Equality,* by George Chauncey; *Gay Marriage: Why It Is Good for Gays, Good for Straights, and Good for America,* by Jonathan Rauch; and Evan Wolfson's *Why Marriage Matters: America, Equality, and Gay People's Right to Marry.* For those wanting additional reading by scholars the History News Network provides links to more than twenty-five relevant articles under "Gay Marriage" at http://hnn.us/articles/5216.html. It is unlikely that the topic will pass from the scene any time soon.

This book began with the question "Was Lincoln Gay?" and examined different answers (yes, no, not sure) as a way of introducing the complexities of GLBT U.S. history (see Chapter 1). To the question of Lincoln's sexuality we might add another, a version of "who cares?" or "why even ask?" Hopefully the necessity of acknowledging the presence and influence of GLBT people simply in the interest of historical truth is evident in this volume. That individuals not merely famous but respected might also not conform to heterosexuality (as understood in the 20th century) might cause a reevaluation of antigay sentiments. At the same time, there is an irony in the claims for Lincoln when there is equal or better evidence of the queerness of Lincoln's immediate predecessor, President James Buchanan. "In life," wrote James Loewen in *Lies Across America,* "Buchanan was not very far in the closet." He added that Buchanan and Senator William Rufus King (D-AL) lived together for years and were "inseparable," and quoted contemporaries calling King "Miss Nancy," "Aunt Fancy," and Buchanan's "better half" and "wife." This is presented in the context of his study of the ways U.S. historic sites present the past; in this case, when a staff member at Buchanan's Pennsylvania home was asked whether the former president was gay the reply was, "'He most definitely was not.'" Loewen suggested that this represents "bad history," as does the site's silence about Buchanan's pro-slavery politics. Further, though, is the possibility

A panel of the cartoon strip *Dykes to Watch Out For* by Alison Bechdel. In this installment, "Nostalgic Fallacy" (#483), Sydney perfectly captures the problems historians face in attempting to over-generalize the past. (© Alison Bechdel)

he raised that the two areas are connected—that, since King was a slaveholder, the Buchanan–King relationship likely had implications for U.S. domestic and foreign policies of a key era of American history.[11] So the issue seems not only whether we have had a gay president, but which president(s) they might have been. With figures like Lincoln, Washington, or Eleanor Roosevelt there is public outcry and denial on one side and the willingness of GLBT people to "claim" them on the other. When someone's legacy is less savory then the situation is reversed and accompanied by less publicity. If nothing else, these reactions are one gauge to the state of GLBT America at the beginning of the 21st century.

A natural sequel to the question of whether the United States has ever had a (closeted) gay president is whether it ever will have one *openly* GLBT (after all, there has yet to be an openly GLBT senator). Given the media fixation, as this book nears completion, of the possibility our next president will be a female, an African American, or a Mormon, one can only imagine the reaction if a candidate came out as anything but straight in the near future. This is not to say there has been no change—even "progress"—over the last hundred years. GLBT visibility may very well be here to stay and many mainstream goals are closer to fulfillment than seemed predictable even twenty years ago. However, as this book attempts to demonstrate, conditions and goals have varied widely, within GLBT communities and across eras, and progress is in the eye of the beholder. As Sydney of *Dykes to Watch Out For* remarks in the strip, "Nostalgic Fallacy," "Things were worse in the past, but also better." When the history of 21st-century GLBT life is written it may come to the same conclusion (though it probably will be titled differently); then again, maybe true progress will occur and the book will not be needed.

DEBATE: HOW USEFUL IS QUEER THEORY?

In 2005 at the annual "Lesbian Lives" conference hosted by University College Dublin a panel was devoted to the question, "Are We Post-Queer Yet? Does Queer Theory Have a Future?" Topics ranged from the term's various applications (as noun, adjective, verb) to the contributions of older theories and whether any remain relevant. Of necessity, the presentations and the discussion that followed were concerned as much with "queer" as with "post-queer." How do we determine if we are post-queer if we are not sure how to draw lines, so to speak, around queer? What the panel illustrated is that definitions and applications of queer are contested, with queer theory most representative of disputed ground. In subsequent conversations it was also clear that people's age and politics contribute to their ideas and reactions regarding queer theory.[12]

Queer theory is only about twenty-five years old. It arose in the political and social context of AIDS and amid the intellectual questioning within several disciplines then moving away from "modernism." This questioning eventually was lumped under the heading "postmodern" and included movements such as deconstruction in literature and poststructuralism in the social sciences. Most areas of study were soon affected, including the arts and even history. Terms varied but the movements had several core ideas in common: a rejection of objective truth— such as an essential "beauty" in art or a "fact" in history—that need only be discovered by a disinterested observer. Greater emphasis is placed on the act of interpretation as a way to understand power relations in society rather than as a means to a correct "reading" (of a book, a painting, a past event). Multiple perspectives, causing multiple interpretations, are analyzed, and cultural products (books, paintings, films, historical events, and even people can be "texts"), are presented as stories. About these stories we are encouraged to ask who is allowed to "tell" them, who is allowed to interpret them, and *in whose interest it is* to present a story in a particular way. In both history and politics these kinds of questions make notions of "progress" meaningless: things change but do not necessarily happen in a linear way (from "A" to "B") and do not necessarily get better or worse.

Not coincidentally, postmodernism developed in tandem with queer theory and by some of the same thinkers. Michel Foucault and Judith Butler, for example, have been important in both areas, contributing to what is called "destabilization" of categories, and consequently of previously accepted ideas of sex, gender, history, and political strategy. In particular, queer theory rejects the dualities of heterosexual/homosexual and masculine/feminine as human constants, promoting instead a continuum of possibilities limited only by the time and place one lives/ has lived. Gender is among those attributes that are *performed* though the performance may be unthinking and simply according to societal mores. As summarized by Annamarie Jagose, queer, as used theoretically, "focuses on mismatches between sex, gender and desire...[It] locates and exploits the incoherencies in those three terms which stabilise heterosexuality. Demonstrating the impossibility of any 'natural' sexuality, it calls into question even such apparently unproblematic terms as 'man' and 'woman.'"[13] The primary target, as coined by queer theorists, is "heteronormativity" and they emphasize that it is a standard not universal but created over time for the purposes of people in power.

Disputes over queer theory often focus on practical politics and just as often fall along generational lines (as noted in Chapter 1, the term queer itself is problematic to many people, especially those old enough to remember it in the context of national Cold War paranoia against homosexuals). Lesbian and queer theorists sometimes divide by age and (to lesbians) sex/gender: at the Dublin conference, for example, lesbians over forty that identified with lesbian feminism (see Chapter 6) were more likely to critique queer theory. In fact, some older activists see theory in general as less productive than action in the "real world." Among lesbian feminists there is a sense that queer theorists ignore or dismiss the contributions of lesbian feminist theory (especially in its pioneering critiques of "compulsory heterosexuality" and gender). Some lesbian feminists also object to erasing men and women as meaningful categories, and many older thinkers and doers, male and female, question whether queer is too broad and diffuse a concept to be usable politically.

Critics of queer theory are most concerned, perhaps, with its potential applications in a political world based on the identity politics of the 20th century (see Chapter 4). Queer theory is political, though, and its great potential lies in its vision of true sex and gender liberation. That liberation rests on the idea of fluid rather than fixed genders and sexualities, and on eliminating regulation of bodies by government rather than lobbying for more equal treatment of the categories gay, lesbian, bisexual, and transgendered. In queer theory, all laws eventually fall short (or are in danger of repeal) while to those schooled in identity politics, liberals and radicals, queer theory not only is less applicable to everyday life but also could undermine the gains made in protecting GLBT people from harassment, discrimination, and violence. Undoubtedly the debate will continue and it remains to be seen when and how queer and "post-queer" theory will be developed and used.

NOTES

1. Quotes taken from two articles: Christine Carrie Fien, "'We Are the Same as Any Other Couple,'" *Gates-Chili Post,* May 5, 2004, 1A, 6A; and Jim Memmott, "Women Denied License Will Marry Today Anyway," *Democrat and Chronicle,* April 29, 2004, 1A, 10A.

2. Statement made September 13, 2001; Falwell did retract his remarks later that day, according to CNN article, "Falwell Apologizes to Gays, Feminists, Lesbians," September 14, 2001 (http://archives.cnn.com/2001/US/09/14/Falwell.apology/).

3. "Why You Should Ignore the 'Millennium March'," *Off Our Backs,* October 1998 (http://findarticles.com/p/articles/mi_qa3693/is_199810/ai_n8825099).

4. Walter L. Williams and Yolanda Retter, eds., *Gay and Lesbian Rights in the United States: A Documentary History* (Westport, CT: Greenwood Press, 2003), 282–84.

5. Stephen Tropiano defines the "gaycom" in *The Prime Time Closet: A History of Gays and Lesbians on TV* (New York: Applause Books, 2002), 245.

6. Mark Simpson, "Meet the Metrosexual—He's Well Dressed, Narcissistic and Obsessed with Butts. But Don't Call Him Gay," Salon.com, July 22, 2002, at http://dir.salon.com/story/ent/feature/2002/07/22/metrosexual/index.html.

7. Hank Stuever, "The Bomb with a Loaded Message: For Gays in America, Even Heroism Isn't a Ticket to Inclusion," *The Washington Post,* October 27, 2001, C1.

8. Quoted in Kevin Jennings, ed., *Becoming Visible: A Reader in Gay & Lesbian History for High School & College Students* (Boston: Alyson Publications, 1994), 232.

9. *Lawrence v. Texas* (02-102) 539 U.S. 558 (2003), at http://www.law.cornell.edu/supct/html/02-102.ZS.html.

10. *The Washington Post,* July 13, 2003, B03, at http://www.sodomylaws.org/usa/usnews089.htm. Also see George Chauncey, "'What Gay Studies Taught the Court': The Historians' Amicus Brief in *Lawrence v. Texas,*" *GLQ: A Journal of Lesbian and Gay Studies* 10, no. 3 (2004): 509–38.

11. James W. Loewen, *Lies Across America: What Our Historic Sites Get Wrong* (New York: The New Press, 1999), 367–70.

12. This author participated in that panel, with "The Incredible Shrinking Lesbian: Salvaging Lesbian Feminism for (Post) Queer Studies."

13. Annamarie Jagose, *Queer Theory: An Introduction* (New York: New York University Press, 1996), 3.

SUGGESTED RESOURCES

Chauncey, G. (2004). *Why marriage? The history shaping today's debate over gay equality.* New York: Basic Books.

Eaklor, V.L. (1998, July). Learning from history: A queer problem. *Journal of Gay, Lesbian, and Bisexual Identity, 3*(3), 195–211.

Eaklor, V.L. (2001). Where have we been, where are we going, and who gets to say? In A.M. Black (Ed.), *Modern American queer history* (pp. 285–299). Philadelphia: Temple University Press.

Morland, I., & Willox, A. (Eds.). (2005). *Queer theory.* New York: Palgrave Macmillan.

Rauch, J. (2004). *Gay marriage: Why it is good for gays, good for straights, and good for America.* New York: Times Books.

Sullivan, A. (1997). *Same-sex marriage, pro and con: A reader.* New York: Vintage Books.

Wolfson, E. (2004). *Why marriage matters: America, equality, and gay people's right to marry.* New York: Simon & Schuster.

BIBLIOGRAPHY

ANTHOLOGY, PRIMARY, REFERENCE

Abelove, H. (Ed.). (1993). *The lesbian and gay studies reader*. New York: Routledge.

Beam, J. (Ed.). (1986). *In the life: A black gay anthology*. Boston: Alyson Publications.

Bergman, D. (1994). *The violet quill reader*. New York: St. Martin's Press.

Blasius, M., & Phelan, S. (Eds.). (1997). *We are everywhere: A historical sourcebook of gay and lesbian politics*. New York: Routledge.

Comstock, G.D., & Henking, S.E. (Eds.). (1997). *Que(e)rying religion: A critical anthology*. New York: Continuum Publishing.

Currah, P., & Minter, S. (2000). *Transgender equality: A handbook for activists and policymakers*. New York: Policy Institute of the National Gay and Lesbian Task Force.

Denny, D. (1994). *Gender dysphoria: A guide to research*. New York: Garland Publishing.

Dynes, W.R. (Ed.). (1990). *Encyclopedia of homosexuality*. New York: Garland Publishing.

Fletcher, L.Y., & Saks, A. (1990). *Lavender lists: New lists about lesbian and gay culture, history, and personalities*. Boston: Alyson Publications.

Hogan, S., & Hudson, L. (1998). *Completely queer: The gay and lesbian encyclopedia*. New York: Henry Holt.

Johnson, E.P., & Henderson, M.G. (Eds.). (2005). *Black queer studies: A critical anthology*. Durham: Duke University Press.

Katz, J.N. (1983). *Gay/lesbian almanac: A new documentary*. New York: Harper & Row.

Katz, J.N. (1992). *Gay American history: Lesbians and gay men in the U.S.A.* (Rev. ed.). New York: Penguin Meridian.

Leyland, W. (Ed.). (1991). *Gay roots: Twenty years of gay sunshine: An anthology of gay history, sex, politics, and culture*. San Francisco: Gay Sunshine Press.

Morgan, R. (Ed.). (1970). *Sisterhood in powerful: An anthology of writings from the women's liberation movement*. New York: Vintage Books.

Ochs, R. (Ed.). (2001). *Bisexual resource guide* (4th ed.). Boston: Bisexual Resource Center.

Ridinger, R.B.M. (Ed.). (2004). *Speaking for our lives: Historic speeches and rhetoric for gay and lesbian rights (1892–2000)*. Binghamton, NY: Haworth Press.

Roscoe, W. (Ed.). (1988). *Living the spirit: A gay American Indian anthology*. New York: St. Martin's Press.

Rutledge, L.W. (1992). *The gay decades*. New York: Plume.

Sanlo, R.L. (Ed.). (1998). *Working with lesbian, gay, bisexual, and transgender college students: A handbook for faculty and administrators.* Westport, CT: Greenwood Press.

Smith, B. (Ed.). (1983). *Home girls: A black feminist anthology.* New York: Kitchen Table Women of Color Press.

Stein, M. (Ed.). (2004). *Encyclopedia of lesbian, gay, bisexual, and transgender history in America.* Detroit, MI: Gale.

Williams, W.L., & Retter, Y. (Eds.). (2003). *Gay and lesbian rights in the United States: A documentary history.* Westport, CT: Greenwood Press.

Witt, L., Thomas, S., & Marcus, E. (Eds.). (1995). *Out in all directions: The almanac of gay and lesbian America.* Collingdale, PA: Diane Publishing.

Zimmerman, B. (Ed.). (2000). *Lesbian histories and cultures: An encyclopedia.* New York: Garland Publishing.

glbtq: An encyclopedia of gay, lesbian, bisexual, transgender, and queer culture. http://www.glbtq.com

ARTICLES, BOOKS, PAPERS

Abbott, S., & Love, B. (1972). *Sappho was a right-on woman: A liberated view of lesbianism.* New York: Scarborough House.

Abelove, H. (2003). *Deep gossip.* Minneapolis: University of Minnesota Press.

Adam, B.D. (1995). *The rise of a gay and lesbian movement* (Rev. ed.). New York: Twayne Publishers.

Albertson, C. (1972). *Bessie.* New York: Stein and Day.

Aldrich, R. (Ed.). (2006). *Gay life and culture: A world history.* New York: Universe Publishing.

Allen, P.G. (1986). *The sacred hoop: Recovering the feminine in American Indian traditions.* Boston: Beacon Press.

Anderson, E. (2005). *In the game: Gay athletes and the cult of masculinity.* Albany, NY: SUNY Press.

Andriote, J.-M. (1999). *Victory deferred: How AIDS changed gay life in America.* Chicago: University of Chicago Press.

Angelides, S. (2001). *A history of bisexuality.* Chicago: University of Chicago Press.

AP. (1981, June 6). A pneumonia that strikes gay males. *The San Francisco Chronicle,* p. 4.

Armstrong, E. (2002). *Forging gay identities: Organizing sexuality in San Francisco, 1950–1994.* Chicago: University of Chicago Press.

Armstrong, E.A., & Crage, S.M. (2006). Movements and memory: The making of the Stonewall myth. *American Sociological Review, 71*(5), 724–751.

Atkins, G.L. (2003). *Gay seattle: Stories of exile and belonging.* Seattle: University of Washington Press.

Atkinson, T.-G. (1974). *Amazon odyssey.* New York: Links Books.

Avila-Saavedra, G. (2006, August). *The construction of queer memory: Media coverage of Stonewall 25.* Paper delivered at the Association for Education in Journalism and Mass Communication, San Francisco. Accessed at http://list.msu.edu/cgi-bin/wa?A2=ind0610d&L=aejmc&P=2281.

Bad Object-Choices. (Ed.). (1991). *How do I look? Queer film and video.* Seattle, WA: Bay Press.

Bauman, R.E. (1986). *The gentleman from Maryland: The conscience of a gay conservative.* New York: William Morrow.

Bawer, B. (1993). *A place at the table: The gay individual in society.* New York: Poseidon.

Bean, B. (2003). *Going the other way: Lessons from a life in and out of major league baseball.* New York: Marlowe & Co.

Beemyn, B. (Ed.). (1997). *Creating a place for ourselves: Lesbian, gay, and bisexual community histories.* New York: Routledge.

Bell, A. (1971). *Dancing the gay lib blues: A year in the homosexual liberation movement.* New York: Simon & Schuster.

Benemann, W. (2006). *Male-male intimacy in early America: Beyond romantic friendships.* Binghamton, NY: Harrington Park Press.

Benshoff, H.M., & Griffin, S. (2006). *Queer images: A history of gay and lesbian film in America.* Lanham, MD: Rowman & Littlefield.

Bergman, D. (1991). *Gaiety transfigured: Gay self-representation in American literature.* Madison: University of Wisconsin Press.

Bérubé, A. (1990). *Coming out under fire: The history of gay men and women in World War Two.* New York: The Free Press.

Black, A.M. (Ed.). (2001). *Modern American queer history.* Philadelphia: Temple University Press.

Boag, P. (2003). *Same-sex affairs: Constructing and controlling homosexuality in the Pacific Northwest.* Berkeley: University of California Press.

Boag, P. (2004, Spring). 'Does Portland Need a Homophile Society?' Gay culture and activism in the Rose City between World War II and Stonewall. *Oregon Historical Quarterly, 105,* 6–39.

Boag, P. (2005, Winter). Go west young man, go east young woman: Searching for the *Trans* in western gender history. *Western Historical Quarterly, 36,* 477–497.

Bornstein, K. (1994). *Gender outlaw: On men, women and the rest of us.* New York: Routledge.

Boyd, N.A. (2003). *Wide open town: A history of queer San Francisco to 1965.* Berkeley: University of California Press.

Boykin, K. (1996). *One more river to cross: Black & gay in America.* New York: Doubleday.

Boykin, K., & Harris, E.L. (2005). *Beyond the down low: Sex, lies, and denial in Black America.* New York: Carroll & Graf.

Brenner, C. (with Ashley, H.) (1995). *Eight bullets: One woman's story of surviving anti-gay violence.* Ithaca, NY: Firebrand Books.

Bronski, M. (1998). *The pleasure principle: Sex, backlash, and the struggle for gay freedom.* New York: St. Martin's Press.

Bronski, M. (2003). *Pulp friction: Uncovering the golden age of gay male pulps.* New York: St. Martin's Press.

Bull, C. (Ed.). (2001). *Come out fighting: A century of essential writing on gay and lesbian liberation.* New York: Thunder's Mouth Press.

Bull, C., & Gallagher, J. (1996). *Perfect enemies: The battle between the religious right and the gay movement.* New York: Crown Publishing.

Bullough, V.L. (1994). *Science in the bedroom: A history of sex research.* New York: Basic Books.

Bullough, V.L. (Ed.). (2002). *Before Stonewall: Activists for gay and lesbians rights in historical context.* Binghamton, NY: Harrington Park Press.

Bullough, V.L., & Bullough, B. (1993). *Cross dressing: Sex and gender.* Philadelphia: University of Pennsylvania Press.

Burg, B.R. (1995). *Sodomy and the pirate tradition.* New York: New York University Press.

Burgess, L.C. (Ed.). (1994). *An uncommon soldier: The Civil War letters of Sarah Rosetta Wakeman, alias Private Lyons Wakeman, 153rd Regiment, New York State Volunteers, 1862–1864.* New York: Oxford University Press.

Burke, G., Sherman, E., & Sherman, M. (1995). *Home: The Glenn Burke story.* Manchester, UK: Excel Publishing.

Butler, J. (1990). *Gender trouble: Feminism and the subversion of identity.* New York: Routledge.

Cain, P.A. (1993, October). Litigating for lesbian and gay rights: A legal history. *Virginia Law Review, 79*(7), Symposium on Sexual Orientation and the Law, 1551–1641.

Cain, P.A. (2000). *Rainbow rights: The role of lawyers and courts in the lesbian and gay civil rights movement.* New York: Westview Press.

Califia, P. (2003). *Sex changes: The politics of transgenderism* (2nd ed.). San Francisco: Cleis Press.

Capsuto, S. (2000). *Alternate channels: The uncensored story of gay and lesbian images on radio and television.* New York: Ballantine Books.

Carby, H. (1987). It jus be's dat way sometime: The sexual politics of women's blues. *Radical America, 20*(4), 9–22.

Carter, D. (2004). *Stonewall: The riots that sparked the gay revolution.* New York: St. Martin's Press.

Charles, C. (2003). *The Sharon Kowalski case: Lesbian and gay rights on trial.* Lawrence: University Press of Kansas.

Chasin, A. (2000). *Selling out: The gay and lesbian movement goes to market.* New York: Palgrave.

Chauncey, G. (1994). *Gay New York: Gender, urban culture, and the making of the gay male world 1890–1940.* New York: Basic Books.

Chauncey, G. (2004). *Why marriage? The history shaping today's debate over gay equality.* New York: Basic Books.

Clendinen, D., & Nagourney, A. (1999). *Out for good: The struggle to build a gay rights movement in America.* New York: Simon & Schuster.

Constantine-Simms, D. (Ed.). (2001). *The greatest taboo: Homosexuality in black communities.* Boston: Alyson Publications.

Cook, B.W. (1993). *Eleanor Roosevelt.* New York: Penguin Books.

Cooney, C. (2005). 'Prove It On Me' migration, urbanization and the making of an autonomous, black lesbian culture. Unpublished paper.

Corber, R.J. (1997). *Homosexuality in Cold War America: Resistance and the crisis of masculinity.* Durham: Duke University Press.

Cory, D.W. [Edward Sagarin]. (1951). *The homosexual in America: A subjective approach.* New York: Greenberg Press.

Cruikshank, M. (Ed.). (1982). *Lesbian studies: Present and future.* Old Westbury, NNY: Feminist Press.

Cruikshank, M. (1992). *The gay and lesbian liberation movement.* New York: Routledge.

Dahl, L. (1984). *Stormy weather: The music and lives of a century of Jazzwomen.* New York: Pantheon Books.

Daly, M. (1973). *Beyond God the Father: Toward a philosophy of women's liberation.* Boston: Beacon Press.

Daly, M. (1978). *Gyn/ecology: The metaethics of radical feminism.* Boston: Beacon Press.

Dangerous Bedfellows. (Eds.). (1996). *Policing public sex: Queer politics and the future of AIDS activism.* Boston: South End Press.

Davis, A.Y. (1998). *Blues legacies and black feminism: Gertrude "Ma" Rainey, Bessie Smith, and Billie Holiday.* New York: Vintage Books.

DeBold, K. (Ed.). (1994). *Out for office: Campaigning in the gay nineties.* Washington, DC: Gay and Lesbian Victory Fund.

Deford, F. (1976). *Big Bill Tilden: The triumphs and the tragedy.* New York: Simon & Schuster.

D'Emilio, J. (1992). *Making trouble: Essays on gay history, politics, and the university.* New York: Routledge.

D'Emilio, J. (1983, 1998). *Sexual politics, sexual communities: The making of a homosexual minority in the United States, 1940–1970.* Chicago: University of Chicago Press.

D'Emilio, J. (2002). *The world turned: Essays on gay history, politics, and culture.* Durham: Duke University Press.

D'Emilio, J. (2004). *Lost prophet: The life and times of Bayard Rustin.* Chicago: University of Chicago Press.

D'Emilio, J., & Freedman, E.B. (1989). *Intimate matters: A history of sexuality in America.* New York: Harper Perennial.

D'Emilio, J., Turner, W.B., & Vaid, U. (Eds.). (2000). *Creating Change™: Sexuality, public policy, and civil rights.* New York: St. Martin's Press.

Dews, C.L., & Law, C.L. (Eds.). (2001). *Out in the south.* Philadelphia: Temple University Press.

Duberman, M. (1986). *About time: Exploring the gay past.* New York: Gay Presses of New York.

Duberman, M. (1991). *Cures: A gay man's odyssey.* New York: Dutton.

Duberman, M. (1993). *Stonewall.* New York: Plume.

Duberman, M. (1996). *Midlife queer: Autobiography of a decade 1971–1981.* Madison: University of Wisconsin Press.

Duberman, M., Vicinus, M., & Chauncey, G., Jr. (Eds.). (1989). *Hidden from history: Reclaiming the gay and lesbian past.* New York: New American Library.

Duggan, L. (2000). *Sapphic slashers: Sex, violence, and American modernity.* Durham: Duke University Press.

Duggan, L., & Hunter, N.D. (1995). *Sex wars: Sexual dissent and political culture.* New York: Routledge.

Eaklor, V.L. (Ed.). (1994, Summer). Lesbian histories. Special issue, *Historical Reflections/ Réflexions Historiques, 20*(2), 165–333.

Eaklor, V.L. (1998, July). Learning from history: A queer problem. *Journal of Gay, Lesbian, and Bisexual Identity, 3*(3), 195–211.

Edmonds, S.E. (1999). *Memoirs of a soldier, nurse, and spy: A woman's adventures in the Union Army (1865).* DeKalb, IL: Northern Illinois University Press.

Ehrenstein, D. (1998). *Open secret: Gay hollywood 1928–2000.* New York: William Morrow.

Endean, S. (2006). *Bringing lesbian and gay rights into the mainstream.* (Vicki L. Eaklor, Ed.). Binghamton, NY: Haworth Press.

Epstein, J., & Straub, K. (Eds.). (1991). *Body guards: The cultural politics of gender ambiguity.* New York: Routledge.

Erenberg, L. (1981). *Steppin' out: New York nightlife and the transformation of American culture, 1890–1930.* Chicago: University of Chicago Press.

Eskridge, W.N., Jr. (1999). *Gaylaw: Challenging the apartheid of the closet.* Cambridge, MA: Harvard University Press.

Estes, S. (2005). Ask and tell: Gay veterans, identity, and oral history on a civil rights frontier. *Oral History Review, 32*(2), 21–47.

Estes, S. (2007). *Ask & tell: Gay and lesbian veterans speak out.* Chapel Hill: University of North Carolina Press.

Evans, N.J., & Wall, V.A. (Eds.). (1991). *Beyond tolerance: Gays, lesbians, and bisexuals on campus.* Alexandria, VA: American College Personnel Association.

Faderman, L. (1981). *Surpassing the love of men: Romantic friendship and love between women from the Renaissance to the present.* New York: William Morrow.

Faderman, L. (1992). *Odd girls and twilight lovers: A history of lesbian life in twentieth-century America.* New York: Penguin Books.

Faderman, L. (1999). *To believe in women: What lesbians have done for America—a history.* Boston: Houghton Mifflin.

Faderman, L. (2003). *Naked in the promised land: A memoir.* Boston: Houghton Mifflin.

Faderman, L., & Timmons, S. (2006). *Gay L. A.: A history of sexual outlaws, power politics, and lipstick lesbians.* New York: Basic Books.

Feinberg, L. (1992). *Transgender liberation: A movement whose time has come.* New York: World View Forum.

Feinberg, L. (1996). *Transgender warriors: Making history from Joan of Arc to Rupaul.* Boston: Beacon Press.

Fellows, W. (1996). *Farm boys: Lives of gay men from the rural midwest.* Madison: University of Wisconsin Press.

Firestein, B. (1996). *Bisexuality: The psychology and politics of an invisible minority.* Thousand Oaks, CA: Sage Publications.

Firestone, S. (1970). *The dialectic of sex: The case for feminist revolution.* New York: William Morrow.

Forrest, K.V. (2005). *Lesbian pulp fiction: The sexually intrepid world of lesbian paperback novels 1950–1965.* San Francisco: Cleis Press.

Foster, J. (1956). *Sex variant women in literature: A historical and quantitative survey.* New York: Vantage Press.

Foster, T.A. (2006). *Sex and the eighteenth-century man: Massachusetts and the history of sexuality in America.* Boston: Beacon Press.

Foucault, M. (1980). *The history of sexuality, volume I: An introduction.* New York: Vintage Books.

Foucault, M. (1990). *The history of sexuality, vol. II: The use of pleasure.* New York: Vintage Books.

Fout, J.C., & Tantillo, M.S. (Eds.). (1993). *American sexual politics: Sex, gender, and race since the civil war.* Chicago: University of Chicago Press.

Fuss, D. (1991). *Inside/out: Lesbian theories, gay theories.* New York: Routledge.

Gallo, M.M. (2006). *Different daughters: A history of the Daughters of Bilitis and the rise of the lesbian rights movement.* New York: Carroll & Graf.

Gamson, J. (1998). *Freaks talk back: Tabloid talk shows and sexual nonconformity.* Chicago: University of Chicago Press.

Garber, M. (1991). *Vested interests: Cross dressing and cultural anxiety.* New York: Routledge.

Gerassi, J. (1966, 2001). *The Boys of Boise: Furor, vice, and folly in an American city.* New York: Macmillan; Seattle: University of Washington Press.

Gingrich, C. (with Bull, C.) (1997). *The accidental activist: A personal and political memoir.* New York: Touchstone.

Gorman, M.R. (1998). *The empress is a man: Stories from the life and times of Jose Sarria.* Binghamton, NY: Haworth Press.

Grahn, J. (1980). *The work of a common woman: The collected poetry of Judy Grahn, 1964–1977.* New York: St. Martin's Press.

Grahn, J. (1984). *Another mother tongue: Gay words, gay worlds.* Boston: Beacon Press.

Greenberg, D.F. (1990). *The construction of homosexuality.* Chicago: University of Chicago Press.

Grier, B. (1981). *The lesbian in literature* (New rev. 3rd ed.). Tallahassee, FL: Naiad Press.

Griffin, H.L. (2006). *Their own receive them not: African American lesbians and gays in black churches.* Cleveland, OH: The Pilgrim Press.

Gross, L. (1993). *Contested closets: The politics and ethics of outing.* Minneapolis: University of Minnesota Press.

Gross, L. (2002). *Up from invisibility: Lesbians, gay men, and the media in America.* New York: Columbia University Press.

Gustav-Wrathall, J.D. (1998). *Take the young stranger by the hand: Same-sex relations and the YMCA.* Chicago: University of Chicago Press.

Hadleigh, B. (1994). *Hollywood lesbians.* New York: Barricade Books.

Hadleigh, B. (2001). *The lavender screen: The gay and lesbian films—their stars, makers, characters, and critics.* New York: Citadel Press.

Halberstam, J. (2005). *In a queer time and place: Transgender bodies, subcultural lives.* New York: New York University Press.

Halley, J. (1999). *Don't: A reader's guide to the military's anti-gay policy.* Durham: Duke University Press.

Halperin, D.M. (2004). *How to do the history of homosexuality.* Chicago: University of Chicago Press.

Handy, D.A. (1998). *The International Sweethearts of Rhythm: The ladies jazz band from Piney Woods Country Life School* (Rev. ed.). Lanham, MD: The Scarecrow Press.

Hansen, K.V. (1995, August). 'No Kisses Is Like Youres': An erotic friendship between two African-American women during the mid-nineteenth century. *Gender and History, 7,* 153–182.

Harris, D. (1997). *The rise and fall of gay culture.* New York: Hyperion.

Harwood, G. (1997). *The oldest gay couple in America: A seventy-year journey through same-sex America.* New York: Birch Lane Press.

Hatheway, J. (2003). *The gilded age construction of modern American homophobia.* New York: Palgrave Macmillan.

Hawkeswood, W.G. (1996). *One of the children: Gay black men in Harlem.* (A.W. Costley, Ed.). Berkeley: University of California Press.

Hemphill, E. (Ed.). (1991). *Brother to brother: New writings by black gay men.* Boston: Alyson Publications.

Holcomb, G.E. (2007). *Claude McKay, code name Sasha: Queer black marxism and the Harlem Renaissance.* Gainesville: University Press of Florida.

Holobaugh, J. (with Hale, K.) (1993). *Torn allegiances: The story of a gay cadet.* Boston: Alyson Publications.

hooks, b. (1981). *Ain't I a woman: Black women and feminism.* Boston: South End Press.

Howard, J. (Ed.). (1997). *Carryin' on in the lesbian and gay south.* New York: New York University Press.

Howard, J. (1999). *Men like that: A southern queer history.* Chicago: University of Chicago Press.

Hubbs, N. (2004). *The queer composition of America's sound: Gay modernists, American music, and national identity.* Berkeley: University of California Press.

Humphrey, M.A. (1990). *My country, my right to serve: Experiences of gay men and women in the military, World War II to the present.* New York: HarperCollins.

Humphreys, L. (1972). *Out of the closets: The sociology of homosexual liberation.* Englewood Cliffs, NJ: Prentice Hall.

Hunter, T. (with Muller, E.) (2005). *Tab hunter confidential: The making of a movie star.* Chapel Hill, NC: Algonquin Books.

Hutchins, L., & Kaahumanu, L. (Eds.). (1991). *Bi any other name: Bisexual people speak out.* Boston: Alyson Publications.

Irvine, J.M. (1990). *Disorders of desire: Sex and gender in modern American sexology.* Philadelphia: Temple University Press.

Jackson, R., & Paris, B. (1994). *Straight from the heart: A love story.* New York: Warner Books.

Jacobs, S.-E., Thomas, W., & Lang, S. (Eds.). (1997). *Two-spirit people: Native American gender identity, sexuality, and spirituality.* Urbana: University of Illinois Press.

Jagose, A. (1996). *Queer theory: An introduction.* New York: New York University Press.

Jay, K. (2000). *Tales of the lavender menace: A memoir of liberation.* New York: Basic Books.

Jay, K., & Young, A. (Eds.). (1992). *Out of the closets: Voices of gay liberation (1972).* New York: New York University Press.

Jennings, K. (Ed.). (1994). *Becoming visible: A reader in gay & lesbian history for high school & college students.* Boston: Alyson Publications.

Johnson, D.K. (2004). *The lavender scare: The cold war persecution of gays and lesbians in the federal government.* Chicago: University of Chicago Press.

Johnson, S.L. (2001). *Roaring camp: The social world of the California Gold Rush.* New York: W.W. Norton.

Johnston, J. (1973). *Lesbian nation: The feminist solution.* New York: Simon & Schuster.

Jones, A. (1996). *All she wanted.* New York: Pocket Books.

Jorgensen, C. (with a new introduction by Stryker, S.). (2000). *Christine Jorgensen: A personal autobiography* (2nd ed.). San Francisco: Cleis Press.

Kaiser, C. (1997). *The gay metropolis, 1940–1996.* Boston: Houghton Mifflin.

Katz, J.N. (1995). *The invention of heterosexuality.* New York: Dutton.

Katz, J. (2001). *Love stories: Sex between men before homosexuality.* Chicago: University of Chicago Press.

Kehoe, M. (Ed.). (1986). *Historical, literary, and erotic aspects of lesbianism.* New York: Harrington Park Press.

Kennedy, E., & Davis, M. (1993). *Boots of leather, slippers of gold: The history of a lesbian community.* New York: Routledge.

Kepner, J. (1998). *Rough news, daring views: 1950's pioneer gay press journalism.* Binghamton, NY: Haworth Press.

King, J.L. (2004). *On the down low: A journey into the lives of "straight" black men who sleep with men.* New York: Broadway Books.

Kirk, M., & Madsen, H. (1990). *After the ball: How America will conquer its fear & hatred of gays in the 90s.* New York: Plume.

Knutson, D.C. (Ed.). (1979). *Homosexuality and the law.* Binghamton, NY: Haworth Press.

Kopay, D. (1977). *The David Kopay story: An extraordinary self-revelation.* New York: Arbor House.

Kornfeld, E. (1997). *Margaret Fuller: A brief biography with documents.* Boston: Bedford Books.

Krahulik, K.C. (2005). *Provincetown: From pilgrim landing to gay resort.* New York: New York University Press.

Legg, W.D. (1994). *Homophile studies in theory and practice.* San Francisco: GLB Publishers and ONE Institute Press.

Lehman, C. (2007). Polemical science: 'Gay Gene' theory and the subversion of progressive feminist politics. Unpublished paper.

Leong, R. (Ed.). (1995). *Asian American sexualities: Dimensions of the gay and lesbian experience.* New York: Routledge.

LeVay, S. (1996). *Queer science: The use and abuse of research into homosexuality.* Cambridge, MA: MIT Press.

Lorde, A. (1982). *Zami: A new spelling of my name.* Freedom, CA: Crossing Press.

Lorde, A. (1984). *Sister outsider.* Freedom, CA: Crossing Press.

Louganis, G. (with Marcus, E.). (1995). *Breaking the surface.* New York: Random House.

Loughery, J. (1998). *The other side of silence: Men's lives and gay identities: A twentieth-century history.* New York: Henry Holt.

Madsen, A. (1995). *The sewing circle, Hollywood's greatest secret: Female stars who loved other women.* Secaucus, NJ: Carol Publishing Group.

Mann, W.J. (2002). *Behind the screen: How gays and lesbians shaped Hollywood, 1910–1969.* New York: Penguin Books.

Marcus, E. (2002). *Making gay history: The half-century fight for lesbian and gay equal rights.* New York: Harper Perennial.

Martin, D., & Lyon, P. (1983). *Lesbian/woman* (Rev. ed.). New York: Bantam Books.

Maupin, A. (1989). *Sure of you.* New York: Harper & Row.

McCaffrey, J.A. (Ed.). (1972). *The homosexual dialectic.* Englewood Cliffs, NJ: Prentice-Hall.

McCourt, J. (2003). *Queer street: The rise and fall of an American culture, 1947–1985.* New York: W.W. Norton.

McGarry, M., & Wasserman, F. (1998). *Becoming visible: An illustrated history of lesbian and gay life in twentieth-century America.* New York: Penguin Studio.

McLellan, D. (2000). *The girls: Sappho goes to Hollywood.* New York: St. Martin's Press.

Meeker, M. (2006). *Contacts desired: Gay and lesbian communications and community, 1940s–1970s.* Chicago: University of Chicago.

Meyer, L.D. (1996). *Creating G.I. Jane: Sexuality and power in the women's army corps during World War II.* New York: Columbia University Press.

Meyer, R. (2002). *Outlaw representation: Censorship and homosexuality in twentieth-century American art.* New York: Oxford University Press.

Meyerowitz, J. (2002). *How sex changed: A history of transsexuality in the United States.* Cambridge, MA: Harvard University Press.

Michael, R.T., Gagnon, J.H., Laumann, E.O., & Kolata, G. (1994). *Sex in America: A definitive survey.* Boston: Little, Brown.

Middlebrook, D.W. (1998). *Suits me: The double life of Billy Tipton.* Boston: Houghton Mifflin.

Miller, M. (1971). *On being different: What it means to be homosexual.* New York: Random House.

Miller, N. (1990). *In search of gay America: Women and men in a time of change.* New York: Harper & Row.

Miller, N. (2002). *Sex-crime panic: A journey to the paranoid heart of the 1950s.* Boston: Alyson Publications.

Millett, K. (1970). *Sexual politics.* New York: Doubleday.

Minton, H.L. (2002). *Departing from deviance: A history of homosexual rights and emancipatory science in America.* Chicago: University of Chicago Press.

Mixner, D. (1996). *Stranger among friends.* New York: Bantam Books.

Moraga, C., & Anzaldúa, G. (Eds.). (1981). *This bridge called my back: Writings by radical women of color.* New York: Kitchen Table Press.

Morland, I., & Willox, A. (Eds.). (2005). *Queer theory.* New York: Palgrave Macmillan.

Morris, B.J. (1999). *Eden built by Eves: The culture of women's music festivals.* Boston: Alyson Publications.

Murdoch, J., & Price, D. (2001). *Courting justice: Gay men and lesbians v. the Supreme Court.* New York: Basic Books.

Murphy, J. (1971). *Homosexual liberation: A personal view.* New York: Praeger Publishers.

Nestle, J. (1987). *A restricted country.* Ithaca, NY: Firebrand Books.

Nestle, J., Wilchins, R., & Howell, C. (Eds.). (2002). *Genderqueer: Voices from beyond the sexual binary.* Boston: Alyson Publications.

Newton, E. (1993). *Cherry Grove, Fire Island: Sixty years in America's first gay and lesbian town.* Boston: Beacon Press.

Newton, E. (2000). *Margaret Mead made me gay: Personal essays, public ideas.* Durham: Duke University Press.

Norton, R. (1997). *The myth of the modern homosexual: Queer history and the search for cultural unity.* London: Cassell.

Pallone, D. (with Steinberg, A.). (1990). *Behind the mask: My double life in baseball.* New York: Viking Press.

Peiss, K., & Simmons, C. (Eds.) (with Padgug, R.A.). (1989). *Passion and power: Sexuality in history.* Philadelphia: Temple University Press.

Perry, T.D. (with Swicegood, T.L.P.). (1990). *Don't be afraid anymore: The story of Reverend Troy Perry and the metropolitan community churches.* New York: St. Martin's Press.

Pharr, S. (1997). *Homophobia: A weapon of sexism.* Berkeley, CA: Chardon Press.

Plummer, D. (1999). *One of the boys: Masculinity, homophobia, and modern manhood.* Binghamton, NY: Harrington Park Press.

Pohlman, H.L. (1999). *The whole truth: A case of murder on the Appalachian trail.* Amherst: University of Massachusetts Press.

Poling, J.D. (2005, Spring). Standing up for gay rights. *Chicago History, 33,* 4–17.

Queen, C., & Schimel, L. (Eds.). (1997). *PoMoSexuals: Challenging assumptions about gender and sexuality.* San Francisco: Cleis Press.

Rader, R. (1983). *Breaking boundaries: Male/female friendship in early Christian communities.* New York: Paulist Press.

Rauch, J. (2004). *Gay marriage: Why it is good for gays, good for straights, and good for America.* New York: Times Books.

Rich, A. (1979). *On lies, secrets, and silence: Selected prose 1966–1978.* New York: W.W. Norton.

Rich, A. (1980, Summer). Compulsory heterosexuality and lesbian existence. *Signs: Journal of Women in Culture and Society, 5,* 631–660.

Richards, D.A.J. (2005). *The case for gay rights: From Bowers to Lawrence and beyond.* Lawrence: University Press of Kansas.

Richmond, L., & Noguera, G. (Eds.). (1973). *The gay liberation book.* San Francisco: Ramparts Press.

Ridinger, R.B.M. (2002). Things visible and invisible: The leather archives and museum. *Journal of Homosexuality, 43*(1), 1–9.

Rimmerman, C.A. (Ed.). (1996). *Gay rights, military wrongs: Political perspectives on lesbians and gays in the military.* New York: Garland Publishing.

Rimmerman, C.A. (2002). *From identity to politics: The lesbian and gay movements in the United States.* Philadelphia: Temple University Press.

Rofes, E. (1998). *Dry bones breathe: Gay men creating post-AIDS identities and cultures.* Binghamton, NY: Haworth Press.

Rofes, E. (2005). *A radical rethinking of sexuality and schooling: Status quo or status queer?* Lanham, MD: Rowman & Littlefield.

Roscoe, W. (1992). *The Zuni man-woman.* Albuquerque: University of New Mexico Press.

Roszak, B., and Roszak, T. (Eds.). (1969). *Masculine/feminine: Readings in sexual mythology and the liberation of women.* New York: Harper & Row.

Rothblum, E.D. (Ed.). (1996). *Classics in lesbian studies.* Binghamton, NY: Haworth Press.

Rubenstein, W.B. (Ed.). (1993). *Lesbians, gay men, and the law.* New York: New Press.

Rupp, L. (1999). *A desired past: A short history of same-sex love in America.* Chicago: University of Chicago Press.

Rupp, L., & Taylor, V. (2003). *Drag queens at the 801 Cabaret.* Chicago: University of Chicago Press.

Ruskin, C. (1988). *The QUILT: Stories from the NAMES project.* New York: Simon & Schuster.

Russell, I. (Ed.). (1993). *Jeb and Dash: A diary of gay life, 1918–1945.* London: Faber & Faber.

Russo, V. (1981; 1987). *The celluloid closet: Homosexuality in the movies.* New York: Harper & Row.

Rust, P.C.R. (Ed.). (1999). *Bisexuality in the United States: A social science reader.* New York: Columbia University Press.

Schulman, S. (1994). *My American history: Lesbian and gay life during the Reagan/Bush years.* New York: Routledge.

Schwarz, J. (1982). *Radical feminists of heterodoxy: Greenwich Village 1912–1940.* Lebanon, NH: New Victoria Publishers.

Scott, W., & Stanley, S.C. (Eds.). (1994). *Gays and lesbians in the military: Issues, concerns, and contrasts.* Piscataway, NJ: Transaction Publishers.

Sears, J.T. (1997). *Lonely hunters: An oral history of lesbian and gay southern life, 1948–1968.* New York: Westview Press.

Sears, J.T. (2001). *Rebels, rubyfruit, and rhinestones: Queering space in the Stonewall South.* Piscataway, NJ: Rutgers University Press.

Sears, J.T. (2007). *Behind the mask of the Mattachine: The Hal Call chronicles and the early movement for homosexual emancipation.* Binghamton, NY: Haworth Press.

Seidman, S. (2002). *Beyond the closet: The transformation of gay and lesbian life.* New York: Routledge.

Shilts, R. (1982). *The mayor of Castro Street: The life & times of Harvey Milk.* New York: St. Martin's Press.

Shilts, R. (1987). *And the band played on: Politics, people, and the AIDS epidemic.* New York: St. Martin's Press.

Shilts, R. (1993). *Conduct unbecoming: Gays and lesbians in the U.S. military.* New York: St. Martin's Press.

Signorile, M. (1993). *Queer in America: Sex, the media, and the closets of power.* New York: Random House.

Simmons, C. (1979). Companionate marriage and the lesbian threat. *Frontiers, 4*(3), 54–59.

Simmons, R., & DiMarco, D. (2005). *Out of bounds: Coming out of sexual abuse, addiction, and my life of lies in the NFL closet.* New York: Carroll & Graf.

Sinfield, A. (1999). *Out on stage: Lesbian and gay theatre in the twentieth century.* New Haven, CT: Yale University Press.

Smith, B. (2000). *The truth that never hurts: Writings on race, gender, and freedom.* Piscataway, NJ: Rutgers University Press.

Smith, P.J. (Ed.). (1999). *The queer sixties.* New York: Routledge.

Smith-Rosenberg, C. (1975). The female world of love and ritual: Relations between women in nineteenth-century America. *Signs, 1,* 1–29.

Somerville, S. (2000). *Queering the color line: Race and the invention of homosexuality in American culture.* Durham: Duke University Press.

Stannard, D.E. (1992). *American holocaust: Columbus and the conquest of the New World.* New York: Oxford University Press.

Stansell, C. (2000). *American moderns: Bohemian New York and the creation of a new century.* New York: Henry Holt.

Steffan, J. (1992). *Honor bound: A gay naval midshipman fights to serve his country.* New York: Villard Books.

Stein, M. (2004). *City of sisterly and brotherly loves: Lesbian and gay Philadelphia, 1945–1972.* Philadelphia: Temple University Press.

Stein, M. (2005, Fall). *Boutilier* and the U.S. Supreme Court's sexual revolution. *Law and History Review, 23*(3), 491–536.

Stepto, M., & Stepto, G. (Trans.). (1996). *Lieutenant Nun: Memoir of a Basque Transvestite in the New World.* Boston: Beacon Press.

Storr, M. (Ed.). (1999). *Bisexuality: A critical reader.* New York: Routledge.

Streitmatter, R. (1995). *Unspeakable: The rise of the gay and lesbian press in America.* Collingdale, PA: Diane Publishing.

Stryker, S. (2001). *Queer pulp: Perverted passions from the golden age of the paperback.* San Francisco: Chronicle Books.

Stryker, S., & Van Buskirk, J. (1996). *Gay by the bay: A history of queer culture in the San Francisco Bay area.* San Francisco: Chronicle Books.

Sullivan, A. (1995). *Virtually normal: An argument about homosexuality.* New York: Alfred A. Knopf.

Sullivan, A. (1997). *Same-sex marriage, pro and con: A reader.* New York: Vintage Books.

Sullivan, M.K. (Ed.). (2004). *Sexual minorities: Discrimination, challenges and development in America.* Binghamton, NY: Haworth Press.

Sullivan, N. (2003). *A critical introduction to queer theory.* New York: New York University Press.

Teal, D. (Ed.). (1971). *The gay militants.* New York: Stein and Day.

Terry, J. (1999). *An American obsession: Science, medicine, and homosexuality in modern society.* Chicago: University of Chicago Press.

Thompson, K., & Andrzejewski, J. (1989). *Why can't Sharon Kowalski come home?* San Francisco: Aunt Lute Books.

Thompson, M. (Ed.). (1994). *Long road to freedom: The advocate history of the gay and lesbian movement.* New York: St. Martin's Press.

Thompson, M. (Ed.). (2004). *Leatherfolk: Radical sex, people, politics, and practice.* Los Angeles: Daedalus Publishing.

Timmons, S. (1990). *The trouble with Harry Hay: Founder of the modern gay movement.* Boston: Alyson Publications.

Tobin, K., & Wicker, R. (1972). *The gay crusaders.* New York: Paperback Library.

Tocqueville, A. de. (1840; 1980). *Democracy in America.* New York: J. & H.G. Langley; New York: Alfred A. Knopf.

Trexler, R.C. (1995). *Sex and conquest: Gendered violence, political order, and the European conquest of the Americas.* Ithaca, NY: Cornell University Press.

Tripp, C.A. (2005). *The intimate world of Abraham Lincoln.* New York: The Free Press.

Tropiano, S. (2002). *The prime time closet: A history of gays and lesbians on TV.* New York: Applause Books.

Tuaolo, E. (2006). *Alone in the trenches: My life as a gay man in the NFL.* Naperville, IL: Sourcebooks.

Tucker, N. (Ed.). (1995). *Bisexual politics: Theories, queries, and visions.* Binghamton, NY: Harrington Park Press.

Turner, W.B. (2000). *A genealogy of queer theory.* Philadelphia: Temple University Press.

Vaid, U. (1995). *Virtual equality: The mainstreaming of gay & lesbian liberation.* New York: Doubleday.

Velazquez, L.J. (1972). *The woman in battle: A narrative of the exploits, adventures, and travels of Madame Loreta Janeta Velazquez (1876)* (C.J. Worthington, Ed.). New York: Arno Press.

Vicinus, M. (2004). *Intimate friends: Women who loved women, 1778–1928.* Chicago: University of Chicago Press.

Walters, S.D. (2001). *All the rage: The story of gay visibility in America.* Chicago: University of Chicago Press.

Warner, M. (1993). *Fear of a queer planet: Queer politics and social theory.* Minneapolis: University of Minnesota Press.

Warner, M. (1999). *The trouble with normal: Sex, politics, and the ethics of queer life.* New York: The Free Press.

Wat, E. (2002). *The making of a gay Asian community: An oral history of pre-AIDS Los Angeles.* Lanham, MD: Rowman & Littlefiled.

Weinberg, M.S., Williams, C.J., & Pryor, D.W. (Eds.). (1994). *Dual attraction: Understanding bisexuality.* New York: Oxford University Press.

Weiss, A. (1993). *Vampires and violets: Lesbians in film.* New York: Penguin Books.

Welter, B. (1966). The cult of true womanhood: 1820–1860. *American Quarterly, 18,* 151–174.

Werth, B. (2002). *The scarlet professor: Newton Arvin: A literary life shattered by scandal.* New York: Anchor Books.

Williams, W.L. (1986). *The spirit and the flesh: Sexual diversity in American Indian culture.* Boston: Beacon Press.

Williams, C.J., & Weinberg, M.S. (1971). *Homosexuals and the military: A study of less than honorable discharge.* New York: Harper & Row.

Wolfson, E. (2004). *Why marriage matters: America, equality, and gay people's right to marry.* New York: Simon & Schuster.

Woods, W.J., & Binson, D. (Eds.). (2003). *Gay bathhouses and public health policy.* Binghamton, NY: Harrington Park Press.

Woog, D. (1997). *Jocks: True stories of America's gay male athletes.* Boston: Alyson Publications.

Wright, L. (Ed.). (1997). *The bear book: Readings in the history and evolution of a gay male subculture.* New York: Harrington Park Press.

Wright, L. (Ed.). (2001). *The bear book II: Further readings in the history and evolution of a gay male subculture.* New York: Harrington Park Press.

Wright, L. (2004). Tangled memories of a wounded storyteller: Notes on bear history and cultural memory.*Torquere: Journal of the Canadian Lesbian and Gay Studies Association, 6,* 66–90.

Wright, W. (2005). *Harvard's secret court: The savage 1920 purge of campus homosexuals.* New York: St. Martin's Press.

Yeager, K. (1999). *Trailblazers: Profiles of America's gay and lesbian elected officials.* Binghamton, NY: Haworth Press.

Young, A.F. (2004). *Masquerade: The life and times of Deborah Sampson, continental soldier.* New York: Alfred A. Knopf.

Zimmerman, B., & McNaron, T.A.H. (Eds.). (1996). *The new lesbian studies: Into the twenty-first century.* New York: Feminist Press.

Zipter, Y. (1988). *Diamonds are a dyke's best friend: Reflections, reminiscences, and reports from the field on the lesbian national pastime.* Ithaca, NY: Firebrand Books.

FILM/VIDEO/DVD

This is not intended as an exhaustive list, but as suggestions for the interested viewer, and many are mentioned in the text. The focus is on U.S.-produced films with significant GLBT content. With a few exceptions they were made 1980–2005, and most are available on VHS or DVD.

The Adventures of Sebastian Cole (1998)
Advise and Consent (1962)
Alexander: The Other Side of Dawn (TV 1977)

And the Band Played On (TV 1993)

Andre's Mother (TV 1990)

Angels in America (TV 2003)

Any Mother's Son (TV 1997)

As Is (TV 1986)

The Badge (2002)

Basic Instinct (1992)

Beautiful Thing (1996)

The Birdcage (1996)

Bobbie's Girl (TV 2002)

Bound (1996)

Boys Don't Cry (1999)

The Boys in the Band (1970)

Boys on the Side (1995)

Breaking the Surface: The Greg Louganis Story (TV 1996)

Brokeback Mountain (2005)

Brother to Brother (2004)

Buddies (1985)

Capote (2005)

The Children's Hour (1961)

The Christine Jorgensen Story (1970)

Chutney Popcorn (1999)

Citizen Cohn (TV 1992)

Claire of the Moon (1992)

The Color Purple (1985)

Common Ground (TV 2000)

Consenting Adult (TV 1985)

Cruising (1980)

Desert Hearts (1985)

Dog Day Afternoon (1975)

Dressed To Kill (1980)

An Early Frost (TV 1985)

Ed Wood (1994)

Flawless (1999)

Fried Green Tomatoes (1991)

Further Tales of the City (TV 2001)

Gia (TV 1998)

A Girl Thing (TV 2001)

Glen or Glenda? (1953)

Go Fish (1994)

Gods and Monsters (1998)

Holiday Heart (TV 2000)

If These Walls Could Talk, 2 (TV 2000)

In & Out (1997)

In the Gloaming (TV 1997)

The Incredibly True Adventures of Two Girls in Love (1995)

Jack (TV 2004)

Jeffrey (1995)

The Killing of Sister George (1968)

Lianna (1983)

Longtime Companion (1990)

Love! Valour! Compassion! (1997)

Making Love (1982)

The Matthew Shepard Story (TV 2002)
More Tales of the City (TV 1998)
My Own Private Idaho (1991)
Myra Breckinridge (1970)
Normal (TV 2003)
Our Sons (TV 1991)
Parting Glances (1986)
Personal Best (1982)
Philadelphia (1993)
Prick Up Your Ears (1987)
The Rocky Horror Picture Show (1975)
Roommates (TV 1994)
Salmonberries (1991)
Saving Face (2004)
Second Serve (TV 1986)
Serving in Silence: The Margarethe Cammermeyer Story (TV 1995)
Soldier's Girl (TV 2003)
Stonewall (1995)
Swoon (1991)
Tales of the City (TV 1993)
Tea and Sympathy (1956)
That Certain Summer (TV 1972)
To Wong Foo, Thanks for Everything, Julie Newmar (1995)
Torch Song Trilogy (1988)
Transamerica (2005)
The Truth About Jane (TV 2000)
The Twilight of the Golds (TV 1997)
Victor/Victoria (1982)
Waiting for the Moon (1987)
Watermelon Woman (1995)
The Wedding Banquet (1993)

DOCUMENTARIES

After Stonewall (1999)
Before Stonewall (1984)
The Brandon Teena Story (1998)
Brother Outsider (2003)
The Celluloid Closet (1995)
Coming Out Under Fire (1994)
Common Threads: Stories From The Quilt (1989)
Fight Back, Fight AIDS: 15 Years of ACT UP (2002)
For Love and For Life: The 1987 March on Washington for Lesbian and Gay Rights (1988)
Gay Pioneers (2004)
Gay USA (1977)
Gendernauts (1999)
Hand on the Pulse (2002)
Hope Along the Wind: The Life of Harry Hay (2002)
International Sweethearts of Rhythm (1986)
It's Elementary: Talking About Gay Issues in School (1996)
The Laramie Project (2002)
Last Call at Maud's (1993)
Lavender Limelight: Lesbians in Film (1997)

Let Me Die a Woman (1978)
Lifetime Commitment: A Portrait of Karen Thompson (1993)
Looking for Langston (1989)
No Secret Anymore (2003)
Out at Work (1996)
Out of the Past (1998)
Paris Is Burning (1990)
Paris Was a Woman (1995)
Radical Harmonies (2002)
The Real Ellen Story (TV 1998)
Scout's Honor (2001)
Screaming Queens: The Riot at Compton's Cafeteria (2005)
Silent Pioneers: Gay and Lesbian Elders (1985)
A Simple Matter of Justice: The 1993 March on Washington for Lesbian, Gay and Bi Equal Rights and Liberation (1993)
Sis: The Perry Watkins Story—Gays in the Military (1994)
Southern Comfort (2001)
Stop the Church (1990)
The Times of Harvey Milk (1984)
Tiny and Ruby: Hell Divin' Women (1988)
Tongues Untied (1991)
Totally Gay (TV 2003)
Totally Gayer (TV 2004)
TransGeneration (2005)
Two-Spirit People (1991)
Trembling Before G-d (2001)
Venus Boyz (2002)
Voices From the Front (1991)
Word Is Out (1977)

INDEX

Note: Page numbers in italics indicate references to photographs.

ABOUT THE AUTHOR

VICKI L. EAKLOR is Professor of History at Alfred University. She has edited, authored, and contributed to numerous works including *Bringing Lesbian and Gay Rights Into the Mainstream: Twenty Years of Progress;* "Where Have We Been, Where Are We Going, and Who Gets to Say?" in *Modern American Queer History;* and "Striking Chords and Touching Nerves: Myth and Gender in *Gone With the Wind*," in *Images: A Journal of Film and Popular Culture,* www.imagesjournal.com.